THE NEW COUNTERINSURGENCY ERA

Additional praise for *The New Counterinsurgency Era*

"David Ucko has taken on one of the most important and perplexing dilemmas in contemporary American defense policy and has created a pioneering work. Reflecting a sound grounding in history and a mastery of official policy and doctrine, Ucko places the counterinsurgency debate within its larger strategic context. Both scholars and strategists will find this book provocative and informative. All will benefit from reading it."

—**Steven Metz**, Strategic Studies Institute, U.S. Army War College

"The U.S. military that invaded Iraq in 2003 was neither designed nor trained for counterinsurgency. Its experience of adapting to these new requirements offers a crucial source of potential insight for students of organizational change, irregular warfare, strategy, and defense policy. David Ucko presents the history of this process of adaptation with skill and analytical acuity."

—**Stephen Biddle,** senior fellow for defense policy, Council on Foreign Relations

"David Ucko has written a provocative and thorough, and sometimes troubling, study about how the American military has learned and adapted in the cauldron of contemporary conflict. That capability will be an essential attribute for any organization hoping to deal with the dangerous, complex, and often irregular challenges in the current and future security environment."

—**Conrad C. Crane**, U.S. Army Military History Institute, and lead author of
Field Manual 3-24/MCWP 3-33.5

"*The New Counterinsurgency Era* is a valuable resource for military leaders as well as academics who wish to understand the true forces of military change. It is a warning to both sides of the debate that the battle for the future of the American military is not over."

—**Janine Davidson,** George Mason University

"David Ucko's *The New Counterinsurgency Era* will make a major contribution to the ongoing debate about such operations and about American military culture. Readers interested in this subject will find this to be an invaluable source and future historians of the Iraq War will no doubt look to it too."

—**Michael P. Noonan**, managing director, Program on National Security, Foreign Policy
Research Institute and Operation Iraqi Freedom veteran

"This is a timely book on an exceedingly important and controversial topic. . . . The argument is persuasive . . . the author's conclusions are sound and his predictions and prescriptions are reasonable."

—**Anthony James Joes**, St. Joseph's University, and author of *Urban Guerrilla Warfare,*
Resisting Rebellion: The History and Politics of Counterinsurgency,
America and Guerrilla Warfare

"David Ucko's excellent portrayal of the U.S. military's repeated learning and unlearning of counterinsurgency is a stark reminder that even today there is no guarantee that the U.S. military will remember what it has learned in Afghanistan and Iraq."

—**Heather Peterson**, project associate, RAND Corporation

THE NEW COUNTERINSURGENCY ERA
TRANSFORMING THE U.S. MILITARY FOR MODERN WARS

DAVID H. UCKO

Foreword by
Lt. Col. John A. Nagl, USA (ret.)

GEORGETOWN UNIVERSITY PRESS / WASHINGTON, D.C.

Georgetown University Press, Washington, D.C. www.press.georgetown.edu

The image used on the cover is with permission from the U.S. Department of Defense. The use of this image constitutes no intended or implied endorsement of this book by the Department of Defense.

Library of Congress Cataloging-in-Publication Data

Ucko, David H.
  The new counterinsurgency era : transforming the U.S. military for modern wars / David Ucko ; foreword by John A. Nagl.
     p. cm.
  Includes bibliographical references and index.
  ISBN 978-1-58901-487-9 (cloth : alk. paper)—
ISBN 978-1-58901-488-6 (pbk. : alk. paper)
     1. Counterinsurgency—United States. 2. Iraq War, 2003- 3. Military planning—United States. 4. United States—Military policy. I. Title.
U241.U256 2009
355.02'180973—dc22

                                                              2008048353

⊗This book is printed on acid-free paper meeting the requirements of the American National Standard for Permanence in Paper for Printed Library Materials.

15 14 13 12 11 10 09   9 8 7 6 5 4 3 2
First printing

Printed in the United States of America

CONTENTS

Foreword   vii

Acknowledgments   ix

Introduction   1

List of Abbreviations   7

1 Framing the Reorientation   9

2 A Troubled History   25

3 Revisiting Counterinsurgency   47

4 Innovation under Fire   65

5 Counterinsurgency and the QDR   81

6 FM 3-24 and Operation Fardh Al-Qanoon   103

7 The Ambivalence of the "Surge"   119

8 Innovation or Inertia   141

Conclusion: Kicking the Counterinsurgency Syndrome?   169

Notes   183

Bibliography   219

About the Author   245

Index   247

FOREWORD

When an insurgency erupted in Iraq in the hot summer of 2003, the U.S. military was unprepared to counter it. Since then, the Department of Defense has painfully relearned a number of old lessons about the nature and conduct of successful counterinsurgency campaigns. In *The New Counterinsurgency Era*, David Ucko traces the process by which this relearning occurred, creating a worthy successor to Douglas Blaufarb's *The Counterinsurgency Era* and Richard Downie's *Learning from Conflict*.

The historical record suggests that a future scholar may have to write yet another book chronicling a similar relearning process. Although the U.S. military has spent more of its history fighting "small wars" than conventional ones, it has generally opted not to institutionalize the lessons it has paid for with blood and treasure. America's top military leaders from George Washington onward have demonstrated varying degrees of antipathy toward preparations for irregular warfare, generally viewing it as an uncivilized and irrelevant anomaly. Dabbling in counterinsurgency is commonly seen as a distraction from the more important business of preparing for major combat operations against comparable enemy forces. Counterinsurgency is something of an affront to the organizational culture of America's military; as one anonymous U.S. Army officer reportedly declared of efforts to adapt the U.S. Army for success in Vietnam, "I'll be damned if I permit the United States Army, its institutions, its doctrine, and its traditions to be destroyed just to win this lousy war."

In that light, the strides made by the U.S. military to adapt to the demands of irregular warfare during the past several years have been impressive. However, the harder task is institutionalizing these adaptations so that the painful and costly process of relearning counterinsurgency does not have to be repeated. The innovations of operational- and tactical-level commanders in Vietnam were purposefully forgotten by a traumatized military that vowed "no more Vietnams" and refocused on major combat operations, relegating irregular warfare expertise and capabilities to a marginalized Special Operations community. Although the post-Vietnam rebuilding of the Army created the all-volunteer force that triumphed in Operation Desert

Storm, apparent military supremacy was highly deceptive. The enemy has a vote, and our foes have chosen to fight us not on our terms but on theirs. During the occupation of Iraq, they have turned to insurgency and terrorism, the classic strategies of the weak, updated and made more lethal thanks to the globalization of communications and improvements in weapons technology. The idea that the United States could avoid irregular warfare was wrong; irregular warfare found the United States, and suddenly the counterinsurgency lessons of Vietnam are again in high demand.

The United States will someday have to fight a major conventional war against another state actor, but today America's wars are against insurgents, militias, and terrorists that leech off of disaffected indigenous populations for recruits and support for their extremist ideologies. Combating these enemies effectively requires U.S. forces that are thoroughly trained for counterinsurgency and nation building. While neither popular nor convenient, this focus is not a temporary excursion from preparing for a large-scale war; it must be an enduring priority for the U.S. military.

Ucko's study reveals that behind the scenes there is still considerable resistance to prioritizing irregular warfare. The 2006 Quadrennial Defense Review offered rhetorical support but failed to link strategy for the "Long War" with new development priorities. What Secretary of Defense Robert Gates calls "Next-war-itis," coupled with a "no more Iraqs" backlash within the military, could once again wipe out the hard-learned lessons of irregular warfare that will then have to be learned again when the next enemy of the United States decides to avoid our strengths and attack our relative weaknesses.

The question of how military forces adapt to strategic change is an enormously important one, both for military organizations and for the nations that depend on them for their security and safety. David Ucko has done a great service in tracking the process by which the Department of Defense has adapted to the demands of counterinsurgency in the wake of the September 11 attacks, and his work is of more than academic interest. It has the potential to shape future decisions about the direction in which the Department of Defense allocates resources that will influence the course of the wars in Iraq, Afghanistan, and the broader Long War that David Kilcullen has called a "global counterinsurgency campaign." This is not just a work of history, but a book that may help to make it.

Lt. Col. John A. Nagl, USA (ret.)
President, Center for a New American Security

ACKNOWLEDGMENTS

I owe debts of gratitude to a number of people who have contributed significantly to the completion of this study. At the Department of War Studies, King's College London, I am in the first place thankful to Mats Berdal for his generous support, thoughtfulness, and friendship from the very beginning of the process. I am also thankful to Sir Lawrence Freedman for his constant availability and sound advice. Large parts of this book were written at the Institute of National Strategic Studies at the National Defense University (NDU), which accepted me as a visiting fellow for three valuable months in 2007. I am indebted to their staff, who made my stay not only productive but also enjoyable. In particular, I wish to recognize the extraordinary generosity, helpfulness, and intellectual contributions of Col. Michael Bell, U.S. Army, and Lt. Col. James Laughrey, U.S. Army.

I have benefited tremendously from the input and advice of a number of academics, thinkers, and analysts from various institutions. I am indebted to Lt. Col. Frank Hoffman (ret.) at the Center for Emerging Threats and Opportunities, USMC, for having shared his wealth of knowledge and material. My thanks go to Terry Terriff, University of Calgary, for having read through a previous draft and for providing valuable feedback on the nature of institutional change in the Marine Corps. I would also like to recognize the intellectual contributions and kind support of Christopher Coker, London School of Economics and Political Science, and of Brig. Gen. H. R. McMaster, U.S. Army, whose guidance and availability have been invaluable. I am grateful to Hans Binnendijk of the Center for Technology and National Security Policy, NDU, for the many meetings and interviews. Benjamin Buley merits special mention for his advice during the early years, Scott Kofmehl for helping me tremendously with previous drafts, and Jeffrey Michaels for having shared his insights into the workings of the U.S. Department of Defense.

I also think it is important to recognize all those who accepted to be interviewed and consulted for this study, who offered their time to answer my questions or to help me understand my own research better. Along with those who preferred to remain anonymous, I would therefore like to thank

Col. John Agoglia, U.S. Army; Brig. Gen. Joseph Anderson, U.S. Army; Col. Michael Bell, U.S. Army; Stephen Biddle; Hans Binnendijk; Lt. Col. James Boozell, U.S. Army; Col. J. B. Burton, U.S. Army; Joseph J. Collins; Conrad C. Crane; Ambassador James Dobbins; Richard Downie; Maj. Gen. David Fastabend, U.S. Army; John T. Fischel; Col. T. X. Hammes (ret.), USMC; Lt. Col. Frank Hoffman (ret.), USMC; Donna L. Hopkins; Andrew F. Krepinevich Jr.; Lt. Col. Richard A. Laquement Jr., U.S. Army; Lt. Col. James Laughrey, U.S. Army; Thomas Mahnken; Thomas A. Marks; Dayton L. Maxwell; Montgomery McFate; Brig. Gen. H. R. McMaster, U.S. Army; Lt. Col. John Nagl (ret.), U.S. Army; Robert M. Perito; Heather C. Peterson; Col. Kevin Reynolds (ret.), U.S. Army; Vikram Singh; Terry Terriff; and J. Clint Williamson. All of those mentioned contributed to a vastly improved final product; remaining weaknesses and errors are entirely my own.

I wish to express my gratitude to Georgetown University Press and to Donald Jacobs in particular, whose support and input helped me through the publication phase of the study. The manuscript also benefited from the two anonymous readers who reviewed a previous draft and provided valuable comments and suggestions.

Finally, I would like to thank my parents, Hans and Agneta, my brother Daniel, my sister Hanna, and my brother-in-law Alexander for their patience, wisdom, and humor. A special thanks, also, to Kate for her love and support.

INTRODUCTION

(ii) *The primary functions of the Army are:*

. . .

(G) To provide forces for the occupation of territories abroad, including initial establishment of military government pending transfer of this authority.
(iii) *The collateral functions of the Navy and Marine Corps include the following:*

. . .

(E) To establish military government, as directed, pending transfer of this responsibility to other authority.

—U.S. Code of Federal Regulations, Title 32, vol. 2, sec. 368.6

The U.S. military has historically paid little attention to the nature and requirements of counterinsurgency and stability operations. Missions pitting the U.S. military against insurgents, or forcing it into stabilization tasks and policing duties abroad, have tended to be dismissed as beyond the military's remit or as "lesser-included" operations.[1] The emphasis has instead been on achieving primacy against the armed forces of nation-states, involving an anticipated adversary shaped and operating very much like the U.S. military itself. This prioritization of "high-intensity" or "conventional" war has remained even though the U.S. military has faced "unconventional" or "irregular" challenges at a greater frequency and in campaigns of greater duration and cost.[2] Indeed, even the major combat operations waged by the United States have often preceded or involved a less conventional phase, entailing postconflict stabilization or state-building.[3] Notwithstanding these historical trends, the U.S. military has—in its doctrine, education, training, and, more broadly, its culture—prioritized the destruction of military targets far above the different means of creating or consolidating a new political order.[4]

Counterinsurgency and stability operations share certain characteristics that make them particularly problematic and that explain to a large degree why the U.S. military has sought to avoid such missions. In these campaigns,

the military effort is but a subset to the much more complex task of building and strengthening a new political compact, an objective that can require
years if not decades, is prone to setbacks, and depends as much on local conditions as on the actions of the intervening force. Stability operations will
also typically involve reconstruction activities, the provision of basic services, and the establishment of governance. Although these tasks are best
conducted by civilian and humanitarian agencies, the frequent inability of
the latter to operate in insecure conditions has and will yet force military
troops to assume responsibility for these areas as well, alongside the provision of security.

Militarily, foreign and local forces are confronted with "asymmetric" or
"irregular" armed threats: guerrillas, insurgents, or rebels that are indistin-
guishable from the population among which they operate and appear only
for short instances to conduct an attack. Effective operations require identifying, locating, and closing in on an elusive adversary—a demanding challenge, even more so in a foreign land where the language barrier is high, the
local police structures are weak, and the loyalties of the population are split.
Whereas the U.S. military is certainly not lacking in firepower, the use of
force in urban settings risks large-scale destruction and the disaffection of
the local population and can easily be counterproductive. Even when precise and discriminate, however, the physical elimination of insurgents will
have little meaning unless it occurs alongside a comprehensive strategy that
can alienate the insurgency group, minimize its support, and prevent it from
attracting fresh recruits—a challenge far more demanding than locating and
striking targets.

No wonder, then, that the U.S. military has sought to steer clear of these
complex operations. The fundamental problem with this stance is that it
confuses the undesirability of these missions with an actual ability to avoid
them. This proclivity has unnecessarily complicated the U.S. military's, *mal-
gré tout*, repeated engagements with both counterinsurgency and stability
operations. As retired Army Lieutenant Colonel Ralph Peters wrote in
1999, "One way or another, we will go. Deployments often will be unpre-
dictable, often surprising. And we frequently will be unprepared for the
mission, partly because of the sudden force of circumstance but also because our military is determined to be unprepared for missions it does not
want, as if the lack of preparedness might prevent our going."[5]

The flaws in the U.S. military's logic were made clear in the early years
of the War on Terror, when it failed to anticipate and then struggled to contain the "postconflict" instability that came to characterize both Operation
Enduring Freedom and Operation Iraqi Freedom. Though the setbacks
faced by the United States in Afghanistan and Iraq cannot be understood
monocausally, it is generally recognized that the U.S. military was itself in-
appropriately prepared and configured to carry out the stabilization tasks

that both of these campaigns demanded. In Iraq in particular, this factor contributed, both directly and indirectly, to popular disenchantment and resentment of the U.S. mission and, ultimately, to a rise in violence directed against the occupying forces and the political institutions that they had put in place.[6]

Following this unanticipated rise in low-level violence, the U.S. Department of Defense (DoD) launched a number of initiatives to improve the armed forces' ability to conduct counterinsurgency. A military more adept at stabilization, it was reasoned, would be able to establish the conditions in Iraq necessary for a U.S. withdrawal from this troubled campaign. In the aftermath of the September 11 terrorist attacks on the United States, some also perceived a stability-operations capability as enabling the U.S. military to intervene in weak or failing states, seen as offering sanctuary to terrorist organizations. To others still, the reorientation was justified simply as providing the military with a means of consolidating its future combat victories, to "win the peace" as well as the war. Whatever the motivation, the reorientation soon gathered momentum: departmental instruction, concept papers, training exercises, organizational changes, and doctrinal field manuals emerged, all relating specifically to counterinsurgency and stability operations.

The reforms and restructuring within DoD and the armed services suggested a potential turning point in the history of the U.S. military. By that very fact, the reorientation necessarily also challenged the institution's orthodoxy and culture. Throughout its history, it has been an axiom of the U.S. military that it does not sacrifice in any significant way the pursuit of conventional primacy for the sake of "lesser" tasks. For the U.S. military to "learn counterinsurgency," DoD would need to overcome this institutional hindrance, which has blocked earlier instances of organizational learning. In other words, it would need to embrace change from the top down; treat and prioritize stability operations as an integral slice in the spectrum of operations; prepare and train its soldiers to conduct such campaigns; and, most important, tackle the challenge of counterinsurgency without trying to define it as something more manageable than what it really is.

This book offers an assessment of DoD's efforts to transition to a new strategic environment during the early years of the War on Terror. It focuses on three broad questions. First, what steps did the U.S. military take in this period to improve its ability to conduct stability operations? Second, how effective were these measures in prompting institutional learning? Finally, how can one best account for the particular level of success experienced as part of this learning process?

The focus throughout is on counterinsurgency and stability operations, but the learning process under scrutiny has far wider implications. Indeed, this is the study of how the United States military has transformed itself for *modern wars:* engagements that, whether irregular or conventional, will in virtually all cases carry a certain complexity for which the counterinsurgency learning process is particularly relevant. Certainly, when ground troops are involved, they will need to operate in urban settings, interact with civilian populations, fend off various irregular adversaries, and understand the local political and social environments—that is, the type of knowledge, skills, and awareness that are also called for and emphasized in counterinsurgency theory. This more than anything is what makes the learning of counterinsurgency so important, particularly for a military with global expeditionary ambitions.

The study follows in the footsteps of previous studies of the U.S. military's learning of counterinsurgency, such as Douglas Blaufarb's *The Counterinsurgency Era*, which assessed the efforts of the U.S. government to develop a capability for counterguerrilla warfare in the 1960s, and Richard Downie's *Learning from Conflict*, which examined the U.S. military's development of doctrine for "low-intensity conflict" during the 1970s and 1980s.[7] The current period of learning coincides roughly with George W. Bush's tenure as U.S. president—an eight-year period in which DoD transitioned from an exclusive focus on high-intensity combat to the growing realization that counterinsurgency presented a critical challenge. Although arguably more targeted and significant in scope, this learning process has yet to undergo a similarly systematic analysis.

One problem in assessing a more recent learning process is, of course, that insufficient time has passed to enable a definite statement on where the U.S. military is heading. In recognition of this fact, the aim of this study is not to determine whether the U.S. military had, at the time of publication, "learned counterinsurgency." Nor is the primary aim to prophesy about the eventual outcome of a most probably never-ending process of change. Instead, the focus is on the achievements and challenges of DoD's *initial institutional response to unforeseen strategic and operational challenges.* Close scrutiny of the institutional encounter with stability operations reveals the first steps of a possible reorientation and the immediate tendencies and assumptions to have marked this process. Through this assessment, it is possible to determine whether there were not signs, even in the early stages, of a learning process compromised in both orientation and ambition.

A recurring theme in this narrative is the concept of "learning"—a seemingly simple abstraction that can gain unforeseen complexity in the context of a vast organization such as the U.S. Department of Defense. The meaning and implication of organizational learning is examined in detail in chapter 1, which also seeks to frame the reorientation under review. Even though extensive elaboration on definitions and terminology is usually an uninspiring point at which to start, the discussion of stability operations and of counterinsurgency is notorious for its semantic ambiguity. Because imprecision of terms and meaning has in the past served to distort or deviate institutional learning, it is imperative to set out exactly what type of innovation is needed and, as importantly, why.

Another recurring theme is the tension between the U.S. military's retention of conventional primacy and its development of a counterinsurgency capability. Merely positing stability operations as a "gap" in U.S. military know-how is misleading, for it suggests that the competence to conduct these highly challenging missions can simply be added to the range of tasks already under the U.S. military's control. Quite aside from the need to reallocate finite resources, the learning of stability operations would also require deep-rooted cultural reform—particularly given the U.S. military's singular focus on high-intensity combat throughout history. By tracing the U.S. military's troubled relation with counterinsurgency, chapter 2 illustrates the great friction involved in transforming an institution that has actively sought to avoid stability operations into one that is to perceive them as equal in importance to major combat operations. The chapter also looks at two previous attempts, both unsuccessful, by the U.S. military to institutionalize a counterinsurgency capability, first in the 1960s and then in the 1980s. The analysis points to specific tendencies that have subverted previous learning processes and that may yet exert a powerful influence today.

Chapter 3 elaborates on the motivation for the U.S. military to revisit the topic of counterinsurgency at the dawn of the War on Terror. The analysis examines the U.S. military's attitude toward counterinsurgency and stability operations at the turn of the twenty-first century, framed here as a function of its interpretation of the 1990s' peacekeeping operations and, to a lesser extent, the Vietnam War. The chapter then traces the process by which counterinsurgency emerged as an important preoccupation to the U.S. military, focusing on the initial effect of the September 11 attacks and the later impact of operational experiences in Afghanistan and Iraq.

Chapter 4 provides an account of how DoD's reorientation toward counterinsurgency and stability operations fared in the 2004–2005 period—the moment at which the reorientation truly took off. Central to this account is a group of personalities within the military—a "COIN community"—who were, due to their experience and against a backdrop of changed strategic circumstances, given positions where they could influence the wider institution. At the same time, this period of flux also illustrates the friction involved in changing priorities and upsetting established norms.

Chapter 5 assesses DoD's 2006 Quadrennial Defense Review (QDR), a major review of defense policy. This document is held as representing the prevailing priorities of the institution, and a close analysis is therefore provided of its treatment of counterinsurgency and of stability operations. Along with the provisions and assumptions relating directly to such missions, the focus is also on the implications of two concepts introduced in the QDR: "irregular warfare" and "support for stability, security, transition, and reconstruction (SSTR) operations."

Chapter 6 engages with the U.S. military's learning of counterinsurgency during 2006. The worsening security conditions in Iraq during this year gave continued meaning to the learning of counterinsurgency, translating into a number of initiatives related to these types of missions. This process culminated in the publication of the U.S. Army and Marine Corps counterinsurgency field manual in December 2006. The chapter assesses the conceptualization of counterinsurgency presented in this publication and examines its value in furthering the U.S. military's understanding of these types of campaigns. The chapter concludes with an examination of how the field manual came to inform the U.S. military's strategy in Iraq.

With the launch of Operation Fardh al-Qanoon in February 2007, the U.S. military embarked on a comprehensive counterinsurgency campaign to bring stability to Iraq. The notion of the U.S. military directing its troops to conduct counterinsurgency was in itself revolutionary. Yet, the new operation, what came to be called the "surge," would be a mixed blessing for the future of counterinsurgency as a U.S. military priority. Chapter 7 assesses the origins of the "surge," its outcomes on the ground, and the effect of this change in strategy on the U.S. military's ongoing institutionalization of counterinsurgency.

With the U.S. military having released an interservice counterinsurgency field manual and also conducting counterinsurgency operations "by the book" in Iraq, chapter 8 assesses whether this moment can be seen as the beginning of a U.S. military "counterinsurgency capability." The analysis concludes with an overview of two of the most fundamental variables in the configuration of a military force—its defense budget and force structure—and the steps taken to reorient each in line with the demands of counterinsurgency and stability operations.

To what extent did this moment signify institutional learning and innovation—a break with the U.S. military's historical tendency to marginalize counterinsurgency within its training, education, doctrine, and resource allocation? How effective was the U.S. military as a learning institution during these years? These questions are addressed in the conclusion, which also identifies the factors determining the particular level of success experienced in this reorientation. This concluding chapter also offers a prognosis of the future of counterinsurgency as a U.S. military priority, an analysis that draws heavily on the likely fallout of the U.S. military's engagement in Iraq and the impact of this experience on the Pentagon's future stance toward counterinsurgency.

ABBREVIATIONS

AC	Active Component
AFP	Armed Forces of the Philippines
AQI	al-Qaeda in Iraq
ASG	Abu Sayyaf Group
BCT	brigade combat team
CAOCL	Center for Advanced Operational Culture Learning
CAP	Combined Action Platoon (program)
CCJO	Capstone Concept for Joint Operations
CENTCOM	Central Command
CGSC	Command and General Staff College
CJCS	Chairman of the Joint Chiefs of Staff
CJTF-HOA	Combined Joint Task Force Horn of Africa
CLIC	Center for Low-Intensity Conflict
COIN	counterinsurgency
CORDS	Civil Operations and Revolutionary Development Support
CS	combat support
CSBA	Center for Strategic and Budgetary Assessments
CSS	combat service support
DoD	Department of Defense
DSB	Defense Science Board
ESAF	El Salvador Armed Forces
FCS	Future Combat System
FID	foreign internal defense
FM	field manual
FMLN	Farabundo Marti National Liberation Front
HTT	Human Terrain Team
GAO	Government Accountability Office
IDA	Institute for Defense Analyses
IED	improvised explosive devices
ISG	Iraq Study Group
IWJOC	Irregular Warfare Joint Operating Concept
JCS	Joint Chiefs of Staff
JFCOM	Joint Forces Command
JOC	Joint Operations Concept
JSF	Joint Strike Fighters
LIC	low-intensity conflict
LID	light infantry divisions

MNF-I	Multi-National Force-Iraq
MOOTW	Military Operations Other Than War
MOS	military occupation specialties
MRAP	Mine Resistant Ambush Vehicle
NDS	National Defense Strategy
NDU	National Defense University
NLF	National Front for the Liberation of South Vietnam
NMS	National Military Strategy
NSAM	National Security Action Memorandum
NSPD	National Security Presidential Directive
ORHA	Office of Reconstruction and Humanitarian Assistance
OSD	Office of the Secretary of Defense
OUSD(P)	Office of the Under Secretary of Defense for Policy
PDD	Presidential Decision Directive
PME	Professional Military Education
PRT	Provincial Reconstruction Team
PSYOPS	psychological operations
QDR	Quadrennial Defense Review
RC	Reserve Component
RMA	Revolution in Military Affairs
S/CRS	Office of the Coordinator for Reconstruction and Stabilization
SF	Special Forces
SOCOM	Special Operations Command
SOF	Special Operations Forces
SSTR	stability, security, transition, and reconstruction
TRADOC	Army Training and Doctrine Command
USAF	U.S. Air Force
USAID	U.S. Agency for International Development

1
FRAMING THE REORIENTATION

This book assesses the efforts of the U.S. Department of Defense since 2001 to improve the U.S. military's ability to conduct counterinsurgency and stability operations. It is a topic that raises inevitable definitional and theoretical issues that must be resolved. What is meant by "stability operations," and how do they differ from "counterinsurgency" campaigns? What do we mean by "learning," and how does this process apply to an institution as opposed to an individual? What type of innovation would one expect as part of a reorientation toward counterinsurgency and stability operations? And, perhaps most fundamentally, why are these types of missions so important, today and in the future?

THE NATURE OF THE MISSION

To understand the U.S. military's reorientation toward counterinsurgency and stability operations, it is necessary to understand the types of missions that lie at the heart of the learning process. What is meant by "stability operations," by "counterinsurgency," how do they differ from one another, and what, specifically, distinguishes these types of operations from the conventional combat campaigns with which the U.S. military is more familiar? As definitions can often obscure more than they reveal, it may suffice to group the operations of concern to this book not by what they are called but by the characteristics that they share. In so doing, the operations of key import are those that share three specific attributes:

(1) A medium-to-high level of hostile activity targeting the "stabilizing" forces, whether foreign or local; this is also known as a *nonpermissive operational environment.*

(2) An underlying state-building initiative, of which the military stabilization effort is but a subset. *State-building* is here loosely understood

as primarily nonmilitary assistance in the creation or reinforcement of state structures, culminating in the formation of a government that is, at the very least, able to maintain stability in the territory under its jurisdiction.

(3) The deployment of ground troops to conduct operations in the midst of a local civilian population.

It is when these three characteristics have coexisted within one area of operation that the U.S. armed forces have struggled to achieve its desired results. Andrew Krepinevich captures the conundrum: "The emphasis is on light infantry formations, not heavy divisions; on firepower restraint, not its widespread application; on the resolution of political and social problems within the nation targeted by insurgents, not closing with and destroying the insurgent's field forces."[1]

Missions that share these characteristics are commonly called either *"counterinsurgency campaigns"* or *"stability operations."* Although the terms are not entirely interchangeable, these types of campaigns clearly overlap, as both comprise simultaneous military, political, and economic efforts to help a government stabilize and consolidate order in its own territory.[2] Efforts to learn counterinsurgency are thus often relevant, if not entirely congruent, to those relating to stability operations. Aside from their respective connotations, the one true variable separating these two types of operations is the level and organization of armed opposition facing the stabilizing forces. But as it is often armed opposition that forces the military to engage in the first place, the difference between stability operations and counterinsurgency campaigns is often not very pronounced, if at all extant.[3]

However termed, a narrow understanding of the operations under scrutiny, based on the three above attributes, allows for appropriate and insightful historical parallels. The focus is not on the conventional phase of war, though it should be said that delineations between the conflict and postconflict phase are often all-too crude.[4] Peacekeeping and peace-building operations also form inappropriate bases of comparison; whereas peace operations are often consensual in nature, stabilizing forces actively seek to bolster one party at the expense of another—there is no pretense of neutrality. Counterterrorism operations are similarly beyond the remit, as they do not necessarily involve the creation of a new political order or the sustained presence of ground troops. Furthermore, in DoD jargon, counterterrorism is commonly interpreted as predominantly "enemy-centered," that is, "aimed at dissuading, deterring, and defeating adversaries, principally through kinetic means [combat]."[5] In contrast, counterinsurgency and stability operations are, in theory at any rate, "population-centered," that is, "aimed at assuring, persuading, and influencing indigenous populations through the provision of security, humanitarian assistance, basic services, infrastructure, institution-building, support for the rule of law."[6] This distinction makes these two types of operations highly incongruent, though counterterrorism will often feature as one component of a wider counterinsurgency campaign.

Based again on the three above attributes, a critical distinction is made between those counterinsurgency operations that involve the deployment of foreign ground troops and those that do not. In assisting an insurgency-threatened government, an intervening state has a choice whether to deploy its own troops to conduct operations within the host country, or to limit its support to training, advice, and assistance in the hope that the security forces of the host nation are sufficiently capable and reliable to conduct operations on their own. Whereas both these approaches to counterinsurgency can be effective depending on circumstance, the focus here is on those campaigns that necessitate the actual deployment of ground troops by the intervening state, also termed a "direct engagement." These operations have historically been the most challenging, and they are also those that involve the armed forces to the greatest degree.

To isolate these three variables is not to suggest that all operations that share them are in some way amenable to a similar solution. It is sufficient to consider the sharp contrasts between the British campaign in Malaya, the American experience in Vietnam, and its later engagement in Iraq to realize that nominally similar campaigns often share few commonalities. Not only is each campaign marked by its specific circumstances and context, but each is also uniquely shaped by its political essence. For example, the methods, approaches, and best practices implemented in Malaya, widely deemed a counterinsurgency success story, would not have resulted in victory had they not also been framed within a strategic context that foresaw Malayan independence: "Had the British simply refused to leave, we would most likely be talking about a misguided British defeat—yet another Aden."[7]

Yet, despite their unique political setting and circumstances, these campaigns do for the most part conform to a set of broad principles, identified in many scholarly and military works on counterinsurgency. These touch upon the importance of achieving a nuanced political understanding of the campaign, operating under unified command, using intelligence to guide operations, isolating insurgents from the population, using the minimum amount of force necessary to achieve security, and assuring and maintaining the perceived legitimacy of the counterinsurgency effort in the eyes of the populace.[8] While some of the principles verge on the commonsensical, they do nonetheless provide an insight into the elusive logic of these operations and illustrate how significantly they differ from exclusively combat-oriented campaigns. Even when taken together, however, they do not provide a "solution" to counterinsurgency.

Some analysts have suggested that "classical" counterinsurgencies, such as those seen in Malaya and in Vietnam, differ in important respects from more recent operations. The argument centers on a set of new, or seemingly new, variables—mass media, urbanization, globalized connectivity, religious extremism, suicide terrorism—that are said to add fresh considerations to an already challenging type of operation.[9] Critically, however, even those seeking to identify such new dimensions also tend to emphasize the continued relevance of many of the broad counterinsurgency principles alluded to above; this is also the assessment of most practitioners of counterinsurgency in Iraq and Afghanistan.[10] The goal, therefore, has been to revise rather than discard old theory, with the underlying message that while counterinsurgency principles provide a useful conceptual guide, there simply is no "silver-bullet" solution to what will always be sui generis and intensely complex campaigns.

WHY LEARN COUNTERINSURGENCY?

Partly due to the complexity and demands of counterinsurgency, it is often argued that the U.S. military should not get involved in such campaigns or include them as part of their remit. The tasks associated with counterinsurgency, it is argued, are best conducted by civilian agencies, or by special operations forces rather than general-purpose troops, or by local security forces rather than the U.S. military.[11] Most fatalistic is the suggestion that insurgencies cannot be stopped, certainly not through outside intervention, and that peace is best achieved by "giving war a chance."[12] Common to all of these arguments is the premise that U.S. soldiers and Marines should not and will not regularly or in the foreseeable future be sent to conduct counterinsurgency or stability operations and that the Iraq and Afghanistan campaigns are somehow the exception to this rule.

Although some of these arguments have merit, they sit badly with today's strategic environment, one in which stability operations appear to be a growth business. A RAND report published in 2003 demonstrated that not only did the frequency of "nation-building" efforts increase since 1945 but that "each successive post–Cold War U.S.-led intervention has generally been wider in scope and more ambitious in intent than its predecessor."[13] In terms of frequency if not of scope, the ongoing War on Terror is likely to extend rather than curb this trend, as the military's role in this struggle will seemingly be to assert control over "contested zones," where government capacity is weak and terrorist groups seek sanctuary.

Clearly, intervention in these areas of the world is best conducted by local security forces, but it would appear equally clear that this preference cannot always be accommodated. It should be recalled that the original intent for both Afghanistan and Iraq was precisely for the postwar stabilization to be achieved *indirectly*, through the use of surrogate forces. Stability operations in Afghanistan were to be conducted by local forces and NATO peacekeepers, but not by U.S. troops. In Iraq, the initial U.S. occupation plans foresaw only a brief stabilization phase, concluded with the fairly rapid withdrawal of most U.S. forces. As U.S. Army Brig. Gen. H. R. Mc-Master and others have argued, these assumptions "betrayed linear thinking [and] neglected the interaction with determined enemies."[14] When the sought-after proxies proved unable, unwilling, or insufficient, U.S. combat troops were soon needed to fill the gap.

Future presidents may, of course, be more cautious and resist entangling U.S. troops if and when the advisory approach fails. This would, however, limit U.S. strategic options, and it is questionable whether such restraint will be maintained when vital national security issues are deemed to be at stake. History also shows the many ways in which soldiers and Marines can be dragged into a counterinsurgency campaign that is unforeseen or even mis-understood by both the military and political leadership at the time. From the counterinsurgency campaign in the Philippines in the late 1800s, to the Vietnam War during the Cold War, and finally to the current campaigns in Afghanistan and Iraq, the record of unanticipated engagements in coun-terinsurgency is century-long. Added to the list are various stabilization or peace enforcement campaigns in Panama, Haiti, Somalia, and Kosovo, to name only the most recent and high-profile of efforts.

Nor is there any real evidence to suggest that this record of engagement will end with the current campaigns. Instead, and for many reasons, the like-lihood of facing irregular challenges (either expectedly or not) appears to be getting higher rather than lower. The U.S. military today enjoys a clear primacy in terms of conventional combat capabilities, but it has had to work hard when faced with insurgents. Future adversaries will observe this trend and will likely respond by resorting to asymmetric or irregular means in-volving concealment among civilian populations, hit-and-run attacks, and dispersion.[15] As long as the U.S. military fails to prepare for direct engage-ment in counterinsurgency, it will further encourage its would-be adver-saries to employ these types of tactics. Once deployed, a lack of relevant instruction will also complicate the U.S. military's response to irregular challenges or interaction with civilian populations, which will in itself risk inflaming the situation on the ground and give rise to further confronta-tions. In this way, too, failing to prepare for stability operations only in-creases the likelihood of becoming embroiled.

Finally, although it may be some time before the U.S. military embarks on another "counterinsurgency operation" or "stability operation" per se, the operations it will conduct will nonetheless inevitably involve a similar range of tasks. If territory is to be seized, for example, stabilization of that terri-tory will be an unavoidable requirement. Also, most future operations will by force be conducted in urban environments where the local population cannot be ignored but, more often, must be co-opted and even protected against attack.[16] More generally, and as Mats Berdal has argued, the post–Cold War period as a whole reveals "as one of its most striking characteristics, the widespread practice of external intervention undertaken with the express aim of 'building sustainable peace' *within* societies ravaged by war and violent conflict."[17]

The aim of the required institutional innovation is therefore not necessarily to "learn counterinsurgency" in a narrow sense but rather to learn how to conduct modern wars, the complexity of which simply cannot be wished away. Whatever we call it, troops involved in modern wars will benefit from the relevant instruction: how to engage with a civilian population, how to establish and maintain order, how to collect and process human intelligence, how to operate in foreign culture, how to provide basic services, and so on. In Michael Howard's words, "The military may protest that this is not the kind of war that they joined up to fight, and taxpayers that they see little return for their money. But . . . this is the only war we are likely to get: it is also the only kind of peace. So let us have no illusions about it."[18]

THE U.S. MILITARY AS A LEARNING ORGANIZATION

The differences in opinion within DoD regarding its future priorities and likely roles and missions are indicative of the heterogeneity of the organization itself. Officially, the U.S. military is composed of "the Office of the Secretary of Defense (OSD), the Military Departments, the Chairman of the Joint Chiefs of Staff (JCS), the Combatant Commands, the Inspector General of the Department of Defense, the Defense Agencies, the DoD Field Activities, and such other offices, agencies, activities and commands established or designated by law, or by the President or by the Secretary of Defense."[19] Within this superstructure of entities, layers, and actors, achieving a coherent policy and direction is often challenging. Analytically tackling such an institution can also present distinct challenges.

For the purposes of this book, it is not necessary to view the U.S. military in its entirety. Instead, as an exploration of institutional change, the most relevant sections of the DoD are those that help set its policy and priorities: the Office of the Secretary of Defense, the Joint Chiefs of Staff, the Combatant Commands, and the departments of the various uniformed services—particularly the Army and Marine Corps, who have traditionally been the most involved in the types of operations under scrutiny. The special operations community clearly also has an important role to play in counterinsurgency operations. Nonetheless, it should be emphasized that whereas special operations forces commonly operate indirectly, through proxies, or conduct isolated strikes against discrete targets, the focus here is specifically on *direct*, population-centered, and protracted engagement in counterinsurgency and stability operations, which often turns out to be a job for the regular services.

Examining the U.S. military also requires an appreciation for the many ways in which its behavior can be understood. Drawing on an analytical framework put forward by Graham Allison and Philip Zelikow, the U.S. military, or any large institution, can be seen in three ways: as a rarefied "rational actor"; a "conglomerate of loosely allied organizations, each with a substantial life of its own"; or as a combination of players—groupings of key personalities, forming coalitions and engaging in bargaining and compromises, or "the pulling and hauling that is politics."[20]

The rational-actor perspective is in many ways inadequate for the study of institutional learning. While viewing organizations as cohesive entities can be useful for heuristic purposes, this conceptualization fails to explain the complex or even idiosyncratic manner in which organizations make decisions and evolve.[21] As should become clear, this process is best understood through the second and third levels of analysis described above: through the competition of institutional subunits and individuals, each with their respective interests, culminating in a resultant policy that may, from the outside, seem irrational or unresponsive to external conditions. It must also be recognized that the rationality of organizational decision making is strongly bounded by the institution's culture, defined by James Q. Wilson as "a persistent, patterned way of thinking about the central tasks of and human relationships within an organization."[22]

The three-tiered structure advanced by Allison and Zelikow points to the heterogeneity of any large organization and the possibility of innovation occurring in a disaggregated manner and in different parts of the organization at any one time.[23] The framework also illustrates that change can be motivated by a range of factors, not all of which relate to the organization's external environment or threat perception. However, the framework does not provide much contextual detail on the many ways in which change can be impelled or the process by which it occurs. Various theories have sought to fill this gap.[24] Indeed, the literature on military innovation suggests several distinct drivers of institutional learning: civilian direction and pressure; competition between different military services for finite resources; competition between different elements of the same service; or changes in the organization's culture brought on by new leadership, external shocks, or cross-national professional militaries ties.[25] There is no consensus on precisely which agent of change is the most influential in prompting military innovation. Plausibly, such a ranking would depend on the particular institution and the circumstances facing it.

It should also be added that these sources of military innovation are not mutually exclusive. Indeed, one means of synthesizing the different models is through Richard Downie's "integrative approach" to military learning, which he applied to the U.S. military's development of doctrine for low-intensity conflict during the 1970s and 1980s. Lacking perhaps in theoretical neatness but benefiting from greater verisimilitude, the approach "offers a means to bridge the theoretical gaps" between more parsimonious frameworks of analysis and provides a coherent and multifaceted model to understand the process by which the military learns.[26] It acknowledges that change can derive from a multitude of sources and for a multitude of reasons and that one must therefore focus on the "dynamic relationship involving the external conditions that make . . . change necessary and the timing and development of the military's cyclical institutional learning process in responding to those conditions."[27]

Downie's research reveals two basic, overarching prerequisites for institutional change: institutional consensus that a particular problem requires attention, and institutional consensus on how to respond.[28] This consensus is shaped and broken by the combination of factors identified in the wider literature on institutional innovation: changes in the external environment, the influence of intervening outsiders, the role of the organization's leadership, and the sway of well-placed individual "mavericks" within the organization. By merging these variables, rather than selecting one or two for isolated analysis, Downie's framework provides a useful conceptual model for the analysis of the U.S. military's attempts to learn counterinsurgency.

Whether the factors prompting change are taken individually or synthesized, most models of military innovation view learning as being driven from the top down.[29] To Adam Grissom, this overriding focus on top-down innovation obscures the critical role played by bottom-up initiatives in pushing an organization forward.[30] Indeed, bottom-up learning is particularly salient to the development of a counterinsurgency capability: with Western militaries typically failing to prepare adequately for counterinsurgency, low- to middle-ranking officers involved in such operations have often had to formulate an improvised response on the ground. This was certainly the case with the British counterinsurgency campaign in Malaya, where the British forces arrived at a since venerated approach to counterinsurgency through trial and error.[31] Similarly, the U.S. campaigns in Afghanistan and Iraq have seen a number of units in the field internalize best practices through ad hoc adaptation.[32]

It is thus necessary to make a distinction between bottom-up adaptation and top-down learning and to realize the role each plays within military innovation. Whereas the former suggests changes in tactics, techniques, and procedures implemented on the ground and through contact with an unfamiliar operating environment, the latter involves the institutionalization of these practices through changes in training, doctrine, education, and force structure. The learning provides a foundation of knowledge, but adaptation allows the troops in theater to mold the prescribed approach to particular circumstances. Adaptation thus fills the inevitable gap between what is learned and what is experienced, but the learning is indispensable in making this gap as small as possible. In the words of Brigadier General McMaster, "You are never going to get it right before the war, but the key is to not be so wrong that you can't adapt once the complexity of the problem is revealed to you."[33]

In its history with counterinsurgency, the U.S. military has often adapted in the field but failed to institutionalize lessons learned at the operation's close. At this juncture, it has been typical for the U.S. military to discard whatever wisdom was accrued, forcing a renewed process of hurried adaptation once troops are again committed to a similar mission. This pattern is what renders the top-down process of institutionalization so critical, a point made by Ambassador Eric S. Edelman, U.S. undersecretary of defense for policy, with regard to the ongoing adaptation seen in Iraq: "Great progress has been made on the ground by our civilians and our military, who have learned to work together and have adapted in innovative ways to meet these challenges. But for every ingenious adaptation we see in the field, we should ask ourselves—what institutional failure were they trying to overcome? What tools did we fail to provide them?"[34]

Edelman points to the need to institutionalize a capability to deal with the challenges faced in Iraq and Afghanistan, not in any way to discredit adaptation, but to prepare troops for stability operations before the act. This book responds to the urgent need to focus more closely on the process of top-down institutionalization. As such, it shies away from operational analysis, except to show causality between top-down initiatives and performance on the ground or to illustrate how and when the top-down institutional learning process was driven by bottom-up adaptation in theater. The onus is instead on the lead agencies of the U.S. military, on the manner in which they have framed and prioritized stability operations, and the capabilities they have developed to help its soldiers face these types of operations in theater.

EVIDENCE OF LEARNING

The assessment of the U.S. military's learning requires clear indicators of progress. In an attempt to achieve parsimonious theory, some studies of military learning have sought to isolate *one* specific metric—often published doctrine—and use it as a yardstick for institutional change.[35] While this approach offers an enviable degree of analytical tidiness, there are risks involved in employing monocausal frameworks, particularly if the chosen metric in fact possesses only limited explanatory power. The value of published doctrine is, for example, often overstated: Although "doctrine can serve as evidence of institutional learning," it is less certain that it is "central to how militaries execute their missions."[36] As should become clear, the existence of doctrine really offers no guarantee that it is pushed by the institution or internalized by the troops in theater.

A broader framework is needed, one that captures the various manifestations of institutional learning. Through this wider lens, organizational learning can be thought of as involving three closely related steps:

- gaining an *understanding* of what counterinsurgency entails and requires;
- *prioritizing* counterinsurgency as a mission that the U.S. military will conduct; and
- *developing a capability* to conduct such missions through various institutional adjustments and reforms.

In many ways, these three steps must overlap to be effective: It serves no purpose to understand counterinsurgency without also prioritizing it as a mission, and it would be difficult to prioritize counterinsurgency without also developing the attendant operational capability. Most fundamentally, perhaps, the value of that capability depends on the realism and clarity of the initial understanding of counterinsurgency on which it is based.

If these are the requirements of learning, what are its manifestations? In a military organization such as DoD, a good indicator of institutional *understanding* can be found in doctrine and concept papers. In this context, two variables are of key concern: First, what does the *content* of these publications reveal about the institution's interpretation of a particular challenge? And second, to what degree do these publications represent the understanding of the wider institution? In answering the second question, the author of a publication and its position in the institutional hierarchy can be as important as its content. Given the multitude of field manuals and military publications, it is critical not to confuse the lucid analysis of one particular publication with the policy and mind-set of the entire institution.

Indicators of *prioritization* are manifold and can include the prominence of a particular topic in the military's professional military education (PME) programs and training exercises, as well as the incidence of official publications devoted to the topic.[37] More broadly, the U.S. military's force structure reveals to a large degree the types of missions for which it is optimized. Similarly, a clear indication of prevailing priorities can be seen in the manner in which the institution allocates its budget and the types of capabilities in which it invests.

The U.S. military's prioritization of counterinsurgency relates also to its historical neglect of such missions. Prioritizing counterinsurgency as a mission that the U.S. military will be ready to conduct would thus signify deep-rooted change to the institutional culture at DoD. In the broadest terms, the first step involves recasting stability operations as integral to U.S. national security rather than as missions that detract from combat readiness. In this regard, the role of leadership should not be underestimated, as it is uniquely placed to define the institution's agenda, oversee its recruitment and promotions, and thereby affect its self-identification and culture. Evidence of such a reprioritization would be clearest in statements of policy, strategy papers, changes in personnel, and the issuing of directives to be followed or, better yet, their implementation.

Related to the understanding and prioritization of a challenge is the *development of a capability* to meet it. Among scholars of counterinsurgency and stability operations, there is surprisingly little controversy as to the nature of such a capability. In fact, "nearly all who have studied or experienced previous cases agree on the salient lessons to be drawn."[38] Four main areas requiring change are often identified, some of which were touched on above: technology; concepts and doctrine; culture, education, and training; and organizational structures.[39]

Setting out these categories should in no way suggest that success in stability operations—highly political campaigns—can be guaranteed through bureaucratic tinkering or structural reform alone. Michael Shafer makes the point that even with the right capabilities "there is no counterinsurgency 'master key' and efforts to apply one will fail."[40] This is certainly correct, and it should be stressed that no amount of institutional optimization will compensate for the lack of a clear and well-implemented political strategy. At the same time, a certain level of preparation and institutional readiness, based on the requirements identified in past and current campaigns, will undoubtedly increase the likelihood of success. In practical terms, therefore, the required change and the categories in which it might be anticipated can be understood as follows.

Technology

The process of acquiring technological assets for stability operations is the least complicated means of innovation, especially for the U.S. military, which has a comparative advantage in this field. The analysis here centers on the development of new and adaptation of existing capabilities to meet the military requirements of urban settings, such as crowd control, surveillance, nonlethality, and technological countermeasures against improvised explosive devices (IEDs).[41] The analysis must also consider what may in fact be a more important indicator of institutional change: the balance struck in DoD budget requests between big-ticket weapons platforms for rapid decisive operations and those assets more suited toward counterinsurgency and stability operations.

The resource allocation that goes into high- versus low-intensity technology development relates also to the alleged alliance known as the "Iron Triangle," that is, the "special relationship" between the Pentagon, Congress, and the private defense industry. Each partner in this alliance is said to have an interest in sustaining programs and technologies that are labor-intensive and designed primarily toward high-intensity combat operations. Defense companies have a monopoly on the manufacture of expensive combat equipment, whereas the less costly and smaller technologies that are often most relevant to stability operations can as easily be procured from commercial firms—"in short, there is little money for the defence industry in irregular warfare."[42] Members of Congress, meanwhile, have often been unwilling to cut any existing defense program if it means losing industrial jobs in their district or home state. Finally, the U.S. military services often individually pursue costly and advanced weapons systems and platforms, which justify bigger budgets, higher profiles, and greater roles in major combat operations. In general, therefore, "technologies that do not fill a warfighting need are less likely to be funded or accepted by the military."[43] Against this backdrop, any assessment of DoD's attempts to transform for stability operations must account for the distorting effects and vested interests of the iron triangle.

Concept and Doctrine

The publication of relevant doctrine and concept papers is often taken as solid evidence of institutional learning. Although this assumption needs to be unpacked, it is clear that any attempt by the U.S. military to augment its capability to conduct counterinsurgency and stability operations would include the development of relevant, appropriate doctrine. This is often the first step toward developing a capability, as the content of the doctrinal manuals and concept papers gradually filters down into military education and training. Yet, there is nothing ineluctable about this process: "In theory, doctrine jumpstarts the other 'engines of change.' But each engine is in a separate car with its own driver, already headed toward an important destination."[44] The assessment of doctrine must therefore also take into account its impact on the wider institution.

Culture, Education, and Training

The development of a capability to conduct stability operations would also involve a reorientation of the U.S. military's education and training. In her study of U.S. military culture, Leigh C. Caraher provides a list of character-istics that would be required for effective soldiering in stability operations and that should therefore be stressed in stability operations–related in-struction. Along with the initiative and decision-making capabilities re-quired for all military operations, the list also emphasizes several civil-military skills geared toward interaction with nonmilitary personnel, as well as politico-military awareness, a broad intellectual background, and an appreciation for history and culture.[45]

Innovations in education and training must be enveloped by a shift in the U.S. military's cultural disposition toward counterinsurgency and stability operations. Rather than being derided as "escorting kids to kindergarten"—Condoleezza Rice's famous quip about nation building in 2000, these en-deavors must be cast as a complex but highly critical part of the spectrum of operations, central to the very utility of U.S. military force in the twenty-first century.[46] Along with changes in recruitment, instruction, and resource allocation, a critical gauge of cultural change on this front would be whether or not a soldier's experience and excellence in such campaigns are rewarded by the larger system at hand.

Organizational Structures

Together, the U.S. Army and Marine Corps hold several occupational "fields" that would be relevant to stability operations: military police, engineers, medical, civil affairs and psychological operations (PSYOPS), public affairs, trainers and advisers, linguists, transportation, legal services, law enforce-ment, special forces, counter/human intelligence, and ammunition and ex-plosive ordnance disposal. Within these fields lie "military occupation specialties," with yet more specific roles, many of which would also be use-ful in conducting counterinsurgency and stability operations.[47] However, having relevant skill sets distributed across the force provides a very differ-ent level of preparedness from having units organized and directly tasked with conducting stability operations.

For example, by one estimate the U.S. Army had 37,350 troops trained for various stability operations tasks in theater in Iraq on May 1, 2003.[48] These troops included 17,230 engineers, 10,400 military police and 7,280 medical, 1,800 civil affairs, and 640 PSYOPS staff. In one sense, the prob-lem facing the U.S. military in conducting the subsequent stability opera-tions was not a lack of expertise or numbers; rather, the troops in theater had not been organized for such tasks and did not perceive them as part of their mandate. A second, less immediate problem was that the majority of troops with skills relevant to stability operations were drawn from the U.S. Army's Reserve Component (RC), which complicated their prolonged deployment abroad.[49] Furthermore, the relevant troops from the Active Component (AC) were "organic to combat formations," which meant that "they were assigned to stabilization missions as secondary to their primary combat support role."[50]

Thus even though the required skills and capabilities might have been in theater in Iraq, there was no "dedicated command and control for the post-conflict mission [or] plans for the rapid, integrated employment of such forces."[51] The ensuing difficulties also revealed a capability gap within the U.S. military force structure: It had not established organizational units suited, specifically or as an additive capability, for stability operations. There are many means of filling this gap, but all involve important trade-offs and significant changes in force structure.

First, those service members in fields or with MOS that relate to stability operations would need to be trained for the specific challenges of such missions. "A combat engineer battalion will possess the assets needed to create defensive positions, keep roads open, and clear battlefields of mines. But it may lack the S&R [stability and reconstruction] assets needed to repair damaged office buildings, reconnect electrical power grids, and restore sewage and water systems."[52] Second, the RC and AC could be rebalanced so that the latter holds more of the personnel with the needed skills and training for such operations. At the same time, reservists (particularly civil affairs) often derive their utility in stability operations from their civilian careers; rebalancing must therefore somehow occur without depleting the RC's wide range of expertise.[53] Third, the resources already in place for stability operations could be organized and consolidated, either through the broadening of existing structures or the standing up of new specialized units. In either case, the relevant people and skills must be pooled, coordinated, and able to conduct various stabilization tasks as and when needed. Fourth, because these operations are widely accepted as requiring a whole-of-government approach, it might also be possible or even necessary for DoD to establish structures that cut across federal departments. A critical point in this respect, however, is that so long as civilian agencies and departments lack the resources to conduct stability operations, the military will be asked to undertake the associated tasks in their stead.

CONCLUSION

Counterinsurgency campaigns and stability operations can be understood as featuring three specific characteristics: a nonpermissive operational environment; an underlying state-building process; and military operations conducted by foreign ground troops in the midst of a civilian population. It is when these three characteristics have coexisted within one area of operations that the U.S. military, and those of many Western powers, have struggled to accomplish their stated objectives.

In part, the enduring difficulty of such missions relates to their political essence and to the difficulty of imposing order in a foreign land. These campaigns rarely lend themselves to decisive victories and often require years if not decades to be resolved. They also demand a carefully attuned response on all levels of operations, from the tactical to the strategic. This complexity explains in part why the U.S. military, particularly given its traumatic experience in Vietnam, has sought to avoid engagement in counterinsurgency. Yet despite the inherent complications of counterinsurgency and stability operations, these types of campaigns do not appear to be avoidable—a lesson that became clear soon after the September 11, 2001, attacks on the United States.

Although subsequent operations have highlighted the need for the U.S. military to learn about counterinsurgency, the attendant reorientation is likely to face resistance. The U.S. military is a massive and complex organization; like most bureaucracies it is also expected to oppose change. The institutional-cultural aversion of the U.S. military toward stability operations is also likely to play a strong role in shaping its response to the post-9/11 strategic environment. To turn its back on decades, if not centuries, of neglect—to truly innovate—the U.S. military would need to acknowledge that its ability to conduct counterinsurgency is lacking and that such a capability is also needed.

Developing such a capability would involve three related steps. First, the process would require a clear appraisal of what counterinsurgency is and what it requires. Second, the institution would also have to prioritize these operations, not least because of their cyclical reappearance and the perennial problems of the U.S. military in handling them. Finally, and based on these two preceding factors, the learning of counterinsurgency would also involve the development of a capability to conduct such operations. Developing this capability entails making changes in several key areas, technology; concepts and doctrine; culture, education, and training; and organizational structures. This process would also help institutionalize the adaptation to counterinsurgency seen on the ground in Iraq, Afghanistan, and elsewhere.

For the U.S. military, this period of institutional change has the potential of marking a historically significant turning point. A reevaluation by DoD of its approach and prioritization of counterinsurgency would denote an institutional-cultural transformation—the end of the U.S. military's so-called "Vietnam Syndrome."[54] Yet as Lawrence Freedman has suggested, a failed or subverted learning process would have the potential to foment a new syndrome—an "Iraq Syndrome," possibly resulting in a "renewed, nagging and sometimes paralyzing belief that any large-scale U.S. military intervention abroad is doomed to practical failure and moral iniquity."[55]

Ultimately, the current opportunity to come to grips with stability operations is matched in magnitude only by the cost of failing to do so. Learning how to conduct stability operations is necessary to consolidate combat
victories and to add utility to the U.S. military's use of force. As the link between the use of military force and the attainment of particular political objectives, a successful stability operation is, in other words, also foundational
to strategy.

2

A TROUBLED HISTORY

"It is useful to learn from your mistakes, but abject foolishness to define yourself by them."

Lt. Col. Ralph Peters (ret.), U.S. Army

The U.S. military's learning of stability operations cannot be fully understood, nor its significance grasped, without some awareness of this institution's troubled relation to counterinsurgency. Throughout history, the U.S. military has typically neglected counterinsurgency as a mission—despite repeated operational experience with such campaigns. This is a cyclical pattern—one might call it a *"counterinsurgency syndrome"*—that has also affected the U.S. military's conduct of such operations.

Only in a few instances has the U.S. military sought to consolidate its experience with counterinsurgency operations by incorporating these missions into its doctrine, education, and training. And even though some of these efforts have been moderately successful, they have consistently been marred by unclear conceptual thinking, causing a poorly targeted learning process. Accordingly, these attempts to learn counterinsurgency have commonly resulted in the further perfection and broadening of war-fighting capabilities or the development of methods that, though focused on irregular campaigns in general, have been inadequate for the specific challenges of counterinsurgency.

This chapter elaborates on two such learning processes: the U.S. military's efforts to enhance its ability to counter guerrilla warfare in the 1960s, and low-intensity threats in the late 1980s. Although an in-depth historical account of these two periods is beyond the scope of this book, a brief assessment is nonetheless valuable in providing historical perspective and a comparative baseline for DoD's most recent reorientation. This analysis illustrates how the institutional preferences and idiosyncrasies of the U.S. military can divert or even subvert the necessary learning process.

In particular, both previous learning processes reveal strikingly similar tendencies that have hitherto prevented the development of a genuine counterinsurgency capability. These tendencies can be seen most forcefully in the *assumptions* with which the U.S. military as a whole engaged with counterinsurgency conceptually and in the attendant development of an *approach and capability* to conduct such missions. The critical question is whether these tendencies will again exert an influence on this most recent of learning processes.

THE U.S. MILITARY'S "COUNTERINSURGENCY SYNDROME"

The U.S. military's troubled history with counterinsurgency stems most fundamentally from its self-perception as a force intended for major combat operations.[1] With a firm foundation in European strategic thinking, the American military was from the outset configured for battlefield wars conducted against the military formations of other nation-states. This was how George Washington initially sought to fight the Revolutionary War (1775–1783), though Britain's superiority in this domain ultimately forced the Continental Army to adopt guerrilla tactics. With victory, however, the U.S. military instinctively returned to the topic of conventional war, its initial experience with irregular operations having done little to inform its later evolution.[2]

This concentration on the "conventional" at the exclusion of the "irregular" has characterized the U.S. military ever since. Following the Civil War, the U.S. Army focused on large-scale warfare and military engineering while dismissing the frontier, counterguerrilla, and peacekeeping operations of the time as skirmishes and police work.[3] At the turn of the twentieth century, Secretary of War Elihu Root framed the Army's sole objective to prepare for and fight the nation's wars, which translated into a twin focus on the defense of the U.S. Atlantic coastline against a European amphibious raid and the possibility of a conventional threat to its interests on the Pacific Coast.[4] And in the second half of the twentieth century, the U.S. military was primarily concerned with the threat of a Soviet armored advance across Europe. Despite its successful state-building enterprises in Germany and Japan following World War II, it did not institutionalize or prepare for any similar contingencies. Following the Cold War, the focus shifted to the need to develop capacities to fight two major regional campaigns in the Middle East and Asia.[5] The contemporaneous experiences in peacekeeping and stabilization operations made only a marginal impact and were generally perceived as detracting from the military's need to maintain readiness against anticipated conventional foes.[6]

At no time, however, has the U.S. military's prioritization matched the types of operations under way. In the nineteenth century "the U.S. Army embraced the conventional Prussian military system as [a] paragon of professionalism at the same time that the American Army was engaged in the frontier war against the Indians—the most unorthodox of the U.S. Army's 19th-century enemies."[7] Similarly, the roles and missions of the U.S. military delineated by Root hardly reflected the "era of small wars" that was the 1900–1940 period, in which the U.S. military was once again called upon to conduct a number of irregular engagements, including a counterinsurgency campaign in the Philippines and a nineteen-year stability operation in Haiti.[8] During the Cold War, the U.S. military's preoccupation with the Soviet threat in Europe and the Chinese threat in Asia did not prevent it from embroiling itself in an intense counterinsurgency campaign in Vietnam.[9] In the post-Vietnam era, the U.S. military was involved in a series of unconventional operations and postconflict stabilization campaigns, and with the end of the Cold War it once again found itself engaging in peacekeeping and stabilization operations at an increasing rate, with deployments to Kuwait, Somalia, Haiti, Bosnia, Kosovo, Afghanistan, and, most recently, Iraq.

The U.S. military's singular focus on conventional combat appears paradoxical given its record of frequent engagement in irregular operations. This discrepancy between theory and practice, between discourse and reality, has also had powerful implications on the U.S. military's engagement with counterinsurgency. It has engendered the U.S. military's "counterinsurgency syndrome," a cyclical condition involving three components: anticipation, adaptation, and learning.[10]

Anticipation

John D. Waghelstein has noted that "there is seemingly something in the Army's DNA that historically precludes it from preparing itself for the problems of insurgency or from studying such conflicts in any serious way until the dam breaks."[11] Of course, the diagnosis is in part self-fulfilling, as preempted insurgencies often leave no mark in the annals of history; one could arguably cite the co-option of militia in the South, including the Ku Klux Klan, following the Civil War, and the reconstruction of Germany following World War II, as two successful U.S. stabilization efforts.[12] Nonetheless, the point remains that, despite its history, and besides the occasional field manual or relevant pamphlet, the U.S. military never developed the training, education, and doctrine necessary to prepare for counterinsurgency campaigns. As Russell F. Weigley explains, "Whenever after the Revolution the American Army had to conduct a counter-guerrilla campaign—the Second Seminole War of 1835–1842, the Filipino Insurrection of 1899–1903, and in Vietnam in 1965–1973—it found itself almost without an institutional memory of such experiences, had to relearn appropriate tactics at exorbitant costs, and yet tended after each episode to regard it as an aberration that need not be repeated."[13]

Adaptation

The failure to anticipate and prepare for counterinsurgencies has put the onus squarely on the U.S. military's ability to adapt while in operation. The record here is mixed. The Philippines counterinsurgency in the early twentieth century illustrates a comparatively positive scenario and reveals the importance of individual experience to compensate for a lack of institutional memory. There was still no formal doctrine, no relevant instruction or training, but the troops sent to the Philippines were familiar, thanks to their experience in previous similar campaigns, with the exigencies of irregular operations.[14] This body of individual experience flattened the learning curve and undoubtedly contributed to the comparative level of success experienced in the Philippines campaign. Similarly, during the Vietnam War elements of the U.S. armed forces were able to develop successful counterinsurgency methods, as seen most clearly in the Civil Operations and Revolutionary Development Support (CORDS) and Combined Action Platoon (CAP) programs.[15]

While the U.S. military has at times adapted to the threat of insurgency, the lack of preparation for such contingencies has more often resulted in the application of inappropriate strategies, typically of a conventional flair and involving the overwhelming and indiscriminate use of force that is often counterproductive in counterinsurgencies. So-called "collective punishment" was apparent in the Second Seminole War, in which, from 1838 onward, the U.S. Army recruited Native American tribes as proxies to kill, enslave, and harass the Seminole civilian population.[16] Indiscriminate violence and the targeting of civilians were also hallmarks of the Indian Wars. During the Civil War, the Union campaign against an Arkansas guerrilla movement raised by Confederate forces in June 1862 involved retributive measures against guerrillas and populations alike, such as the destruction of villages deemed complicitous and the mass arrests and confiscation of property from suspected sympathizers.[17] Even the Philippines campaign was marked by brutality, collective punishment, and civilian casualties; it would be fair to say that "the success of the U.S. counterinsurgency effort was due not to committing atrocities . . . but by paying attention to the rudiments of counterinsurgency strategy."[18]

This form of "total counterinsurgency" seems to flow naturally from a military culture bent on conventional wars of attrition, in which the endgame was the annihilation of the enemy.[19] As Gen. Fred C. Weyand, U.S. Army field commander in Vietnam, put it, "The American way of war is particularly violent, deadly and dreadful. We believe in using 'things'—artillery, bombs, massive firepower—in order to conserve our soldier's lives."[20] A similar understanding was expressed a century earlier by Gen. William Tecumseh Sherman: "War is cruelty. There is no use trying to reform it. The crueler it is the sooner it's over."[21]

Learning

Even when sustained engagement in counterinsurgency campaigns has generated a body of knowledge and theory, the acquired wisdom has often been discarded.[22] At times, relevant doctrine has been produced—most notably the U.S. Marine Corps' 1940 *Small Wars Manual*—but such publications are rare and have also had a limited impact on the U.S. military as a whole.[23] More commonly, engagements with counterinsurgency have been cast as aberrations, justifying the lack of attention paid to their nature and complexity. This absence of learning relates intimately to the subsequent failure to anticipate; together, they form a cyclical inability to come to terms with the particular logic of counterinsurgency until it is too late, necessitating the type of improvised adaptation alluded to above.

This cycle has a long history. With time the U.S. military formed a moderately successful counterguerrilla approach against the Seminoles, but the lessons learned were never codified or passed on throughout the institution. As a result, the military had to relearn the relevant methods to overcome the several other Native American tribes it faced during the remainder of the nineteenth century.[24] However, any knowledge thus acquired was lost by the time of the Philippines insurgency, at which point the U.S. troops were "caught unawares by an unexpectedly robust insurgency" and had to "struggle . . . to develop and implement an effective counterinsurgency strategy."[25] Having subdued the insurgency, the U.S. military left the Philippines and, with it, most of what it had learned about counterinsurgency during the campaign, shifting its gaze instead toward conventional threats and capabilities. The focus was at this time on the Russo-Japanese war of 1904–1905, which caught the imagination of the U.S. military and seemed to justify an exclusive investment in conventional doctrine and training. "Believing that it was finally preparing for a Big War . . . the Army with some satisfaction turned to constructing coastal defenses and exercising brigades. Not for many more years would the need to relearn the lessons of pacification, peacekeeping, and occupation once again intrude upon the Army's consciousness."[26]

A similar shift in priorities followed the Vietnam War, when the U.S. military turned its attention from the small wars of Southeast Asia and toward the prospect of a conventional and possibly nuclear confrontation in Europe against the Soviet Union. Given the complications of the Vietnam War—the military's perception of excessive civilian meddling in its decision making, the high number of U.S. casualties, mounting domestic dissension over the campaign, and the ultimate strategic defeat—there was simply no will to dwell on the issue of counterinsurgency or to contemplate future such engagements. There were also good reasons to concentrate on Europe: Beyond all sorts of budgetary and institutional motivations, the focus on the European theater was clearly warranted by the need to mount a credible counterweight to the buildup of Soviet armor on the Central Front.[27] The fact that this shift in focus comprised a simultaneous and total neglect of counterinsurgency, however, was a result of the U.S. military's particular reading of its experience in Vietnam and its relation to counterinsurgency. Generally, the senior U.S. military staff felt that as a result of Vietnam "the Army had lost a generation's worth of technical modernization while gaining a generation's worth of nearly irrelevant combat experience."[28] The same feeling prevailed in the Marine Corps; in 1971 USMC Commandant Gen. Leonard F. Chapman observed that "we got defeated and thrown out . . . the best thing we can do is forget it."[29] Accordingly, in a subsequent attempt to define itself out of future "Vietnams," the Pentagon "gradually eliminated much of the infrastructure for fighting such conflicts."[30]

PAST COUNTERINSURGENCY ERAS

In a select few instances the U.S. military has sought to combat its "counterinsurgency syndrome" by integrating such missions into its doctrine, training, and education. The most distinctive of these efforts occurred in 1960s, when the U.S. military began to focus on counterguerrilla operations, and in the 1980s, when the spotlight was on "low-intensity conflict" (LIC). Both attempts at institutional learning offer insightful precursors to DoD's latest attempt to transform for stability operations. What makes these efforts so informative is not only the significant number of characteristics that they share but also the fact that neither period ultimately saw a significant improvement in the U.S. military's counterinsurgency capabilities. In that sense, both periods highlight a critical distinction between learning and the *appearance* of learning.

The first shared characteristic of the 1960s' and 1980s' learning processes relates to the initial motivation for examining counterinsurgency and other irregular operations. In each case the reorientation toward small wars was prompted by a perception of third world subversion, either as a Soviet-administered extension of power or as a phenomenon from which the Soviet Union could profit. President John F. Kennedy's personal interest in developing a national counterguerrilla capability was grounded in "concern over troubles with communists in Laos and in Vietnam, ideological doubts regarding African decolonization, and unfinished business in Cuba—where efforts were underway to slap down the first successful communist revolution in America's 'backyard.'"[31] The perceived threat of global communist subversion gained added urgency following an address by Nikita Khrushchev on January 6, 1961, in which he endorsed "wars of national liberation" in the third world.[32] In a speech delivered on April 27, 1961, Kennedy characterized the threat as a "monolithic and ruthless conspiracy that relies primarily on covert means for expanding its sphere of influence—on infiltration rather than invasion [and] on guerrillas by night instead of armies by day."[33] This new Soviet strategy required a U.S. counterstrategy.

The investment in LIC capabilities in the 1980s followed a similar rationale. Instead of featuring the anticipated conventional showdown in Europe against the Soviet Union, the late 1970s saw growing instability in the third world. During 1974–1980 the United States witnessed the ascendance of left-learning and Soviet-backed regimes in several states, including many former U.S. client states: Ethiopia (1974), Mozambique (1975), Angola (1976), Grenada (1979), and Nicaragua (1979). The Soviet invasion of Afghanistan in 1979, the Iranian revolution that same year, and the subsequent hostage crisis further demonstrated the volatility of international order and the vulnerability of U.S. partners without its support. As in the 1960s these developments were perceived through the lens of the Cold War and as offering opportunities to the Soviet Union to enhance its power and influence internationally.[34] The conclusion drawn within the U.S. government was that the contest with the Soviet Union had widened from the high-intensity theater in Europe and would now be fought globally, requiring greater worldwide deployability, power projection, and capabilities to conduct "low-intensity" operations.[35]

Though the motivation for concentrating on irregular campaigns was arguably simplistic, the U.S. military did take steps, first in the 1960s and again in the 1980s, to prepare and develop capabilities for such operations.[36] In the 1960s the action taken by the military was largely a response to pressure from the White House, specifically President Kennedy himself. In February 1961, one month after his inauguration, Kennedy issued National Security Action Memorandum (NSAM) 2, which "requested that the Secretary of Defense . . . examine means for placing more emphasis on the development of counter-guerrilla forces."[37] On January 18, 1962, issuing another NSAM, Kennedy established a high-level interagency committee, the Special Group (Counter-Insurgency), concerned specifically with the threat of insurgency. The group was mandated to ensure "proper recognition throughout the U.S. Government that subversive insurgency . . . is a major form of politico-military conflict equal in importance to conventional warfare" and "that such recognition is reflected in the organization, training, equipment and doctrine of the U.S. Armed Forces."[38]

The U.S. armed services responded to this pressure by making changes to its doctrine, training, and curricula. In April 1962 the Joint Chiefs of Staff issued the Joint Counter-Insurgency Concept and Doctrinal Guidance, which was superseded that August by the U.S. Overseas Internal Defense Policy, setting forth "a national counterinsurgency doctrine for the use of U.S. departments and agencies concerned with the internal defense of overseas areas threatened by subversive insurgency."[39] That same year the JCS appointed Maj. Gen. Victor H. Krulak as "special assistant for counterinsurgency and special activities," a post intended to provide an institutional focal point for these types of operations.[40] Also in 1962 both the ground services published doctrine relevant to counterinsurgency, with the Marine Corps issuing Fleet Marine Force Manual 8-2, *Operations against Guerrilla Forces*, and the Army including, for the first time, two chapters on countering irregular forces and on "situations short of war" in its edition of Field Manual 100-5.[41]

A 1962 report by the JCS detailing the "counterinsurgency accomplishments" of the U.S. military since the previous year noted the introduction of nine new counterinsurgency courses, a significant increase in hours-per-year spent studying counterinsurgency campaigns, and a growing commitment to developing linguistic skills.[42] Military training had likewise been adapted: The report declared that "it is now obligatory throughout the armed forces . . . to conduct field exercises addressed specifically to counterinsurgency."[43] Douglas Blaufarb adds that some schools even built mock Asian villages so as to provide troops with more realistic training conditions (this at a time when U.S. military advisers were assisting South Vietnam with its counterinsurgency campaign).[44]

The 1980s featured a similar reorientation, this time prompted by a combination of international incidents, operational setbacks, and subsequent congressional pressure. In 1981 the U.S. Army released FM 100-20, *Low Intensity Conflict*, thus ending a decade of silence on such operations. In 1984 the Combined Arms Operations Research Activity at Fort Leavenworth, Kansas, launched the "Absalon" training simulation, which reproduced the conditions of guerrilla warfare.[45] In 1986 the Army updated its capstone FM 100-5, *Operations*, which for the first time in more than a decade emphasized the need for the Army to master operations across the spectrum, including counterinsurgency.[46]

The activity was such that some spoke of the 1980s having "ushered in a new counterinsurgency era."[47] The Army configured and started developing light infantry divisions that would be more appropriate for less-than-conventional war. In 1986 the Army and Air Force established the Center for Low-Intensity Conflict (CLIC) "to improve the Army/Air Force posture for engaging in low-intensity conflict [and to] elevate awareness throughout the Army/Air Force of the role of military power in low-intensity conflict."[48] CLIC subsequently helped create a substantial two-volume study, *Joint Low-Intensity Conflict Project Final Report*, that set out recommendations for U.S. defense policy with regard to LIC, a part of the conflict spectrum it defined as "diplomatic, economic and military support for either a government under attack by insurgents or an insurgent force seeking freedom from an adversary government."[49]

To reinforce the new direction, Secretary of Defense Caspar Weinberger sponsored a two-day counterinsurgency conference at the National Defense University in 1986, bringing together a selection of experts and high-level policymakers to discuss the new strategic environment, the nature of low-intensity threats, and the optimal U.S. response.[50] The following year Congress mandated President Ronald Reagan to establish the Board for Low Intensity Conflict within the National Security Council "to coordinate the policies of the United States for low intensity conflict."[51] It was a priority apparently shared by Reagan's secretary of defense, who in his annual report to Congress in 1987 described as "the most plausible scenario for the future . . . a continuous succession of hostage crises, peacekeeping operations, rescue missions, and counterinsurgency efforts" and urged the development of a capability to respond to these threats and contingencies.[52] This senior-level attention to counterinsurgency came in sharp contrast to the outlook of the Pentagon leadership during the immediate post-Vietnam years.

LEARNING–OR THE APPEARANCE OF LEARNING

Despite the efforts outlined above both the 1960s' and 1980s' learning processes ultimately fell short of developing a U.S. military counterinsurgency capability. In terms of the U.S. military's understanding, prioritization, and capability to conduct such missions, neither process produced significant and sustained change.

At the most basic level it was a matter of bad timing. The reorientation in the 1960s was arguably too rushed; commenting on the "military counterinsurgency accomplishments" in its 1962 progress report, the JCS cited the great difficulty of turning the armed forces "from sophistication to simplicity, from total attention upon great weapons to serious consideration of humble ones, from an environment where technology is pre-eminent to one where improvisation plays a key part."[53] Furthermore, the 1960s' reorientation was in a sense interrupted by the 1965 decision to commit U.S. troops to the Vietnam War. Although that conflict did include an important counterinsurgency element in the form of the National Front for the Liberation of South Vietnam (NLF), the conventional threat of a North Vietnamese invasion was generally regarded as more pressing and therefore received more attention. In the 1980s the issue related not only to the time needed to internalize a new mind-set but also to the recent and traumatic memory of Vietnam, which unnecessarily complicated the U.S. military's reengagement with counterinsurgency. More than anything it was the failed intervention in

Southeast Asia that engendered the "Vietnam syndrome"—the U.S. military's overriding aversion to prolonged and costly on-the-ground engagement in intensely political campaigns.

To reduce the issue to one of timing would, however, be to obscure three critical and related factors that were instrumental in undermining both learning processes, in the 1960s and 1980s. First, both reorientations were underpinned by an unclear conceptual framework that conflated counterinsurgency with other less-than-conventional operations. This bundling together of distinct types of operations revealed a lack of appreciation for the specificity of counterinsurgency and resulted in it being either overlooked or misunderstood. Second, the military sought to delegate counterinsurgency missions to various special forces units on the perilous assumption that regular ground forces would not be needed. Although the initiatives and reforms associated with this approach gave the appearance of institutional learning, the approach in and of itself was problematic. Third, in the absence of a clear focus on counterinsurgency, particularly its nonmilitary aspects, and the delegation of counterinsurgency as a whole to special forces, the regular military was never compelled to challenge or abandon its strictly conventional, strike-oriented mind-set. More typically, this mind-set was broadened and even made to apply to the new missions of the decade, including counterinsurgency.

Confusion and Conflation

In both the 1960s and 1980s, the development of counterinsurgency capability was hampered by the failure to delineate the challenge precisely and to provide the military with a clear idea of its anticipated role in such campaigns. More specifically the effort to understand irregular warfare did not include a separate and realistic evaluation of the unique demands of counterinsurgency campaigns, principally the frequent need to deploy a significant number of appropriately trained ground forces for protracted periods, and for those forces to conduct tasks that are broader in range and very different from those of more limited combat operations. Through the construction of complex taxonomic structures and the employment of vague umbrella terms, these requirements for an effective counterinsurgency strategy were effectively obscured, resulting in a critical gap in the respective learning processes.

Charles Maechling Jr. notes that even though President Kennedy was fascinated with guerrilla warfare and counterinsurgency "the two were wholly confused in his mind."[54] This ambiguity contributed to the military's muddled understanding as to its function and role in the anticipated operations.[55] Throughout the 1960s "a variety of publications attempted to explain the difference between unconventional, guerrilla, counterguerrilla, counterinsurgency and special warfare, as well as between indigenous, irregular, partisan and guerrilla forces."[56] As it turns out counterinsurgency was considered but one of three components of "special warfare," a category that also included psychological operations and unconventional warfare, itself comprising guerrilla warfare, escape and evasion, and subversion versus hostile states.[57] Within this conceptual structure the focus throughout the 1960s was on sponsoring U.S.-friendly guerrilla movements and on training foreign militaries to combat local insurgents, with the prospect of direct U.S. engagement with counterinsurgency receiving comparatively little attention.[58] Accordingly, doctrine, education, and training relevant to guerrilla warfare tended "to be oriented toward waging such warfare, as against resisting it," with the former suiting the U.S. military's combat-oriented culture more so than the civil-military complexities of counterinsurgency.[59]

When the initiatives of the 1960s did focus specifically on counterinsurgency the mission was characterized as a predominantly military problem geared toward the elimination of insurgents through conventional means. In education and training, the instruction "stressed the proper employment of air power, armor, and artillery against insurgents in swamps, while civil programs got short shrift."[60] With regard to doctrine the Marine Corps' 1962 publication *Operations against Guerrilla Forces* emphasized firepower far above the nonmilitary aspects of counterinsurgency or the principle of minimum force.[61] Five years later the Army's FM 31-16, *Counterguerrilla Operations*, framed counterinsurgency as a collateral mission tagged on to the regular combat duties of divisions and brigades: "The Army prescribed no changes in organization nor any scaling down of the firepower to be used in fighting an insurgency."[62] Similarly the infrequent references to counterinsurgency in the professional military journals during the 1960s revealed an overall attempt "to fit counterinsurgency doctrine into something approximating traditional Army operations."[63]

In the 1980s, counterinsurgency was nominally subsumed under the term "low-intensity conflict," but as in the 1960s the use of this vague umbrella term often blurred the specific meaning and requirements of counterinsurgency. The definition was certainly descriptive of counterinsurgency: LIC was a "limited politico-military struggle to achieve political, social, economic, or psychological objectives" that "is often protracted," "ranges from diplomatic, economic, and psychosocial pressures," and is "often characterized by constraints on the weaponry, tactics, and level of violence."[64] However, *as interpreted* LIC did not relate primarily to counterinsurgency but instead to various distinct and far more strike-oriented operations that were also included in this category, ranging from special forces raids, counterterrorism to pro-insurgency operations, and even contingency campaigns with "mid-intensity" characteristics. As a result of this conflation, interest in LIC did not ultimately address the U.S. military's approach to counterinsurgency but various unrelated concerns: "the failure of the 1980 Iranian hostage rescue attempt . . . ; the withdrawal of U.S. Marines from Lebanon in 1983 after a terrorist bombing attack; the coordination problems that beset the U.S. Special Operations Forces during Operation 'Urgent Fury' . . . ; and problems associated with the SOF operational reaction to the *Achille Lauro* hijacking incident in 1985."[65]

Too often, operations were deemed low-intensity not because they signaled restraint on the use of force or military operations conducted among the people but because they were less total than the foreseen armored and possibly nuclear exchange against the Soviet Union. Further indicative of this interpretation was the assertion in the U.S. Army's 1986 capstone FM 100-5, *Operations*, that "while Air Land Battle Doctrine (ALB) focuses primarily on mid- to high-intensity warfare, the tenets of [ALB] apply equally to the military operations characteristic of low intensity war."[66] The prescription of a blitzkreig-like ultra-conventional mode of engagement to a category of conflicts intended to include counterinsurgency gives some measure of its marginalization within that category. Indeed, in the aftermath of Vietnam there was really no desire to revisit that particular topic.

The Advisory Approach

Flowing from the rushed nature of the reorientation and the concurrent conflation of concepts, the military displayed both an inability and an unwillingness to appreciate the unique logic of counterinsurgency and to develop the required capabilities. In the 1960s and 1980s the sluggishness of institutional innovation caught the attention of the White House and Congress respectively, resulting in new measures to compel the military to diversify. This added pressure was successful insofar as it prompted the emergence of "an approach" to counterinsurgency. However, during both the decades the approach to emerge assured that regular U.S. ground troops were not to feature in these missions, and that special forces units would instead be deployed to advise and train the security forces of the insurgency-threatened government.[67] This constituted a mutually acceptable compromise between the military and its civilian leaders, amounting—it would seem—to a counterinsurgency capability but posing no threat to the regular services' resource allocation or priorities.[68] However, as we shall see, the approach itself was problematic, and because it emerged in lieu of, rather than to complement, a capability for direct engagement in counterinsurgency within the regular services, it also served to justify the services' continued neglect of such missions.

In both decades, faith in the advisory approach to counterinsurgency resulted in dramatic boosts to the capabilities and authorities of various special forces components. In the early 1960s Special Warfare units, principally the Special Forces, were reinforced and given additional resources along with a wider remit. Kennedy upgraded the Special Forces headquarters at Fort Bragg, creating the Special Warfare Center, which had a broader mandate and was to be commanded by a brigadier general.[69] The other U.S. armed services followed suit: "The navy produced the SEALs, combat paratrooper frogmen who could do everything the Special Forces could do and more. The air force was rather more ambitious, establishing its First Air Commando Group in April 1961, and inaugurating its own Special Air Warfare Center at Eglin Air Force Base in Florida the following year."[70]

A similar phenomenon occurred in the 1980s. Whereas much of the U.S. military's Special Operations Forces (SOF) infrastructure had been dismantled following the Vietnam War, a series of Third World crises and setbacks prompted President Reagan to boost SOF funding from $440 million in FY1981 to $2.5 *billion* in FY1988.[71] As part of this ramping up, the U.S. Army established 1st Special Operations Command in 1982, which "activated and developed a complete array of SOF units [including] the Rangers, psychological warfare, and counter-terrorism units."[72] In the following years a number of new Special Operations groups and combat units were formed.[73] Finally, through the 1987 Defense Authorization Act the U.S. military consolidated the reemerging SOF capabilities by establishing the Special Operations Command (SOCOM), whereby SOF was made part of the unified command level.

The advisory approach to counterinsurgency is in many respects theoretically sound. It limits the deployment of combat troops and thus appears more respectful of the host nation's sovereignty. By producing a lighter "footprint," it results in interventions that are more discreet and less politically problematic, both for the U.S. and the threatened government. It also shields the U.S. military from active engagement in what were and still are considered to be the most complex and difficult types of operations: counterinsurgencies. These are instead undertaken by local troops who have the required linguistic skills, cultural awareness, and familiarity with the conflict-affected society.

Although this approach does have advantages, the manner in which it emerged and was applied in the 1960s and 1980s provided for an inadequate counterinsurgency capability. First, the value of military advisers related directly to the nature of the advice given and therefore demanded a sophisticated understanding of counterinsurgency that was often lacking. Second, the reliance on advisers presumed a level of cooperation with the host government that was and would not always be forthcoming. Third, it was never the actual deployment of U.S. troops that hindered the effective prosecution of a counterinsurgency campaign but rather their lack of training and familiarity with these types of missions. To exclude them altogether was thus to limit severely the range of options available to the U.S. military as it sought to assist insurgency-threatened governments.

Nothing illustrates the weaknesses of the advisory approach better than its actual implementation, first in support of the government of South Vietnam in the years leading up to the 1965 deployment of U.S. ground troops, and then in support of the El Salvador government against the Farabundo Marti National Liberation Front (FMLN) in 1981–1992. In Vietnam the U.S. military's institutional predilection toward conventional conflicts informed the guidance offered, which in turn affected the planning and conduct of operations by the local security forces. "We tried to build the ARVN [Army of the Republic of Vietnam] into conventional divisions just like we were," recalls Maj. Gen. John Tillson, a participant in the advisory effort.[74] As a result "the South Vietnamese Army, when it went on the offensive at all, followed the U.S. philosophy of wide-reaching sweeps and massive expenditure of firepower," tactics that "killed civilians and devastated the countryside without rooting out the guerrillas."[75]

The Vietnam experience also showcased the lack of leverage achieved through the advisory approach. Indeed, even when the U.S. military was able to contribute effectively to the development of a "homegrown" or otherwise promising counterinsurgency strategy, there was no assurance that the South Vietnamese government or armed forces would toe the line, particularly as the U.S. advice would often call upon the threatened government to compromise its own power and authority in order to save itself.[76] As it happened, American impatience with the Ngo Dinh Diem regime, which was unwilling or unable to implement the recommended reforms, resulted in a U.S.-sponsored coup that opened the door to the commitment of American ground troops in 1965.

Similar impediments marked the U.S. advisory effort in El Salvador. In this instance U.S. advisers were more familiar with the basic precepts of counterinsurgency, emphasizing time and again the need for social and political reform as paths toward victory.[77] They were also able to establish and train a number of specialized counterinsurgency units, such as the Atlacatl, Atonal, and Belloso battalions, which readily adopted small-unit approaches appropriate for counterguerrilla warfare.[78] Yet, not only were the successes of these units overshadowed by the atrocities and human rights abuses they inflicted on civilian populations; their understanding of counterinsurgency, such as it was, also contrasted with the general reluctance of the El Salvador Armed Forces (ESAF) to adapt to the nature of the conflict and abandon their big-war approach to operations.

As in Vietnam some blame could be placed on the nature of U.S. training, which at times remained colored by the U.S. military's own culture.[79] More critically, the advisers, many of whom were well versed with counterinsurgency, found it nearly impossible to influence the ESAF's conduct of operations; much like in Vietnam, exogenous efforts to change the local security forces encountered a distinct lack of leverage. In El Salvador this problem was exacerbated by the deliberate U.S. efforts to keep its footprint exceedingly small. Because of public (and congressional) aversion to a large-scale engagement—"another Vietnam"—the Reagan administration had restricted the maximum number of U.S. advisers deployable to El Salvador at any time to fifty-five and prohibited them from going on operations.[80] The approach thus relied on the El Salvador military being willing and able to follow the guidance given by these few advisers. Neither of these eventualities proved correct.

Commenting on the lack of leverage, one senior officer involved in the campaign asserted that "'observer' would be far more accurate [a] term than 'advisor' or 'trainer,'" adding that "these latter two terms require either a willingness of the host nation to accept advice/help, or lacking that, some sort of power base from which to implement change in spite of local resistance."[81] Furthermore, ESAF also had a free hand in the allocation of U.S. financial assistance and preferred to "purchase heavy weapons—105mm howitzers, 90mm recoilless rifles, and 72mm light antitank weapons—of little utility in a counterinsurgency," yet purchases with which the U.S. advisers would acquiesce, either by choice or necessity.[82] In the end "the assumption that the host nation would be willing to do what the United States recommended because they 'must,' did not hold."[83]

While ESAF's predilection toward conventional weaponry and tactics mattered less during the more conventional phase of the campaign in 1981–1984, it resulted in strategic stalemate once the FMLN adapted to ESAF's victories by dispersing and mounting hit-and-run attacks.[84] "To be sure," argue Andrew J. Bacevich and others, "tactical air support, heavy weapons, and battalion-size operations helped ESAF turn the tide in the war's early, desperate phase," but subsequently "ESAF's unsuitability for the 'other war' became apparent."[85] In this latter phase ESAF remained "a conventional army [using] conventional tactics to fight an unconventional war . . . a Salvadoran Army that is most comfortable operating in battalion-size formations, that relies on helicopters and trucks for mobility, and that has become dependent upon heavy firepower: close air support, attack helicopters, indirect fire, and antitank weapons."[86] As Robert Ramsey concludes his account of the campaign, "ESAF had averted defeat, but success against the insurgency had proved elusive."[87]

STICKING TO YOUR GUNS

The advisory approach had some inherent flaws but could have contributed to the toolkit of U.S. military options for countering insurgents. As it happened, both in the 1960s and 1980s there was no such toolkit, as the advisory approach was developed as the sole means of conducting counterinsurgency; ground troops were not to get involved. During the Kennedy administration the military "emphasized both the practical and political advantage of minimizing the direct involvement of U.S. combat forces in unconventional warfare."[88] In the 1980s the stance toward counterinsurgency followed the 1969 Nixon Doctrine, which stipulated that the United States would "furnish military and economic assistance [but] look to the nation directly threatened to assume the primary responsibility of providing the manpower for its defense."[89]

In both instances, the stances adopted were defensible, as the engagement of troops to establish stability in foreign lands ranks as one of the more risk-prone and complicated of all military operations. Nonetheless, this fact has not prevented these types of campaigns from taking place, which is, after all, what prompted the U.S. military's various efforts to learn counterinsurgency in the first place. Whether the U.S. footprint was minimized with operational efficaciousness or with risk-aversion in mind, the failure to anticipate the involvement of U.S. ground troops in counterinsurgency revealed a lack of foresight and, perhaps, a measure of wishful thinking. Notably missing in this analysis was the possibility that the deployment of advisers would lead to the deployment of troops, or the notion of having to intervene directly in failed or postconflict states where local powers are weak or nonexistent and therefore unable to provide the needed leverage.

In the 1960s as in the 1980s, this failure of foresight helped stultify the development of the military skills and capabilities needed for counterinsurgency. What one finds instead is a military sticking to its conventional remit and finding within its own conceptual misunderstanding of counterinsurgency a suitable validation for its lack of investment on this front. At worst the conventional approach of the U.S. military was even broadened and made to apply to the new types of operations under review.

In the 1960s' reorientation the scope for reform within the regular services was, according to Blaufarb, "more or less predetermined by the reluctance of the Joint Chiefs to accept at face value the president's commitment to a radical revision of its combat style, weaponry, and tactics."[90] The military was simply unwilling to sign on to the proposition that the new types of operations, principally counterinsurgency, would require a different approach to those practiced on the conventional battlefield.[91] Despite the training, education, and doctrinal efforts under way, the predominant feeling at senior echelons of the armed services was that any soldier trained for major war could also take on counterinsurgency duties—that these were, in fact, lesser-included operations.[92] Investment in counterinsurgency capabilities was therefore to be discouraged, lest it divert energy and resources from the military's core mission: preparing for conventional battle in Europe.[93] This predisposition affected the Army's promotion system, with Lloyd Norman and John B. Spore contending in 1962 that "the whole field of guerrilla operations was the burial ground for the future of any officer."[94]

There was thus a disconnect between the focus on counterguerrilla operations in doctrine and training and the mind-set instilled in most U.S. military officers.[95] At worst "the conventionally trained officer appears to feel that guerrilla operations are beneath his dignity."[96] At best he would regard counterinsurgency as a branch of conventional combat and seek to apply similar methods. Blaufarb concludes his study of the counterinsurgency era of the 1960s with a downbeat assessment: "With the exception of a few voices . . . they clung to the assumption that the principal role of *military force* in a counterinsurgency situation is to find and destroy the armed enemy rather than accepting the prior importance of protecting the population in order to separate the insurgents from their base." The latter approach, Blaufarb adds, "was viewed as a defensive strategy and anathema was pronounced upon it."[97] As seen from the discussion above, this is in line with the U.S. military's traditional approach to counterinsurgency.

A similar intransigence marked the 1980s' learning process, though its manifestations were different. As in the 1960s, the focus on LIC did not change the basic fact that "the Army's favored paths to promotion and career success led through service in conventional Army units" rather than through experience with counterinsurgency.[98] In this instance, however, the broad understanding of LIC meant that the U.S. military appeared as if it was innovating while it was in fact perfecting and broadening the application of conventional practices, which the U.S. armed forces then demonstrated to good effect in the 1989 invasion of Panama and the 1991 Gulf War.

In 1973 the U.S. military's *Restricted Engagement Options* study emphasized the need for greater interservice jointness in the prosecution of counterinsurgency operations.[99] Yet, even though jointness was one of the major defense preoccupations of the 1980s, it grew not out of the lack of coordination in Vietnam or the need to prepare specifically for other counterinsurgency campaigns but in response to the interservice dysfunction in conventional mid-intensity or special operations, principally the failed Iran hostage-rescue operation in 1980 and the invasion of Grenada in 1983.[100] Thus even though the changes to service relations brought on by the Goldwater-Nichols Reorganization Act of 1986 enabled the conventional victories in Panama and Iraq, the U.S. military's approach to counterinsurgency operations remained static.

In 1983 Robert Kupperman released a study, sponsored by the Army's Training and Doctrine Command (TRADOC), of the Army and the threat of LIC, here roughly interpreted as a typical counterinsurgency campaign. The study advocated the creation of the light infantry division (LID) to improve the U.S. military's ability to perform such missions.[101] The 1980s did see the standing-up of LID, yet while they could have played an important role in counterinsurgency campaigns—either as constabulary forces or through their increased tactical mobility—their application to LIC made them little more than deployable versions of the heavy forces in Europe, with a mandate to respond to new, but nonetheless conventional, threats in non-European theaters.[102] Various early documents outlining the intended purpose and structure of the LIDs suggested that they be designed "to seize beachheads and airheads, repel counterattacks, and ready an area of operations for the arrival of heavy forces"; to "attack or defend to delay or disrupt enemy armored forces"; and that "attacks by infiltration, air assault, ambush, and raid . . . be the norm."[103] In fact, and as Gen. Paul F. Gorman contended in 1986, "the main reasons for restructuring the division—intercontinental mobility—had little to do with low intensity conflict."[104]

The USMC's search for mobility during this time was also rooted in conventional war. In the post-Vietnam years, the Marine Corps deliberated how to balance the adoption of a role on the Central Front with the retention of its "mystical competence" in amphibious warfare, an identity-furnishing capability of the Corps but one whose likelihood of being used was then in decline.[105] The expansions of the Pentagon's horizons in the late 1970s provided part of the answer; the other was found within the Corps itself, where innovative thinkers were setting out the origins of what was later to crystallize into the USMC concept of "maneuver warfare."[106] This new concept, combining mechanization with mobility, propelled the Marine Corps toward the adoption of "light" wheeled armored carriers to become a "mechanized Marine amphibious force" with greater deployability and maneuverability.[107] However, the adversary to be combated through this approach to warfare remained armored forces—far from the minds of Marine Corps strategists and thinkers was the notion of its conducting "small wars" such as counterinsurgency and stability operations.

Any pretense that the U.S. military was seriously considering counterinsurgency in the 1980s should have been abandoned with the promulgation of the so-called "Weinberger Doctrine" by the then secretary of defense, Caspar Weinberger, on November 28, 1984. This influential doctrine set out conditions for the use of American military power; in the words of Robert Cassidy, it was "a prescription for the use of force that essentially proscribe[d] anything other than conventional war."[108] When deployed, the U.S. military would maintain domestic support by employing overwhelming force and thereby achieve a quick victory, presumably the destruction of the targeted enemy. Among other prerequisites for the commitment of U.S. troops, it precluded the use of force unless there was a clear exit strategy and U.S. troops were "committed wholeheartedly and with the clear intention of winning."[109] Messy, limited, and protracted counterinsurgency campaigns were clearly somehow to be avoided.

Unsurprisingly, both in the 1960s and 1980s, the failure to anticipate a role for regular units in counterinsurgency campaigns and to prepare accordingly resulted in repeated operational difficulties once troops were deployed for precisely those missions. Robert Doughty maintains that "American units were much better prepared [for counterinsurgency] when they entered combat in South Vietnam" than they had been in 1962.[110] That may certainly be the case, and the experience with CAP and CORDS did prove to be comparatively successful. Nonetheless there was still an overriding lack of understanding regarding the nature of effective counterinsurgency, and despite the many initiatives of the decade the military's approach remained distinctly combat-oriented. As Douglas Blaufarb explains, "It left the combat division unchanged in organization and equipment but required it to fight in the counterinsurgency mode."[111] This type of intransigence revealed the failure of the Kennedy administration to persuade the military institution to adapt; as one general is reputed to have exclaimed: "I'll be damned if I permit the United States Army, its institutions, its doctrine, and its traditions, to be destroyed just to win this lousy war."[112]

Importantly, the problem in Vietnam was not the use of conventional operations per se, as they certainly had their place against a North Vietnamese enemy able to respond in kind. The problem was instead the basic inability to shift gears and engage in counterinsurgency tasks as and when required.[113] Whether facing the standing armies of Hanoi or the guerrilla forces of the Vietcong, the standard U.S. military response would too often consist of large-unit operations employing overwhelming firepower. "The solution," as Gen. William Depuy is reputed to have opined, was "more bombs, more shells, more napalm . . . 'til the other side cracks and gives up."[114] The results of this approach were predictably devastating: "Villages and hamlets controlled or infiltrated by the Viet Cong were labeled enemy territory—and then all of the destructive power of high explosives intended for heavily fortified enemy positions was brought to bear on primitive bunkers and in straw-thatched villages."[115] Although these attacks may at times have rattled the NLF command structure, the misapplication of conventional tactics "proved too destructive to permit anything but transitory success in a purely military sense."[116]

The 1980s also reveal an overall failure to learn counterinsurgency. This conclusion is borne out by a cursory comparison of the U.S. military's blistering victory in Panama in December 1989 and its subsequent difficulties in stabilizing the country following the removal of Manuel Noriega and his regime. The invasion of Panama was an "overwhelming military success" that generated great enthusiasm for the U.S. military within DoD and beyond.[117] Building on the very same reforms that were to have improved the

U.S. military's ability to perform low-intensity operations, the conventional campaign was a joint endeavor, involving light deployable infantry as well as special operating forces. Analyzing the operation, Lorenzo Crowell reasoned that the overwhelming use of precise military force had not only destroyed the combat capability of the Panama Defense Forces but also "prompt[ed] all concerned to accept the United States' replacement of the Noriega regime with the Endara government."[118]

This enthusiasm was in no significant way dented by the substantial problems faced by the U.S. military during Blind Logic, the postconflict stabilization phase of the Panama operation, for which it had made no coherent plans. Specifically the U.S. military was unprepared and unable to deal with the wave of looting and criminality that followed the collapse of the government.[119] The regional commander-in-chief, Gen. Max Thurman, later remarked: "I did not even spend five minutes on *Blind Logic* during my briefing as the incoming CINC. . . . We put together the campaign plan for *Just Cause* and probably did not spend enough time on the restoration."[120] More than a lack of policy and plans, the U.S. military was also "programmatically and structurally ill-equipped for the situation that followed the fighting."[121] There was no training, concepts, or doctrine to fall back on, resulting in the "loss of order in Panama, severe economic damage, and a stability and crime problem."[122] In a 2004 study, the Defense Science Board concluded that, ultimately, Operation Just Cause "provides an illustrative example of how *not* to approach stabilization and reconstruction operations. Virtually every aspect of reestablishing a coherent Panamanian government was bungled."[123]

CONCLUSION: LEARNING FROM HISTORY

The U.S. military's effort to learn counterinsurgency can be understood as an attempt to break a cyclical and century-long tendency to marginalize such operations. Throughout history, the U.S. military has typically failed to prepare for counterinsurgency before the act, forcing it into hurried adaption once in operation. What renders the U.S. military's experience with counterinsurgency so cyclical is its seeming inability to learn either from its lack of preparation or from its subsequent adaptation in the field, but to revert instead to a singular focus on high-intensity warfare. This tendency can be thought of as the U.S. military's "counterinsurgency syndrome."

Previous attempts by the U.S. military to "kick" this syndrome have on the whole been unsuccessful. Assessing the 1960s' learning process, Blaufarb concludes that "the apparatus we have just described and the programs it generated did not, in fact, come to serious grips with the problems they were intended to solve."[124] And commenting on the U.S. military's learning effort in the 1980s, Downie concludes that "despite its considerable—and generally unsuccessful—experience with counterinsurgency operations in Vietnam and El Salvador, the Army made no conceptual change to its published counterinsurgency doctrine from the Vietnam War to the mid-1990s."[125]

In both decades three different but closely related reasons stand out as having impeded the military's effort to learn:

(1) Lack of conceptual clarity: The effort to understand irregular warfare did not include a separate evaluation of the specific and in many ways unique characteristics of counterinsurgency operations.

(2) Engagement frontloaded with assumptions: The approach formulated by the U.S. military to respond to insurgencies relied precariously on a number of prerequisites that would, in theory, obviate the deployment of U.S. ground troops.

(3) Culture of military: The strong offense-oriented culture of the U.S. military served to shape the learning process, resulting in the further perfection and broadening of conventional practices, most of which were inappropriate for counterinsurgency operations.

The 1960s' and the 1980s' efforts were predicated on similar conceptualizations of counterinsurgency as bundled together with a host of other less-than-conventional military engagements. This conflation of different types of operations resulted in the relative marginalization and misunderstanding of counterinsurgency, as well as a learning process that was not sufficiently targeted to be effective.

In both decades, the high faith placed in SOF as the agents of counterinsurgency was particularly problematic. While the advisory approach does present some intrinsic advantages, advisers have less leverage, both politically and militarily, compared with ground troops. More critically, investments in special forces were made on the assumption that their deployment would *preclude* that of U.S. combat troops; this approach hoped to displace counterinsurgency combat duties from the U.S. military to the indigenous armed forces of the host nation. In the end, however, such hope was misplaced and served to stunt the development of a counterinsurgency capability within the U.S. military's regular services. In theory excluded from future counterinsurgency operations, the regular services instead perfected what they already knew best: conventional force-on-force combat.

What relevance do these findings have for the U.S. military's latest attempt to develop a counterinsurgency capability? At the most immediate level, the experiences help explain why the U.S. military had not, by the turn of the century, done more to prepare for counterinsurgency operations.

On a deeper level these two episodes provide potentially significant precursors to subsequent learning efforts.

First, the two learning processes demonstrate the importance of basing any reorientation on a firm and realistic understanding of what counterinsurgency may require, particularly in terms of U.S. troop participation. History clearly shows that engagement in counterinsurgency is not optional and that it often requires the deployment of a large number of ground troops to engage in a range of civil and military tasks. The reliance on surrogates will, of course, remain a strategically wiser response, but only as long as these surrogates exist and are sufficiently competent and reliable to undertake the task at hand. As illustrated in Afghanistan after 2001 and Iraq after 2003, this is not always the case. The regular services must therefore be included in the reorientation, lest their capability to conduct counterinsurgency remain underdeveloped, as in the 1960s and 1980s.

Second, both learning processes illustrate that the appearance of change does not necessarily denote actual change. The emergence of the advisory approach to counterinsurgency did allow the U.S. military to appear as if it was innovating, even though the formulated approach rested on shaky premises. It is also evident that published doctrine does not in itself signify learning. Nor can a range of activity covering various types of irregular operations compensate for a lacking counterinsurgency capability; this latter type of engagement is in many ways unique and requires specific attention. This distinction between learning and the appearance of learning will be critical in the analysis of the U.S. military's most recent attempt to reorient toward stability operations.

3

REVISITING COUNTERINSURGENCY

The U.S. military's attitude toward stability operations at the turn of the twenty-first century can be understood as a combination of disinterest and aversion. The defense reviews and planning documents of the time made token nods to the need to prepare for "full-spectrum" operations or to counter "asymmetric" threats but skirted over the complexities and possibility of conducting stability operations in contested environments. By late 2005, however, the very same institution had issued a directive that placed precisely such operations on equal footing with conventional war-fighting—historically the core mission of the U.S. military—and that tasked the various components of the organization to prepare and structure themselves accordingly.[1] The about-face was dramatic, not least because the U.S. military has traditionally considered counterinsurgency and stability operations as beyond its remit. Moreover, it occurred under a president (George W. Bush) and secretary of defense (Donald Rumsfeld) who had entered office in 2001 seeking to minimize the use of U.S. troops in "nation building."

This chapter examines the initial phase of this reorientation. First, it identifies the mind-set and priorities of the U.S. military as it transitioned into the twenty-first century. The perspective gained through this assessment helps uncover the tensions that marked the U.S. military's subsequent engagement with stability operations. Particularly relevant in this regard is the manner in which the U.S. military interpreted the operations it had conducted during the 1990s, a decade marked by nearly continuous engagement in "peace operations" and by the ascendance of the so-called "Revolution in Military Affairs (RMA)."

The chapter then assesses the changes to U.S. defense policy brought on by the "War on Terror," or the U.S. military's campaign against al-Qaeda in the aftermath of the September 11, 2001, attacks on the United States. Albeit in many ways a significant turning point, 9/11 did not fundamentally change the U.S. military's understanding and prioritization of irregular war. Nor did the campaign in Afghanistan initially prompt the U.S. military to view stability operations and counterinsurgency in a new light. It would take the encounter with low-level violence in Iraq to compel a shift within DoD. Even then, however, institutional resistance against revisiting counterinsurgency and stability operations remained palpable.

MOOTW AND THE RMA

The U.S. military's operational experience with peacekeeping and peace enforcement during the 1990s, in Somalia, Haiti, Bosnia, and Kosovo, strongly affected its understanding and prioritization of stability operations as it moved into the twenty-first century. It might have been expected that virtually uninterrupted institutional experience with what came to be termed Military Operations Other Than War (MOOTW) would have prepared the armed forces for stability operations. After all, both stability operations and MOOTW tend to be protracted civil-military affairs, occurring principally in urban environments and requiring restraint, legitimacy, and political astuteness on the part of the intervening force. And indeed there were some notable initiatives relating to such campaigns during the 1990s, such as the opening of the Peacekeeping Institute in 1993 by Army Chief of Staff Gen. Gordon Sullivan and the issuing of the Army's FM 100-23, *Peace Operations*, in 1994 and of Joint Publication 3-07, *Joint Doctrine for Military Operations Other than War*, in 1995.[2] Yet, while "support to counterinsurgency" was in theory included in the category "MOOTW," and while "the restoration and maintenance of order and stability" was included in the term "peace operations," the experience gained by the U.S. military in the 1990s did not in the end prepare it for the challenges it was to face in Afghanistan and Iraq, or even for stability operations in general.[3] Instead, it more often served to *delay* and *deter* the U.S. military's reengagement with such missions.

Most fundamentally, the overlap between the 1990s' peace operations and the stability operations since 2000 was smaller than might be expected. With the important exception of the Somalia intervention in 1992–1994, the missions of the decade were all conducted in permissive environments, where U.S. ground troops would only rarely face armed resistance. The Somalia experience was the exception to confirm this rule. Although it, too, had originally been conceived as a humanitarian and relatively risk-free "peace operation," the interests pursued by the first United Nations Operation in Somalia (UNOSOM) put it on a collision course with warlord Mohamed Farrah Aideed and his militia. When the U.S. military began targeting Aideed's bases and weapons sites it unwittingly designated itself a combatant in the country's struggle for power.[4] It thus embroiled itself in an escalating confrontation with Aideed's forces, culminating in the shooting down of two U.S. Black Hawk helicopters in early October 1993 and a subsequent firefight in Mogadishu in which eighteen U.S. soldiers and thousands of Somalis were killed.[5]

Rather than reassess the grounding assumptions of peace operations and prepare for future missions conducted in nonpermissive environments, the U.S. government reacted to the Mogadishu experience by seeking to avoid any peace operation that might risk U.S. combat troops.[6] "The bottom line" of Bill Clinton's Presidential Decision Directive (PDD) 25 on peacekeeping, issued shortly after the withdrawal from Somalia, was "that the United States will only commit ground troops with a peace enforcement mandate and with robust forces, after a peace agreement has been signed."[7] Future humanitarian adventures were also to operate according to a clear timetable and exit strategy. In short, the Weinberger Doctrine was applied to peace operations, to the degree possible, and with a view to reduce risks to U.S. combat forces.[8]

These principles were foundational to the design and running of future peace operations. During Operation Restore Democracy—the U.S. military deployment to Haiti in 1994–1995—the Army leadership in particular "kept force protection at the forefront" and failed to change this policy "either to reflect the virtual absence of resistance or . . . the sense of the mission."[9] Though the Marine Corps detachment did interpret its rules of engagement less narrowly, the Army preferred to retain its neutrality for the sake of force protection; as intended, therefore, the "Kevlar zone" saw no Army casualties.[10] Meanwhile, the exit strategy in Haiti was precisely defined and occurred according to schedule, leading one scholar to suggest that "the exit strategy became the mission."[11] Adding nuance to this charge, others contended that "the key conditions for departure—basic order, the return of Aristide, and the conduct of a presidential election resulting in a peaceful transfer of power—were met" but added that the scorecard looked good only because of "the Army's tendency to focus on process and the successful execution of specific jobs, rather than the long-term political objective" and "that little in Haiti had fundamentally changed in terms of the big picture."[12] James Traub notes, for example, that "the military made no serious effort to disarm rival factions, which ensured that violence would flourish as soon as the troops left . . . and the troops left quickly."[13]

The later peace operations in the Balkans conformed to similar conditions. Both the Bosnia and Kosovo operations occurred in largely permissive environments, where peacekeeping troops would not be targeted. The only difference was that U.S. withdrawal now hinged on conditions on the ground rather than timetables elaborated in Washington. This tendency not to commit troops to nonpermissive circumstances, but to do so for consensual peacekeeping, nonetheless became characteristic of Bill Clinton's administration and was articulated by the president himself at the onset of the Kosovo campaign: "If NATO is invited . . ., our troops should take part in that mission to keep the peace. But I do not intend to put our troops in Kosovo to fight a war."[14]

Whereas some of the lessons learned in these campaigns might be relevant to stability operations, the institutional experience with peace operations was too firmly wedded to the notion of maintaining a permissive and consensual operating environment. This precondition of engagement was a strategic luxury of the 1990s, yet the notion that it may not always apply was given no serious consideration.[15] As it turned out, the 1990s' peace operations operated by an entirely different logic to the much bloodier campaigns in Afghanistan and Iraq and therefore constituted poor prototypes for these missions.

The permissiveness of the 1990s' campaigns had two other pernicious effects on the U.S. military's understanding and prioritization of stability operations. First, it encouraged a view within the U.S. military that operations short of war were "lesser-included" cases, simpler than high-intensity combat and requiring no special training or knowledge that could not be imparted immediately prior to deployment.[16] By this logic it was natural and justifiable for DoD to devote most of its attention and resources to high-intensity war and to marginalize all types of MOOTW, including stability operations. This bias was reflected in doctrine. Although the field manuals of the 1990s talked of "full-dimensional operations," this was taken to mean "employing all means available to accomplish any given mission decisively and at the least cost"—hardly language suited for stability operations, which are seldom decisive or low in cost.[17] Furthermore, and despite occasional nods to the lower end of operations, the capstone doctrine of the 1990s consistently revealed the institution's combat-oriented mind-set, emphasizing time and again the need for the Army "to win quickly with minimum casualties."[18] As the U.S. military moved into the twenty-first century, it regarded MOOTW, including (implicitly) stability operations, as eminently manageable by a force trained and optimized for conventional combat.

Second, by making the lower end of operations seem easy to conduct (if not to bring to a close), the constant permissiveness of the 1990s' peace operations eventually led to a negative view of having American soldiers participate in such missions. Precisely because these operations were conducted in consensual environments, the argument emerged that MOOTW were not worthy of the U.S. military, eroded its readiness for conventional combat, and could just as well be conducted by someone else.[19] Condoleezza Rice put it sardonically when she argued that "we don't need to have the 82nd Airborne escorting kids to kindergarten."[20] This type of reasoning gathered momentum with the lack of political progress seen in Bosnia and Kosovo, as the U.S. commitments to MOOTW were made to seem never-ending. Over time, questions surfaced within the U.S. military and beyond regarding the strategic relevance of having American troops rotate in and out of the Balkans' seemingly dormant conflict zones.

Importantly, the distaste for peace operations extended to all operations short of war and therefore also tainted the prospect of committing U.S. troops to stability operations. The confusion of peacekeeping with counterinsurgency and stability operations was based on the U.S. military's erroneous (and typical) conflation of all operations other than conventional war into one analytical category. Whereas it could be argued that the experiences with peace operations provided some familiarity with less conventional campaigns, the larger effect of these campaigns was to entrench the historically consistent tendency of the U.S. military to dismiss the entire "lower end" of the conflict spectrum as a distraction.

This trend was reinforced by the U.S. military's experiences with conventional campaigns during the 1990s, in which the emerging technologies associated with the RMA—including satellites, precision bombing, and information technology—had appeared to provide a means of avoiding the pitfalls of complex ground operations. The coercive engagements over Bosnia and Kosovo were dominated by precision bombing from a virtually risk-free altitude and the notable absence of U.S. ground forces, whose role was instead played by local allies (the Croat forces in Bosnia and the Kosovo Liberation Army in Kosovo). This approach to war seemed to provide leverage while drastically limiting the U.S. footprint and, with it, the risk of casualties. It also fit hand-in-glove with various theories on the nature of future war that had thrived within the Pentagon during this so-called "strategic pause" and all of which, interestingly, predicted a technology-dominated, high-intensity vision of engagements to come.[21] With theory and practice apparently pointing in the same direction, proponents within DoD began pushing for accelerated investment in RMA-related capabilities, seeing here an "opportunity to use the new information technology to change the very nature of our military, in a way that could reinvigorate American political, diplomatic, and economic leadership."[22] Yet, this investment would not be possible, it was argued, as long as the U.S. military was stuck with "keeping the peace" in the Balkans.[23]

It was against this backdrop that George W. Bush was elected president in 2000. During his presidential campaign and first few months in office, Bush made no secret of where he stood with regard to U.S. military participation in stability operations. "I don't think our troops ought to be used for what's called nation-building," Bush contended during the 2000 presidential debate. "I think our troops ought to be used to fight and win war."[24] It was a position also shared by Condoleezza Rice, Bush's foreign policy adviser during the campaign and, following the inauguration, his National Security Advisor. In an article published in January 2000, Rice articulated what was to become Bush's stance on U.S. military participation in "lower-end" operations: "Using the American armed forces as the world's '911' will degrade capabilities, bog soldiers down in peacekeeping roles, and fuel concern among the great powers that the United States has decided to enforce notions of 'limited sovereignty' worldwide in the name of humanitarianism."[25] Strongly informed by the Balkan campaigns, the Bush administration erroneously assumed that future "nation-building" missions would be peripheral to the U.S. national interest and easily managed by the armed forces of other nations more suited to the task. It was a mind-set that assigned any "military operation other than war" to irrelevance.

Instead of conducting state-building, Bush wanted the U.S. military to take advantage of the "strategic pause" in international relations to make the RMA a reality. In an address in 1999, Bush set out the foundations of what was to become his defense policy: "Power is increasingly defined, not by mass or size, but by mobility and swiftness. Influence is measured in information, safety is gained in stealth, and force is projected on the long arc of precision-guided weapons. . . . The best way to keep the peace is to redefine war on our terms. . . . The real goal is . . . to use this window of opportunity to skip a generation of technology. . . . Our forces in the next century must be agile, lethal, readily deployable, and require a minimum of logistical support."[26]

To implement this agenda, Bush appointed Donald Rumsfeld to become secretary of defense on January 20, 2001. Rumsfeld took immediate steps to capitalize on the seemingly revolutionary developments in information technology; in his own words, he sought to "build a military that takes advantage of remarkable new technologies to confront the new threats of this century."[27] The RMA was rebranded as "Transformation" and became a dominant theme in the Pentagon's September 30, 2001, Quadrennial Defense Review (QDR), which also made no mention of stability operations or counterinsurgency.[28]

For all this, transformation was not primarily a reaction to the U.S. military's involvement in stability and peace operations. Instead it was a response to the institution's adherence to the Weinberger Doctrine of overwhelming force, which had since its articulation in 1984 circumscribed when the United States ought to commit its troops to combat. As seen from the analysis in chapter 2, the Weinberger Doctrine restricted the use of U.S. military power to operations in which vital national interests were threatened; troops were committed with the intention and ability to achieve decisive victory; public and congressional support could be maintained; and use of force was a last resort.[29] If those conditions were satisfied, the U.S. military would mass and attack with overwhelming force to guarantee a swift and unambiguous victory. Elaborated in the aftermath of an abortive peacekeeping mission in Lebanon, which ended with a terrorist attack that killed 241 U.S. servicemen, the Weinberger Doctrine was a reaction against U.S. participation in seemingly open-ended and uncertain missions. It was also a reaction to the business-management approach to war elaborated by Secretary of Defense Robert S. McNamara during the Vietnam War, which had sought to use limited force to achieve limited political outcomes.[30] Gen. Colin Powell, a proponent of the Weinberger Doctrine, rejected this strategy of "gradual escalation," warning against the "so-called experts" who called for "a little surgical bombing or a limited attack." "History," he added, "has not been kind to this approach to war-making."[31]

This outlook put the adherents of the Weinberger Doctrine on an intellectual collision course with those driving the transformation process, a group that included Donald Rumsfeld and George W. Bush.[32] With its emphasis on massing an overwhelming force before acting, the Weinberger Doctrine came to be seen by its critics as risk-averse, paralyzing, and as unimaginative in its use of American military power. In its place, transformation enthusiasts perceived the ascendance of information-age technology and concepts as an opportunity to employ precise military means to create specific political "effects."[33] The U.S. military was thus to become faster and more agile, able to intervene more often and more effectively, not by massing unwieldy military formations but through the creative exploitation of information-age capabilities, especially precision-guided munitions. One slogan of the time was "replace mass with information."[34]

Notably, neither the adherents of transformation nor of the Weinberger Doctrine gave much notice to the prospect of U.S. military engagement in counterinsurgency. For different reasons both camps grounded their respective visions for the U.S. military on the questionable assumptions that counterinsurgency operations did not pose a specific challenge or could simply be avoided. For adherents of the Weinberger Doctrine there was little to be gained and much to be lost by committing U.S. troops to campaigns that promised neither a clear exit strategy nor the prospect of a decisive victory, particularly as they also presented significant risk to the U.S. soldiers involved. Meanwhile, counterinsurgency did not attract much attention within the growing literature on transformation or was presented as amenable to the precision-strike toolkit offered through the information revolution.[35] To the extent that the literature considered irregular operations at all, the focus was overwhelmingly "on the aspects of OOTW that looked most like conventional war. . . . It did not really consider the central feature of OOTW, the operation of forces in a complex civilian environment, at all."[36]

While fighting it out in this moment of institutional change, these two camps expunged one of the more demanding types of military operations from their theoretical baselines. This left a third group, much marginalized and even maligned, that had experience in the peace operations of the 1990s and perceived repeated engagement in "low-intensity" or "irregular" confrontations, particularly in nonpermissive environments, not only as very likely but also as very challenging. The main message of this group, as phrased by USMC Gen. Charles Krulak, was that "the threat in the early years of the next century will not be the 'son of Desert Storm'—it will be the 'stepchild of Chechnya.'"[37]

The influence of this third group upon the wider military is well illustrated by General Krulak's own attempts, as commandant, to familiarize the Marine Corps with complex urban operations. Krulak helped create the "Urban Warrior" experiment, which focused on operations conducted in populated areas and was based in part on the Corps' earlier experience in Somalia. The concept behind Urban Warrior was the so-called "three-block war," the term coined by General Krulak to describe the simultaneity of combat operations, peacekeeping, and humanitarian relief within a single urban campaign. In 1999 Urban Warrior evolved into Project Metropolis, another attempt to develop an approach to military operations in urban terrain. Although these measures constituted promising evidence of Marine Corps innovation, the learning did not take. According to one scholar, "The corps during and after Krulak's command maintained a strong emphasis on being able to fight in its traditional style as the amphibious shock troops in conventional warfare."[38]

The episode is representative of the wider U.S. military at this time. In a limited way, the Army's and the Marine Corps' institutional experience with peacekeeping, peace enforcement, urban, and stability operations was being codified in doctrine, education, and training. More generally, however, these types of operations did not capture the military's attention. The databank of relevant information was further depleted as the U.S. military embraced transformation and ramped down in the Balkans. At this point the main repository of knowledge and experience relating to stability and peace operations rested in the minds of those officers convinced of the importance, difficulty, and likelihood of such campaigns.

THE WAR ON TERROR: CONTINUITY AND CHANGE

The U.S. military was in the middle of a transition when America was attacked by al-Qaeda on September 11, 2001: President Bush was actively reducing the U.S. contribution to the peacekeeping operations in the Balkans, and the U.S. military as a whole was being pushed to implement the transformation agenda of Donald Rumsfeld.[39] With its emphasis on military freedom of action and global reach, transformation gained new adherents in the wake of 9/11, as it answered to the U.S. public's clamoring for swift and decisive retribution against those who had sponsored and conducted this attack.[40]

The QDR released on September 30 outlined Rumsfeld's vision for the U.S. military, which overnight found itself confronting a new strategic environment. As stated, there was no mention either of stability operations or of counterinsurgency in this QDR. The document did specify that "the inability of some states to govern their societies, safeguard their military armaments, and prevent their territories from serving as sanctuary to terrorists and criminal organizations can also pose a threat to stability and place demands on U.S. forces."[41] The QDR also declared that the capability to achieve decisive victory "will include the ability to occupy territory or set the conditions for regime change if so directed," something that would presumably involve stabilization and reconstruction activities.[42] Yet even though it noted the "increasing challenges and threats emanating from the territories of weak and failing states," there was as yet no focus on how the U.S. military could prepare and posture itself to conduct postconflict operations, counteract state failure, and reinforce weak governments.[43]

Instead there was a heavy combat-oriented touch to the document. The six goals it set out as the focus of transformation included various conventional deterrent tasks and the development of a global precision-strike complex; the language was of "protecting critical bases of operations"; "defeating anti-access and area-denial threats"; "assuring information systems in the face of attack"; "enhancing . . . space systems"; and the development of "an interoperable, joint C4ISR [Command, Control, Communications, Computers, Intelligence, Surveillance, and Reconnaissance] architecture and capability."[44] The only objective that spoke of irregular threats was, it too, geared toward the development of strictly combat-oriented capabilities: "Denying enemies sanctuary" would mean "providing persistent surveillance, tracking, and rapid engagement with high-volume precision strike, through a combination of complementary air and ground capabilities."[45] But nowhere was it anticipated that the U.S. military would conduct stability or counterinsurgency operations; the two or three sentences dealing with military occupation, state failure, and regime change were grossly outweighed by the verbiage of transformation and C4ISR.

With the short time span separating 9/11 and the publication of the 2001 QDR, the lack of focus on irregular threats may not be all that surprising, particularly as the "review and the accompanying report were largely completed before the September 11 . . . terror attacks."[46] Nonetheless, rather than suggest that a new vision might be needed to address an apparently new threat, the document instead stated that the 9/11 attacks "confirm[ed] the strategic direction and planning principles that resulted from this review."[47] Given the QDR's strong focus on conventional capabilities, and the patently unconventional nature of the al-Qaeda threat, this statement is revelatory of the U.S. military's understanding of irregular warfare at the time.

Transformation thus continued unabated in the months following 9/11 and, with it, the general neglect of counterinsurgency and stability operations. In October 2001 Secretary Rumsfeld created the Office of Force Transformation within OSD. In late 2001 he began personally interviewing officers for two- and three-star promotions, an unprecedented practice for any secretary of defense, so as to ensure a shared vision of force transformation.[48] In 2002 Joint Forces Command (JFCOM) was made a lead agency of DoD's overall transformation process. Soon thereafter the U.S. military services were requested to submit yearly Strategic Transformation Assessments to OFT to ensure their adherence to this new vision.[49]

Because sustained engagement in stability operations did not fit within the theory espoused by the transformation community, any prospect of engaging in such operations was largely overlooked. Central incompatibilities related to the concentration of troops, the duration of their deployment, and the tasks they were asked to undertake. Whereas transformation was geared toward achieving light footprints and swift victories, stability operations often require the protracted deployment of a sufficiently sizeable ground force, one that is able to provide security and basic services pending transfer to local authorities. More fundamentally, transformation was predicated on striking targets, yet this is not the main function of a military force engaged in stability operations. Neither are precision-guided munitions—the anticipated means of attack through transformation—of particular use in counterinsurgency operations, in which the adversary typically disperses to avoid detection or operates in urban settings, forcing politically delicate decisions regarding missile precision and collateral damage to civilians and nonmilitary targets.[50] These and other inconvenient incompatibilities made the integration of counterinsurgency within U.S. military priorities all the more difficult during this time of force transformation.[51]

The faith in transformation and the concomitant neglect of "lower-end" operations colored the manner in which the United States approached and carried out Operation Enduring Freedom, its campaign in Afghanistan against the Taliban and al-Qaeda. As in the 2001 QDR a disconnect between rhetoric and action could be detected. One of the main objectives of the campaign had been to "make it increasingly difficult for the terrorists to use Afghanistan freely as a base of operations," an aim that rested precariously on the ability of the newly installed Afghan regime to extend control over the country's large ungoverned areas.[52] In an interview with the *Washington Post* in December 2001, Rumsfeld recognized this war aim, stating that "we don't want Afghanistan a year from now to go back to being a place that harbors terrorists, so it is in our interest to be attentive to what kind of government comes along."[53]

Yet while pointing to the importance of stabilizing Afghanistan, however, the White House and Pentagon approach to Enduring Freedom saw no role for the U.S. military in the international stabilization force, the International Security Assistance Force, or in stability operations more generally.[54] Instead its remit in Afghanistan remained limited to strike missions against specific Taliban and al-Qaeda targets in the south and east of the country. As Rumsfeld explains in the same *Washington Post* interview: "We don't think of ourselves as being part of the security force in Kabul. We know what we want to do and when we have done it, we can go do it someplace else. What we want to do is to capture or kill the senior Taliban leadership and see that they are punished. . . . With respect to al Qaeda, we want to capture or kill the senior leadership and catch and imprison the remainder. . . . When those things are accomplished from a military standpoint, we will have done our job."[55]

The refusal to commit U.S. troops for stabilization tasks drew significant criticism, particularly because the Afghan government was at this time severely undercut by flagging international support and was experiencing instability outside of Kabul, a proliferating narcotics industry, and feuds between rival warlords.[56] The debate as to whether the U.S. military should have acted otherwise is beyond the scope of this book, although it does seem clear that the light-footprint approach and the rush to exit Afghanistan did adversely impact the subsequent stabilization effort.[57] The point, however, is that these types of operations were not included in the U.S. military's remit, even though the rhetoric emerging from the White House and Pentagon acknowledged the radical threats that could grow out of ungoverned areas and failed states—Afghanistan in particular.

There were many reasons behind the reluctance to commit U.S. troops to the stabilization of Afghanistan. Two factors stand out as fundamental, and both stem directly from the U.S. military's reading of its operational experiences in the 1990s. First, the missions in the Balkans persuaded both the Pentagon and the White House under George W. Bush that its European coalition partners were more than capable, and certainly more suited, to undertake stabilization tasks. In a press conference on April 17, 2002, Secretary Rumsfeld explained that "if it's appropriate to put in more forces for war-fighting tasks, the United States will do that" but that "there are plenty of countries on the face of the Earth who can supply peacekeepers."[58] The rationale behind this burden-sharing, Rumsfeld continued, was that the U.S. military should, given its size and operational commitments, conduct only strike and advisory missions. This stance was informed by the U.S. military's growing disregard for MOOTW, including stability operations, as interminable and as of lesser importance—a mind-set shaped by its memory of the 1990s' peacekeeping campaigns. Indeed, by using precisely that word, "peacekeepers," Rumsfeld seemed to suggest that the mission in Afghanistan would resemble those conducted in the Balkans—a misinformed yet, in this context, very revealing assumption.

Second, and as argued by Rumsfeld, there was a belief that the commitment of troops would, more than that of international aid, create an Afghan dependence on the United States. As Rumsfeld put it, "The objective is not to engage in what some call nationbuilding. Rather it's to try to help the Afghans so that they can build their own nation."[59] Drawing directly on the Clinton administration's experience in the Balkans, particularly the peacekeeping operation in Kosovo, Rumsfeld warned that "a long-term foreign presence in a country can be unnatural" and have "unintended adverse side effects."[60] Seemingly well intentioned, this position did presume that the new government of Afghanistan could, with the help of a coalition force, quickly develop the means by which to assert control over its territory and deliver security as well as basic services.

This assumption was to be disproved in subsequent years. The sought-after NATO peacekeepers did not show up in sufficient numbers, and the new regime in Kabul was too weak to assert control over its territory and resolve the other substantial obstacles facing it.[61] The Pentagon's anticipated surrogates were thus unwilling or unable to take on the burden of postconflict stabilization, creating, in conjunction with the U.S. military's exclusive focus on counterterrorism, a capability gap that would have severe implications for the viability of the Afghan state.

For a time, however, the Afghan campaign was perceived as having vindicated Rumsfeld's enthusiasm for transformation. In Washington, D.C., the image of U.S. SOF and combat air controllers on horseback calling in precision strikes from bombers overhead encapsulated the imagination, agility, and innovation of the transformation ideal. Within the senior echelons of the White House and Pentagon, the instant wisdom that emerged from Enduring Freedom was that this "proving ground" for transformation showcased how "innovative doctrine and high-tech weaponry can shape and then dominate in an unconventional conflict."[62]

As in the 1960s and 1980s, the precise meaning of the term "unconventional" was not in substance so different from the traditional strike operations of conventional combat. Neither did the use of SOF test or demand much more than direct action and combat skills. The value of having boots on the ground and of engaging closely with the host society in order to dislocate one's irregular adversary, both politically and physically, had not been grasped. And as in previous times, this mind-set had very little to do with the existence or nonexistence of relevant doctrine: Only four months prior to Enduring Freedom the Army had released FM 3-0, *Operations*, a capstone field manual that devoted two separate chapters to stability and support operations.[63] Naturally it often takes time for doctrine to affect training, education, and exercises. Even so, it is clear that the existence of relevant field manuals did not in itself affect the design of operations, the tasks assigned to U.S. soldiers, or the training and instruction provided to them before the mission.

THEORY MEETS PRACTICE: AFGHANISTAN AND IRAQ

It was against this backdrop that the U.S. military invaded Iraq in March 2003. Rumsfeld's vision for transformation appeared to receive a second boost with the U.S. military's three-week blitz to the gates of Baghdad. In planning for the attack Rumsfeld had forced the military to reduce the footprint of the invading force in line with the promise of transformation to substitute mass for information.[64] Because Baghdad was taken so quickly and with a force comprising only 120,000 U.S. ground troops, his wager seemed to have paid off; the transformation agenda was arguably at its peak of persuasion. In April 2003 DoD released *Transformation Planning Guidance*, which again set out a hyperconventional image for the U.S. armed forces, culminating in a precision-strike capability to locate, track, and hit targets anywhere in the world.[65] Stability operations, counterinsurgency, and peace operations of any type were not included or mentioned.

Yet, as DoD's *Transformation Planning Guidance* rolled out, events in Afghanistan began to signal the importance of consolidating combat victories through effective stabilization. With the security situation in Afghanistan deteriorating, the U.S. administration gradually realized that its input in Afghanistan—strike operations against suspected terrorists, financial aid, and military training—was failing to protect the new government from implosion. Reacting to the worsening conditions, the U.S. military laid out plans "to disperse teams of combat soldiers, civil affairs specialists and Afghan troops around the nation to help secure the countryside and boost reconstruction efforts."[66] On February 1, 2003, the U.S. military deployed its first Provincial Reconstruction Team (PRT) to Gardez, comprising "Civil Affairs, the 82nd Airborne Division, assorted Special Forces units and support staff," with a mission to "provide a safe environment for humanitarian activities; exchange information between the central government, the Army and non-governmental organizations; and help the Afghan government project its presence outside of Kabul."[67] Although this was a tentative and arguably insufficient effort given the scale of the problem, the shift in approach constituted the first steps in the U.S. armed forces' reorientation toward stability operations.[68]

The reorientation was accelerated by the U.S. military's experience in Iraq. There the successful overthrow of the Saddam Hussein regime in April 2003 was giving way to a protracted phase of instability, marked by political uncertainty, a rapidly deteriorating security situation, and violent attacks on U.S. forces, their Iraqi partners, and international workers. Because precipitous withdrawal from Iraq was not considered an option, the U.S. military was tasked with containing the escalating violence and carrying out the basic functions of state until a new political regime could be installed. In other words the U.S. military in Iraq assumed control over a stability operation larger in scale and complexity than anything it had previously undertaken, at the very least since the Vietnam War. The Bush administration further complicated this already ambitious endeavor by disbanding the Iraqi military and subjecting the Iraqi government to a deep-rooted process of de-Baathification, resulting in the creation of a large pool of disgruntled former soldiers and the hollowing out of Iraq's civil service.[69]

The task entrusted to the U.S. military far exceeded its capacity and preparation for postconflict stabilization. Pentagon planning for "Phase IV," the "postconflict" phase, had been conducted on the assumption that the destruction of the regime would lead quite seamlessly to the installation of Iraqi exiles and other caretaker figures in a new transitional government. DoD's postwar planning thus concerned other matters, primarily the recuperation of Saddam's alleged stocks of weapons of mass destruction, the provision of humanitarian assistance, and the resettlement of displaced civilians.[70] Although some thought was given to the future of the Iraqi government and military, a declassified Central Command (CENTCOM) preinvasion war plan dated August 2002 reveals the dangerous assumptions underlying Phase IV planning as a whole: "Opposition groups will work with us"; "co-opted Iraqi units will occupy garrisons and not fight either U.S. forces or other Iraqi units"; the U.S. Department of State "will promote creation of broad-based, credible provisional government—prior to D-Day"; and the number of U.S. troops in theater will be reduced to 5,000 by December 2006.[71] In retrospect these assumptions were clearly unrealistic.

Lack of planning, however, did not mean lack of involvement. The U.S. military had planned to delegate the postconflict phase to the Office of Reconstruction and Humanitarian Assistance (ORHA)—a coordinating body set up within OSD but involving personnel detailed from other agencies—but this division of labor failed in practice.[72] Not only did ORHA lack resources, expertise, and policy coherence; it also had no mandate or capacity to address the growing insecurity of postwar Iraq, a fundamental prerequisite for reconstruction to occur.[73] Left with the consequences of this capability gap, U.S. combat troops were forced to undertake tasks for which they had no plans, preparation, and guidance.

Facing criminality, looting, and escalating violence U.S. troops in Iraq developed improvised responses to an unfamiliar operating environment. A few units managed to devise fairly sophisticated counterinsurgency strategies; these units were often commanded by officers with either firsthand knowledge of the 1990s' peace operations or advanced education, including doctoral degrees, in counterinsurgency-related topics.[74] Working on the individual, as opposed to institutional, memory of prior campaigns these units tended to adapt successfully and achieve comparatively promising results in a challenging situation lacking real strategic direction. The learning curve was, however, highly uneven, with several units adopting a predominantly enemy-centered approach to their area of operations, geared almost exclusively toward the physical elimination and incarceration of those opposing the U.S. effort. With a narrow focus on rooting out terrorists and Saddam sympathizers, yet with scant intelligence on the adversary, these units conducted indiscriminate sweep and cordon-and-search operations, whose aggressiveness generally served to alienate Iraqi civilians and generate more resistance.[75]

This latter approach was a logical extension of the rhetoric flowing from the Pentagon and the White House. During the immediate postconflict phase, the senior leadership at DoD dismissed the resistance as temporary, terrorist in nature, and with no real prospects of challenging the wider U.S. project in Iraq. The complexity and ambition of establishing a political, economic, and social order in Iraq perceived as legitimate by all sides had not yet been fully grasped. Instead Rumsfeld actively sought to downplay the political instability as the activity of "dead-enders" and of "former-regime loyalists."[76] Reacting to the looting of Iraqi government ministries, infrastructure, factories, hospitals, and museums in spring 2003, Rumsfeld remarked that this was the "untidiness of freedom."[77] When the instability escalated during that summer Rumsfeld continued to deny that the violence amounted to an insurgency. His argument was that the "looters, criminals, remnants of the Ba'athist regime, foreign terrorists. . . , and those influenced by Iran" constituted "five different things," which "doesn't make it anything like a guerrilla war or an organized resistance" but instead "function[s] much more like terrorists."[78] This stance was representative of the Pentagon leadership throughout the remainder of the year: There was not yet any talk of this operation, never mind that in Afghanistan, representing the U.S. military's return to counterinsurgency.

CONCLUSION

The U.S. military underwent a significant transformation during the first years of the "War on Terror." Having embraced a particular vision of defense innovation that took little notice of stability operations, the U.S. military was gradually forced to conduct precisely such campaigns. For various historical, strategic, and institutional reasons this transition was neither immediate nor unfettered.

The initial motivation to consider stability operations stemmed from the 9/11 attacks, which illustrated forcefully the threat that instability abroad could pose to U.S. security at home. Intervening and assisting in the stabilization of weak or failing states thus moved from being an exclusively humanitarian endeavor to one intimately tied with U.S. national security. Yet, even though this link was clear in rhetoric, it did not affect DoD policy. In three related ways the reorientation toward stability operations was delayed by the U.S. military's particular reading of its operational experiences of the 1990s, both conventional and otherwise.

First, the ascendance of the RMA increasingly made information warfare seem like an effective means of avoiding the operational pitfalls of more complex and protracted on-the-ground campaigns. Throughout the engagements of the 1990s the U.S. military's faith in low-risk, high-impact, high-technology war was repeatedly confirmed, whether positively (as in Iraq, Bosnia, and Kosovo) or negatively (as in Somalia). This steered U.S. defense policy away from the "lower end" of the conflict spectrum, involving the deployment of troops and uncertain exit strategies, and toward investment in information-age capabilities for swift and decisive combat operations.

Second, the peace operations of the 1990s occurred within permissive operating environments. Not only was this inadequate preparation for the bloodier insurgencies the U.S. military was to face in Afghanistan and Iraq; it also made MOOTW seem easy and thus as below the calling of the U.S. armed forces. To the Pentagon these operations were better suited to the militaries and constabulary forces of its allies, leaving the U.S. military to prepare for apparently more demanding conventional threats. Of course, the ability to call in allies was a result of the specific political conditions of the 1990s, just as the permissiveness of these operations was in fact a precondition for engagement imposed by the politico-military leadership of the time. Despite the historical specificity of the conditions, no consideration was given to the possibility that they would not pertain to future campaigns.

Third, the lack of political progress associated with peace operations, principally in Kosovo but also in Bosnia, made MOOTW seem open-ended and as eroding the U.S. military's readiness to face conventional threats. Within DoD this argument gained particular salience with the ascendance of the RMA and its subsequent mutation into "transformation." The costs of neglecting what came to be seen as an opportunity to redefine war on the United States' own terms had never been higher, and engagement in "strategically irrelevant lower-end operations"—all lumped together into one category—was not to get in the way. Integral to this mind-set was the assumption that MOOTW of any type was by definition less critical to the U.S. national interest than traditional combat operations.

Effectively institutionalized by Secretary of Defense Donald Rumsfeld, transformation also had a distorting effect on DoD's understanding of counterinsurgency, as it encouraged undue faith in the strategic utility of precision-guided strikes. The 9/11 attacks prompted the U.S. military to accelerate its pursuit of a global precision-strike complex—now to hit terrorist targets worldwide without needing to establish a firm foothold or gain the political buy-in within the affected country and region. The Afghanistan campaign was conducted on such a basis, and faith in this new approach appeared justified when the Taliban were quickly routed by a handful of SOF and a limited number of ground troops enabling the efforts of local allies. The support for transformation was taken to new heights with the initial victory over Saddam Hussein in 2003, a campaign in which this approach to combat had appeared to ensure swift and decisive victory. Yet, critically, transformation as conceived precluded serious consideration of stability operations and counterinsurgency. Not only were these operations generally dismissed as irrelevant; they also jarred with the light-footprint and strike-oriented approaches advocated through transformation, something that contributed to their marginalization in prioritization and planning.

This is not to say that state-building and stability operations were entirely absent from the minds of senior defense officials. DoD planning for both the Afghanistan and Iraq campaigns recognized, rhetorically, the need for some sort of consolidating effort to follow the cessation of hostilities. Nonetheless the ideological skepticism within the Bush administration and OSD regarding the commitment of U.S. military troops to any operation falling short of conventional war encouraged the ill-founded notion that stabilization could be delegated to allies and civilian partners. In Afghanistan Rumsfeld looked to NATO to volunteer for the expansion of the International Security Assistance Force, and in the prewar planning for Iraq it was the Department of State that was to provide a political solution once the bullets had stopped flying—even though it had effectively been sidelined from the planning process. In both instances DoD mistook its tangible dislike for stabilization for the ability of its partners to take on such missions in its stead.

This mind-set, and the attendant vision of transformation, was forcefully tested by the U.S. military's postwar operations in Iraq. Having successfully dismantled Saddam Hussein's regime, the U.S. military found itself with minimal coalition support and no prospect of imminent withdrawal, thus having to devise a strategy ad hoc to stabilize "postwar" Iraq. The lack of preparation for this contingency engendered a counterproductive response. More than the rhetorical "securitization" of state failure through 9/11, it was the ensuing operational difficulties faced in Iraq and, to a lesser degree, Afghanistan that launched DoD's reorientation toward counterinsurgency and stability operations. Even so, it would take a year of increasing instability in both theaters before the term "counterinsurgency" reentered the DoD lexicon.

4

INNOVATION
UNDER FIRE

One year into the Iraq campaign counterinsurgency gradually became more relevant to the senior echelons of the Pentagon. At this point, the DoD leadership came to see the instability in postwar Iraq as a crucial challenge to the installation of a democratic and stable regime.[1] From a virtual silence on stability operations in previous years, the DoD began signing off on several efforts aimed at augmenting the military's ability to conduct such missions. More than anything this constituted the Pentagon's return to the thorny issue of counterinsurgency.

One of the earliest manifestations of the change in direction was OSD's request in January 2004 for the Defense Science Board (DSB) to focus its yearly Summer Study on the "transition to and from hostilities." The terms of reference for the commissioned study acknowledged that "we have and will encounter significant challenges following conventional military successes as we seek to ensure stability, democracy, human rights and a productive economy."[2] When the report was released, in December 2004, it framed stability operations as an unavoidable and expensive "growth industry" that the U.S. military had to face head-on and made specific recommendations for how it might develop a capability to conduct such missions.[3] The report also warned of the limited role of transformation in fostering capabilities for stability operations and emphasized the implications of such missions for the U.S. military force structure.[4]

The urgency accorded to stability operations in the DSB report echoed that of the Strategic Planning Guidance 2006–11, released by DoD in March 2004 to provide vision and policy direction to the armed services. Envisaging greater U.S. engagement in stability operations, SPG 2006-11 ordered the armed forces to "adjust their doctrine, organizations, training, and exercise plans . . . develop a core competency in stability operations capabilities [and] either create standing units focused on stability operations or develop the capability to rapidly assemble, within their respective services, modular force elements that achieve the same effect as standing units."[5]

The U.S. military also took action to improve the armed forces' immediate suitability for counterinsurgency. Although military training had emphasized urban operations long before and throughout the 1990s, there was now a renewed urgency to such exercises. In 2004, the Army constructed additional mock villages at its Joint Readiness Training Center at Fort Polk, Louisiana, and recruited Arabic-speakers to play the roles of Iraqi civilians and security forces.[6] Mock villages were also constructed at the National Training Center at Fort Irwin, California, to provide counterinsurgency training in urban areas.[7] The Marine Corps underwent a similar process, incorporating a greater emphasis on urban operations, cultural sensitivity, languages, and explosive ordnance disposal into its predeployment training.[8]

The sudden relevance of counterinsurgency also translated into the development of new doctrine and concepts. JFCOM, the organization originally mandated to oversee DoD's transformation agenda, became the lead agency working toward a shared joint conceptual understanding of stability operations. In September 2004 it released *Stability Operations Joint Operating Concept* (*Stability Operations JOC*), a "living" document subsequently refined to reflect the operational learning occurring in Afghanistan and Iraq. Even in its initial form, however, this document revealed some of the lessons learned in Iraq: It emphasized interagency coordination, the need to balance force with restraint, and the importance of establishing and sustaining the perception of legitimacy. It also set out four different theoretical contingencies that could lead to U.S. military participation in stability operations—upon request; during and after major combat; within a failed state; and to counter a nonstate organization—but deliberately limited its scope to the second contingency, it bearing the closest resemblance to the situation in Iraq. JFCOM concluded the analysis with the forceful statement that "stability operations must be a core mission of the military services and civil agencies."[9]

In October 2004, after only five months of drafting, the U.S. Army issued FMI 3-07.22, *Counterinsurgency Operations*, an interim field manual on counterinsurgency and the first doctrinal publication devoted exclusively to the topic since 1986. In producing FMI 3-07.22 the Army sought advice and collaboration from the Marine Corps, the British Army, and the U.S. Army Special Warfare Center. The final product was only a stopgap, meant to provide preliminary guidance while a more developed manual could be produced. Nonetheless this 180-page document was already able to offer an extensive overview of the main characteristics of counterinsurgency, of the Army's role in such campaigns, and of the nature and importance of PSYOPS and intelligence. In broad terms FMI 3-07.22 reiterated many of the principles laid out in the *Stability Operations JOC*, emphasizing, for example, the political nature of counterinsurgencies and the attendant need for close integration of military and civilian operations in support of the host nation.[10] It further recognized the complexity of conducting security operations as part of a counterinsurgency campaign and was clear on the need for U.S. forces to "separate insurgents from the population" and to "conduct themselves in a manner that enables them to maintain popular domestic support."[11]

With insurgencies mounting in Iraq and Afghanistan, the importance of irregular operations was increasingly recognized in the policy statements and publications of OSD, the Joint Staff, and the ground services. In December 2004 Army Chief of Staff Gen. Peter Schoomaker revised the Army Focus Areas by adding the goal of augmenting the service's capabilities for stability operations. He also directed TRADOC to review the Army's existing capabilities and to make recommendations on how to fill any gaps thus identified. This direction culminated in the release of an Army Strategic Policy Guidance document in January 2005, which reiterated the directive for the Army to "improve capabilities for stability operations" and to "improve proficiencies against irregular challenges."[12] The Marine Corps was following a similar course. In April 2005 Commandant Gen. Michael Hagee issued an All Marine Message in which he specified that "our future will be characterized by irregular wars."[13] The message contrasted sharply with the commandant's first All Marine Message of January 2003, in which he emphasized that Marines will "remain 'soldiers of the sea'" and that the Corps' main effort should be "excellence in war-fighting."[14]

INAUSPICIOUS BEGINNINGS

These efforts denoted the urgency with which the U.S. military reengaged with counterinsurgency and stability operations. How significant were they, however, in realigning U.S. military priorities? It should be recalled that previous *failed* efforts to enhance the U.S. military's capability to conduct counterinsurgency also featured streams of promising initiatives, ranging from reworked training exercises and doctrine to reforms in educational curricula. To gain a more informed understanding of this period of change—to gauge the extent to which it truly represented a watershed in the U.S. military's approach to counterinsurgency—it is necessary to go beyond a mere list of reforms and activity. Indeed, although the above initiatives offer firm evidence of a U.S. military effort to familiarize troops with the types of operations then faced in Iraq, they also belied a fundamental misunderstanding of counterinsurgency and, in other cases, a continued low prioritization of such missions by DoD as a whole. In terms of augmenting the U.S. military's understanding of counterinsurgency, this initial effort was flawed, perhaps inevitably so, given the organization's culture and orthodoxy.

In the first place the conceptual treatment of counterinsurgency—in both the *Stability Operations JOC* and FMI 3-07.22—betrayed DoD's assumption that well-resourced and operationally capable civilian agencies would be present to undertake all of the "nonmilitary" components of the campaign: the provision of basic services, the development of functioning administrative services, and the establishment of governmental structures. As seen in Iraq and similar operations, this has often not been the case. Few civilian agencies perceive stability operations as part of their remit, those that do are seldom fully included in military planning, and all have typically struggled to deploy sufficient numbers in a timely manner, particularly where security conditions are still precarious. The result has been that the military is forced to assume tasks best conducted by civilians, adding to the complexity of the operation. Regardless, neither document considered the possibility of a civilian shortfall of this kind or the implications for the military of having to fill the ensuing capability gap.

In listing the types of support to be tendered by the U.S. military in a counterinsurgency campaign, FMI 3-07.22 included only military tasks—security assistance, exercises, intelligence and communications sharing, logistics, and the use of U.S. combat forces—all geared toward the destruction of the enemy rather than the provision of security, of services, or of basic governance.[15] Even though state-building is central to counterinsurgency, the manual characterized as "extreme" the need for U.S. forces "to creat[e] elements (such as local forces and government institutions) of the society they have been sent to assist"; accordingly it committed only a single paragraph to the "nonstandard" implications of such an eventuality.[16] Moreover, and despite the shortfall in civilian stability operations capabilities noted above, FMI 3-07.22 stated without qualifications that the U.S. Agency for International Development (USAID) "is the U.S. government agency responsible for nation building."[17]

In contrast to the interim field manual, the *Stability Operations JOC* stressed from the outset that "the joint force . . . will provide security, initial humanitarian assistance, limited governance, restoration of essential public services, and other reconstruction assistance."[18] Upon closer inspection, however, the *Stability Operations JOC* was also at best unclear on the need for the military to assume nonmilitary tasks in the absence of able civilian agencies. The confusion here stemmed from the deliberate conflation of civilian and military actors and agencies into a single "joint force," a term whose usage throughout the concept paper prevented any analysis of the ideal and likely division of labor.[19] When the *Stability Operations JOC* did distinguish between civilian and military organizations, it contented itself with the ill-founded assumption that "the military and interagency community will achieve synergy in planning and execution."[20] In postcombat stability operations, the military was thus to be the "supporting" element, "expand[ing] its imposition of security throughout the countryside to shape favorable conditions so that civilian-led activities can begin creating the 'new and better' conditions from which the 'new normal' grows."[21] There was, in other words, no recognition of the fact that civilian agencies often lack the organization, resources, and mandate to assist effectively in stability operations conducted in nonpermissive environments, or what this would mean for the military's planning and running of operations.

In a sense the military's narrow focus on security operations reflected its approach to operations in Iraq and Afghanistan at this time. In both campaigns the U.S. military was conducting operations geared predominantly toward the neutralization of the enemy—an approach consistent with its combat-oriented rooting. In Iraq this mode of engagement persisted well into 2004 despite the realization that the instability there constituted more than the death throes of a defeated regime.[22] A number of commanders did devise more comprehensive counterinsurgency strategies and generally experienced a higher degree of success in their respective areas of operation. On the whole, however, their improvised approach constituted the exception to the rule.

Despite their flawed conceptualization of counterinsurgency and stability operations, the two publications did at least denote greater prioritization of these types of missions. Even here, however, the picture is mixed. The *Stability Operations JOC*, although certainly significant for those engaged with such missions on a conceptual level, gained little traction within the uniformed services; it was not doctrine, had no binding power, and was produced by a command—JFCOM—that many perceived as peripheral and obscure.[23] Regardless of its content the publication did not reflect and was unlikely to change institutional priorities.

Similarly, while FMI 3-07.22 did constitute the first doctrinal publication on the topic since the 1980s, the significance of this fact was uncertain. First, the appearance of a drastic discontinuity was largely misleading. Certainly, counterinsurgency had been neglected, but U.S. military doctrine had of late paid increasing attention to stability operations, which clearly enjoy a substantial overlap with counterinsurgency. In February 2003 the Army had released *Stability Operations and Support Operations* (FM 3-07), and it devoted two chapters to these types of operations in its 2001 edition of FM 3-0, *Operations*—a capstone manual.[24] This backdrop of existing doctrine contextualizes the significance of the interim counterinsurgency field manual. More important, none of the previous publications on stability operations had signaled a change in the culture of the U.S. military or the manner in which its soldiers conducted such operations; they clearly did not do much in terms of preparing the Army for stability operations in Iraq. Beyond reintroducing the term "counterinsurgency," it is uncertain whether FMI 3-07.22 would make a difference where it mattered. For sure, its treatment of counterinsurgency was more rigorous than in previous manuals, but this would not in itself guarantee a greater effect.

The point here is not that the more recent of manuals were redundant; instead it is necessary to recognize that the release of publications, FMI 3-07.22 and the *Stability Operations JOC* included, rarely reflects a genuine and deep-running shift in institutional priorities.[25] Much depends instead on the manner in which they are received by the wider institution, and here the evidence was hardly promising. Indeed, beyond the initiatives outlined above there is much evidence to suggest that DoD was at this time fundamentally unconvinced of the importance of learning counterinsurgency or lagging, at the very least, in its acknowledgment that these types of operations mattered.

In its institution-wide strategy papers, for example, DoD would typically assert the importance of stability operations and of irregular warfare more generally yet also present a consistently inadequate understanding of these missions or marginalize them completely. In the 2004 National Military Strategy (NMS) the Joint Chiefs of Staff acknowledged that "winning decisively will require synchronizing and integrating major combat operations, stability operations and significant postconflict interagency operations."[26] Yet, beyond a smattering of references to stability operations and two paragraphs devoted entirely to the topic, the main thrust of the document related to combat operations and counterterrorism. The three priorities of the Chairman of the Joint Chiefs of Staff listed in the 2004 NMS—"winning the War on Terrorism, enhancing joint warfighting and transforming for the future"—had only the most tenuous of links with counterinsurgency and stability operations.[27] The same applied to the 2004 NMS's elaboration of desired force attributes (fully integrated, expeditionary, networked, decentralized, adaptable, decision superiority, lethality) and capabilities (applying force, deploying and sustaining military capabilities, security battle space, achieving decision superiority)—which instead betrayed a distinct continuity with Donald Rumsfeld's transformation agenda.[28] By contrast the document did not once mention counterinsurgency—and this at a time when the U.S. military was actively engaged in two full-blown counterinsurgency campaigns. Indeed, the writers of the strategy paper were specifically instructed not to mention Iraq in the document, as the secretary of defense perceived it as a temporary distraction that would soon be over.[29]

A similar mismatch in rhetoric and provisions marked the March 2005 *National Defense Strategy* (NDS) released by OSD. The document stated that "our experience in the war on terrorism points to the need to reorient our military capabilities to contend with . . . irregular challenges more effectively."[30] At the same time, this NDS was mute on the need for the U.S. military to learn how to conduct counterinsurgency and stability operations. Similarly, even though the strategic objectives set out in this publication pointed to the need to "strengthen peace" when the latter is threatened by "dangerous political instability, aggression or extremism," no detail was provided as to how the U.S. military would develop the capabilities necessary to meet that objective.[31] The publication also acknowledged the difficulty of deterring "terrorists and insurgents inspired by extreme ideology" but gave no indication of how the military would overcome such challenges.[32]

Further inconsistencies could be seen in the JCS's August 2005 update to the *Capstone Concept for Joint Operations* (CCJO), a publication identifying the demands of the joint force in 2012–2025. The document stressed that the U.S. military may be "required to establish a secure environment and initiate reconstruction efforts to facilitate transition to civilian control" involving the provision of "security, initial humanitarian assistance, limited governance [and the] restoration of essential public services."[33] It also recognized that the current interagency capability of the U.S. government was inadequate.[34] However, the CCJO was less forthcoming on how the dysfunctional interagency system would impact DoD operations, and it committed only one paragraph to the nature of stability operations. Given that the U.S. military was at this point two-plus years into simultaneous counterinsurgency campaigns, it is also striking that "counterinsurgency" was not mentioned once in the entire document. Instead, and much like in the NMS, the desired force characteristics listed in the CCJO related overwhelmingly to combat operations or were distinctly transformation-like in their associations.[35]

It is possible to discern a number of interpretations of counterinsurgency within the U.S. military during 2004–2005. Within some quarters learning counterinsurgency was clearly perceived as an important undertaking, primarily due to the Iraq conflict. However, both in theory and in practice the U.S. military's role in counterinsurgency was limited to various combat- and security-related tasks; the notion that troops might have to assume political and reconstruction duties had not yet been fully acknowledged and internalized. More generally DoD tended to regard the counterinsurgency campaign in Iraq as a "temporary spike" in activity that would not affect its preexisting direction and vision.[36] This view was presented most clearly in institution-wide strategy briefs and papers. Ultimately, therefore, the U.S. military's initial engagement with counterinsurgency reveals a tendency either to treat these operations as an aberration or to interpret them as primarily enemy-centered and combat-oriented in nature, at least as far as DoD is concerned. As seen in chapter 2 this is also consistent with the U.S. military's approach to counterinsurgency throughout history.

2005: A COMMUNITY EMERGES

DoD's fragmented attitude toward counterinsurgency during 2004–2005 resulted in an institutional behavior that would at times appear inconsistent, even schizophrenic. Among the mixed messages one can nonetheless discern a clear ascendance of counterinsurgency as a U.S. military preoccupation throughout 2005. This gradual shift occurred as a result of the protracted nature and undiminished intensity of the Iraq operation, which ensured the continued relevance of counterinsurgency doctrine, concepts, training, and education. At the same time, given the reluctance with which DoD as a whole approached counterinsurgency and stability operations, many of the early initiatives were minor in scale and slow in coming.

On February 14, 2005, for example, the department's Defense Language Transformation Roadmap was approved, laying out a strategy for linguistic training within DoD and the armed services. The document acknowledged that "language skill and regional expertise are not valued as Defense core competencies yet they are as important as critical weapon systems."[37] Seeking to remedy this deficiency, DoD established the Defense Language Office in May 2005. The new office was to "ensure a strategic focus on meeting present and future requirements for language and regional expertise" and to set policy for the "development, maintenance, and utilization of language capabilities."[38]

The guiding assumption in the Defense Language Transformation Roadmap was clearly that U.S. soldiers would regularly be participating in operations where understanding of and good relations with the local population are necessary. A similar logic compelled the Marine Corps to place greater emphasis on the importance of the so-called "human terrain": the "social, ethnographic, cultural, economic and political elements of the people among whom a force is operating."[39] In May 2005 the Marine Corps established the Center for Advanced Operational Culture Learning (CAOCL) at Quantico, Virginia, to help educate the service on the cultural dimension of combat. CAOCL was the brainchild of Lt. Gen. James N. Mattis, who at that time was commanding general of the USMC Combat Development Command, and whose tours in Afghanistan and Iraq had convinced him of the need for greater cultural awareness within the Marine Corps.[40] To that end CAOCL was mandated to "provide the Marine Corps with the linguistic and cultural knowledge and awareness necessary for them to operate in foreign countries; gather and disseminate information about cultures deemed of strategic interest; and provide oversight over Marine Corps educational establishments so as to produce an integrated and synchronized education that involved cultural training."[41]

Also in May 2005 the Wargaming Division of the USMC Warfighting Laboratory at Quantico revamped and launched the Small Wars Center of Excellence to act as a repository for counterinsurgency-relevant information, ranging from "cultural intelligence seminars and conferences, academic papers, after action reports, lessons learned, and key insights and observations from current operations information."[42] Around the same time, the

Marine Corps and JFCOM cosponsored a five-day wargame, Joint Urban Warrior 05, that focused heavily on the challenges of Gen. Charles Krulak's "three-block wars," the analytical construct capturing the simultaneity of combat, stability, and humanitarian operations in urban campaigns.[43]

Clearly these measures were important indicators of the new relevance of counterinsurgency and of military operations conducted amid the people, but again their significance to and effect on the wider military should not be overstated; in general these measures were small-scale and peripheral to the main muscle of the military. CAOCL, for example, was set up with a "skeleton staff" and therefore had to struggle to achieve significant results across the Marine Corps.[44] Presented online as a "Center of Excellence," it was in fact "located in a rickety trailer parked next to some railroad tracks" and represented only thirty-nine staff for a force then composed of 180,000 active-duty Marines and 40,000 reservists.[45] In a similar vein the Small Wars Center of Excellence for a long period consisted of a simple website with links to counterinsurgency-related material but with no resources, mandate, or momentum to influence the Corps as a whole. DoD's Defense Language Transformation Roadmap, meanwhile, has been criticized for its "shameful chronology": One scholar describes how the rollout involved twenty-one months of committees, needs assessments, and stalling, only to produce a nineteen-page document that no doubt set out important required actions but also provided "dawdling deadlines" for their implementation.[46] The issuing of guidance on how to manage the implementation of the Roadmap had, for example, an eleven-month closing date.

In recognition of the effort required to reorient the U.S. military toward stability operations the undersecretary for defense for acquisition, technology, and logistics in August 2005 mandated the DSB to issue a second report on stability operations, this time to determine what organizational changes would be needed to improve DoD's ability to conduct or support such operations.[47] One of the more forceful recommendations in the ensuing report, released the following month, was for the secretary of defense to sign as soon as possible a draft directive on stability operations that would see DoD prioritize such missions on par with conventional combat.[48] This directive would also set out a strategy for the development of skills, resources, and procedures dealing with future stability operations.

DoD Directive 3000.05: Military Support for Stability, Security, Transition, and Reconstruction (SSTR) Operations was finally signed on November 28, 2005. The document "provides guidance on stability operations" and "establishes DoD policy and assigns responsibilities within the Department of Defense . . . to conduct and support stability operations."[49] The directive's most notable provision was its policy statement that "stability operations are a core U.S. military mission that the Department of Defense shall be prepared to conduct and support" and that they "shall be given priority comparable to combat operations and be explicitly addressed and integrated across all DoD activities, including doctrine, organizations, training, education, material, leadership, personnel, facilities and planning."[50]

To ensure smooth implementation, Directive 3000.05 assigned eighty-three tasks of varied specificity to various sections within DoD. Each affected section was also mandated to "develop measures of effectiveness that evaluate progress in achieving the goals" set out in the relevant part of the document. Furthermore, these efforts were to be overseen by the Stability Operations Office within OSD.[51] The issue of implementation received strong emphasis throughout the directive, perhaps because the lack of follow-up in previous efforts to enhance the U.S. government's ability to conduct stability operations, such as Bill Clinton's PDD 56 and PDD 78, had made them generally short-lived.

As Directive 3000.05 was being finalized, the prevailing understanding of the challenge in Iraq also began to change. With the conflict showing no sign of abating it became clear that the offensive-oriented approach of the U.S. military was not effective in stabilizing the country. In contrast, those commanders who had through improvisation adopted a more comprehensive counterinsurgency strategy could, for the most part, boast a relative level of success in stabilizing their respective areas of operations. Appreciation for this trend reached the White House in late 2005, after which time the enemy-centered approach to counterinsurgency came to be increasingly discredited, at least in rhetoric.

In October 2005 Secretary of State Condoleezza Rice elaborated a new strategy for Iraq that recalled counterinsurgency best practices from Vietnam, Malaya, and elsewhere. She explained that "our political-military strategy has to be to clear, hold, and build: to clear areas from insurgent control, to hold them securely, and to build durable, national Iraqi institutions."[52] In contrast with the previous approach, this new strategy emphasized the so-called "oil-spot" technique, used to good effect against earlier insurgencies, whereby countrywide stability is ensured gradually by consolidating control in specific cities and regions at a time. The new strategy was steeped in classic counterinsurgency theory; as Rice acknowledged, it had "profited from the insights of strategic thinkers, civilian and military, inside and outside of government who have reflected on our experience and on insurgencies in other periods of history."[53] One of the major intellectual progenitors of the new approach was Andrew Krepinevich, a prominent defense analyst, retired officer, and director of the Center for Strategic and Budgetary Assessments. In a *Foreign Affairs* article published in October 2005, Krepinevich argued that the provision of security in Iraq should be emphasized over the killing and capturing of insurgents.[54] He elaborated that "since the U.S. and Iraqi armies cannot guarantee security to all of Iraq simultaneously, they should start by focusing on certain key areas and then, over time, broadening the effort—hence the image of an expanding oil spot."[55]

The new strategy was also based on the operational experience of those commanders who had achieved a comparative level of success in Iraq. The experience freshest in the minds of the administration was that of Army Colonel H. R. McMaster, who had commanded the 3rd Armored Cavalry Regiment in Tal Afar from May 2005 to February 2006. Prior to deployment McMaster had trained his troops for the cultural and operational complexities specific to Iraq: He instructed them to take elementary language classes, learn about Iraqi culture and history, and familiarize themselves with the basic precepts of counterinsurgency.[56] By adopting a community-oriented approach his unit was able to minimize violence in Tal Afar, turning a stronghold of insurgent activity into a U.S. success story in counterinsurgency. The achievement was used to epitomize the administration's new approach to counterinsurgency; in an address on the new American strategy in Iraq, President Bush spoke at length of the transformation of Tal Afar and the work done by Colonel McMaster, framing it as a "concrete example of progress."[57]

Bush's mention of Colonel McMaster formed part of a wider trend in which commanders who demonstrated proficiency in counterinsurgency were identified, elevated, and promoted to positions where they could share their knowledge and expertise. The most radical example of this trend was the appointment in late 2005 of Lt. Gen. David Petraeus to the post of commanding general at Fort Leavenworth, Kansas, where he would oversee the U.S. Army Combined Arms Center, the Command and General Staff College, and the Army's lessons-learned process. His selection for this position was based partly on his impressive performance as commander of the 101st Airborne Division in Mosul, Iraq, in summer 2003: He had successfully implemented a strategy to stabilize the city, rebuild its basic infrastructure, and provide limited governance.[58] His approach displayed a familiarity with these types of missions that may have stemmed from his deployments to three peacekeeping missions in the 1990s, and his doctoral thesis, which had examined the U.S. Army in the counterinsurgency campaign of Vietnam.

At Fort Leavenworth Petraeus was given positional authority to make a difference on the next generation in terms of education, doctrine, training, and thinking. The Command and General Staff College had already begun modifying its officers' course in late 2004, placing greater emphasis on cultural awareness, counterinsurgency, and stability operations. Petraeus was able to cement this shift in priorities: By early 2006 the ten-month course included 201 hours of instruction on counterinsurgency and related topics out of a total of 555 hours of core curriculum contact time—and this did

not include the forty hours that the average student spent on counterinsurgency-related electives.[59] The core counterinsurgency instruction included an overview of the classic texts on the topic, an assessment of the
concepts and theory of counterinsurgency, historical and current case studies, and a discussion of existing doctrine.[60]

Along with McMaster and Petraeus, another rising star was Lt. Col. John
Nagl, who like Petraeus had completed his doctoral dissertation on the particular logic of counterinsurgency, comparing the British and American approaches to the threat of insurgency in Malaya and Vietnam. Initially
published in 2002, the thesis was released in paperback in 2005 with the
endorsement of Army Chief of Staff Gen. Peter J. Schoomaker, whose foreword stressed the continued need for the U.S. military to learn counterinsurgency.[61] To that end Schoomaker also distributed the book to all
four-star generals in the U.S. Army, including Gen. George W. Casey Jr., the
new commander of Multi-National Force Iraq (MNF-I). Having served a
tour in Iraq with the 82nd Airborne Division, Nagl was subsequently appointed military assistant to the deputy secretary of defense at OSD, placing him in a position to influence and oversee the process of learning
counterinsurgency then taking place at the Pentagon.

Based on Britain's success in Malaya, one of the recommendations in
Nagl's book was for the development of educational and training institutions within the host nation so as to accelerate the adaptation of incoming
military units. This idea was taken onboard by the U.S. military in November 2005, when General Casey opened the COIN Academy (using the military shorthand for "counterinsurgency") at Camp Taji, Iraq. Supplementing
the often uneven instruction in counterinsurgency that incoming troops
were receiving prior to deployment, the academy provided a five-day
course on topics ranging "from counterinsurgency theory and interrogations
to detainee operations and how to dine with a sheik."[62] The course was designed to familiarize troops with the particular workings of counterinsurgency in Iraq and the important ways in which these types of operations
differ from traditional combat campaigns.

One of the driving forces behind the COIN Academy was Kalev I. "Gunner" Sepp, a former Special Forces officer who in 2005 conducted his fourth
tour in Iraq. Based on his operational experience and understanding of
counterinsurgency, urban warfare, psychological operations, and civil affairs,
Sepp was able to contribute regularly and meaningfully to the growing body
of literature on counterinsurgency that was beginning to appear in U.S. military journals and periodicals at this time. In the summer of 2005 Sepp authored a piece for the U.S. Army's *Military Review*, "Best Practices in
Counterinsurgency," in which he provided a retrospective of twentieth-cen-
tury counterinsurgency campaigns, from which he then distilled a number
of best practices. The article would directly inform the drafting of the

Army-Marine field manual on counterinsurgency, then scheduled for release in 2006.[63]

Articles such as Sepp's were proliferating in the military's own publications, indicating not only an increased interest in counterinsurgency but also the growing influence of those officers and experts most familiar with these types of missions. In 2004, during the first full year of the Iraq campaign, *Military Review* featured at most nine articles relating to counterinsurgency; in 2005 the number rose to twenty-nine. In the U.S. Army War College quarterly *Parameters*, the figure rose from three counterinsurgency-related articles in 2004 to eleven in 2005. Most important, many of the articles were based on direct operational experience and embraced counterinsurgency's civilian as well as military components.

One such article was coauthored by Maj. Gen. Peter W. Chiarelli and Maj. Patrick R. Michaelis and published in the summer 2005 issue of *Military Review*. Titled "Winning the Peace: The Requirement for Full-Spectrum Operations," the article reflected the authors' operational experience in Baghdad in 2004 and set out a multifaceted approach to counterinsurgency built around five "lines of operations": combat operations, training of security forces, essential services, promotion of governance, and economic pluralism.[64] Chiarelli and Michaelis's construct was subsequently reproduced both in the 2006 field manual on counterinsurgency and in DoD's reports on Directive 3000.05 implementation.[65] His concept of "SWET operations"—denoting close attention to *s*ewers, *w*ater, *e*lectricity, and *t*rash—also gained some prominence within the military and helped propagate the notion of a more-than-combat-oriented approach to counterinsurgency.

The very same issue of *Military Review* featured an article titled "Iraq: The Social Context of Improvised Explosive Devices" by Montgomery McFate, an anthropologist by training who had crossed over to work with various U.S. defense agencies.[66] In the article McFate exhorted the military to focus on the social context of the threat in Iraq, to engage with its host society, and to acquire human intelligence on its main actors and networks so as to conduct more successful counterinsurgency operations. McFate published three articles in *Military Review* that year; all pushed the importance of anthropological knowledge of the host society in the prosecution of a counterinsurgency campaign.[67] The following year McFate, like Sepp, would contribute directly to the drafting of the Army-Marine field manual on counterinsurgency.[68]

Another anthropologist turned counterinsurgency expert to emerge at this time was David Kilcullen, a former Australian army officer whose Ph.D. dissertation had examined the Darul Islam rebellion in West Java, Indonesia. Kilcullen attracted the attention of DoD through his later writings and lectures on counterinsurgency, al-Qaeda, and the War on Terror, and in 2004 he was asked by Deputy Secretary of Defense Paul Wolfowitz to help draft

DoD's forthcoming QDR.[69] Also, in 2005, Kilcullen wrote "Countering Global Insurgency," an influential article on the War on Terror that argued that this new struggle ought to be conceived as a *counterinsurgency* campaign on a global level.[70] Kilcullen would, too, contribute to the Army-Marine counterinsurgency manual.

Following a string of conceptual treatises on how to understand, plan, and conduct a counterinsurgency campaign, *Military Review* published an article by British Brig. Nigel R. F. Aylwin-Foster titled "Changing the Army for Counterinsurgency Operations."[71] The piece was a scathing critique of the way in which the U.S. Army conducted its operations in Iraq, accusing it of being excessively heavy-handed, morally self-righteous, and culturally blind to the environment, bordering on "institutional racism."[72] Aylwin-Foster also argued that the Army was overly centralized and conformist, severely reducing the scope for adaptation and change. The piece had already appeared on a Marine Corps website in late 2005, but its republication in *Military Review*, an official publication, was indicative of the Army's effort to learn from its mistakes and become a more proficient counterinsurgency force.

Thus, by late 2005, there was discernable momentum to the U.S. military's learning of counterinsurgency and stability operations. The enemy-centered approach to counterinsurgency had been discredited, at least in theory, and this shift had enabled the ascendance of several commanders and academics versed in the finer points of counterinsurgency—a group of experts seeking to spread their knowledge and familiarity with such missions throughout the armed forces. This "COIN community" was acting against the backdrop of an institution—the Department of Defense—that was itself gradually rolling out new initiatives to augment the military's ability to conduct counterinsurgency and stability operations. And even though momentum for this process was at times lacking, particularly given the urgency of the ongoing Iraq campaign, OSD had now released Directive 3000.05, which charted a roadmap for the institutionalization of stability operations across the armed forces.

CONCLUSION

DoD's effort to develop a more effective counterinsurgency capability grew primarily from its experience in postwar Iraq. In 2004 the Pentagon gradually came to acknowledge that adopting some awareness of counterinsurgency would help U.S. forces achieve the necessary stability in Iraq to initiate reconstruction and set up a visible new government. This realization spawned a number of efforts to familiarize U.S. soldiers with the operational specificities of the Iraqi counterinsurgency campaign, ranging from reworked training exercises and educational initiatives to publication of various doctrinal manuals and concept papers. In contrast to the largely enemy-centered approach to counterinsurgency adopted in Iraq in 2003, the new publications explicitly framed counterinsurgency as a predominantly political endeavor and therefore urged stronger civil-military coordination in the planning and running of operations.

Although significant, it is questionable whether these early initiatives can be taken as firm evidence of institutional learning. First, the conceptualization of counterinsurgency advanced in early doctrine and concept papers gave proof of an inadequate understanding of the challenge. While careful to stress the political nature of counterinsurgency and stability operations, these publications also tended to set the military exclusively combat- and security-related tasks, thereby assuming that civilian actors would be ready and able to manage "the rest." In Iraq this assumption did not hold, although this state of affairs did not significantly alter the predominantly combat-oriented orientation of U.S. military operations there. DoD's marginalization of the "nonmilitary" facets of the campaign, in both theory and practice, revealed an unwillingness to address counterinsurgency as it presented itself and a tendency to interpret it instead according to DoD's own preferences. Second, the U.S. military displayed in its institution-wide strategy and policy papers a distinct lack of interest in counterinsurgency. The 2004 *National Military Strategy* as well as the 2005 *National Defense Strategy* were focused primarily on conventional war and gave some attention to counterterrorism but were silent as to counterinsurgency and stability operations—striking given the fact that the U.S. military was at that time engaged in two such campaigns.

Such ambivalence notwithstanding, DoD's efforts to learn counterinsurgency were given a significant boost in 2005. As the security situation in Iraq failed to improve, senior members of the administration came to perceive a more holistic (read: less combat-oriented) approach to counterinsurgency as a possible solution to the continued violence there. Although still a substream of wider DoD policy, the emergence of counterinsurgency-related initiatives gathered steam in mid-2005, featuring a number of efforts to improve the military's linguistic skills, its ability to operate in civil-military environments, and its understanding of traditional counterinsurgency imperatives tried and tested in nominally similar campaigns.

The impetus for this drive manifested itself in two ways, one relating to Iraq specifically, the other to counterinsurgency more generally. In the first instance, the White House and Pentagon gradually acknowledged the relative level of success experienced by those commanders who had implemented broader counterinsurgency strategies in Iraq vis-à-vis those who had confined themselves to strike operations and raids. This acknowledgment resulted in the elevation of these very same commanders to positions in which they were able to affect Iraq policy. Also elevated in this manner were other experts, both military and civilian, who were familiar with the nature of counterinsurgency through previous operational experience, academic study, or both. Based on the advice of this increasingly influential COIN community, the White House officially announced in late 2005 a shift in strategy in Iraq, abandoning the strike-dominated, enemy-centered approach for a "clear-build-hold" strategy based on classical counterinsurgency theory.

DoD's reorientation was also geared toward counterinsurgency more generally, that is, beyond Iraq. Sections within the Pentagon concerned with the military's general lack of familiarity with counterinsurgency and stability operations sought to remedy this deficiency by spreading awareness on these types of operations. This effort was accelerated and also epitomized by DoD Directive 3000.05, released in November 2005, which set out to overhaul the U.S. military's prioritization of stability operations, placing them on the same level as major combat operations. Although Directive 3000.05 notably did not assign an executive agent to ensure the smooth implementation of its many tasks, it did include specific guidelines for follow-up and tasked various Pentagon departments to update OSD on their progress in institutionalizing a stability operations capability.

Together these two tracks helped generate significant momentum for the learning of counterinsurgency. However, it remained uncertain whether this momentum resonated with the Pentagon leadership—whether it would, given time, attract new converts and change the course of DoD policy. For now the coexistence of entrenched interests and the ascendance of counterinsurgency as a military priority resulted in an overall direction to DoD policy that would often appear contradictory. Furthermore, in this immediate phase of learning DoD also remained fragmented in its understanding of counterinsurgency. Amid this state of flux, many looked to the forthcoming Quadrennial Defense Review as a guide to the direction DoD was heading.

5

COUNTERINSURGENCY
AND THE QDR

The gathering pace of DoD's reorientation toward counterinsurgency in late 2005 generated great anticipation for the upcoming Quadrennial Defense Review, scheduled for release in early 2006. The practice of reviewing and setting policy through department-wide quadrennial reports began in 1996. The official purpose of these reports is to examine the "national defense strategy, force structure, force modernization plans, infrastructure, budget plan, and other elements of the defense program and policies of the United States with a view toward determining and expressing the defense strategy of the United States and establishing a defense program for the next 20 years."[1] These are considered to be major strategic publications, reflecting DoD's interpretation of trends and the capabilities needed to meet extant and emerging threats.

While these publications typically attract the attention of defense analysts and strategy pundits, the 2006 QDR was greeted with heightened interest from much further afield. This QDR was the second one published under Secretary of Defense Donald Rumsfeld and arrived in the midst of U.S. military involvement in two major campaigns, Afghanistan and Iraq, neither of which conformed to the vision of war set out in previous QDRs. Questions abounded regarding the direction of DoD as set out in the report. Would the QDR signal the official abandonment of Rumsfeld's transformational vision of rapid decisive operations in favor of a defense posture that regarded counterinsurgency and major combat operations as equally important? What would be the programmatic and budgetary implications of such a shift? And how explicit could DoD be about reversing its own policy? Acknowledging the unusual level of anticipation, Ryan Henry, principal deputy undersecretary of defense for policy, argued that "the need to transform our military has elevated the role of the QDR from a tool of periodic refinement to a fulcrum of transition to a post-9/11 world."[2]

A TROUBLING INCONSISTENCY

Compared to previous QDRs the 2006 iteration was explicit about the growing importance of irregular war and the need for the U.S. military to adapt accordingly. The 1997 QDR had built on the U.S. military's *Joint Vision 2010* (*JV2010*), a "conceptual template" released in 1996 and geared toward "dominant maneuver, precision engagement, full dimensional protection, and focused logistics."[3] *JV2010* did acknowledge the need to dominate across the spectrum of conflict: "We will move," it asserted, "toward a common goal: a joint force—persuasive in peace, decisive in war, preeminent in any form of conflict."[4] Yet for all this verbiage the focus of *JV2010* was overwhelmingly on emerging conventional RMA capabilities, with the "lower end" of the spectrum coming as a mere afterthought. The same view of war dominated the 1997 QDR, which to a large degree constituted an attempt to channel funds into making the RMA happen (including one proposal to cut the total U.S. force structure by 60,000).[5]

The 2001 QDR, analyzed in chapter 3, had also pushed for greater investment in information warfare and paid virtually no attention to counterinsurgency or stability operations. In sizing and structuring U.S. forces it outlined a 1-4-2-1 paradigm, predicated on homeland security, four small-scale operations, and two near-simultaneous conventional campaigns, of which one could be won decisively. Even while giving unprecedented attention to "smaller-scale operations," the 2001 QDR did not appreciate the possibility that a less-than-conventional campaign could be more demanding than a major combat operation. These were instead dismissed as "lesser included" eventualities, threatening only in their ability to erode the force's readiness to conduct more important and apparently more challenging conventional campaigns. As to the vision of war, Frederick W. Kagan contends that the 2001 QDR "had inherited from the growing momentum of the infowar movement the conviction that war was about the destruction of the enemy's ability to fight, either by precision, attrition or by targeting centers of gravity."[6] The very different logic of stability operations was not grasped.

The 2006 QDR seemed to chart a new course. It asserted that "in the post–September 11 world, irregular warfare has emerged as the dominant form of warfare confronting the United States, its allies and its partners" and that, accordingly, "guidance must account for distributed, long-duration operations, including unconventional warfare, foreign internal defense, counterterrorism, counterinsurgency, and stabilization and reconstruction operations."[7] To that end the 2006 QDR laid out a vision of the future joint force as equally "proficient in irregular operations, including counterinsurgency and stabilization operations, as they are today in high-intensity combat. . . . They will understand foreign cultures and societies and possess the ability to train, mentor and advise foreign security forces and conduct counterinsurgency campaigns."[8]

This vision prompted a number of initiatives intended to augment the U.S. military's ability to conduct various types of irregular operations. DoD would, for example, "expand Psychological Operations and Civil Affairs units by 3,700 personnel," which represented a 33 percent increase and a significant shift given that these troops are often required but seldom available in sufficient numbers during stability operations.[9] The 2006 QDR also advocated reviewing U.S. military training so as to incorporate irregular warfare and complex stabilization operations.[10] Moreover, a number of statements referred to efforts "to place linguistically capable individuals at all levels of the military—from the tactical squad to the operational commander."[11] To that end, this latest QDR spoke of increased funding for various language-training programs, increased predeployment linguistic training, and greater recognition for linguistic abilities than in the past.[12]

The focus on irregular war also informed the force-sizing construct advanced in the 2006 QDR. It laid out a vision of the U.S. military as able, at a steady state, to "employ general purpose forces continuously to interact with allies, build partner capability, conduct long-duration counter insurgency operations and deter aggressors through forward presence."[13] The QDR further stated that the military should have a surge capacity to "conduct a large-scale, potentially long-duration irregular warfare campaign including counterinsurgency and security, stability, transition and reconstruction operations"—something akin to the "current level of effort associated with operations in Iraq and Afghanistan."[14] These protracted irregular campaigns were effectively elevated to the position held by conventional war in the 2001 QDR; whereas it had spoken of the need to fight two near-simultaneous major combat operations, of which one could be won decisively, the 2006 QDR envisaged a military that would be able to conduct, simultaneously, either two major combat operations or a major combat operation and a prolonged irregular engagement.[15]

The 2006 QDR clearly gave unprecedented attention to the challenges of irregular warfare, including counterinsurgency. However, the document also presented a number of fundamental contradictions. While emphasizing the importance of incorporating counterinsurgency as part of the U.S. military's remit, there were few substantive directives on what would be required for this to occur. The focus on linguistic skills, the few mentions of revamping the military's training programs, and the boosts in PSYOPS and civil affairs were all well received by those who had anticipated a major reworking of U.S. defense policy, but there was little else to suggest a radical change in direction. The lack of genuine progress on this front was particularly noticeable given the change in strategic environment since 2001 and the rhetoric in the QDR itself regarding the importance of irregular war.

The ambitious vision of a military as proficient in counterinsurgency as in combat operations translated into only six major decisions, none of which related directly to the learning of counterinsurgency. The QDR stated that DoD would:

- "rebalance capabilities by creating modular brigades in all three Army components";
- "transform Army units and headquarters to modular designs";
- "incorporate FCS [Future Combat System] improvements into the modular force";
- "expand the Air Force Joint Tactical Air Control program";
- "stabilize the Army's end strength at 482,400 Active and 533,000 Reserve Component personnel by Fiscal Year 2011"; and
- "stabilize the Marine Corps' end strength at 175,000 Active and 39,000 Reserve Component personnel by Fiscal Year 2011."[16]

Even a cursory review of these decisions reveals the significant mismatch between the vision and the provisions set forth. Most forcefully, the decisions relating to the end strengths of the ground forces represented a cut of 5,000 Marines and a return to pre-2001 levels for the active-duty Army by 2011. Yet, as these very same forces were finding in Iraq and Afghanistan, counterinsurgency operations require a large ground force to clear, hold, and build on contested territory.[17] The reduction in ground force end strength thus seemed to signal a retreat rather than an embrace of counterinsurgency. Furthermore, how would a ground force reduced in size be expected to conduct a conventional war *and* a protracted counterinsurgency operation simultaneously, as stipulated in the QDR, when the U.S. military of 2006 was already struggling to meet the manpower demands of the Iraq campaign alone?

There is, of course, some truth to the argument that the cuts in ground forces were "driven more by budgetary constraints than by the force planning construct itself."[18] Michèle Flournoy, who was involved in producing the 1997 and 2001 QDRs, describes how the military's remit had expanded while its funding shrunk, culminating in an untenable end state.[19] Having increased dramatically in the years following 9/11, from $337 billion in FY2000 (in FY06 constant dollars) to $480 billion in 2004, the U.S. national defense budget then declined, hitting a relative low ($420 billion) in 2006.[20] Meanwhile "the growth of the overall federal deficit to some $317 billion, or 3.8 percent of the gross national product, ha[d] returned deficit reduction to a national priority, increasing the competition for limited discretionary funds."[21] Already worried about the soaring costs of personnel, health care, and retirement and the wearing-out of equipment in operations, DoD was thus an organization intent on limiting rather than extending its expenditures, yet this was at a time when the nation was facing a new type of resource- and manpower-intensive military mission, namely counterinsurgency. This financial quandary may explain why the QDR cut the end strength of the ground forces, even though doing so contravened the stated aim of increasing the military's ability to conduct the more demanding of irregular campaigns.

Although the budgetary constraints on the Pentagon were significant, they were not in themselves deterministic of policy. Indeed, there is something faintly ironic about an agency enjoying an estimated 20.8 percent of unified federal funding yet being unable, due to financial constraints, to implement its own vision and policy.[22] More than an *inability* to go through with the reorientation toward counterinsurgency, the lack of progress on this front would instead appear to represent institutional priorities; there was simply insufficient interest in increasing the size of the ground forces and in the types of missions they were then struggling to conduct.

This charge is borne out when examining the other four main programmatic decisions cited above, which while *presented* as leading the way to greater proficiency in irregular war were at best only tangentially related to counterinsurgency or stability operations. The creation of "modular brigades in all three Army components" was framed in the QDR as "significantly expanding its capabilities and capacity for the full range of military operations, including irregular warfare and support to security, stability and transition operations."[23] This statement is not entirely untrue, but it requires closer scrutiny.[24] In brief, Army modularization, an initiative that predated both 9/11 and the Iraq War, was to have two major effects on the force. First, the Army was forming new "brigade combat teams" (BCTs) that would each contain its own support elements and therefore be able to deploy without "borrowing" those components from other units. By making these brigades more self-sufficient, modularization would enable more deployments at any one time along with smoother troop rotations. Second, BCTs were made modular, meaning that functional components could be added or withdrawn from the brigade to suit a particular mission. Although these changes were undoubtedly important, neither directly addressed the U.S. Army's ability to conduct stability operations. Although self-contained and easier to rotate, a BCT will bring the same capabilities as any other conventional Army unit. And although modular BCTs could in theory be optimized for stability operations by including the components needed for such campaigns, the QDR provided no indication of how or whether this would occur.[25] Instead, the prevalent Army blueprint of the BCT structure at that time was firmly geared toward major combat operations.[26]

The decision to "incorporate the Future Combat System (FCS) into the modular force" was even further removed from the aim of developing a counterinsurgency capability. Much like modularization, FCS predated 9/11 and the Iraq War; neither emerged in response to the irregular challenges of the new strategic environment. In fact, FCS was highly conventional or, perhaps, "transformational" in its orientation, predicated on the interlacing of manned and unmanned Army vehicles and into a network able to gain superior "battle-space awareness" through information-sharing. Although this system may have extended the U.S. military's primacy in conventional combat, its contribution to counterinsurgency operations would appear peripheral at best.[27] Nonetheless, the QDR cited the integration of FCS "rollouts" into the force as a main accomplishment in the Army's re-orientation toward irregular warfare.[28] And in making the further incorporation of FCS one of the QDR's six primary decisions, DoD clearly perceived this system as a convincing means of developing a force as "proficient in irregular operations, including counterinsurgency and stabilization operations, as they are today in high-intensity combat."

Some proponents of FCS have claimed that the system will be relevant also to irregular campaigns, offering the potential for greater coordination and shared awareness—assets of undoubted value in any military operation.[29] However, David Isenberg makes the point that "even if the need for the FCS system is accepted, questions remain about the program's technical feasibility and affordability. Some experts doubt that the army can develop and test the necessary technologies in time to start producing lightweight manned vehicles by 2012—a requisite for meeting the deadline to field them, according to the army's current schedule."[30] Given the ambitious goal of expanding the Army's portfolio, it is questionable whether investment in the FCS still constituted the best use of scarce funds. Furthermore, networked connectivity had never really been the missing link in the U.S. military's engagements with stability operations. To invest more on this front would, at best, merely extend a mostly irrelevant overmatch and at a great opportunity cost.

Finally, the decision to "expand the Air Force Joint Tactical Air Control program" revealed that DoD still perceived irregular challenges as adequately manageable through precision strikes. The primary functions of the Air Force's joint tactical air controllers are to "direct combat strike aircraft against enemy targets" and to "coordinate artillery fire with air strikes."[31] Although conducive to the elimination of specific targets, investment in this program was a far cry from the type of reforms needed to ensure a higher capability to conduct counterinsurgency or stability operations, which require much more than the destruction of targets.

The continued and strictly conventional mind-set revealed in the QDR was even more pronounced in the defense budget request for fiscal year 2007, submitted by President Bush to Congress as the QDR was released. Despite the rhetoric of a change in strategic environment and in institutional priorities, the FY07 defense budget did not cancel any of the U.S. military's high-cost weapons systems, all of which were primarily or exclusively suited for conventional war. As Max Boot argued at the time, "The Pentagon is continuing to fund three ruinously expensive short-range fighters—the F/A-22 Raptor, the F/A-18E/F Super Hornet and the F-35 Joint Strike Fighter—even though we already have total dominance in the air. The entire budget for language and cultural training—$181 million—comes to less than the cost of one F-35."[32] Similarly, the budget called for the increased production of the hugely expensive Virginia-class nuclear attack submarines, a Cold War relic that had by 2006 been remarketed as "tools for gathering intelligence . . . and inserting Special Forces units into enemy water."[33] Other big-ticket items consuming the budget were the CVN-21 next-generation aircraft carrier, the DD(X) destroyer and—on the Army side—the FCS.[34]

These platforms and systems were clearly not suited for counterinsurgency, and their cost per item was also out of proportion with the funding that would have been necessary for most counterinsurgency-related initiatives. It would be fair to conclude that DoD, rather than being financially unable to fulfill its vision for irregular warfare, instead did not sufficiently prioritize this objective to make it happen. Indeed, in his account of internal Pentagon dealings surrounding the QDR journalist Bob Woodward reveals the sense of satisfaction felt by some senior DoD officials at having produced a QDR that did not threaten existing priorities: "The good news," Ryan Henry is quoted as saying, "is that not one defense program had to be cut."[35] Clearly to those driving the QDR process maintaining existing defense programs was more important than the development of a counterinsurgency capability, and the QDR, which Henry had himself described as a "fulcrum of transition to a post-9/11 world," therefore failed to chart a radically new direction for the U.S. military. This endgame engendered the "frequent complaints," made "off the record, by officers home from Iraq, that visiting the Pentagon can be like visiting a distant planet where the war is just a speck in the sky."[36]

The disconnect between vision and provisions had many roots, ranging from the industrial sunk costs involved in rolling out labor-intensive weapons systems, the employment opportunities that such projects create, and the institutional inertia at DoD. This is, however, only half the story, as the QDR did in fact include many decisions relating to irregular warfare. In a curious manner, however, they, too, contributed to the marginalization of counterinsurgency and the continued investment in conventional capabilities. Much as in times gone by, DoD managed to devise an apparent solution to the problem of irregular warfare that did not to any significant degree include the U.S. regular services, which in turn justified their exclusion from the wider reorientation and continued investment in conventional combat. This outcome was the product of DoD's particular definition of "irregular warfare" and on its framing of stability operations, and this highlights once again the critical distinction between learning and the appearance of learning.

THE CONCEPTUAL CONFUSION OF IRREGULAR WARFARE

Even though the QDR contained several provisions to boost the U.S. military's ability to conduct irregular warfare, these initiatives did not significantly augment the U.S. armed forces' ability to conduct counterinsurgency—despite the fact that counterinsurgency was nominally included within the category of irregular war. To a large degree this apparent contradiction in the QDR stemmed from DoD's *particular interpretation of "irregular warfare."* By defining irregular warfare broadly as "operations in which the enemy is not a regular military force of a nation-state," the QDR arbitrarily grouped together various types of distinct operations, including "long-duration unconventional warfare, counterterrorism, counterinsurgency, and military support for stabilization and reconstruction efforts."[37] Much like "low-intensity conflicts" and "MOOTW" during previous decades, the phrase "irregular war" became an umbrella term conflating the specific nature of counterinsurgency with a series of other less-than-conventional (but significantly different) types of engagements.[38] Then as now, within this broad range of irregular campaigns the type of counterinsurgency operations typified by Iraq did not receive much attention.

First, counterinsurgency tended to be overshadowed by counterterrorism. These two types of operations can in theory overlap: Both benefit from close relations with local populations (to gain valuable human intelligence) and the ability to locate, track, and target individuals (rather than combat systems). However, DoD tended to conceive of counterterrorism as an almost exclusively strike-oriented endeavor and therefore as distinct from counterinsurgency, which is often characterized by a protracted political initiative to create or stabilize a particular order or government, requiring the co-option, through a variety of military and nonmilitary means, of those who would otherwise support the insurgency.[39] As interpreted, these types of missions were thus made to be widely different, requiring different force packages, training, education, and doctrine.

Second, counterinsurgency was also conflated and subordinated to various "train-and-equip" programs designed to augment the ability of friendly states to control their own territory so as to prevent the possible use of ungoverned areas by terrorist organizations. As it was framed, irregular war recalled "foreign internal defense" (FID), a military term denoting the "participation by civilian and military agencies of a government in any of the action programs taken by another government or other designated organization to free and protect its society from subversion, lawlessness, and insurgency."[40] In focusing on this type of intervention, rather than the deployment of U.S. ground troops, DoD assumed that future counterinsurgency campaigns would involve a sufficiently developed indigenous state capability, supported by a strictly limited U.S. footprint of advisers and SOF—an approach most closely associated with the El Salvador counterinsurgency campaign in the 1980s.

Grouped in the same category, but distinct in nature and implementation, counterterrorism, FID, and counterinsurgency were competing for finite resources and—just as important—for the finite space that the U.S. military, bent on conventional campaigns, was willing to provide to accommodate the irrefutable ascendance of irregular war. A close reading of the QDR reveals that in this battle counterterrorism and FID prevailed and counterinsurgency was subordinated, if not neglected. The mere twelve references to counterinsurgency throughout the ninety-two-page document failed to match the QDR's consistent focus and heavy emphasis on terrorism and counterterrorism. More to the point, the QDR listed "defeating terrorist networks" as one of DoD's four focus areas; there was no equivalent emphasis on why the U.S. military should learn counterinsurgency or what such an endeavor would entail.[41]

Similarly, with regard to FID, the 2006 QDR heralded and advocated the "indirect approach" to irregular war, whereby small teams of U.S. troops, typically special operations forces, would be distributed over large areas and help friendly states police their own territory in order to remove the types of sanctuaries believed to be so attractive to al-Qaeda and its affiliated groups.[42] Via the QDR, DoD stressed that it should acquire the "authorities and resources to build partnership capacity, achieve unity of effort, and adopt indirect approaches to act with and through others to defeat common enemies—shifting from conducting activities ourselves to enabling partners to do more for themselves."[43] There was no similar urge to transform the regular services to engage directly should the "enabling partners" of the indirect approach be in any way inadequate or even nonexistent.

This emphasis on counterterrorism and FID to the exclusion of counterinsurgency was perhaps most evident in the decisions taken in the QDR. Throughout the document, SOF were elevated as the lead force in conducting counterterrorism operations across the globe, either by training indigenous ground forces or by conducting "direct-action" strikes and raids.[44] SOF, rather than regular forces, were to be the agents of irregular warfare. Accordingly the QDR proposed a one-third increase in active Special Forces battalions; the establishment of a 2,600-person Marine Corps

Special Operations Command to "train foreign military units and conduct direct action and special reconnaissance"; an increase in the Navy's "SEAL team force levels to conduct direct action missions"; the establishment of a SOF unmanned aerial vehicle squadron "to locate and target enemy capabilities in denied or contested areas"; and enhanced capabilities "to support SOF insertion and extraction into denied areas from strategic distances."[45] In budgetary terms these measures translated into $5.1 billion to increase SOF by 4,000 in 2007 and nearly $28 billion for a further increase of 14,000 by 2011.[46]

These steps built on previous initiatives. In March 2005 President Bush had signed off on Unified Command Plan 2004, which effectively designated Special Operations Command as the lead command for the War on Terror.[47] From 2001 to September 2005 SOCOM staff levels increased by 6,000 to 51,441 and enjoyed a budgetary hike from $3.8 billion to $6.6 billion.[48] The QDR further specified that "the Army Special Forces (SF) School [had] increased its training throughput from 282 new active duty enlisted Special Forces personnel in 2001 to 617 new personnel in 2005—the equivalent of an additional SF Battalion each year—with a further goal of increasing to 750 students per year."[49]

The approach to irregular warfare promoted in the QDR had already been put into practice. The QDR itself praised the 1,700-strong Combined Joint Task Force Horn of Africa (CJTF-HOA) as a prototype of the "indirect approach," stating that it was "operating across large areas . . . using only small detachments" and was "helping to build host-nation capacity in Kenya, Ethiopia and Djibouti."[50] According to the QDR, CJTF-HOA involved "military, civilian, and allied personnel work[ing] together to provide security training and to perform public works and medical assistance projects"; this style of operations, the QDR added, had helped to "improve . . . local conditions and set the stage to minimize tribal, ethnic, and religious conflict, decreasing the possibility of failed states or ungoverned spaces in which terrorist extremists can more easily operate or take shelter."[51] The QDR also cited the European Command's Counterterrorism Initiative, which involved training the security forces of the trans-Sahara region to help them police national territories, with the ultimate aim of countering emerging terrorist threats. The QDR elaborated that "in Niger, for example, a small team of combat aviation advisors has helped Niger's Air Force hone its skills to prevent the under-developed eastern part of the country from becoming a safe haven for transnational terrorists."[52]

A third example of this approach, not mentioned in the QDR, was the U.S. military's engagement in the Philippines, where various SOF elements had since 2002 teamed up with the Armed Forces of the Philippines (AFP) in their counterinsurgency campaign against the Abu Sayyaf Group (ASG), a purportedly Islamist outfit engaged in kidnappings, violence, and crime.

The U.S. forces provided training to the AFP and, stationed in the area of operations, were also able to assess the needs and nature of the counterinsurgency campaign, as well as interact with the local population. The U.S. troops set up medical facilities to build legitimacy and, with limited discretionary funds, initiated a number of projects for the areas most touched by conflict. Robert Kaplan, who spent time with the U.S. forces there, explains that "the objective was always to further legitimize the AFP among the islanders. The Americans went nowhere and did nothing without Filipino troops present to take the credit."[53] Alongside the armed operations of the AFP, the presence, measures, and training programs of SOF helped drive the ASG from its former stronghold on Basilan Island, although the group did retain a presence in the country.[54]

The SOF-led approach to irregular warfare is highly appealing. Not only does it circumvent the many pitfalls of deploying large numbers of soldiers and Marines; the presence of U.S. troops would also be discreet and therefore reduce the political risks of the associated operations. Indeed, the indirect approach seemed particularly promising when compared to the situation in Iraq, where U.S. troops were struggling with a classic counterinsurgency campaign that was highly costly and deadly and that even its supporters predicted would take a very long time. Some deduced from this comparison that the regular military was simply the wrong tool for counterinsurgency and that these operations, and irregular operations in general, should instead be conducted by SOF, which had the low profile and adaptability necessary to thrive in these complex environments.[55] With its overwhelming focus on SOF in its irregular warfare–related directives, the QDR seemed to suggest a similar division of labor. In that sense, it echoed the elevation of SOF seen during the 1960s and 1980s, which were also grounded on the premise that SOF, rather than the regular services of the armed forces, would be the ones to conduct irregular warfare.[56]

The indirect approach brings undeniable advantages, but it also has strictly limited applicability—which is what made the QDR's virtually exclusive emphasis on this approach so disconcerting. The indirect approach relies on "building and leveraging partner capacity . . . and the employment of surrogates"; however, situations have and will arise where local surrogates are unwilling, unable, or too unreliable to fulfill their end of the bargain.[57] In these instances, and where the mission at hand is of sufficient strategic importance to the United States, its own ground forces have had to step into the breach. The U.S. effort in Vietnam began as an advisory effort but soon escalated into direct intervention; in Afghanistan the initially small footprint of the U.S. military grew with each year as planners confronted the inadequacy of local security forces and NATO partners; and in Iraq similar constraints indefinitely postponed the desired redeployment of U.S. ground forces, as they were instead called upon to conduct counterinsurgency operations themselves. It is this finding—the cyclical inevitability of engaging in counterinsurgency—that has motivated the U.S. military's repeated attempts to learn how to prosecute such missions, but it also appears to be the first cognitive casualty of this process.

Furthermore the QDR's nearly exclusive investment in SOF betrayed an assumption that irregular campaigns are separate from conventional combat—that they occur in different places and can therefore be conducted by different troops. Yet, as seen with the invasion of Iraq in 2003 there is a need, both during and following conventional operations, to stabilize and initiate reconstruction so as to consolidate the military objectives achieved through the use of force. The decisions advanced in the QDR did little to prepare the regular forces for this task. Not only is this something that would have to be conducted by the regular troops in theater, it is also a task that small and dispersed SOF teams would struggle to fulfill, principally due to their smaller size and the immediate need to project a presence to the local population.

By focusing most of its attention and resources on irregular operations employing a light footprint, and so little on the specifics of counterinsurgency, DoD seemed to presume that these more demanding types of challenges could be avoided—an assumption that has marked DoD's understanding of counterinsurgency throughout history. The U.S. military was thus structuring its force according to the types of irregular operations that it was willing to conduct rather than those it had been driven to undertake in Iraq and Afghanistan. Despite the many merits of the indirect approach the QDR thus represented a failure to fill the capability gap exposed in these conflicts.

The QDR's virtually exclusive reliance on SOF as the agent of irregular war belied a third difficulty, relating to the exact purpose of SOF troops. Far from uniquely devoted to irregular operations SOF and the related community are functionally heterogeneous, tasked to conduct a series of missions, including foreign internal defense and unconventional warfare as well as direct action, special reconnaissance, counterterrorism, and counterproliferation. Depending on the particular unit and mission, SOF activity can thus be as combat-oriented as any mission conducted by regular troops, although the manner in which they go about the operation may differ.[58] Accordingly it is far from certain that investment into SOF will produce a superior capability to conduct irregular operations, much like the boosting of conventionally trained regular forces would be an inadequate means of building a counterinsurgency capability.

This point gains particular relevance when one considers the institutional bias of the U.S. military's SOF community. Hy S. Rothstein, a retired career special forces officer, argues that the core of the community has traditionally prioritized direct action and strike missions and that SOF specializing in civil affairs, PSYOPS, and unconventional warfare (the organization, training, equipping, and support of surrogate forces) have typically been fewer and less powerful within the organization.[59] Max Boot echoes this point, arguing that SOCOM "is overly focused on what is known in the trade as Direct Action—on rappelling out of helicopters, kicking down doors, and capturing or killing bad guys."[60] He also notes the "widespread concern within Army SF circles that their 'softer,' but no less vital, missions are being shortchanged by SOCOM in favor of sexier SWAT-style raids."[61]

There are many reasons for such bias within the SOF community. Prior to the 1986 Goldwater-Nichols legislation, special operations forces were closely integrated into the conventional military and lacked the autonomy to pursue alternative missions and skills. SOF were dependent on their parent service for promotions, equipment, and resources—a relation that let the regular service dictate its functions and uses. At this time, and even today if to a lesser degree, the U.S. military was suspicious of these "elite units," a distrust based on a number of more or less well-founded criticisms: "that they have limited utility; require a disproportionate amount of support; take the best personnel from other units; gain undeserved public attention, thus damaging the morale of other units; have a tendency toward individualism; exhibit barbaric behavior; and resist traditional discipline."[62] The effect of this institutional tension on SOF was to force conformity with the regular services' overarching ethos, even though this limited their ability to offer an alternative to the conventional use of force. The establishment of SOCOM in 1987 helped safeguard SOF from the conventional bias of the regular services, but by this time, the SOF community had to a large extent internalized the orthodoxy of its parent institution.

The conventionalization of the SOF community is also a product of its own culture and mind-set. From the outset the special-warfare community has struggled with the question of what it is that makes them special: "Are these essentially conventional soldiers with a very high level of proficiency? Or are they something else, dedicated to purposes and functions that are different and using methods that are outside the conventional mold of most military forces"?[63] In answering these questions the SOF leadership, much like its counterparts in the regular services, has often been unduly swayed by the immediate attraction of direct action. Whereas unconventional warfare is protracted and collaborative and requires civil-military coordination and a community-oriented approach, direct action is quick, decisive, unilateral, and, this is important, glamorous. Tellingly, senior SOF positions are generally filled by officers with experience in direct action rather than unconventional warfare; within SOCOM the latter camp has tended to be marginalized.[64]

For these and other reasons SOF has on the whole historically identified itself as a hyperconventional rather than unconventional force. Accordingly, even though the above efforts to expand SOF did include increases to Special Forces, civil affairs, and PSYOPS, the best part of the additional resources was allocated to direct-action capabilities, such as Special Mission Units and their supporting units.[65] All of this being said, it is uncertain whether the QDR's faith in SOF as the sole agent of irregular warfare was particularly well placed. Noting that "there is less of a gap between SOF and the regular services than you would expect," Thomas A. Marks—an authority on counterinsurgency and so-called people's war—warns of the "absolutely disastrous impact, possibly, of taking the most tactically oriented commando mentality and putting it in charge strategically of irregular warfare when there is not even clarity between counterterrorism and counterinsurgency."[66] In a similar vein Hy Rothstein, writing in 2006, concluded that "the U.S. military is not able to wage unconventional warfare despite significant investment in special operations capabilities."[67]

Ultimately, exclusive investment in the SOF-dominated "indirect approach" did little to prompt the development of a counterinsurgency capability within the regular armed forces. For the reasons outlined above the emergence of the indirect approach was at best peripheral to the U.S. military's learning of counterinsurgency; at worst it provided a convenient cover for the regular services' lack of preparation and familiarity with such missions. This fig-leaf function of the indirect approach might help explain the disconnect between the QDR's soaring rhetoric regarding the importance of irregular warfare and the lack of directives targeting the regular services' ability to conduct such campaigns. DoD appeared to have convinced itself of the infallibility of its chosen approach to irregular warfare, by which logic the regular services could focus on conventional and other initiatives unrelated to counterinsurgency. In effect it had innovated in accordance with *its own* interpretation of the challenge, even though that interpretation hardly matched the operational realities of Iraq, Afghanistan, or any future and nominally similar campaign.

SSTR AND THE ELUSIVE "INTERAGENCY"

A careful reading of the QDR reveals a second source of conceptual ambiguity that further helps explain the QDR's mismatch between rhetoric and related action. This second "fig leaf" for the U.S. military's lack of counterinsurgency capability is found in the elevation, subtle throughout the document, of U.S. civilian agencies and government departments as the likely torchbearers in future stability operations. Here, too, the QDR expressed a high level of faith, most of it misplaced, in the ability of others to conduct the operations that DoD would evidently most like to avoid. In this case the emphasis centered on the Department of State and the U.S. Agency for International Development and their role in what came to be termed "stability, security, transition, and reconstruction" operations, or SSTR for short.

From the very outset the QDR spoke of giving "greater emphasis to the war on terror and irregular warfare activities, including long-duration unconventional warfare, counterterrorism, counterinsurgency, and *military support* for stabilization and reconstruction efforts."[68] The implication of this phrasing was clearly that the military would take the lead in the initial three types of operations, which were interpreted as primarily combat-oriented tasks, but that it would only *support* stability operations, which were instead to be conducted by other (by default) civilian agencies. In the QDR's final chapter ("Achieving Unity of Effort") DoD elaborated on this theme, suggesting that stability operations ought to involve the civilian government departments to a greater degree, which would in turn minimize the role played by the military.[69]

In theory the division of labor vied for in the QDR made perfect sense. First, the problem of instability cannot be solved by military means alone; the key lies instead in finding a political compromise that can gain the buy-in of the majority of the affected population. In essence this means that the immediate security provided by the military is secondary to the more fundamental political bargaining—a diplomatic task that is best undertaken by the political leadership of the host and intervening nations. Second, stability operations often take place in countries with weak or lacking infrastructure. There is often a need for the intervening state to create, reinforce, or momentarily take over state institutions and to provide basic services to the population. Stability operations will thus frequently involve a series of traditionally "civilian" tasks, ranging from sewage treatment and water filtration to the organization of elections and the kick-starting of the economy. Although the military holds some relevant expertise in these areas, it is generally felt that such tasks are better performed by civilian organizations—international financial institutions; international and nongovernmental agencies; the intervening state's departments of agriculture, international development, and justice—who have the skills needed to create at least the semblance of a functioning state.

This division of labor, although ideal in theory, is difficult to implement in practice. The overriding problem is that it relies on the ability of civilian agencies and departments to deploy a sufficient number of experts within an acceptable time frame. Typically this does not occur, as civilian agencies (contrary to the military) cannot forcibly deploy staff and often lack the numbers and operational capability to match the military's resources in the field.[70] As a result the military has typically been forced to conduct political and reconstruction tasks for which it is untrained and generally unsuited. This is a historically consistent challenge, summarized effectively in 1964 by David Galula, the French military officer and counterinsurgency theorist: "To confine soldiers to purely military functions while urgent and vital tasks have to be done, and nobody else is available to undertake them, would be senseless. The soldier must then be prepared to become . . . a social worker, a civil engineer, a schoolteacher, a nurse, a boy scout. But only for as long as he cannot be replaced, for it is better to entrust civilian tasks to civilians."[71]

To devise an *effective* all-of-government approach to stability operations is to ensure that civilian agencies undertake civilian tasks *as far as possible* but also that the military, with its advantage in resources and deployability, retains ownership of those mission components for which the civilian agencies are inadequately prepared. As far as DoD is concerned, such an approach would be consistent with its 2005 directive on stability operations, which stated as DoD policy that "many stability operations tasks are best performed by indigenous, foreign, or U.S. civilian professionals," but that "U.S. military forces shall be prepared to perform all tasks necessary to establish or maintain order when civilians cannot do so."[72] It would also be consistent with the U.S. Code of Federal Regulations, which includes, as one of the Army and Marine Corps' functions, the provision of forces "for the occupation of territories abroad, including initial establishment of military government pending transfer of this authority."[73]

The QDR, however, revealed a DoD tendency to promote not a workable division of labor based on existing and likely civilian capabilities but instead a wholesale transfer of responsibility for stability operations, particularly the nonmilitary components, to civilian agencies regardless of their ability to conduct those tasks. While repeatedly limiting the military's role to *supporting* SSTR, there was no real discussion in the QDR as to the identity, capabilities, and mandate of the agencies to be thus supported. Skirting such an assessment, the QDR at once overestimated the civilian agencies' ability to conduct stability operations and underestimated the range of tasks to be assumed by the military itself.

This charge is based on the weakness of civilian agencies to conduct stability operations and the likelihood of this weakness enduring in the medium to long terms. For years leading up to the 2006 QDR the U.S. government had tried various means of augmenting the capabilities of civilian departments to resource and deploy for stability operations. Tellingly, even the most ambitious of these initiatives, the establishment within the Department of State of the Office of the Coordinator for Reconstruction and Stabilization (S/CRS), had paid no real dividend on this front.

Founded in 2004, S/CRS was mandated to "lead, coordinate and institutionalize U.S. Government civilian capacity to prevent or prepare for post-conflict situations, and to help stabilize and reconstruct societies in transition from conflict or civil strife."[74] To that end S/CRS was also to stand up a corps of 250 civilian experts with the capability to deploy to conflict-torn countries, as well as a "Response Readiness Reserve" of more than 500 civilian experts should a surge capability be required.[75] From the very outset the military saw within this new organization an opportunity to offload or share the burden of stability operations with civilian partners.[76] Testifying before the Senate in June 2005, Ryan Henry explained that "the ability of civilian components of the [U.S. government] to prevent conflict and/or establish a sustainable peace will save lives and money by either obviating the need for military force in the first place or helping our troops come home more quickly."[77]

The problem is that S/CRS suffered from a fundamental lack of capacity and funding. Congress, particularly the appropriations committees, was unwilling to make the important trade-offs to fund this and other state-building initiatives, which were perceived as peripheral to national security.[78] To preempt this congressional hesitancy, the White House deliberately limited the size of S/CRS: It was created with a staff of thirty to forty, and though the figure increased in subsequent years it reached only seventy-five by the time the QDR was published.[79] More generally, the Bush administration regularly downgraded its funding requests for S/CRS, but even these requests were often further slashed or outright eliminated while passing through the House and Senate.

As well as facing enemies on Capitol Hill, S/CRS also suffered from its location within the State Department. The new entity faced rivalry from some of the regional bureaus, which perceived S/CRS as demanding a seat at the table while bringing no funds of its own.[80] The organization also threatened the turf and equities of some of the functional offices, engendering resistance there as well. More generally the new entity "had difficulty in getting a clear mandate from either [Colin] Powell or [Condoleezza] Rice" and received inadequate support from the higher echelons of the organization.[81] The new body was placed in a separate annex outside the main headquarters, and its head was assigned the position of assistant secretary rather than that of undersecretary, undercutting his influence within the department.[82]

Most important in this context, S/CRS was unable to develop a deployable roster of personnel that could significantly alleviate the burden placed on DoD in its engagements in stability operations. Struggling for funding, the efforts of the S/CRS to develop the Active Response Corps culminated in handfuls of experts deployed to various conflict zones where the military had no presence or only a limited one.[83] Notwithstanding whatever contribution these teams, perhaps ten or twenty individuals, could achieve on the ground, this capability was not the type of contribution that the U.S. military had wanted and anticipated from S/CRS. Similarly the efforts to stand up the Civilian Reserve Corps and establish the

Conflict Response Fund (a pool of funds to be quickly allocated in response to unforeseen crises) were repeatedly thwarted in Congress. In fiscal year 2005 the Bush administration requested but was denied $100 million to this end. The following year the process repeated itself, although after heavy lobbying by DoD the House bill did authorize the Pentagon to transfer up to $100 million of its own funds to help the State Department carry out reconstruction and stabilization activities.[84] Even when the Civilian Reserve Corps was finally launched in July 2008, with the help of $75 million of appropriated supplemental funds, a further $250 million was immediately requested for it to grow beyond the minimum requirements. Ultimately these initiatives were insufficient to develop the civilian capability that the military had anticipated.[85]

It is telling that S/CRS nonetheless represented one of the more convincing efforts to develop a civilian capability for stability operations; other U.S. government agencies did not present any better alternatives. The personnel systems of most U.S. government departments continued to resist collaboration with DoD; operational secondments were not encouraged nor rewarded but were instead likely to jeopardize career progression.[86] Even organizations ostensibly oriented toward international assistance, such as USAID, had only a minimal capacity for stability operations. The organization had downsized following the Vietnam War, in which it was heavily involved, and abandoned the prospect of playing a similar role in the future. As a result USAID's deployment to Vietnam was itself larger than the agency's entire staff in 2006.[87] Despite some structural reforms following 9/11 USAID in 2006 was, much like the State Department, lacking a sizeable operational capability and a standing deployable corps: These two organizations could "send a few people quickly, but for such substantial operations as those in Afghanistan or Iraq, both have to recruit staff, write and sign contracts, and conduct training—a time-consuming process for which the situation on the ground can't wait."[88] It is also the case that sections within USAID continued to resist a role for the agency in stability operations conducted in unsecure environments and alongside DoD.[89]

Despite the evident and chronic lack of capable civilian partners, DoD stubbornly formulated policy on the assumption that the burden of stability operations would be shared along civilian-military lines. This mind-set was evident during the rollout of DoD Directive 3000.05, which was delayed by months because of a rift over whether its title should include the language "stability operations" or "military support to stability, security, transition, and reconstruction operations" (i.e., SSTR).[90] Adm. Edmund Giambastiani, vice chairman of the JCS and former commander of JFCOM, finally broke the impasse by opting for "support to SSTR" as the title; for DoD this implicitly signaled that the U.S. military's remit in these operations would be limited to security- and combat-related tasks.[91] This assumption clashed with the demands of the ongoing operations in Iraq and Afghanistan, as well as with every assessment of civilian departments' ability to fill the shortfall.

The notion of a functional civilian capability conducting stability operations was further entrenched with the issuing of National Security Presidential Directive (NSPD) 44 by President Bush in December 2005, which set out an interagency division of labor for "reconstruction and stabilization assistance for foreign states."[92] Highlighting the importance of stability operations for U.S. national security, NSPD 44 clearly states that "the Secretary of State shall coordinate and lead integrated United States Government efforts, involving all U.S. Departments and Agencies with relevant capabilities, to prepare, plan for, and conduct stabilization and reconstruction activities."[93] The NSPD also adds that the State Department must "coordinate such efforts with the Secretary of Defense to ensure harmonization with any planned or ongoing U.S. military operations across the spectrum of conflict."[94] Nonetheless, in giving the State Department the lead for the preparation, planning, and conduct of stability operations, NSPD 44 effectively signals a reduced role for DoD in such engagements, even though State was at this time unprepared to undertake most tasks typical of stability operations, particularly if on a scale like Afghanistan or Iraq.

The 2006 QDR carried forward the idea of the U.S. military having operationally capable partners within the U.S. government. The use of military troops in stability operations, it noted, was to be seen as a "short-term necessity."[95] And rather than recognize the seemingly persistent weakness of other government agencies in carrying out these tasks, the QDR stated that DoD, in its force planning, "will consider a somewhat *higher* level of contributions from international allies and partners, as well as other Federal agencies."[96] This assumption jarred with the finding of a subsequent internal report from OSD on stability operations that "hardly any new deployable civilian capacity in any other departments and agencies has been created in the last several years despite Presidential requests, National Security Directives, and Defense Department urging."[97]

It could be argued that the QDR planned for the future rather than the present—that its provisions should be taken as hortatory expressions of intent rather than as a reflection of the relevant status quo at the time. The QDR did make a number of recommendations for how the sought-after coordination between agencies might be achieved: It laid out DoD's support for legislation "to enable other agencies to strengthen their capabilities so that balanced interagency operations become more feasible" and backed "efforts to expand the expeditionary capacity of agency partners."[98] Yet even though the authors of the QDR cannot be faulted in planning for an ideal, clearly that ideal was wholly detached from time-tested realities. One such reality concerned the historically consistent shortfall in civilian capabilities.

Another was put bluntly in the abovementioned internal DoD report: "Promoting increased deployable civilian capacity must remain a top DoD priority, but the process will take years, if not decades, and require revolutionary Congressional action with respect to budgets and authorities."[99] The assessment effectively contextualizes DoD's lack of consideration of its own role in stability operations, a role that has and will extend beyond the security- and combat-related tracks. This conundrum expressed itself in Iraq and in previous contingencies; it was also what prompted the reorientation toward stability operations in the first place. To a large degree, therefore, the 2006 QDR's failure to acknowledge this fact and to plan accordingly illustrates the Pentagon's continued aversion to stability operations.

Further evidence of this mind-set is the limited focus given to stability operations throughout the QDR—a lack of attention that could be justified only if the military did not see a major role for itself in such missions. As seen above, "military support to SSTR" was, much like "counterinsurgency," conflated with other operations under the rubric of "irregular operations." Furthermore, and despite the 2005 directive to prioritize stability operations on the same level as major combat operations, there were in fact only nine references to stability operations throughout the entire QDR. Most of these simply emphasized that the military could not conduct such operations alone—a statement that, although entirely accurate, belied the point that no other agency could even begin to match the military's resources and operational capability.

CONCLUSION

Great anticipation marked the run-up to the publication of the 2006 QDR. The strategic environment had changed, and DoD appeared to be adapting to the new context. In one sense the QDR did not disappoint expectations of reform. It carried strong rhetoric regarding the importance of counterinsurgency and stability operations, which were grouped together with other less-than-conventional types of engagements under the category of "irregular war." It also repeatedly asserted the dominance of irregular war in the post-9/11 strategic environment and emphasized the need to shape the U.S. military accordingly. The force-sizing construct of the QDR included a prolonged irregular campaign, akin to the counterinsurgency in Iraq, as a mission that the U.S. military should be able to conduct while also defeating a conventional adversary elsewhere.

There was, however, a disconnect between the rhetoric on irregular war and the direction it set for DoD. Only a few provisions in the document related directly to counterinsurgency, striking given the institution's previous neglect of such missions, its acknowledgment of their importance, and the problems faced in countering insurgencies in Afghanistan and Iraq. In places (particularly with regard to the end strength of the ground forces) it seemed as if counterinsurgency, which is often manpower-intensive, did not form part of DoD's vision at all.

This contradiction between vision and provisions had two related roots. First, a close reading of the QDR reveals that its emphasis on irregular war was in fact less representative of institutional priorities than might be assumed. It seems clear from the QDR and the defense budget that the U.S. military maintained an unremittingly combat-oriented mind-set, which reduced the scope for investment in other forms of warfare. In the QDR this inconsistency no doubt stemmed in part from the manner in which this publication is produced: A series of committees and working groups are formed, each is assigned a particular theme, and their collective findings are later embedded within the final product without much triage or prioritization. Even so, the lack of emphasis on counterinsurgency also reflected an institutional reluctance to engage with this challenge with the seriousness it deserved. Certainly the defense budget left no doubt as to DoD's priorities and was notable for not cutting a single conventional big-ticket program. The U.S. military did not sufficiently value the need to invest in counterinsurgency or—at best—underestimated the level of investment that this particular transformation would require.

Second, when the QDR did acknowledge a shift toward irregular operations, it generally assumed that regular forces would play only a marginal role in such missions, which in turn justified the minimal focus on how best to prepare forces for future contingencies. The QDR's particular interpretation of "irregular warfare" was far removed from the counterinsurgency campaigns in Iraq and related instead to SOF conducting counterterrorism and unconventional warfare. Similarly the QDR suggested, or assumed, that civilian agencies would take the lead in conducting stability operations, leaving the military with a purely security-related role. Adherence to these divisions of labor allowed the military to invest minimally, if at all, in developing a capability for stability operations and counterinsurgency within the regular services.

With regard to irregular war and stability operations DoD gave the appearance of an institution learning from the contemporaneous strategic environment. The initial problem with the approach advanced in the QDR was that its underlying assumptions do not hold. Its strategy for irregular war relied on several shaky assumptions and a poor understanding of counterinsurgency; indeed the QDR suffered from many of the same problems as the prior counterinsurgency reforms of the 1960s and 1980s. First, the faith in the SOF community as the agents of irregular war obscured the fact that special forces have specialized in direct action more so than unconventional warfare. Second, even with SOF capable of conducting unconventional warfare, there is still a limit to what special operations can achieve, as the collaborative element of this approach relies on the existence of viable surrogates, which are not always available. Third, the construct seemed to suggest that SOF could manage irregular war, leaving regular forces to pursue other types of missions, and thus glossed over the need for regular forces to conduct stability operations during and after conventional combat (as in Iraq in 2003) or to provide a follow-on force should the commitment of SOF be insufficient (as in Vietnam). Similarly the QDR's approach to stability operations assumed the presence of adequately resourced and operationally able civilian institutions, yet these have not as of yet been established. The QDR's commitment to building this type of capability was welcome and necessary but seemed to have been confused with an existing ability to transfer responsibility for stability operations to civilian agencies.

For all these reasons the QDR disappointed those who had foreseen a radical departure from DoD's traditional preoccupations and the elevation of counterinsurgency and stability operations as missions on par with conventional campaigns. Instead it considerably deflated the momentum gained in that direction in late 2005. The faith in counterterrorism over counterinsurgency proved remarkably impervious to the demands and requirements of the ongoing campaigns in Iraq and Afghanistan. Similarly the lack of civilian resources in those theaters did not dent the military's conviction that it would be shielded from assuming civilian tasks in the future. Ultimately Iraq was not, in the case of the QDR, informing policy.

6

FM 3-24 AND
OPERATION FARDH
AL-QANOON

Throughout its history, the U.S. military has had to relearn the principles of
counterinsurgency while conducting operations against adaptive insurgent
enemies. It is time to institutionalize Army and Marine Corps knowledge of
this longstanding form of conflict.

U.S. Army FM 3-24/Marine Corps WP 3-33.5, *Counterinsurgency*
(December 2006)

Despite the QDR's marginalization of counterinsurgency and stability operations, the ongoing instability in Iraq gave special relevance to the activities of the COIN community, which continued to push the military towards
a greater understanding of such missions. In 2006, this process culminated
in the release of FM 3-24/MCWP 3-33.5, *Counterinsurgency*, a joint
Army–Marine Corps field manual. Receiving a high level of publicity—
mostly due to Iraq—the new field manual became a flagship publication for
those with an interest in counterinsurgency. The manual also indicated the
extent of Army and Marine Corps innovation; having four years ago omitted counterinsurgency as a military mission, these services were now issuing a high-profile field manual whose content was in many ways
anathematic to U.S. military orthodoxy.

Critically, only months after the publication of FM 3-24 the COIN
community was offered an opportunity to implement its emerging wisdom in Iraq. Following a change in the Bush administration's Iraq policy,
the counterinsurgency field manual came—quite unexpectedly—to form
the foundation for U.S. operations in Baghdad and al-Anbar Province. For
the first time, the ensuing Operation Fardh al-Qanoon formally directed
U.S. troops to conduct population-centered counterinsurgency on the
streets of Baghdad and to provide sustained security and services to its
population. Although the manner in which the new strategy was imple-

mented was in some ways flawed, this official shift in the U.S. military's mode of operations was nonetheless testament to a radically changed mindset and understanding.

LEARNING COUNTERINSURGENCY

On February 22, 2006, the al-Askari Mosque in Samarra was bombed and partially destroyed. The attack was attributed to al-Qaeda in Iraq, the Islamist group whose targeting of this Shia holy site was seen as an attempt to ignite ethnic violence between Iraq's Sunni and Shia communities. As expected, the attack, while causing no casualties itself, unleashed a wave of retaliatory violence and tension across Iraq: In its aftermath the daily homicide rate in Baghdad tripled from eleven to thirty-three per day, and 365,000 Iraqis were forced to flee their homes.[1] The Samarra bombing and the ensuing bloodshed provided a powerful indication that the U.S. government needed to overhaul its Iraq strategy if it still entertained any notion of stabilizing the country.

Although some argued that the bombing had turned the Iraqi problem from one of insurgency to one of ethnic civil war, the predominant U.S. government assessment was that the violence would nonetheless have to be controlled and that the role played by the U.S. military would not differ substantially whether it was fighting a counterinsurgency campaign or containing an ethnic conflict.[2] As a result the continued deadliness of the conflict meant that counterinsurgency, despite its marginalization in the QDR, was never excluded entirely from the internal deliberations at DoD. As a byproduct of this line of thinking, the learning of counterinsurgency also retained its relevance, and even gained a new urgency. As in 2005, there was a stream of initiatives aimed at augmenting the U.S. military's understanding and prioritization of COIN campaigns.

In February 2006 U.S. Army Lt. Gen. David Petraeus and USMC Lt. Gen. James N. Mattis convened a two-day conference at Fort Leavenworth to discuss the new counterinsurgency manual, which was being produced at Leavenworth and would replace the interim field manual issued in 2004. Whereas the latter had been drafted in five months, and with minimal consultation from outside the Pentagon, the updated and final version would be the product of discussion and exchange within and beyond DoD. To that end the U.S. military invited a number of critics of the military and of its operations in Iraq, from the human rights community, academia, and the press. Also invited to the conference was Brig. Nigel R. F. Aylwin-Foster, the British officer who in 2005 had authored a scathing critique of the U.S. military's attempts to learn and conduct counterinsurgency—and who was now asked to provide the conference's opening address.[3] As Lt. Col. John Nagl, then the military assistant to the deputy secretary of defense, put it,

"We're inviting our critics to see the sausage being made and to help push the ball forward. . . . I cannot think of another institution that has exhibited a greater interest in evaluating itself closely and looking hard at itself, figuring out what it is doing well and what it is doing poorly and making a real effort to do better. That is the shining example for me of an organization that takes learning seriously."[4]

With the input of civilian agencies and nongovernmental organizations, it became clear that the military could not, as it had done, simply write civilian government agencies into its doctrine. There were also significant misunderstandings across government departments regarding the division of labor in and the very nature of "counterinsurgency," a term much less palatable on the civilian side of the fence.[5] Throughout the coming year, sections and individuals within the U.S. military displayed remarkable self-scrutiny and analytical openness, even humility, in their approach to and understanding of counterinsurgency.

This learning process manifested itself in a series of publications released in 2006 by the Marine Corps, which presaged many of the themes of the counterinsurgency field manual. In March 2006 the USMC issued *Marine Corps Operating Concepts for a Changing Security Environment*, a 131-page document that covered all Marine Corps operations, including counterinsurgency. In the chapter titled "Countering Irregular Threats: A New Approach to Counterinsurgency," the document outlined the practices that had proved successful in such operations. Despite the chapter's title, this approach was not particularly "new," based as it was on classic counterinsurgency theory derived from British, Australian, and U.S. doctrine and the prominent theorists in the field. As a result the document mostly reiterated established counterinsurgency principles: "political primacy in pursuit of objectives"; the importance of "legitimacy and the moral right to govern"; the need to "understand the complex dynamics of the threat"; "the discriminate application of power (including a limitation on the use of force, especially firepower)"; "unity of purpose" between participating agencies; the need to "isolate the irregulars from their physical and moral support base," to have "patience, persistence, and presence," and to maintain a "sustained commitment to expend political capital and resources over a long period."[6]

While some detractors criticized this concept as outdated, it did reflect a broader understanding of the challenge than that set out in the interim field manual of 2004 or in the QDR. Indeed, the document explicitly advocated "an expanded view of campaign design" and presented counterinsurgency as involving, for the Marines, a range of combat, stabilization, and developmental tasks, including "combat operations, training and advising host nation security forces, essential services, promotion of governance, economic development, and information operations."[7] The document was also forthright in asserting that in a counterinsurgency campaign "the military must not only understand the impact that each component may have on campaign success, they must also be prepared to lead activities associated with components that have not traditionally been military responsibilities."[8]

Ironically, and to the embarrassment of some USMC officers, this "new approach to counterinsurgency" was based directly on an Army concept for "full-spectrum operations" advanced by Maj. Gen. Peter Chiarelli in summer 2005.[9] Chiarelli's theory was based on his operational experience in Iraq, where he had implemented a comprehensive counterinsurgency strategy, directing his troops to undertake both security- and civilian-related tasks and, partly as a result, achieved a relative level of success.[10] In a circuitous way, therefore, the emerging USMC wisdom on counterinsurgency was powerfully informed by the best practices unearthed by the more successful "maverick" counterinsurgency commanders on the ground; the merits of their approach were being recognized and disseminated.

In June 2006 the "New Approach" chapter was extended and published as a separate volume, focusing specifically on irregular challenges. This document, *Tentative Manual for Countering Irregular Threats: An Updated Approach to Counterinsurgency*, reiterated the "expanded view" of counterinsurgency and now devoted an entire chapter to each of its campaign components.[11] In each case the manual emphasized the need for the Marine Corps to focus specifically on tasks such as governance and reconstruction and to integrate these with the security component.

With regard to basic services, the manual argued that the Marine Corps "must treat this line of operation with the same emphasis and importance as the other lines and must ensure true integration in planning and execution."[12] The manual did not discourage interagency support for these tasks but was careful not to write nonexistent civilian partners into the theory: Conduct planning, it urged, according to "who else, that is what other organizations or agencies, will likely be involved."[13] As the manual stated, this was not "a means of abrogating responsibility for or even lessening the importance of planning in this line of operation"; indeed, it acknowledged that "the military may likely be the principle [sic] player in all six lines of operation during the initial periods of intervention."[14] This stance contrasted to earlier works on stability operations, where the military has assigned itself only or mainly security-related tasks.

In a similar vein, the *Tentative Manual for Countering Irregular Threats* emphasized the aim of establishing and promoting governance in the host nation, stating that it "may actually be the most important of the lines" of operation, relating as it does to "the ability of the government of the indigenous nation to establish and maintain order, and to perform all necessary governmental activities that pertain to the legitimacy of a sovereign nation."[15] It noted that in the absence of a functioning government and civilian agencies the USMC may "be forced to take on responsibilities that seem to be far outside the traditional military realm—such as working with locals to establish an interim rule of law construct and organizational structure."[16] It also acknowledged that the military "has not developed the intellect, training and skills . . . that this line of operation, promoting governance, will demand," a conundrum that should "cause the military to carefully consider the organic competencies that it has and rightly should have."[17]

A similar recommendation was made with regard to economic development, where the manual again saw a capability gap within the USMC, expressed a desire for greater interagency support, yet acknowledged that in the absence of such assistance "the Marine Corps needs some civil affairs personnel with specific education in the study of economics (and economies), business and business development, and government (public administration)."[18] Again, with regard to the "information" line of operation the manual stressed the need for individual Marines to be cognizant of their ability to affect the strategic direction of the campaign, either positively or negatively, through actions in the tactical realm.[19]

If the USMC publications of the summer of 2006 represented a refinement of the conceptual understanding of counterinsurgency, Joint Publication 3-0, *Joint Operations*, issued in September 2006, carried this process one step farther, primarily by clarifying the nature of stability operations to the joint force. In clear terms, JP 3-0's executive summary stated that joint force commanders "*must integrate and synchronize stability operations . . . with offensive and defensive operations* within each major operation or campaign phase."[20] To reinforce this point, JP 3-0 adopted a new "phasing" construct for operational planning. Previously, joint doctrines had used a sequential four-phase construct, whereby stability operations followed major combat operations temporally and contiguously, thus resulting in the military term "Phase IV" to denote postconflict stabilization activities. In recognition of the need to focus on stability operations during, and even before, major combat, the four-phase construct was now abandoned for a six-phase model in which "stabilizing activities" featured in every phase from the initiation of a crisis or operation.[21]

JP 3-0 took additional steps to elevate the importance of stability operations and counterinsurgency. It formally discontinued the ambiguous term "MOOTW" from the military's lexicon, which had during its heyday in the 1990s unnecessarily conflated widely disparate military missions based on the arbitrary criterion of not constituting all-out war. The publication also added counterinsurgency to the JCS's list of military operations and expanded the "principles of war," traditionally oriented toward combat operations, by adding three with direct relevance to stability operations (restraint, perseverance, and legitimacy).[22] Finally, JP 3-0 provided a new definition of "stability operations," to apply across the services, as "missions, tasks, and activities to maintain or reestablish a safe and secure environment and provide essential governmental services, emergency infrastructure reconstruction, or humanitarian relief."[23] Compared to the previous definition of stability operations (i.e., as missions that "promote and protect U.S. national interests by influencing the threat, political, and information dimensions of the operational environment through a combination of peacetime developmental, cooperative activities and coercive actions in response to crisis"), this new definition was straightforward and clear, reducing the potential for misinterpretation.

The greater clarity in doctrine and concept papers built on an increased interest in counterinsurgency and population-centered operations, which was also reflected in the establishment of new nodes and agencies dedicated to these missions. In February 2006 TRADOC opened its Culture Center, an equivalent in some ways to the Marine Corps' CAOCL and, although similarly understaffed, a useful driver of cultural training and education across the force.[24] In July the Army and Marine Corps cofounded the Counterinsurgency Center at Fort Leavenworth, the first Army institution dedicated exclusively to such campaigns. Mandated initially to review the early drafts and material of the forthcoming counterinsurgency field manual, the Counterinsurgency Center was also involved in incorporating lessons learned in Iraq and Afghanistan as part of the U.S. military's schoolhouse curricula. Alongside these central responsibilities, the center conducted research, hosted seminars, and reached out to organizations with an interest in counterinsurgency, within the U.S. military and beyond.[25] In terms of institutionalizing a stability operations capability, however, the most important step might have been the establishment in September 2006 of the Stability, Security, Transition, and Reconstruction Division within Army Headquarters, which was to serve "as the focal point for the integration of all SSTR activities within the Army."[26] Its Strategy, Policy, and Integration Branch would, for example, be responsible for driving the Army's implementation of the various tasks assigned to it in Directive 3000.05. Other branches—a Security Sector Branch, a Reconstruction Branch, and a Civil-Military Integration Branch—were dedicated to the various aspects of stability operations, both "military" and "civilian."

Interest in counterinsurgency went beyond the personnel at DoD. On September 28–29, 2006, DoD and the Department of State cosponsored a conference, "Counterinsurgency in the 21st Century: Creating a National Framework," in Washington, D.C. It assembled the COIN community that had emerged in the previous years, along with a smattering of academics, think-tank experts, and policymakers in an attempt to "develop a national framework that would aid in building a new counterinsurgency paradigm."[27] If nothing else the conference offered an opportunity to spread awareness about counterinsurgency across government and beyond and to consolidate the network of personalities involved in formulating an approach to these types of operations. As the main recommendations to come out of the conference related to the need for a more robust civilian capacity to conduct counterinsurgency, the event also oxygenated some of the efforts outside DoD to include these types of operations as part of their remit. At the State Department, for example, the Office of Plans, Policy, and Analysis began soon after the conference to draft a guide to counterinsurgency—a civilian equivalent, in some ways, to the forthcoming DoD manual.[28]

FM 3-24/MCWP 3-33.5

Following twelve months of drafting, the Army and Marine Corps' counterinsurgency manual was finally published in December 2006.[29] Titled *Counterinsurgency*, and coded Field Manual 3-24 by the Army and Warfighting Publication 3-33.5 by the Marines, the new publication received substantial publicity from within and outside the DoD: "With over two million downloads after its first two months on the Internet, the counterinsurgency (COIN) manual clearly touched a nerve."[30] For those who actually read it, the manual presented a nuanced conceptualization of counterinsurgency and urged a carefully attuned, all-of-government approach to such operations.

The contribution of FM 3-24 to the U.S. military's understanding of counterinsurgency was significant and manifold. Beyond constituting the first official manual on the topic since the 1980s, it also presented a far more analytically advanced and realistic assessment of COIN operations. Its contribution can be seen especially in three areas, each signaling a distinct break from the treatment of counterinsurgency in previous U.S. military doctrine.

First, FM 3-24 assumed from the outset that counterinsurgency would include a significant deployment of U.S. ground troops. Previous manuals to have touched upon these types of operations had referred to "support to counterinsurgency," either as a possible type of MOOTW or as an example of "complex contingency operations," and all of them presupposed that "generally, U.S. forces do not engage in combat."[31] The predominant model of counterinsurgency was thus the indirect or advisory approach, as practiced in El Salvador during the 1980s and as emphasized in the 2006 QDR. In contrast, FM 3-24 distinguished between "a mission to assist a functioning government" with those operations "where no such viable entity exists or where a regime has been changed by conflict," noting that "the last two situations add complex sovereignty and national reconstruction issues to an already complex mission."[32] With the Iraq campaign providing the obvious backdrop, the counterinsurgency field manual devoted most of its energy to the latter two types of contingencies. Similarly, in listing the different approaches to counterinsurgency, it paid most attention to the "clear-hold-build" and "combined-action" approaches, either of which involves signifi-cant U.S. ground forces. In contrast, the manual glanced over so-called "limited support," the provision of U.S. counterinsurgency assistance—through advisers, fires, and security cooperation—not involving the deploy-ment of "large combat formations."[33]

The second major contribution of FM 3-24 was its emphasis on the need for the U.S. military to take on the full gamut of tasks associated with coun-terinsurgency (if no other agency is there to fill the gap). From the outset it recognized that while "the purpose of America's ground forces is to fight and win" wars, "throughout history . . . the Army and Marine Corps have been called on to perform many tasks beyond pure combat [and that] this has been particularly true during the conduct of COIN operations."[34] In set-ting out the "aspects of counterinsurgency," the manual made it clear that this mission "requires Soldiers and Marines to be ready both to fight and to build."[35] Throughout, the manual stressed the need for the military to un-dertake "nonmilitary" tasks in the absence of adequately resourced and de-ployable civilian agencies, the repetitiousness seemingly an attempt to eliminate any confusion as to whether or not these mission components constituted "the military's job."[36]

The manual was also far from sanguine about the likelihood of having an adequate civilian presence in the area of operations. Setting out a distinc-tion between the "preferred" and "realistic" division of labor in a counterin-surgency campaign, the manual noted that "U.S. and multinational military forces often possess the only readily available capability to meet many of the local populace's fundamental needs" and that "human decency and the law of war require land forces to assist the populace" in their areas of oper-ations.[37] Beyond constituting merely a legal duty or moral obligation, the manual also stated that "most valuable to long-term success in winning the support of the populace are the contributions land forces make by con-ducting stability operations," defined here as those tasks designed "to main-tain or reestablish a safe and secure environment, provide essential governmental services, emergency infrastructure reconstruction, and hu-manitarian relief."[38]

The third major contribution of FM 3-24 was its embrace of the full complexity of counterinsurgency. Rather than present these missions as more manageable than they really are—a tendency that had marked previ-ous doctrinal elaborations of the issue—the 2006 field manual emphasized the intractable challenges of counterinsurgency operations. First, it listed several "historical principles," often repeated in classical counterinsurgency literature (most recently in the above-mentioned USMC publications on the topic): legitimacy as the main objective; the centrality of politics; the importance of unity of effort, of operating within the rule of law, of preparing for the long haul; and the value of environmental understanding, of good intelligence, and of separating the insurgents from the populace.[39] The manual then added to this list a number of principles deemed, somewhat arbitrarily, to be particularly relevant today: the need to manage the expectations of the local populace through "information operations;" the need to use an "appropriate" level of force; the need to "learn and adapt," to "empower the lowest levels" (as initiative is critical and since tactical decisions can have strategic consequences), and to promote the host nation rather than oneself.[40]

But perhaps the most successful means of conveying the complexity of counterinsurgency was through the itemization of various "paradoxes" pertaining to these operations. Through these paradoxes, the authors of the manual were able to explain, succinctly and simply, how counterinsurgency differs from the traditional combat campaigns with which the U.S. military is most familiar and encourage the users of the manual to think independently rather than look for prescribed answers. In most cases these paradoxes also provided pushback to some of the tendencies to have marked the U.S. military's attempt at counterinsurgency in Iraq: the excessive focus on force protection, on offensive operations, and on tactical dominance rather than strategic objectives. On force protection ("Sometimes, the More You Protect Your Force, the Less Secure You May Be") the manual emphasized closer contact with the populace, rather than self-imposed confinement to armored barracks, so as to gain trust and support. On the use of force, the manual stressed that "Sometimes, the More Force Is Used, the Less Effective It Is," that "Some of the Best Weapons for Counterinsurgents Do Not Shoot" and that "Tactical Success Guarantees Nothing" without a strategic framework that also takes into account the perceived legitimacy and adequacy of the host government. Finally, on the need for constant adaptation and initiative, the manual emphasized that "If a Tactic Works this Week, It Might Not Work Next Week; If It Works in this Province, It Might Not Work in the Next."[41]

This last paradox may have been the most important one in that it countered any suggestion that the manual sought to provide a foolproof formula for counterinsurgency campaigns. The authors clearly did not intend for FM 3-24 to represent a silver-bullet solution to these types of operations, to be rigidly implemented, step by step; its purpose was instead to familiarize the military with the counterintuitive logic of counterinsurgency and the many ways in which these endeavors differ from conventional combat. As stated in the foreword, "You cannot fight former Saddamists and Islamic extremists the same way you would have fought the Viet Cong, Moros, or Tupamaros; the application of principles and fundamentals to deal with each varies considerably."[42] The best the manual could do, therefore—and what it did in fact accomplish—was to set out the historical complexity of these operations, the importance of adaptation, and the need to arrive at a carefully tailored response rather than fall back on templates.

At last, therefore, the U.S. military had an official interservice publication setting out, in some detail, the nature, requirements, and challenges of counterinsurgency with full honesty as to what they have historically entailed.[43] In a sense, the manual represented the end product of three years of conceptual learning.

A COUNTERINSURGENCY STRATEGY FOR IRAQ

FM 3-24 was published amid a counterinsurgency campaign in Iraq that was not making much headway. The Samarra bomb attack in February 2006 triggered an increase in violence that the U.S. forces struggled to contain. While various military institutions in the U.S. homeland gained a clearer conceptual understanding of counterinsurgency, the implementation of operations in Iraq did not, with a few important exceptions, reflect this learning curve.[44] This gap between theory and practice became particularly evident with the release of the counterinsurgency field manual. Indeed, its listing of "unsuccessful practices" for counterinsurgency correlated very closely to some of the approaches that had been employed by the U.S. military in operation: "overemphasize killing and capturing the enemy rather than securing and engaging the populace"; "conduct large-scale operations as the norm"; "concentrate military forces in large bases for protection"; and "focus special operations primarily on raiding."[45]

Because the manual was upfront about the requirements of an effective counterinsurgency campaign, it was readily interpreted as something of an attack on the U.S. military's prevailing strategy in Iraq. As it happens, the authors of FM 3-24 were soon given an opportunity "to put up or shut up" by implementing their recently released doctrine in the field. One month following its publication, President Bush announced a new strategy for Iraq, one that approximated closely to the precepts set out in the counterinsurgency field manual and that would be spearheaded by its author, Gen. David Petraeus. With this flagship publication still hot off the press, the COIN community was now charged with turning theory into practice.

This decision to "operationalize" FM 3-24 in Iraq stemmed from three developments and had more to do with the coincidence of disparate events than a calculated change of strategy. In the first place, the adoption of a new approach related closely to shifts in the political landscape back in Washington, D.C. In the congressional elections of November 2006, the Republican Party lost the majority in both the House and the Senate, seemingly over the Bush administration's handling of the Iraq War. The electoral losses and the public outcry over the continued commitment of troops to Iraq strongly suggested to the Bush administration that a change of course was now necessary.

To placate the mounting dissent, Bush announced on November 8, in the wake of the congressional elections, that Secretary of Defense Donald Rumsfeld was to resign. This development was primarily symbolic, designed to appease those calling for a withdrawal from Iraq, or at least a significant change in policy; as the *Washington Post* put it, Rumsfeld was "offered as a sacrificial lamb amid the repudiation of Bush and his Iraq policy."[46] Although noteworthy and significant for an administration then marked by few changes in high-level personnel, the announcement of Rumsfeld's resignation did not in itself suggest a new strategy. And while the appointment of Robert Gates as the new secretary of defense did seem to indicate a change of direction—Gates had been a member of the Iraq Study Group (ISG), a bipartisan advisory board mandated by Congress to identify alternatives to the administration's Iraq policy—there were no clear signs of what that change in policy would entail.[47]

The fact that counterinsurgency came to be the foundation of the new policy in Iraq thus required a second key factor: the refusal of the Bush administration to consider a ramping-down of the military effort there. Although charting a new course for Operation Iraqi Freedom seemed possible, some options, most critically the withdrawal of troops, were effectively off the table, as the Bush administration perceived such an action as leading to both political and strategic failure.[48] "I of all people would like to see the troops come home," Bush had emphasized in several speeches, "but I don't want them to come home without achieving our objective."[49] The Bush administration therefore also chose to interpret the losses in the congressional elections not as unequivocal opposition to the Iraq operation as such but as evidence that "people . . . expect to see a different strategy to achieve an important objective."[50]

President Bush's blanket refusal to reduce the troop commitment in Iraq informed and limited the policy maneuverings of Robert Gates. If the recommendations of the ISG were in any way a reflection of his own policy preferences, the new secretary of defense might in fact have favored such a reduction. Indeed, one of the main recommendations of the ISG was to replace combat troops in Iraq with SOF and military advisers, who would train and equip Iraq security forces to conduct combat operations themselves.[51] The proposed strategy was, of course, reminiscent of the U.S. military's approach to counterinsurgency in El Salvador and in subsequent doctrine and policy. Yet, if this recommendation was also backed by Robert Gates, it was a course of action that he could not pursue once in office.[52]

The Bush administration, and Gates himself, thus faced a dilemma: How could it change course in Iraq without withdrawing the U.S. combat power that was, it was reasoned, holding the country together and thus constituting the linchpin of the Bush administration's project there? It was in seeking to resolve this dilemma that Bush (and as a result the U.S. military) was pushed to accept the idea of a surge of troops and their adoption of a more full-fledged counterinsurgency strategy. The final factor compelling this change in direction was the elevation of the COIN community, gaining momentum since 2004 and coming to the fore with the release, amid all this policy confusion, of FM 3-24. With Bush facing a policy quandary with few promising solutions, the new manual, and its authors and wider constituency, seemed to provide a time-tested means of overcoming insurgencies.

On January 5, 2007, Secretary Gates announced the promotion and appointment of Lt. Gen. David Petraeus as commander of Multinational Force Iraq (MNF-I), a four-star post that put him in command of all U.S. forces in the country. Petraeus spearheaded the drafting of FM 3-24 as commanding general at Fort Leavenworth, and his appointment to commander of MNF-I indicated that U.S. policy in Iraq would henceforth be informed by his expertise with counterinsurgency. As Gates put it, "Petraeus is an expert in irregular warfare and stability operations, and recently supervised the publication of the first Army and Marine counterinsurgency manual in two decades. . . . He'll bring all the tools to enable Iraqi and coalition forces to create a stable and secure Iraq."[53]

The shift to counterinsurgency was made official on January 10, when Bush set out his new strategy for Iraq. Popularized in the press as the "surge," the president's new approach featured an increase in troop levels in Baghdad; a new force posture designed to establish a security presence throughout the city; and a range of nonmilitary measures designed to satisfy the political requirements for stability. Specifically Bush announced that "more than 20,000 additional American troops" would be sent to Iraq, predominantly to Baghdad and al-Anbar Province, to "work alongside Iraqi units and be embedded in their formations." Their mission, Bush continued, would be "to help Iraqis clear and secure neighborhoods, to help them protect the local population, and to help ensure that the Iraqi forces left behind are capable of providing the security that Baghdad needs."[54] These measures were to enable and occur alongside a number of governmental reforms, aimed at undercutting many of the grievances thought to be fueling the violence.[55]

A similar surge of troops had been attempted in August-October 2006 as part of the U.S. military's Operation Together Forward II. That operation involved the redeployment of 3,700 U.S. forces to Baghdad, a bolstering of Iraqi security forces in the capital, and the introduction of curfews and checkpoints. According to the ISG the results of the operation were "disheartening," with "violence in Baghdad—already at high levels—[having] jumped more than 43 percent between the summer and October 2006."[56] Setting out the new strategy, Bush acknowledged the weaknesses of Together Forward II but maintained that the new strategy would correct its deficiencies. First, the surge would involve an increased number of U.S. troops operating in the streets of Baghdad, enabling a sustained presence rather than fleeting raids. And second, the United States military would also acquire the Iraqi government's authorization to enter into the neighborhoods hosting Shia militias.[57] These two changes did answer the ISG's main criticisms of Together Forward II, which had centered on a lack of "capability to hold areas that have been cleared" and the lack of "will to clear neighborhoods that are home to Shiite militias."[58]

A number of brigade commanders had already adopted the new counterinsurgency-oriented approach to their area of operations and achieved unexpected security gains in former insurgency hot spots.[59] Nonetheless, the dominant deployment strategy in Iraq was overly concerned with *minimizing* the visibility of U.S. forces, who were seen by both Gen. George Casey, commander of MNF-I, and Gen. John Abizaid, commander of CENTCOM, as "an 'antibody' in Iraqi society."[60] In general U.S. troops were secluded in armored forward operating bases, and emphasis was placed on getting Iraqi security forces, often unwilling, unable, or unaccountable, to conduct operations in their stead.

The official shift in strategy in early 2007 formalized the turn away from this approach. As General Petraeus told Congress during his confirmation hearing for the new position, "the mission of Multinational Force Iraq will be modified, making security of the population, particularly in Baghdad, and in partnership with Iraqi forces, the focus of the military effort."[61] This shift, Petraeus continued, would "require that our unit commanders and their Iraqi counterparts develop a detailed appreciation of the areas in which they will operate. . . . Together with Iraqi forces, a persistent presence in these neighborhoods will be essential."[62] The approach was in line with FM 3-24, which discouraged the concentration of "military forces in large bases for protection" in favor of keeping a close "focus on the population, its needs, and its security" through the establishment and expansion of "secure areas."[63]

Although critical of Bush's handling of the war and wary of the troop surge, the Senate confirmed General Petraeus as commander of MNF-I, with eighty-one votes in favor to none against, thus setting the course for a comprehensive counterinsurgency effort to be launched in Iraq. The campaign would follow the clear-hold-build format of classic counterinsurgency laid out in FM 3-24: U.S. troops would first clear selected neighborhoods, targeting extremist elements; then maintain a full-time presence in these areas, operating out of small forts or "joint security stations" constructed across the city; and then, with Iraqi security forces gradually assuming the lead, pursue efforts to stimulate the local economy, initiate reconstruction, and improve the infrastructure.[64] The adoption of these counterinsurgency strategies in Iraq would constitute an apex in the U.S. military's learning of counterinsurgency over the previous three years. It would, in fact, be the first time the U.S. military had conducted anything resembling a full-fledged counterinsurgency campaign since Vietnam—a statement of no small significance.

To implement the Baghdad security plan, Petraeus called upon several prominent members of the COIN community. In January 2007 U.S. Army Brig. Gen. H. R. McMaster, of fame for having implemented a successful counterinsurgency strategy in Tal Afar in 2005, joined Petraeus in Iraq to assist in the planning and running of operations. The subsequent month David Kilcullen, instrumental in the drafting of FM 3-24, was deployed to Iraq as senior counterinsurgency adviser to the U.S. effort. U.S. Army Col. Peter Mansoor, military historian and founding director of the Counterinsurgency Center at Fort Leavenworth—was also called to Iraq to serve as Petraeus's executive officer.[65] These individuals, along with other experts with experience and familiarity with counterinsurgency, were now being brought together to implement their theory and findings in the field. From humble origins, the COIN community was now at the helm.

CONCLUSION

By giving short shrift to the prospect of direct engagement in counterinsurgency the February 2006 QDR disappointed those within the COIN community who had driven the U.S. military's learning of such operations during the preceding months. Although frustrated, the commanders and experts involved in this process of institutional learning did not abandon their cause. In fact, with the continued and escalating violence in Iraq in early 2006 the marginalization of counterinsurgency in official DoD policy papers did not matter much: The Bush administration still wanted U.S. troops to stabilize Iraq, and the commanders and experts versed in counterinsurgency were therefore given a platform to influence policy and spread their ideas. Hence, this period saw a stream of initiatives aimed at augmenting the U.S. military's understanding of counterinsurgency.

In contrast to previous initiatives, the publications and activities to come out of DoD in 2006 revealed a more realistic and informed understanding of counterinsurgency. The focus was increasingly on the importance of a population-centered approach to counterinsurgency and on achieving and maintaining the perception of legitimacy. This process of conceptual refinement culminated in the release in December 2006 of an Army-Marine Corps field manual dedicated entirely to the topic of counterinsurgency. FM 3-24 urged and presented a carefully attuned understanding of counterinsurgency in all its complexity. It also asked of soldiers and Marines to undertake, should no one else be there to assist, all lines of operation, including tasks traditionally considered beyond their remit. With the U.S. military having entirely dismissed counterinsurgency just four years earlier, the Army and Marine Corps were giving proof of remarkable innovation.

What made the publication of FM 3-24 all the more significant was the fact that it unexpectedly came to inform the U.S. military's planning and conduct of operations in Iraq. With General Petraeus, a lead author of the counterinsurgency field manual, promoted and appointed commanding general of MNF-I, the U.S. military began to implement formally some of the manual's main principles on the ground. Although applied on a limited scale, Operation Fardh al-Qanoon would see U.S. troops conduct a true counterinsurgency campaign, on the street, in spite of the high risks involved, undertaking both military and nonmilitary actions to gain and maintain the support of the local populace.

7

THE AMBIVALENCE
OF THE "SURGE"

The launch of Operation Faardh al-Qanoon in February 2007 put Gen. David Petraeus and the COIN community squarely in the spotlight. Having developed an approach to counterinsurgency through years of research and writing, Petraeus and other officers were now in charge of putting that approach into practice, in what would be the U.S. military's first true counterinsurgency campaign in decades. In that sense, then, the "surge" of U.S. ground troops in Iraq represented the end of the beginning of a much longer learning process.

At the same time, the surge also threatened to mark the beginning of the end of this counterinsurgency era, which might then be better termed a "counterinsurgency moment." Inasmuch as this was an opportunity for the COIN community to prove itself, its future credibility was now also tied to their ability to stabilize Iraq—no small feat and one further complicated by the many challenges that would mark the application of counterinsurgency doctrine to this conflict. From the unpopular origins of the surge, to the inevitable ambiguity of the situation in Iraq, to the deleterious effect of repeated tours in Iraq on U.S. military readiness and the ground services in particular, many reasons availed themselves to those seeking to abandon Iraq and, with it, the learning of counterinsurgency that this campaign had compelled.

A TRIAL BY FIRE

Even though the adoption of counterinsurgency methods in Iraq in 2007 denoted an unprecedented willingness to conduct such missions on the part of the U.S. military, the shift in strategy did not enjoy much support among the Pentagon's senior brass. Briefing the president and vice president on policy options for Iraq in December 2006, the Joint Chiefs of Staff had discouraged an increased commitment of U.S. forces and advocated instead a shift "from combating insurgents to supporting Iraqi troops and hunting terrorists."[1] Gen. George W. Casey Jr., commander of MNF-I, had reportedly proposed a similar plan: that is, to beef up the training program of Iraqi security forces so that they could conduct combat operations instead of U.S. troops, who would themselves be restricted to a limited number of armored bases.[2] According to the testimony of Gen. John Abizaid, commander of CENTCOM, it had also been the "professional opinion" of General Casey and of most divisional commanders that the deployment of additional troops would not "add considerably to our ability to achieve success in Iraq."[3]

Many of those who opposed the surge saw the U.S. troop presence in Iraq as fueling the violence there and argued that the best way to reduce the bloodshed was to maintain a low profile and concentrate on discrete counterterrorism operations. In terms of stabilizing Iraq, this approach was manifestly failing, mostly because it ignored the inadequacies of the Iraqi security forces and did not address the ethnic and criminal violence that was tearing the country apart. Regardless, the strategy continued to dominate inside the senior ranks of the military, plausibly because of its positive implications for force protection.

Senior Army and Marine Corps officials were also concerned about the increased demands that the surge would place on the force and the further degradation of its combat capability.[4] The repeated tours of the same active duty and reserve forces had resulted in personnel leaving the Army, prompting a scrambled search for recruits and various measures, most notoriously the "stop-loss" provision, intended to prevent an all-out exodus.[5] The senior brass therefore resisted the anticipated increase in operational tempo that would come with the surge. To placate the generals, President Bush agreed to an overall increase in ground forces in December 2006, by which the Army was to grow by 65,000 and the Marine Corps by 27,000.[6] Even so, these expansions would not be completed for many years or address the immediate threats to morale, recruitment, and retention that an expanded deployment and intensified effort in Iraq were thought to signify.

For all these reasons General Petraeus represented a minority within the U.S. military leadership. In spite of his command of U.S. forces in Iraq, his influence in the Pentagon, along with that of the counterinsurgency community that he was seen as championing, was far from assured. Much would come down to whether or not his venture in Iraq succeeded. Given DoD's tentative embrace of counterinsurgency to date—and its opposition to the surge itself—a suboptimal outcome was likely to tarnish not only the new strategy but also those driving it. At the very least such an outcome would cause many within DoD to question the importance of focusing on and learning counterinsurgency. Conversely, only significant progress in Iraq would justify the relevance of counterinsurgency and help establish those most familiar with these types of missions within DoD.

In this sense the surge became the counterinsurgency community's "trial by fire"—progress on the ground equaled influence, setbacks equaled marginalization. This was far from an ideal or fair means of justifying the relevance of counterinsurgency. Indeed, for several reasons the surge was not an opportunity for the COIN community to shine but a poisoned chalice, threatening its influence within DoD and, indeed, its survival.

First, the likelihood of the surge succeeding was undercut by the circumstances of its launch. The counterinsurgency field manual stated that "at the strategic level, gaining and maintaining U.S. public support for a protracted deployment is critical."[7] In this instance U.S public support for the campaign was very low, even before the operation got under way. A Fox News poll conducted on January 16–17, 2007, found that 59 percent of Americans opposed sending more U.S. troops to Iraq; a *Newsweek* poll released later that week put the figure at 68 percent.[8] Amid growing uncertainty regarding the feasibility of salvaging anything positive from Iraq, the proposal to "raise the stakes" by deploying additional troops and exposing them to more danger was plainly not well received.

The counterinsurgency field manual also noted that "insurgencies are protracted by nature" and that "COIN operations always demand considerable expenditures of time and resources."[9] Here as well, the new strategy faced immediate opposition. Within the U.S. Congress the recently installed Democrat majority had taken from the results of the 2006 general election a mandate to draw down the U.S. effort in Iraq. Reacting to the announcement of the troop surge, the House of Representatives passed a nonbinding (but nonetheless significant) resolution denouncing the change in strategy.[10] On April 26 the Senate passed a war-funding bill that would have tied continued funding of the U.S. military in Iraq to a specific timetable for the withdrawal of troops, to be completed by April 2008.[11] As widely predicted, President Bush vetoed the bill.

Though Congress was loathe to cut funding for troops currently in Iraq—one of the few means by which it could prevent the Bush administration from going forward with the surge—it did add benchmarks to the fiscal year 2007 supplemental spending bill and thereby tied continued funding of the surge to its ability to produce quick results.[12] Eighteen benchmarks were laid out in the bill, including provisions to distribute Iraq's oil wealth equitably, enact constitutional reforms relating to ethnic power-sharing, the reworking of de-Baathification laws, preparations for provincial elections, as well as "procedures to form semi-autonomous regions" within Iraq.[13] With regard to Operation Fardh al-Qanoon, the most relevant benchmarks may have been those calling for the enactment and implementation of "legislation establishing a strong militia disarmament program," the establishment of "political, media, economic, and services committee in support of the Baghdad Security Plan"; the standing up of "three trained and ready Iraqi brigades to support Baghdad operations"; the acquisition of the authority, via the Iraqi prime minister, to conduct this operation fully; for the elimination of "militia control of local security"; and a reduction in the "level of sectarian violence in Iraq."[14]

The bill required regular reports on the progress made in meeting the benchmarks, with a first presidential report due on July 15 and a second round of reporting, from both the president and the commander of MNF-I, planned for September 2007, seven months into the new counterinsurgency operation and less than four months after the bill's signing into law. Though the bill did not stipulate the consequences of a failure to meet the rather ambitious objectives within the given time frame, it was generally understood that such an outcome would increase congressional and political pressure on the president to call off the surge or to cut it short.

There was, at worst, no patience for the Baghdad security plan and, at best, a temptation to consider the wisdom of the counterinsurgency field manual as a panacea, to be implemented in Iraq with the expectation of immediate, tangible returns—or otherwise to be abandoned. This political backdrop offered General Petraeus an excruciatingly narrow window of opportunity to put the new strategy into effect. Keenly aware of the typical duration of COIN campaigns, he tried to warn the U.S. public that "historically, counterinsurgency operations have gone at least nine or 10 years" and that "a situation like this, with the many, many challenges that Iraq is contending with, is not one that's going to be resolved in a year or even two years."[15] Equally aware, however, that nothing would change the fundamental lack of patience for the war in the United States—and its intense politicization given the forthcoming 2008 presidential elections—General Petraeus was effectively left with the unenviable task of providing results, quickly. In his own words, he noted that "the Washington clock is moving more rapidly than the Baghdad clock" and that he was therefore trying "to speed up the Baghdad clock a bit and to produce some progress on the ground that can perhaps give hope . . . and perhaps put a little more time on the Washington clock."[16]

His effort to "produce some progress" was undercut by the Iraqi government's lack of authority, capacity, and legitimacy. Although the lifeline of the new strategy depended on the ability of Prime Minister Nouri al-Maliki to push through reform, his freedom of action was critically constrained, as he struggled with a fragmented government and a host of other structural, political, and security-related challenges.[17] As General Petraeus himself conceded, "He does not have a parliamentary majority. He does not have his ministers in all of the different ministries. They are from all kinds of different parties. They sometimes sound a bit discordant in their statements to the press and their statements to other countries. It's a very, very challenging situation in which to lead."[18] Indeed, the sectarian-dominated ministries and various parties of the Iraqi government—incoherent at best and often at cross-purposes—represented no basis for national policy, reform, or compromise, never mind reconciliation.

The attempt to "put more time on the Washington clock" was further complicated by the increase in U.S. casualties that came with the surge. Inevitably, the attempt to provide a modicum of security in Baghdad—which had, after all, been the stated aim of U.S. operations since at least the promulgation of the "clear-build-hold" strategy in late 2005—presented greater risks to U.S. combat troops, who were forced to operate and remain, often on foot, in public areas where they were more vulnerable to attack. The *Washington Post* noted on May 1, 2007, that "the deaths of more than 100 American troops in April made it the deadliest month so far this year for U.S. forces in Iraq."[19] Casualty figures for the subsequent two months showed that this spike was no anomaly; Gen. Peter Pace, chairman of the Joint Chiefs of Staff, even acknowledged publicly the "expectation that this surge is going to result in more contact and therefore more casualties."[20] As it happened, 2007 was the bloodiest year to date for U.S. combat troops in Iraq.[21] The fact that U.S. casualties had not increased statistically in proportion to the total number of soldiers in Iraq did not dampen the domestic criticism of the surge—nor did the security gains made during this period. Throughout the year, *USA Today*/Gallup polls found that 63–75 percent of U.S. respondents thought that the surge was either making no great difference or making matters worse.[22]

Given the widespread and multifaceted disaffection for the war in Iraq, there was really no way the Iraqi populace could have much "confidence in the staying power of both the counterinsurgents and the [host-nation] government," a condition for success emphasized in FM 3-24.[23] The surge was further undermined by several other divergences between what General Petraeus had at hand and what the counterinsurgency field manual had defined as prerequisites for these types of campaigns. The operation did not seem to be guided by what FM 3-24 termed "a clear understanding of the desired end state," which it argued ought to "infuse all efforts, regardless of the agencies or individuals charged with their execution."[24] The levels of democracy and stability sought in Iraq were highly uncertain, and it was also unclear whether these variables mattered as much as the need to find an exit strategy. And for all the talk in the counterinsurgency manual of "unity of effort" and the "synchronized application of military, paramilitary, political, economic, psychological, and civic actions," a major problem in Iraq was "the absence of a political solution to support the campaign plan—the 'National Compact.'"[25]

Militarily, even the increase in troop levels left the U.S. military far below the ideal force ratios identified in FM 3-24. The counterinsurgency manual suggested a tentative *minimum* force ratio of "twenty counterinsurgents per thousand residents," which for Baghdad—with a population of 6 million—would mean a minimum force of 120,000 troops. Even if one accepts General Petraeus's estimate that 85,000 troops—U.S. soldiers and Iraqi security forces—would operate in Baghdad as part of the surge, this would still mean a substantial shortfall.[26] Adding to the troop shortages, the police force in Iraq was often either ineffective or infiltrated by Shia extremist elements guided by sectarian interests rather than loyalty to the state. The messages of FM 3-24—that the "primary frontline COIN force is often the police—not the military" and that "few military units can match a good police unit in developing an accurate human intelligence picture" of their area of operation—were thus either inapplicable or irrelevant to this campaign.[27]

Although the troop shortfall could possibly be worked around in Baghdad, a more critical issue concerned the lack of forces to "secure the populace continuously" throughout Iraq, to "disrupt base areas and sanctuaries," or to "stop insurgents from bringing materiel support across international and territorial borders"—tasks that the counterinsurgency manual presented as critical in the execution of such a campaign.[28] This shortfall would matter: Although 80 percent of all sectarian violence had reportedly occurred within thirty miles of Baghdad when the U.S. military launched the surge, the subsequent massing of troops in the capital had the predictable effect of displacing insurgent activity into neighboring provinces, primarily Diyala, Salah al Din, and Tamim.[29] And as U.S. forces pursued insurgent strongholds in those provinces, the troop concentration in Baghdad and elsewhere dwindled.

It might not always be possible to launch counterinsurgency efforts only when the circumstances are right. Given the typical demands, risks, and duration of these campaigns, however, it is important not to enter into such endeavors without devoting the required resources or in the vain hope of seeing immediate returns. In Iraq General Petraeus was given a very ambitious mandate—to reverse four years of increasing entropy—but few troops and a very limited time frame in which to accomplish that goal. For anyone tracing the learning process of the U.S. military vis-à-vis counterinsurgency since 2003, there was something fundamentally tragic about this outcome. With the U.S. military having finally achieved a conceptually clear and realistic understanding of counterinsurgency, the capital of the COIN community that had driven this process was now being tied to a flawed and widely unpopular White House-directed strategy for progress in Iraq.

Given the domestic unpopularity of the war and the anticipated increases in troops, casualties, and duration of the campaign, there was a high likelihood that this first experiment with counterinsurgency by the U.S. military would be short-lived and deemed unsuccessful. In light of the Pentagon's preexisting bias against the surge, one risk closely associated with such an outcome would be the tarnishing of counterinsurgency in general and, with it, the community of experts and officers who pushed for its integration as part of DoD policy. Although for many reasons an unfair trial, the Iraq campaign—which had provided the initial impetus to consider counterinsurgency—was now threatening to unravel the institutional learning that occurred during the previous four years.

AGAINST THE ODDS

The inauspicious circumstances marking the shift in U.S. strategy made the security gains that resulted from its implementation all the more extraordinary.[30] Even during its initial stages, before all of the additional troops were at hand, the new surge strategy paid a modest but indisputable dividend. Writing in March 2007, Gen. Barry McCaffrey (ret.) provided a wholly negative assessment of the general security situation in Iraq but noted the many ways in which the new strategy had alleviated the situation in Baghdad: following the "green light" from the Maliki government, more than 600 Shia "rogue elements" had been incarcerated; the joint security stations system had resulted in "life . . . springing back in many parts of the city"; and the Iraqis had "committed credible numbers of integrated Police and Army units to the battle of Baghdad."[31] Max Boot came to a similar conclusion, noting in late April 2007 that "the situation in the capital has already shown signs of improvement. . . . The murder rate fell 75 percent in February. March saw a slight increase, but by the beginning of April the numbers of murders in the capital was still down 50 percent since the start of the year."[32] Meanwhile, clearing operations in Ramadi were netting substantial arms caches, dismantling several weapons factories, and causing an overall reduction in attacks per day from around two dozen to four or even less.[33]

The U.S. military was able to sustain this lull in violence through the end of 2007 and into 2008. According to one estimate the number of conflict-related civilian casualties declined from a high of some 3,000 per month in autumn 2006 to around 1,500 in April 2007, when the surge was beginning to take effect, to 300–600 from September 2007 onward.[34] Another estimate by the Brookings Institution's Iraq Index reported Iraqi casualties in January in 2006–2009 as 1,778, 3,500, 750, and 455, respectively.[35] In terms of security incidents—attacks against infrastructure and government facilities, bombs (both detonated and found), small-arms attacks, and mor-

tar, rocket, and surface-to-air missile attacks—MNF-I in April 2008 reported an increase from around 800 per week in early 2006 to 1,400 in
early 2007, followed by a gradual decline, leading to an average of below
600 per week from mid-September 2007 onward.[36] The number of
weapons caches cleared and found went from 2,862 in 2005 to 2,660 in
2006, which increased to 6,963 in 2007 and to around 1,000 per month for
the first three months of 2008.[37] All quantitative measures—although not
the most reliable of metrics—indicated the tentative success of the surge.

Two main factors lay behind this progress. First, the Sunni community
was increasingly turning against the extremist—or *takfiri*—groups such as al-
Qaeda in Iraq (AQI), creating a split in the Sunni-led insurgency. Whereas
the more moderate Sunni rejectionists strove for greater representation and
power in Iraq, the *takfiri* elements were inspired by an Islamist and revolutionary campaign of violence against perceived apostasy in the region. Their
shared Sunni identity and hatred of the central Iraqi government had
brought these two groups together, but differences emerged as AQI began to
seek greater control over its more moderate allies. Henceforth AQI would
render itself deeply unpopular by disrupting and taking over informal business networks, seeking to marry into the higher tribal echelons, and otherwise challenging the sheiks' authority.[38] Seeking to coerce the tribes into
submission, AQI also launched a wave of brutal attacks on the tribes and
their leaders. By late 2006 these efforts had resulted in a backlash.

The second factor behind the reduction in violence was the U.S. military's
change in strategy. The transition from larger isolated bases to smaller joint
security stations helped U.S. troops provide security, which enabled bridges
to be built with local communities seeking greater stability or protection. In
addition, the U.S. military actively assisted and even enabled the decoupling
of Sunni moderates and extremists.[39] In short, U.S. brigades moved from a
narrow and predominantly enemy-centered focus on rooting out the insurgency to a broader effort to "end the cycle of violence," primarily by engaging with its adversaries' initial motivation to take up arms. This helped locate
groups and individuals within the insurgency with whom cooperation would
be possible. By co-opting the middle ground and working with it against
more extreme elements, the U.S. military not only helped achieve common
goals but also contributed to the marginalization of hardliners.

These two factors converged in al-Anbar Province in late 2006, before
the surge even got under way. A split between Sunni moderates and extremists was emerging in the province as local tribes turned against AQI elements operating in the area. The Ready First Combat Team (RFCT—1st
Brigade, 1st Armored Division) devised an approach that capitalized on this
split and presaged the main tenets of the official strategy adopted in early
2007. Through "a deliberate, often difficult campaign that combined traditional counterinsurgency (COIN) principles with precise, lethal opera-

tions," RFCT managed to turn al-Anbar, a former hornet's nest of insurgent activity, into a comparatively peaceful province.[40]

Deploying in June 2006 the RFCT first conducted a thorough review of the population. The study revealed that in this predominantly Sunni province local sheiks did not willingly side with extremists, as previously assumed. Instead AQI was escalating its intimidation and was disliked, yet the tribes were unable to counter the threat for fear of retaliation. Meanwhile, American assurances of an imminent troop withdrawal, intended to placate Sunni tribes, had in fact heightened their fears of AQI intimidation and of an Iranian power grab (conducted directly or indirectly through the Iraqi government, widely seen as a "Persian" stooge).[41] Col. Sean MacFarland, RFCT commander, therefore changed the message and the mission: U.S. troops would not leave but would stand by the sheiks and help their forces provide security and defend the population against AQI retributions and any form of Iranian interference.

A similar partnership was forming in northwest Baghdad. With a highly enemy-centered mission statement "to defeat al-Qaeda and its affiliated movements," 1st Infantry Division's "Dagger Brigade" also initiated its tour in November 2006 by studying the local population.[42] It emerged that, in this ethnically mixed area, the Sunni population felt compelled to side with AQI as an imperfect security guarantee against the incursions of Shia death squads conducting ethnic cleansing. This understanding of the Sunni perspective offered an opportunity to turn moderate fighters in that area: If U.S. troops could help these Sunnis curb Shia violence, they could drive a wedge between "honorable resistance members" and AQI, expand security in the area, and build bridges with former "spoilers."[43]

The partnerships required the adoption of counterinsurgency practices: To gain support, intelligence, and collaboration, the U.S. military needed to demonstrate that its presence would be sustained, that it could provide security, and that it was a reliable partner.[44] Even before the shift from forward operating bases had become official U.S. strategy, Dagger Brigade, the RFCT, and a few other units therefore deployed to and operated from the most volatile sections of their areas of operations. Dagger Brigade established combat outposts on the fault lines separating the Sunni community from Shia incursions. With the first outpost built, the unit "saw an increased partnership on the part of the local nationals," which led to the co-location of volunteer Sunni units and U.S. soldiers, one that soon included Shia security personnel.[45] In Ramadi outposts were constructed where AQI violence was at its highest, where U.S. troops would team up with the sheiks' forces to combat the terrorist threat. In subsequent months tribal fighters joined the security forces en masse and worked with the U.S. military to protect and secure the hospital and other civil institutions against AQI control.[46]

The official shift in strategy in early 2007 helped formalize the practices that Dagger Brigade, the RFCT, and a number of other units had developed ad hoc. Launched officially on February 13, Operation Fardh al-Qanoon divided Baghdad into nine sectors, with the U.S. military constructing twenty-seven joint security stations across the city. In line with theory contained in the counterinsurgency manual, the U.S. military then deployed to the stations together with Iraqi forces and set about providing security at the local level.[47] Areas were subjected to intense yet discriminate infantry security operations and were then cordoned off with checkpoints and barriers; the population was issued identity cards, and any travel to and from the area was strictly controlled.[48] This strategy was also formalized in Ramadi. Building on the achievements of the RFCT, the U.S. military established forty joint security stations and observation posts, all within eyeshot, where U.S. soldiers were stationed to work with their Iraqi counterparts in establishing security, interacting with the population, and initiating reconstruction of streets and buildings damaged by the war.[49] Because these operations are manpower-intensive, they required the surge of five additional brigades; those extra troops (35,000 of them in the end) allowed the U.S. military to extend its reach, provide sustained security, and interact with local communities, who were better protected and more willing to work with the United States.[50]

Co-option and accommodation remained central to the new strategy: As the U.S. military showed itself to be a reliable partner, it found groups of Sunni moderates willing to cooperate in providing security. As various collaborative opportunities emerged, more "Sons of Iraq"—as the volunteers were named—were put on the payroll; by mid-2008 more than 70,000 Sunnis were working with the United States.[51] The recruits were screened and then registered using biometric technology and eventually organized for patrols in their neighborhoods and towns, producing—overall—a nationwide reduction in bloodshed.[52] This was not simply a strategy of bribing and arming militias bent on ethnic cleansing. The Sons of Iraq were neither cohesive as a force nor independently strong: They were carefully screened, derived their strength from U.S. support, and were limited to police missions. Neither did the United States arm these fighters, as the groups were already armed prior to the shift in U.S. strategy. Most important, the tribes were not sectarian but rather secular nationalists, concerned more with their local power base and community.[53] Grievances against extremists were also genuine rather than opportunistic, and the locals therefore did not need to be bought off.

If the adoption of a counterinsurgency strategy and the enlarged U.S. footprint helped pacify the Sunni insurgency, it also compelled the Shia cleric Moqtada al-Sadr to rein in his militia, the Mahdi Army, which had been responsible for much of the violence against Sunnis in 2006. When the U.S. deployed additional troops to Baghdad and acquired Prime Minister al-Maliki's authorization to enter previously off-limits areas hosting Shia militias, including Sadr City, the cleric decided that now was the time to lie low and refrain from further operations. Alongside this coercive leverage, the U.S. military command added a strategy of co-option based on finding common causes and transforming erstwhile adversaries into more peaceful political actors.

As it turns out Sadr was keen to streamline his militia, which had lost coherence and discipline during the previous year of violence. During 2006 Mahdi Army elements operated with no real direction from Sadr and engaged in armed activity for personal self-enrichment: Renegade units turned on each other for war spoils, targeted civilians—even in Shia areas—and attacked anyone opposing their activities.[54] The movement, which had captured the grievances of working-class Shias, was losing legitimacy and jeopardizing Sadr's hopes for greater influence relative, primarily, to the Islamic Supreme Council of Iraq and Dawa, the two major Shia parties in the Iraqi government. Sadr therefore "sought to use the surge as a further opportunity for cleansing his movement, ridding it of notorious troublemakers and giving their names to the government or Coalition forces."[55] Following a firefight between the Mahdi Army and the Badr Organization, the Supreme Council's militia, in Karbala in August 2007, Sadr even imposed a six-month cease-fire, which "lifted the impunity that many groups—criminal gangs operating in the Mahdi Army's name and Sadrist units gone astray—had enjoyed."[56] In early 2008 he also stood up the "Golden Battalion," which was to hunt down rogue Mahdi elements, now referred to as "special groups."[57]

By tapping into the motivations of its enemies, the U.S. military again was able to find common ground for promoting a form of reintegration. It capitalized on the split in the Mahdi Army by supporting moderates and targeting extremists, much as it had done with Sunni communities in al-Anbar and Baghdad. Accordingly the U.S. military supported Sadr's Golden Battalion and reportedly paid some of Sadr's forces to "help keep the peace"— a reversal on previous policy.[58] General Petraeus meanwhile held secret meetings with senior Sadr officials to discuss security cooperation.[59] The goodwill thus engendered was used to goad Sadr toward peaceful political participation: Henceforth U.S. officials were careful to distinguish between "special groups," on whom cease-fire violations would be blamed, and Sadr himself, who was no longer cast as an extremist cleric but as a moderate and important political figure seeking to rein in his militia. In General Petraeus's words, "this is a movement that was built on the principles of the martyr Sadr, Moqtada's father, and it was all about serving the people, not extorting money from them, carrying out criminal actions against them."[60] Most ambitiously, Petraeus "started using the honorific 'seyed' when referring to

Sadr"—used to address descendents of Prophet Mohammad—and "asked U.S. officers to do the same."[61] Overall the strategy appeared to pay some dividends: Despite numerous attacks on Mahdi Army units throughout 2007, Sadr renewed the cease-fire in February 2008 and again, indefinitely, in August 2008. He also took steps toward recasting himself as a national leader, launching a "reform and reconciliation" project to "establish a broad coalition of political parties" and sending his envoys to meet with Sunni tribal leaders and politicians.[62]

As General Petraeus himself pointed out, the pacts and security gains made during the surge were far from irreversible.[63] Much depended on the Iraqi government—and it was unlikely to react constructively to the changing security situation. The empowerment of Sunni tribes and former insurgents presented a threat not only to the dominant Shias in Baghdad but also to the Sunnis in government who had so far posed as the champions of their ethnic constituency. Throughout the surge the Iraqi government therefore prevaricated on its promise to reintegrate Sunni volunteer fighters and to share power with Sunni political leaders. The delays caused frustration and threatened a return to violence.[64] Meanwhile it was also uncertain whether Sadr was willing to renounce violent means altogether or work with the U.S. military over the long term. Given his popularity, Sadr's transformation into a politician was also likely to inflame his rivalry with the incumbent Shia parties who viewed him as a threat to their power and privilege.[65]

Absent unlikely government reforms, the security gains achieved during the surge were fragile. Still, despite the many serious obstacles that remained in the way of reconciliation in Iraq, the new counterinsurgency strategy had, more than any previous approach, succeeded in dramatically reducing the levels of violence across the country, giving Iraq at least a chance for reform and repair. Although the surge was not quite "counterinsurgency by the book," the new approach had given proof of a "conceptual revolution within the military leadership" that enabled unprecedented progress in stabilizing Iraq.[66] For the International Crisis Group, "U.S. field commanders displayed sophistication and knowledge of local dynamics without precedent during a conflict characterised from the outset by U.S. policy misguided in its assumptions and flawed in its execution."[67] Beyond the much-needed improvements for the population of Iraq, all of this augured well for General Petraeus and the COIN community.

RECOGNITION AND REWARD

Clearly tentative yet undeniably positive, the effects of the surge would have three broad effects on the U.S. military's learning of counterinsurgency. First, the stabilization of Iraq gave General Petraeus more time to implement the new strategy. Secretary of Defense Robert Gates, who had initially appeared uncertain about the surge and sought to limit its scope to a few months, increasingly deferred to General Petraeus and President Bush, who wanted to give his top commander in Iraq "all the time he need[ed]" for the new strategy to show results.[68] Congressional opposition to the surge also simmered down: During the September 2007 strategy review General Petraeus and Ambassador Ryan C. Crocker were able to provide a mixed picture of progress to the House and the Senate, gaining cautious approval for continuing the new strategy while pledging to draw down the additional troops of the surge within a year.[69] By the time of the April 2008 hearing, the "surged" troops were approaching the end of their tour; although frustrated, neither Democratic nor Republican lawmakers made much by way of protest when Petraeus requested, and Bush accepted, a temporary freeze on further withdrawals so as to assess the situation as the surge drew down.

Second, the success in Iraq gave General Petraeus and his supporters more influence within the Pentagon. In November 2007 the Army called on Petraeus to chair a promotions board to select the forty colonels (out of more than a thousand applicants) to be promoted to brigadier general.[70] When the list of officers was released in July 2008 it included both Col. H. R. McMaster and Col. Sean B. MacFarland, officers known for sharing Petraeus's understanding of the operational environment in Iraq. McMaster's name had previously twice been omitted from the list of promotions to brigadier general, prompting speculation that the Army was refusing to reward officers who showed innovative thinking and expertise in counterinsurgency; his promotion in 2008, along with that of Colonel MacFarland, suggested that a new course had been set.

The successes on the ground would also result in a promotion for Petraeus, who in April 2008 was nominated by President Bush as the next commander of CENTCOM. Through this move Petraeus would be replacing Adm. William J. Fallon, who had unexpectedly retired in March 2008, reportedly due to frequent disagreements with Petraeus, over CENTCOM priorities and strategy in Iraq, in which Fallon had argued for troop withdrawals.[71] In promoting Petraeus, President Bush and Secretary Gates signaled faith in him and his understanding of irregular warfare. As Gates put it when he announced the promotion, "the kinds of conflicts we are dealing with . . . are very much characterized by asymmetric warfare . . . and I don't know anybody in the United States military better qualified to lead that effort."[72]

Replacing Petraeus would be his deputy, U.S. Army Gen. Raymond T. Odierno, whose promotion to commander of MNF-I signified further continuity with the approach put in place during the surge. Also, as part of this shakeup Gen. Peter Chiarelli, commanding general of Multi-National Corps–Iraq, was nominated as the next vice chief of staff of the U.S. Army.

Known for his success in devising a comprehensive counterinsurgency strategy as commander of 1st Cavalry Division in Baghdad in 2004, Chiarelli's promotion to full general and his high placement within the Army would help institutionalize the comprehensive understanding of operations that he had showcased in Iraq.[73]

Third, the success of the surge added momentum to the ongoing process of institutional learning at the Pentagon, as manifested in a stream of plans, official publications, and field manuals. One of the more important steps taken may have been the August 2, 2007, release of the *Army Action Plan for Stability Operations*, a document that would serve "as the plan for improving Army capabilities and capacities to execute [stability operations], as well as for implementing DoD Directive 3000.05."[74] The detailed plan directed the Army to "identify, develop and institutionalize existing [stability operations] capabilities, establish and address required capabilities and capacities that do not exist, and report progress toward achieving these requirements."[75] To that end it set out a litany of tasks and reforms to be enacted, which it assigned to various units and agencies within the Army. Throughout, the *Army Action Plan for Stability Operations* embraced an understanding of stability operations as comprising developmental, humanitarian, and governance-related tasks that the Army would have to conduct in the absence of capable civilian partners.

Whereas the ground services had thus far been most assertive during this learning process, the Air Force increasingly sought to carve out some turf for itself in irregular warfare and counterinsurgency. On August 1, 2007, it released Air Force Doctrine Document 2-3, *Irregular Warfare*, intended to fill a gap in USAF guidelines.[76] The document was based on a conference organized by the Air University's Air Force Doctrine Center on February 20–23, 2007, at which the Air Force's possible roles in irregular warfare, beyond the support of ground troops, were discussed.[77] The Air University also hosted a counterinsurgency symposium in April 2007, to which it invited prominent members of the COIN community.[78] Through such discussions, USAF was able to propagate its contributions to irregular war, many of which were already being tested and regularly employed in theater: precision strikes using low-yield bombs to limit collateral damage; persistent intelligence, surveillance, and reconnaissance; air mobility; force multipliers including space-based assets (intelligence, communications, weather, and navigational capabilities); and the training and support of the partner nation's air force.[79]

Naturally, Doctrine Document 2-3 dwelled on these and other USAF capabilities. At the same time, Air Force doctrine also echoed the Army and Marine Corps' joint counterinsurgency field manual; it emphasized that irregular warfare is not a "lesser-included form of traditional warfare"; that "legitimacy and influence are the main objectives"; that it "requires a long-term strategy for victory"; and that "winning a protracted war is all about winning the struggle of ideas, undermining the legitimacy of a competing ideology, addressing valid grievances, reducing an enemy's influence, and depriving the enemy of the support of the people."[80] From a service often derided for its reliance on precision bombardment and air strikes, the USAF's new irregular warfare doctrine was surprisingly congruent with the population-centered approach to counterinsurgency developed by the ground services, so much so that one USAF commentator criticized the doctrine for having "undervalue[d] the function of force in suppressing intractable insurgents" and for replicating "FM 3-24's relegation of airpower to an 'enabling' role as opposed to that of an independent maneuver force."[81]

The elaboration of irregular warfare in Doctrine Document 2-3 was to a large degree borrowed from the emerging Irregular Warfare Joint Operating Concept (IWJOC), a first draft of which had been released in February 2007. When the final product was issued on September 11, 2007, it replaced the 2006 QDR's very vague definition of irregular war as "operations in which the enemy is not a regular military force of a nation-state" and instead defined such operations in line with the population-centered approach taken in the counterinsurgency field manual.[82] In the IWJOC, irregular warfare was defined as "a violent struggle among state and non-state actors for legitimacy and influence over the relevant populations."[83] The IWJOC also gave equal importance to all major irregular operations, including counterinsurgency and stability operations, which again distinguished it from the QDR, in which irregular warfare had implicitly denoted counterterrorism and foreign internal defense rather than the population-centered missions also included in that category of operations. The growing influence of the COIN community was apparent.

An additional sign of the counterinsurgency community's influence was the publication of Army Field Manual 3-0, *Operations*, in February 2008. The previous version of this cornerstone document had been released before the 9/11 attacks. Whereas in 2001 it had devoted two chapters to stability operations and support operations, the 2008 version emphasized throughout the need to consider stabilization and reconstruction as pertaining to *all* military operations.[84] It stated, for example, that "with the exception of cyberspace, all operations will be conducted 'among the people' and outcomes will be measured in terms of effects on populations" and that "stability and civil support operations cannot be something that the Army conducts in 'other than war' operations."[85] The manual also picked up on Directive 3000.05's stated DoD policy that stability operations are a core U.S. military mission that should be given equal priority to combat operations—and emphasized the need for the U.S. Army to master "full spectrum operations", that is, simultaneous offense, defense, stability, and civil-support operations.[86] The emphasis on stability operations and the reiterated

definitions and directives relating to such missions were especially important, as the capstone manual referred to *all* U.S. Army missions. Thus it
would reach a wider audience and emphasized, to a greater degree, the priorities of the Army as an institution rather than those of a subsection or interest group.

Underlying and enabling the above changes was Secretary of Defense
Robert Gates, who during 2007 and 2008 became an increasingly vocal proponent for the need of the U.S. military to prepare for ongoing and future
irregular operations. In sharp contrast to his predecessor, Gates became
closely associated with the COIN community and was a chief advocate of
many of its arguments. Following a visit to Iraq in August 2006 he hired
General Chiarelli to serve as his senior military assistant; according to Fred
Kaplan, Chiarelli subsequently shared a draft copy of a forthcoming article
of his with the secretary that argued for a greater focus on small wars, asym-
metrical challenges, and irregular operations.[87] The effect of that article
alone is uncertain, but it remains the case that during 2007 and 2008 Gates
made increasingly pointed remarks, often to military audiences, about the
need to focus closely on stability operations, counterinsurgency, and other
irregular types of campaigns. In an address to the Marine Corps Association
on July 18, 2007, he stated that "it is hard to conceive of any country challenging the United States using conventional military ground forces—at
least for some years to come" and stressed that "irregular forces—insurgents,
guerrillas, terrorists—have for centuries found ways to harass and frustrate
larger, regular armies and sow chaos."[88] Similar themes appeared in Gates's
address to the Association of the United States Army in October 2007, during which he characterized unconventional wars as "the ones most likely to
be fought in the years ahead."[89] Given at a bastion of the Army's old guard,
the speech was certainly provocative, with some calling it a "declaration of
bureaucratic war."[90] Gates's mission in this "war" was clear: "We in defense
need to change our priorities to be better able to deal with the prevalence
of what is called 'asymmetric warfare.'"[91]

BACKLASH

Even though the positive results of the surge enabled members of the
COIN community to gain institutional power and influence, the interpretation of the surge as justifying the need to focus on counterinsurgency was
not uniformly shared inside DoD. Indeed, while the COIN community
gained added momentum it also faced increased resistance and new coun-
terarguments by those unconvinced of their cause: The more that "irregular warfare" and "stability operations" were touted in doctrine and speeches,
the more vocal the opposition would grow.

One of the arguments raised was that learning counterinsurgency was equivalent to learning how to fight the last war—in this case the Iraq campaign, which, while clearly still ongoing, was thought to be in its final stretch. Given the many complications of the Iraq War since the beginning in 2003, contemplating and preparing for a future marked by several more such campaigns was an understandably unattractive proposition. Retired Col. Douglas MacGregor's argument in this context was typical: "Many in the senior ranks . . . ask why the United States would ever willingly seize control of another Muslim country (again), occupy it (again), and then fight a rebellion (insurgency) against the U.S. military's unwanted presence in that country (again)?"—and if no reason could be found, "why they should retool the Army and Marine force structure, doctrine, training and modernization to repeat the folly of Iraq, especially when doing so comes at the expense of the Army's and Marine Corps' ability and preparedness to fight future conflicts against far more capable adversaries."[92]

This line of reasoning confused the unlikelihood of engaging in "another Iraq" with the unlikelihood of engaging in operations that would call for similar skill sets and capabilities. It also falsely presumed that those who advocated a greater focus on counterinsurgency ardently believed that the United States would invade and occupy a succession of Muslim countries in coming years. Instead their message was clearly that global urbanization; the West's superiority in conventional combat; the attractiveness and effectiveness of asymmetric tactics to militarily inferior adversaries; the increased frequency of state-building; and the "securitization" of state failure following 9/11 all pointed to a future of irregular operations conducted among the people and, most often, with the objective of building governmental capacity. These were the trends underlying the need to prepare for counterinsurgency and stability operations beyond Iraq and Afghanistan; they represented, to the COIN community and also to Secretary Gates, the nature of modern warfare.

These trends notwithstanding, resistance to learning counterinsurgency remained palpable. The main argument against it was that the U.S. military had become too focused on counterinsurgency during the Iraq War and that its "traditional" skills had suffered—or as Maj. Gen. Robert Williams, commander of the Army Armor Center, put it, that "the long war is taking a toll on our core competencies" (an unintentionally ironic comment).[93] This contention was already present in late 2006 when Gen. Richard Cody, the Army's vice chief of staff, urged swift redress lest the focus on Iraq produce "an Army that can only fight an insurgency."[94] The chorus intensified during the surge when the apparent success of counterinsurgency operations in Iraq could be counterposed against the atrophy of conventional combat skills. In June 2007, for example, Dennis Tighe, deputy director of the Combined Arms Center for Training, asked whether "while we're doing all this

COIN . . . we have battalions that can still do an attack or a major defense, or brigades that can coordinate three battalions attacking an objective."[95] Upon leaving as commander of JFCOM, Gen. Lance Smith voiced the same concern: "The danger now, of course, is we get so focused on counterinsurgency and irregular warfare that we are not prepared for a different kind of war."[96] By early 2008, Lt. Col. Gian Gentile, a leading Army voice against perceived counterinsurgency "hype" and the chair of the history department at the U.S. Military Academy, concluded with no ambivalence that "due to five years in Iraq and six years in Afghanistan, I believe the U.S. Army has become a counterinsurgency-only force."[97]

Curiously, even while the COIN community and others looked at the surge to justify the utility of learning counterinsurgency, others within DoD used the same evidence to suggest that the time had come to return to more orthodox priorities, counterinsurgency having been amply covered. This sentiment was also evident within the Marine Corps, where the debate played into the Corps' fear of becoming a second ground force to the Army. In the 2006 *Commandant's Planning Guidance*, USMC Gen. James T. Conway acknowledged the importance of counterinsurgency but offered a subtle reminder of the Marine Corps' real calling: "Other types of forces, unique to counterinsurgency and much in demand, will have to be stood up. However, we will maintain robust, contingency response forces required by law to be *'the Nation's shock troops,' always ready—and always capable of forcible entry.*"[98] The implicit message was driven home in subsequent comments in which General Conway suggested that "you can have a major contingency operation kind of capability and still do the 'lesser included' things to include counterinsurgency" but that "the reverse of that statement is probably not true."[99]

It is, of course, true that the military's ability to conduct major combat operations had eroded during the course of the Iraq campaign since 2003. It is, however, inconceivable that after decades of virtually exclusive investment in conventional combat capabilities the balance had now swung so far in the direction of counterinsurgency that remedial action was necessary, either immediately or in the coming years. Instead, the singular focus on "far more capable adversaries" suffered from what Robert Gates would come to term "Next-War-itis"—"the propensity of much of the defense establishment to be in favor of what might be needed in a future conflict" (which by default was assumed to be conventional in nature).[100] As Gates explained, this "inclination is understandable, given the dominant role the Cold War had in shaping America's peacetime military, where the United States constantly strove to either keep up with or get ahead of another superpower adversary."[101] Yet, when engaged in two ongoing and highly demanding counterinsurgency campaigns and in a global strategic environment that promised future irregular campaigns, this obsession with the next (and necessarily conventional) war appeared out of touch with the most pressing of priorities. Indeed, given the current conflicts and those likely on the horizon it seemed more conceivable that the attention devoted to counterinsurgency and stability operations would have to *increase*, particularly if DoD was to treat them on par with high-intensity operations.

To the extent that DoD was accepting the importance of diversifying beyond standard war-fighting, the dominant school continued to regard the appropriate response to an ongoing insurgency as primarily dependent on foreign internal defense, that is, advisers and enabling assistance rather than the direct engagement of U.S. forces, as seen in Iraq.[102] In that sense, the COIN community faced resistance even among those who recognized irregular war as an integral part of the U.S. military's future. Certainly there was a need for the U.S. military to institutionalize a capability to conduct advisory missions targeting insurgents and terrorists in foreign countries— this would allow for greater leverage in a wider span of countries threatened by insurgency and terrorism. The problem, however, was that many proponents of the indirect or vicarious mode of exerting influence also tended to see a very low likelihood of engaging *directly* in counterinsurgency and, therefore, less of a need to develop a capability for such missions. In wishing away the type of counterinsurgency epitomized by Iraq, these advocates of the indirect approach were effectively confusing a widely shared desire to avoid such operations with the actual ability to do so.

This basic split within the irregular warfare community did not fully surface at this time, as the group united in its joint focus on the "lower end of the spectrum." Nonetheless this alliance of convenience did not change the fundamental fact that for many the indirect approach emerged in contradistinction rather than to complement the direct types of engagement most closely associated with the COIN community and, ill-fatedly, to the Iraq campaign. This central incompatibility can be appreciated when the counterinsurgency manual and surge strategy are compared with the QDR's Irregular Warfare Roadmap, a document intended to ensure sustained institutional attention on this category of conflict and determine budgetary decisions for DoD's 2008–13 program objective memoranda.[103]

Signed by Deputy Secretary of Defense Gordon England on April 28, 2006, the Irregular Warfare Roadmap called upon the services and SOCOM to assess "a range of issues, dealing with doctrine, training, leader development, combat equipment and personnel policies," all relating to irregular warfare.[104] Much like the QDR from which it derived, the Roadmap's interpretation of irregular warfare gave short shrift to the requirements for direct engagement in counterinsurgency; the point was to avoid these types of campaigns. Thus whereas FM 3-24 had directed soldiers and Marines to conduct a range of military and nonmilitary actions themselves (if no one else was capable), the Roadmap effectively broadened the indirect approach, initially tailored for SOF, to include general-purpose troops. This course of action has since been referred to as a "step to the right," whereby "SOF need to adapt to new missions [relating to the War on Terror] and general-purpose forces need to take over some of the missions that had characteristically been thought of as special operations missions."[105] In other words when general-purpose troops conduct irregular war they would be engaged in foreign internal defense and counterterrorism strikes, not counterinsurgency.[106]

In the Roadmap, the "step to the right" translated into five "lines of operations," of which one dealt exclusively with SOF and the other four with preparing general-purpose forces for typical SOF missions.[107] One line of operation expressed the need to "rebalanc[e] our general purpose forces to better support irregular warfare," which really meant "increased frequency of operations with host nation security forces and improving our General Purpose Force's ability to train, equip, and advise large numbers of these foreign forces."[108] This line of operation clearly targeted the troops' ability to conduct FID. A second line of operation sought to enhance DoD's "capacity to conduct counter network operations," that is, the military's "ability to identify, find, locate, characterize, and perturb and disrupt extremist cells, networks and individuals."[109] This, in other words, was counterterrorism through special operations–type direct action.

The last two lines of operation emphasized "changing the way we manage the people necessary to support irregular warfare" and "redesigning our joint and service education and training programs to conduct irregular warfare."[110] Although both objectives did seem more relevant to counterinsurgency and stability operations, it is uncertain, given the conceptualization of irregular warfare to dominate the Roadmap, what skills would in fact be emphasized in the new personnel policies and training and education programs. The apparent silence on Iraq-style operations throughout the Roadmap suggested that the sought-after capabilities would instead be geared toward discreet, lighter-footprint, and less operationally demanding missions.

The skills needed for FID and direct-action counterterrorism are valuable and needed also in counterinsurgency campaigns. However, mastering these skills does not in itself augment the organic ability of U.S. troops to conduct counterinsurgency in the absence of local surrogates, or to undertake the nonmilitary tasks that are often central to population-centered campaigns such as stability operations. Moreover the emphasis on "network perturbation" can easily lead to an overly strike-oriented posture for irregular operations. This tendency was alluded to in an internal DoD report on the implementation of Directive 3000.05, which found that DoD "continue[d] to emphasize the kinetic lines of operation, traditional or irregular, at the expense of the non-kinetic."[111] Indeed, the acknowledgment that irregular "lines of operations" can nonetheless also be overly kinetic in design was itself a subtle signal that not everything irregular optimizes or even relates to the military's ability to conduct population-centered campaigns such as counterinsurgency and stability operations. Even when DoD appeared to be going in the right direction, therefore, its learning of counterinsurgency in particular was not guaranteed.[112]

CONCLUSION

The notion of U.S. soldiers successfully conducting comprehensive counterinsurgency operations in Iraq was astonishing, especially given the preexisting aversion to such operations within DoD and the Bush administration. What this says about the U.S. military's learning of counterinsurgency more generally is, however, less straightforward. Operation Fardh al-Qanoon was forced upon the military brass. The resistance on the part of the Army and USMC leadership may not have reflected an a priori aversion to counterinsurgency but rather concerns over the applicability of this strategy to Iraq. Even so, it is clear that General Petraeus and his community of counterinsurgency advisers represented a minority within the U.S. military at this time.

During the surge the COIN community was able to overcome the formidable skepticism and opposition facing it while producing quick results in Iraq. The official shift in strategy also helped familiarize U.S. ground forces with the nature and requirements of counterinsurgency operations; what had previously been embarked upon ad hoc and by only a limited number of units was now the prescribed U.S. military approach. Although the manner in which the surge evolved was unanticipated, its achievements propelled its leaders to higher echelons within DoD. In parallel, the surge also had a trickle-down effect on the Pentagon and accelerated its institutionalization of counterinsurgency and stability operations as missions that the U.S. military will prepare for and conduct.

At the same time, the surge fueled an ongoing debate within DoD as to how much focus should really be given to irregular operations. In some parts an understandable but overly hopeful desire never again to engage in similar operations informed the discussion. Elsewhere Iraq was already being perceived as "the last war," and arguments were made to prepare for the next conflict, unquestionably presumed to be a conventional one. Others saw the continued potential for instability in Iraq and assumed, therefore, that counterinsurgency theory in general was flawed. Even those who

acknowledged the ascendance of irregular warfare offered a counternarra-
tive to the COIN community, emphasizing an indirect approach to future
irregular challenges rather than the deployment of U.S. troops as in Iraq.
With the surge ongoing—and with the final chapter of the Iraq campaign
still in the balance—it remained to be seen whether the new attention given
to the COIN community would have a positive or negative effect on the
future of counterinsurgency as a U.S. military priority. Up to this point the
results were ambivalent.

8

INNOVATION
OR INERTIA

The danger is not that modernization will be sacrificed to fund asymmetric capabilities, but rather that in the future we will again neglect the latter.

—Secretary of Defense Robert Gates, announcing the release of the 2008
National Defense Strategy, July 31, 2008

The U.S. military's prosecution of counterinsurgency in Iraq intensified a polemic within DoD as to how far the learning of counterinsurgency should be allowed to proceed, whether the armed services' traditional capabilities were eroding, and whether a return to conventional priorities was now needed. The debate of how to balance old priorities with new ones is necessary and important. In this case what was too often missing from the debate was any real sense of how much—or how little—had in fact changed since the onset of the reorientation. Any comprehensive attempt to make such an assessment would have uncovered the strong continuity that marked DoD policy in several important respects. Indeed, far from singularly devoted to the topics of counterinsurgency and stability operations, the U.S. military remained, even during the heights of the surge in Iraq, an institution oriented predominantly toward major combat operations and unwilling to upset entrenched priorities and spending patterns. Whether through resistance or inertia, the continuity expressed itself in several ways, but most forcefully in DoD's decisions over its budget and force structures—areas that reveal, to a large degree, the roles and missions for which the military is primarily configured.

These findings contextualize the growing calls by those generals and senior officers seeking a swift return to conventional priorities. Given the strictly limited nature of the reorientation to date, these sentiments seem to echo a familiar tendency in the U.S. military to consider anything that detracts from conventional war-fighting capabilities as eroding the force's readiness, however defined. Readiness to conduct a stability operation or a counterinsurgency campaign was no doubt deemed important, but it was not to encroach on the military's traditional resource allocation.

INSTITUTIONAL CONSTRAINTS

The struggle to overcome established norms and priorities within the Pentagon was documented in an internal DoD report on the implementation of the SSTR directive, intended, it should be recalled, to ensure that the U.S. military treat stability operations on the same level of importance as major combat operations.[1] Titled the *Interim Progress Report on DoD Directive 3000.05, Military Support for Stability, Security, Transition, and Reconstruction (SSTR) Operations*, the report laid out the areas where progress was being seen and those where resistance or inertia had prevented change. While lauding "DoD components" for their "great progress in meeting the exigencies of ongoing stability operations"—in particular with regard to doctrine, training, education, and experimentation—the report also noted a fundamental resistance to the deep-rooted changes necessary to make stability operations a core competence of DoD.[2]

Overall, progress in implementing the directive was characterized as "uneven, ad hoc, and incomplete."[3] More specifically, "shortcomings" were "conspicuous in such areas as overall stability operations capacity, planning, intelligence, and information sharing—despite best efforts by various pioneering and innovative individuals."[4] The intelligence picture of the U.S. military had not, according to the report, adapted to the demands of stability operations, and the military was therefore lacking the means with which to assess and understand the so-called human terrain—foreign civilian populations, systems, and structures. Other issues flagged were more fundamental to the military, relating to the structure and sizing of the force and the defense planning scenarios required to determine those variables.[5]

The September 2006 report gave the impression of a reorientation that was proceeding apace where no real reallocation of resources was necessary or where driven by the right individuals, but that the need to learn stability operations had not taken root within DoD as a whole. It explained that although the value of stability operations had been "absorbed throughout the Defense Department over the last several years at the conceptual level, the Department and the larger U.S. government still spend inadequate effort on population-centered stability operations designed to create conditions inhospitable to the enemy."[6] In that sense, the report provided another valuable insight into the important distinction between learning and the appearance of learning.

Some of the downbeat assessments in the OSD report reappeared in an October 2007 brief issued by the Government Accountability Office (GAO) examining the U.S. government's planning and capabilities for future stabilization and reconstruction operations. As a general conclusion the report stated that "because DOD has not yet fully identified and prioritized stability operations capabilities as required by DOD's new policy, the services are pursuing initiatives that may not provide the comprehensive set of capabilities that combatant commanders need to accomplish stability operations in the future."[7] GAO elaborated on this finding with reference to three major areas of concern.

First, the report noted that DoD had not developed the "measures of effectiveness as required by DOD Directive 3000.05," which was impeding the process of determining the directive's successful implementation. The report explained that there was "significant confusion over how this task should be accomplished and minimal guidance provided by the Office of Policy" and warned that "without clear department-wide guidance . . . progress on this important management tool may be significantly hindered."[8] Second, the military's planning process for contingency operations too often excluded DoD's interagency partners, complicating the synchronization of stabilization and reconstruction tasks across government departments. GAO offered three reasons for this shortcoming: lack of DoD guidance on interagency planning; the Pentagon's policy "not [to] share DOD contingency plans with agencies or offices outside of DOD unless directed by the Secretary of Defense"; and the "differences in the planning capabilities and capacities of all organizations involved."[9] Third, GAO criticized DoD's lessons-learned process as ineffective, in that it did not reliably capture the best practices identified in previous operations. "As a result," the report noted, "DOD heightens its risk of either repeating past mistakes or being unable to build on its experiences from past operations as it plans for future operations."[10]

In part, the limited progress made in implementing the SSTR directive can be explained by the time required to institutionalize new operating procedures and organizational protocols. At the same time, DoD also appeared actively opposed to making certain trade-offs and changes in priorities. Even in such areas as training and education, where progress had been comparatively strong, there were clear signs that major combat operations often continued to dominate. In early 2007, for example, Capt. Scott Cuomo of the Marine Corps commented that "a lack of appropriate training settings and conditions" had rendered "the Urban Warfare Training Center (UWTC) at Twenty-nine Palms the only place where Marines can simulate the complex environment that we've been operating in for the past 15 years"—adding that this particular program lasts only a week.[11] On the Army side, Fred Kaplan noted in August 2007 that "about 70% of the training at the Captains Career Course [at Fort Knox, Kentucky] is for conventional warfare."[12] Commenting in particular on the Aviation Captains Career Course, a 2007 graduate of the program cited an overwhelming focus on "the conventional

Fulda gap–style battle" and lamented the absence of "economics, political situation and cultural awareness" from the exercises included in the curriculum.[13]

Similarly, in terms of professional military education U.S. Army Col. Kevin P. Reynolds (ret.) revealed that during the 2007 academic year at the Army War College only "6.2 percent of the courses offered and approximately 4.8 percent of the hours in the core curriculum" dealt directly with counterinsurgency, "either as a subject of the lesson or as a major sub-section of a lesson."[14] Reynolds also noted that only two of ninety electives offered that year "address[ed] counterinsurgency or a directly related subject."[15] Although the Army War College doubled the amount of time allocated to counterinsurgency in its curriculum the following academic year, the relevant statistics still did do not go much beyond the 10 percent mark.

It is, of course, true that the Army War College focuses on the strategic level of war, whereas many counterinsurgency-related topics would be operational or tactical in nature. Even so there was a lacuna in Army PME with regard to such strategic questions as military governance, infrastructure assessment and repair, force structure for counterinsurgency, weapons system acquisition with utility for counterinsurgency, and force rotation for counterinsurgency. As Reynolds put it, "these are strategic issues that not only impact on how a nation pursues a counterinsurgency campaign, but how the decision to do so affects the nation's ability to meet and respond to its other obligations and challenges."[16] These are, in other words, areas that the Army War College could have tackled more fully but did not.[17]

A similar underrepresentation of counterinsurgency could be found in Marine Corps professional military education. In 2007 Cuomo noted that the Basic Officer Course included thirty-three hours of instruction devoted to counterinsurgency or irregular warfare out of a total curriculum of 1,534 hours; that the Infantry Officer Course spent seventy hours on those subjects out of a total of 730.5; and that the Infantry Squad Leader Course did not touch upon those topics at all in a 1,534-hour curriculum.[18] In other words the time devoted specifically to counterinsurgency *or* irregular warfare at this time ranged between 0 percent and 10 percent of total courses. These statistics resonate with the finding in the September 2006 OSD report that "the degree to which stability operations are incorporated into DoD education programs varies by institution and is not well coordinated."[19]

If the continued conventional leaning of the U.S. military could be discerned in its hesitant implementation of Directive 3000.05, training programs, and educational instruction, the same proclivity was even more pronounced in its budgetary allocations and decisions over force structure. Even while the Pentagon focused on irregular war and conducting counterinsurgency, DoD policy in these areas appeared predicated on the notion that such operations, never mind Iraq, would not form part of its future. This disconnect is in itself significant, in that the structure and budget of an armed force are fundamental to its functioning and indicative of the types of missions for which it is primarily intended.

FOLLOW THE MONEY

The very means by which DoD managed its budget during the first years of the Iraq War illustrates the continuity of its priorities. From the outset the Iraq campaign and other operations relating to the War on Terror were funded through a series of extrabudgetary "emergency" supplemental appropriations. Such measures had been used during the initial phases of previous U.S. military operations, but in the case of Iraq the practice continued even years after the campaign ceased to be an unanticipated emergency.[20] The clear implication was that the "base budget" was not to be unduly affected by the demands of the Iraq campaign, which would be funded on the side. Plausibly, this logic stemmed from the preexisting assumption that the pursuit of transformational capabilities would bestow the U.S. military with full-spectrum dominance and should therefore not be disrupted, and further the assumption that U.S. troops would withdraw from a stable Iraq within months of the initial occupation.[21] Although such assumptions were proved wrong in practice, they nonetheless continued to inform defense spending.

As a result DoD base budget requests continued to push for expensive combat capabilities, making no real adjustment in recognition of the changed strategic environment facing the United States. While the U.S. military was scrambling troops for the counterinsurgency surge in Iraq, for example, DoD's fiscal year 2008 budget request continued to prioritize platforms of little or no direct relevance to ongoing operations: "$27 billion for aircraft programs, up $4.1 billion or 18 percent from [2006]; $14.4 billion for ship programs, up $3.2 billion or 29 percent; and $6 billion for space programs, an increase of $1.2 billion or 25 percent more than Congress authorized in [2006]."[22] Steven M. Kosiak of the Center for Strategic and Budgetary Assessments (CSBA) noted that in terms of research and development (R&D) the budget request prioritized "traditional kinds of weapons programs," and in terms of procurement it "move[d] ahead with the vast majority of the acquisition programs included in the Services' long-range plans—most of which were also projected in the last, pre-9/11, Clinton Administration defense plan."[23] The same priorities prevailed in the fiscal year 2009 budget, which allocated $45.6 billion on aircraft programs, $16.9 billion on shipbuilding and maritime systems, and $10.7 billion on space programs—and which further distinguished itself by once again failing to cut a single major defense program.[24]

If the base budgets focused predominantly on capabilities for major combat operations, it might be supposed that the extrabudgetary "supplementals" would be more relevant to the strategic context prevailing at the time. Yet even though some of the war funds were allocated toward the procurement of COIN-relevant equipment—body armor, protection equipment, armored vehicles, and counter-IED capabilities—these funds were never intended to develop a general capability to conduct counterinsurgency but rather to address specific costs accrued as a result of ongoing operations. By force, therefore, the bulk of the supplementary spending was spent on providing pay and benefits to soldiers and their families and on replacing worn-out equipment.[25]

Even when the supplemental budget request did touch upon materiel and capabilities relevant to counterinsurgency, the sums involved were often comparatively low. For example, the fiscal year 2007 and fiscal year 2008 requests both allocated $3.5 billion for body-armor sets, $7 billion for protection equipment and activities, in addition to funding for various armored vehicles then in frequent use in Iraq. These provisions were generally perceived as modest, to the extent that they were subsequently augmented by Congress.[26] Marking up the fiscal year 2007 supplemental bill, "Congress added $874 million in funding for the Mine Resistant Ambush Vehicle (MRAP), an armored truck with a V-shaped hull that has proven effective in withstanding Improvised Explosive Devices." Notwithstanding this plus-up, DoD requested only $174 million for MRAPs in its fiscal year 2008 supplemental, a sum characterized by the Congressional Research Service as "well below the FY2007 level judged to match production capacity."[27] Reacting to the services' reticence, Secretary of Defense Robert Gates lobbied for the accelerated production and fielding of the MRAP throughout 2007 and also requested that Congress approve a $1.2 billion transfer of funds for that program.[28] Although Gates's influence eventually paid dividends, the immediate utility of the MRAP declined soon afterward as the number of IEDs in Iraq diminished throughout 2007 and 2008. Regardless, the fact that the secretary of defense had to intervene personally in this matter—four years into a war in which IEDs had caused approximately half of all U.S. casualties—underscored the armed services' unwillingness to adapt existing programs and priorities for ongoing and future irregular campaigns.

Some suggestion was made that the services' initial reticence to back the MRAP was due to the vehicle's inappropriateness for counterinsurgency operations, which often require troops to dismount from their armored vehicles to interact with and protect local populations.[29] Although that point has merit, its relevance to the services' decision making is questionable. Indeed, in an address at the Center for a New American Security in October 2007, Gen. James T. Conway, Marine Corps commandant, made it clear that as far as he was concerned the problem lay in the vehicle's weight and its implication for Marine Corps deployability: "Frankly, you can't put them in a helicopter, and you can't even put them aboard an amphibious ship."[30] The conundrum was therefore not one of how best to conduct counterinsurgency but whether the acquisition of MRAPs would transform the Marine Corps into "a second land army."[31] Given this hangup, there was also little enthusiasm within the Marine Corps to reallocate finite funding from other ongoing defense programs, the bulk of which did conform to the Corps' expeditionary aspirations.[32]

More disturbing than the MRAP saga was the occasional use of extra-budgetary bills to fund distinctly *conventional* platforms, supplementing, quite literally, allocations made for high-cost weapons systems in the base budget. In its emergency supplementary budget request for fiscal year 2008, for example, DoD included funding for the procurement of two Joint Strike Fighters (JSF), state-of-the-art advanced fighter jets that the Pentagon itself did not expect to be available until fiscal year 2010.[33] Given the urgent need at that time to address the exhaustion of ground forces in operation, and the fact that the JSF would not be available for years, its inclusion in emergency spending was at the very least dubious.[34] Indeed, Congress ultimately rejected the inclusion of the JSFs, along with the Air Force's argument that the planes, coming in at $189 million per unit, were a necessary replacement for F-16s, costing $20 million each, lost in theater.[35]

Because of the limited congressional oversight over the supplemental budget, the JSF debacle highlighted a wider trend illustrating the unremitting fixation of DoD with conventional capabilities even at a time when priorities lay elsewhere. This practice became more common following a memo by Deputy Defense Secretary Gordon England in October 2006 in which he implicitly gave the services the go-ahead to finance "overall efforts related to the global war on terror" through supplementals rather than only those relating exclusively to operations in Iraq and Afghanistan.[36] In 2007 a congressional report on the defense budget commented on the dramatic rise in war-related equipment costs and noted DoD's "expanded definition" as to "what constitutes war-related equipment replacement."[37] Similarly, seeking to explain the unprecedented cost of operations in Iraq, CSBA's Steven Kosiak noted in 2008 that "war-related funding measures appear to include funding for some programs at best only indirectly related to the ongoing military operations."[38] The lack of transparency in the supplementals was also the main reason why Congress pushed for operational costs to be integrated within the base budget.[39] DoD relented to this pressure in its request for fiscal year 2008, which earmarked $141.7 billion within its base budget for ongoing military operations, although an extrabudgetary $93.4 billion was also requested to supplement this allocation.

To criticize DoD for pursuing war-fighting capabilities is not to suggest that such capabilities were not needed or that the entire defense budget should have been shifted, wholesale, to meet the demands of counterinsurgency. Nonetheless it should be recalled that the U.S. military at this time enjoyed a remarkable superiority in conventional capabilities, was engaging in two counterinsurgency campaigns, was likely to face future irregular operations, and also needed to catch up on decades of underinvestment in counterinsurgency-related capabilities. Against this backdrop it is difficult not to be troubled by the unflinching continuity in Pentagon priorities.

Alongside the need to strike a balance between conventional and counterinsurgency-related capabilities, DoD also had to decide how its budget would allocate funds among the different services. Here, too, one sees remarkable continuity with spending patterns from the 1990s and early 2000s. Writing for the *Wall Street Journal* in December 2006 Greg Jaffe noted that from 1990 to 2005 the Air Force and Navy received 36 percent and 33 percent of funds allocated to weapons systems, whereas the Army took in only 16 percent; he added that "despite the wars in Iraq and Afghanistan, both dominated by ground forces, the ratio hasn't changed significantly."[40] Col. Kevin P. Reynolds (ret.) offered slightly different statistics but noted nonetheless that from fiscal year 2005 to fiscal year 2007 the Army's share of the DoD budget not only remained lower than those of the Navy and Air Force but in fact decreased.[41] So whereas the Air Force and Navy were, according to a CSBA report, "operating relatively close to their traditional peacetime operational tempo," those two services were nonetheless receiving higher levels of funding than the Army and the Marine Corps, which "accounted for the vast majority of the forces deployed in and around Iraq and Afghanistan and represented the bulk of the U.S. military's counter-insurgency capabilities."[42]

This mismatch in roles and funding openly surfaced in the *2007 Army Posture Statement*, which noted pointedly that "today, while providing the largest number of forces for the war on terror, the Army receives the smallest share of programmed Defense resources."[43] Despite this mismatch DoD continued to allocate roughly 31 percent of the budget to the Army, in both the fiscal year 2008 and fiscal year 2009 budget requests, thus continuing a pattern stretching back decades that had no apparent bearing on strategic realities, operational demands, and resource requirements.[44] Fred Kaplan put it well: "Is it remotely conceivable that our national-security needs coincide so precisely—and so consistently over the span of nearly a half-century—with the bureaucratic imperatives of giving the Army, Air Force, and Navy an even share of the money?"[45]

Alongside bureaucratic inertia this underfunding of the Army stemmed from an idiosyncratic interpretation of the challenges faced by the United States in the 1990s, and of how they might best be countered. As Frederick

W. Kagan has argued, "America's land forces today were designed to face a limited number of badly degraded conventional enemies in an environment in which American air power was expected to have decimated those enemies' ability to fight."[46] This assumption underpinned both the RMA and the initial focus on transformation and, eventually, translated into a spending pattern that sought to sacrifice infantry in favor of next-generation precision-strike technology and platforms. Seemingly this assumption was not quashed by either the U.S. military's encounter with counterinsurgency or the attendant lessons learned about the need for capable and sizeable ground forces.

However, the blame cannot be pinned entirely on DoD. With limited resources, the Army and Marine Corps elected to allocate their funds to capabilities of questionable relevance to the types of operations then straining the ground services so badly. Even during the 2007 counterinsurgency surge in Iraq the Army's "largest procurement and research, development, testing and evaluation program remain[ed] the Future Combat Systems, topping $3.7 billion."[47] Its request for the Future Combat System in the fiscal year 2008 budget amounted to "an increase of $300 million" over the previous year.[48] Yet again this troubled pet project of the Army, which it has pushed for since the late 1990s, was gobbling up funding that might otherwise have helped the U.S. Army reorient itself to become a more capable counterinsurgency force. Indeed, in marking up the fiscal year 2008 defense budget request, the House Armed Services Committee felt it necessary to cut $867 million from the FCS, particularly some of its more "exotic elements," and fund instead programs of direct relevance to the ongoing war in Iraq such as the expanded "production of Stryker armored combat vehicles and Mine-Resistant, Ambush Protected (MRAP) troop carriers."[49] The Army obviously took note, as its request for the FCS the subsequent year remained "limited" precisely to $3.6 billion, the figure accepted by Congress the prior year. In this instance the House markup slashed $200 million from the FCS line item; the Senate let it stand without revision.[50]

The allocation of Army funds may be one reason why "younger officers, frustrated with the pace of change, say that any improvements depend more on how the money is spent than on how much is spent."[51] The critique applied also to the Marine Corps. Commenting on the evolution and investments of the USMC, Lt. Col. Frank Hoffman (ret.) concluded that calls for a greater role in small wars and "complex irregular warfare" had to a large degree been ignored and that the Corps had instead "continued apace with concepts and programs that date from the late 1980s for over-the-horizon amphibious assaults."[52] This charge is corroborated by a cursory look at the Corps' major acquisition programs: the V-22 Osprey, the JSF (for which the Navy provided substantial funding), and the Expeditionary Fighting Vehicle. In fiscal year 2009, these programs cost a combined total of $6 billion, yet all of them "would be more useful for refighting the island-hopping campaign of World War II than for policing western Iraq."[53]

The investment in the tilt-rotor V-22 is particularly informative. The development of this vertical-takeoff-and-landing aircraft was marred by technical difficulties, raising questions as to whether the exorbitant levels of funding necessary to sustain the twenty-five-year-old program, and acquire the planned number of V-22s when they became available, would not be better spent either on a less ambitious aircraft or on transitioning the USMC to better handle the counterinsurgency-related tasks that it was increasingly asked to undertake. At a 2005 conference on the future of the Marine Corps, Frank Hoffman made the point that "if it [the Osprey] works as advertised, which is a big 'if' . . . at $100 million a copy . . . it's a pretty steep price to pay, especially when most of its missions could be performed almost as well by [MH-60S Knighthawk helicopters], which cost about $25 million a piece."[54] Despite all of this, and even as the Marines were scrambling to fulfill the surge in al-Anbar, the Marine Corps continued to pour Navy money into the Osprey, with the fiscal year 2008 budget allocating $135 million for R&D and $1.959 billion for procurement.[55] In the fiscal year 2009 budget request procurement had increased to $2.22 billion while R&D slumped to $68.8 million.[56]

Although the Marine Corps extolled the many virtues of the V-22, including its apparent suitability for irregular operations, the aircraft was originally conceived as a key player in the Navy/Marine Corps concept of Operational Maneuver from the Sea. Because the other big-ticket items requested by the Marine Corps also related to its ability to launch amphibious assaults, it would seem that those types of missions represented USMC priorities and vision for its own future. For Terry Terriff this focus on amphibious attack related to the U.S. Marine Corps' institutional paranoia: "Ever concerned that it might come to be seen as little more than a second land army, sustaining its identify as an amphibious force meant that it needed to demonstrate that amphibious warfare still furnished an important and distinctive contribution to the defense requirements of the United States."[57] Max Boot, however, asked the pertinent question, "when was the last time the Corps has staged such a landing?"[58] The spending pattern of the Marine Corps, in the midst of two counterinsurgency campaigns and with official DoD guidance stressing the increased frequency and complexity of irregular campaigns, was simply anachronistic—oriented toward a mission that it had not had to conduct since the 1950 landing at Inchon and would not undertake in the foreseeable future.[59]

The slowness of the Army and Marine Corps to adapt to the needs of ongoing and anticipated operations led to their clash with the increasingly reform-oriented secretary of defense, Robert Gates. Having already noted the growing likelihood of facing "smaller, irregular forces—insurgents, guerrillas, terrorists," Gates eventually made more pointed comments yet on the need for the armed services to adapt to this reality or lose out on increasingly contested defense dollars.[60] At an address in October 2007 Gates emphasized his belief that "any major weapons program, in order to remain viable, [should] have to show some utility and relevance to the kind of irregular campaigns that . . . are most likely to engage America's military in the coming decades," adding that "a program like FCS—whose total cost could exceed $200 billion if completely built out—must continue to demonstrate its value for the types of irregular challenges we will face, as well as for full-spectrum warfare."[61]

Gates's comments revealed the serious lag in the armed services' acquisitions programs. Coming from a secretary of defense these remarks could also signal change: In late June 2008, for example, the Army announced it would rework the development of FCS to focus early spin-off technologies on deploying infantry brigades rather than on heavy brigades as had long been planned.[62] Whatever the effects of this shift, it is more typical for the armed services to "wait out" troublesome civilian officials rather than bend to pressure. Though Gates's continued tenure as secretary of defense in the Obama administration gives grounds for hope, it must be recognized that efforts to reform the armed services' defense programs are always likely to meet with some level of frustration. These are long-term projects whose sunk costs, implications for industry, and strong support from within DoD, Congress, and beyond all militate against meaningful change. And as Gates himself has rightly observed, "unlike the big conventional modernization programs, there has been no strong constituency inside or, for that matter, outside the Pentagon for a long-term resourcing of capabilities for irregular conflict."[63] Until this reality changes, the U.S. defense budget is likely to remain unresponsive to the current strategic environment.

STRUCTURING THE FORCE

The U.S. military defines *force structure* as the "numbers, size, and composition of the units that comprise U.S. defense forces."[64] Along with how a force is financed, the manner in which it is structured—its size, its organization, and the distribution of skills—is central to its ability to conduct specific tasks and missions.

In the view of many defense analysts a force primed for major combat operations will struggle to master and conduct the particular and often nonmilitary tasks required for stability operations. Multitasking, or the use of combat troops for stability operations as needed, might also result in stability operations being overshadowed by the more typical priorities of the armed services. Some defense analysts therefore argue that targeting specific forces for the development of these skills is a more reliable means of guaranteeing their consolidation and maturation.

The notion of forming specialized units for stability operations has, however, met with resistance for several reasons.[65] Hans Binnendijk, author of a high-profile proposal to create specialized units for such missions, perceived within DoD "a reluctance to shift resources to stability and reconstruction areas, particularly as the armed forces are already overstretched; a fear of establishing what would come to be seen as 'second-class units'; and concerns that the preparations for [stabilization and reconstruction] capabilities would eat into the military's war-fighting capability."[66] More reasonably, some analysts claim that a force primed for stability operations would be more vulnerable to attack compared to general-purpose troops. In the words of Maj. Gen. David Fastabend, then the deputy director of the Futures Center at TRADOC: "We cannot decide what force will be needed—it is the adversary's decision. In an uncertain operating environment where the enemy has no pattern, it is necessary to have a broad menu of capabilities."[67]

Although the Army has rejected the creation of separate units, the exigencies of the ongoing Iraq and Afghanistan campaigns subjected it to increased pressure to adapt its force structure in line with the particular demands of stability operations. The conundrum facing the Army was thus how to reorganize itself for this new mission without creating specialized forces. Its proposed solution was four-fold, but as will be illustrated never entirely satisfactory.

Force Modularization

First, the Army sought to envelop its response to the new types of operations it was facing within the ongoing modularization of its force structure, through which the Army was to transition from a division-based force to one centered on self-sustained modular brigade combat teams of 3,500–4,000 soldiers each.[68] The thinking behind modularization was that the U.S. Army seldom deploys entire divisions, but that the deployment of smaller units—such as a task force or a brigade—inevitably breaks up the division and necessitates a mixing and matching of forces that renders many left-behind units combat ineffective. In particular the support forces required to deploy a brigade had to be borrowed from elsewhere within the force structure or from the Reserve Corps, which is then subjected to unnecessary strain. By basing the force on brigades, and by making each brigade self-contained, more units could be deployed at any one time without cutting into the support elements of other units. Characterized by the Army as "the most ambitious restructuring of its forces since World War

II," modularization, it was hoped, would greatly increase the Army's combat power.[69]

Although the modularization program had surfaced before the Iraq and Afghanistan campaigns, it was increasingly cast as a means of solving the force-structure requirements of these and other irregular campaigns. The 2004 *Army Comprehensive Guide to Modularity* stated that "the new modular organizations provide a mix of land combat power that can be task organized for any combination of offensive, defensive, stability, or support operations as part of a joint campaign."[70] In a similar vein the 2006 Quadrennial Defense Review framed modularization as a means of expanding Army capabilities and capacity for irregular warfare and SSTR operations.[71] With a view toward creating a force as proficient in irregular as in conventional wars, the Army would thus "continue to rebalance capabilities by creating modular brigades in all three Army components" and "transform Army units and headquarters to modular designs."[72]

For the Army modularization related to counterinsurgency and stability operations in two principal ways. First, BCTs would be self-sustainable and thus more deployable. This would increase the total number of "boots on the ground" that the Army could provide at any one time—an important consideration given the manpower requirements of stability operations. Second, BCTs were designed to be multifunctional and scalable, with different modules plugged in or removed in line with the demands of the operation. With regard to stability operations, the Army could therefore implant military police units, engineer components, tactical human intelligence, and other modules to meet the challenges characteristic of such campaigns.[73] In that sense, the Army was also meeting the requirement of the 2004 Strategic Planning Guidance, which had directed the military either to "create specialized units for stability operations or modular force elements that could achieve the same effect."[74]

Grounding the adaptation of force structure for irregular campaigns within the ongoing modularization initiative was, of course, convenient in that it seemed to require no real change in direction or the creation of units specially suited for stability operations. However, even though modularization would certainly improve the Army's ability to prosecute stability operations, it was questionable whether it constituted a sufficient response to the operational demands of such campaigns.

Critically, BCTs had not been designed with stability operations in mind. The notion of creating self-sustainable Army units was first articulated in *Breaking the Phalanx*, an influential book by Col. Douglas A. Mac-Gregor published in 1997, and was subsequently picked up by Army Chief of Staff Gen. Eric Shinseki in November 2001 to dovetail with the FCS, his other main initiative.[75] Not only did modularization thus predate the

Army's encounter with counterinsurgency; it was also designed to create a specifically conventional, or transformational, war-fighting capability. In its 2004 summer study of stability operations the Defense Science Board therefore warned that "modularity, in and of itself, does not ensure an effective stabilization capability"; "modularity," it continued, "provides for the aggregation and deployment of current capabilities; but if the military services do not have, in total, enough capabilities, or the right capabilities, they will not be able to meet S&R requirements."[76]

Thus a change of direction *was* necessary. In particular modular elements with skills relevant to stability operations had to be organized on a sufficient scale to improve the Army's capability to conduct such missions. Yet, for BCTs to be thus adapted, stability operations would have to be viewed as a core Army mission that ought to inform its force structure, and it was always doubtful whether this type of thinking was going into the creation of the new brigades. Instead, to many critics the shift to BCTs did little if anything to augment the Army's capability to conduct stability operations, and the arguments put forward by the Army to that effect received substantial criticism.

First, the claim that modularization would increase the number of troops available for deployment at any given time was at best only partially correct. When structuring BCTs the Army opted to incorporate two rather than three maneuver battalions, a reduction of one battalion from the old division-based brigades. In a report commissioned by OSD, the Institute for Defense Analyses (IDA) argued that this decision would result in a 30 percent cut in the number of battalions Army-wide and a downgraded ability to field forces or "put boots on the ground."[77] The cut of one maneuver brigade was made to accommodate the inclusion of a reconnaissance battalion and an expanded headquarters; the Army contended that these would "act as 'force multipliers' to strengthen or 'enable' the more sparsely populated combat troops in each brigade."[78] This calculation was made on the premise that "information technology and more-capable brigade headquarters can effectively substitute for a maneuver battalion at each brigade."[79] In that sense the Army position was concordant with the central tenets of Donald Rumsfeld's transformation initiative, namely the substitution of mass for information. Whereas this notion proved effective in some combat situations, critics worried that it was not applicable or even relevant to counterinsurgency and stability operations, in which the sheer number of troops may be an irreplaceable asset and the added benefits of superior information technology may be less relevant.

The Army contested the IDA's findings, claiming it had misunderstood modularization and given proof of "old think."[80] Yet even if the Army logic is accepted—that each BCT increases combat power—this effect would nonetheless have been counteracted by the decision to scale back on the number of anticipated BCTs. Having initially planned to create a maximum of forty-eight Active BCTs, DoD cut the number to forty-two in the 2006 QDR.[81] Budgetary pressure would, according to other analysts, compel the Army to "stop Active Army modularization at 39 brigades," while some Army insiders anticipated a mere thirty-six AC brigades.[82] Although financial pressures certainly lay at the root of the decrease, it must be recalled that the Army's budgetary priorities were not at this time only, or even mainly, a function of the Iraq War. A Congressional Research Service report on the modularization program revealed that the elimination of "at least one Active BCT and from three to six Guard BCTs" was made "in order to keep the FCS program on track."[83] Clearly this reduction in BCTs would counteract the stated aim of modularization to provide the Army with more boots to deploy and sustain in theater, and in doing so its relevance to manpower-intensive stability operations would also suffer. The fact that the number of brigades was being reduced to fund the overwhelmingly conventional FCS further suggested that the demands of stability operations did not inform the modularization effort. Indeed, it indicated that the conventional, or transformational, thinking behind the entire modularization program had continued to dominate.

The second factor linking BCTs to stability operations related to the ability to undertake plug-and-play with different units, inserting stability operations–relevant modular elements to respond to the demands of such operations as and when needed. Although this concept makes sense in theory, a closer look reveals a more ambiguous reality. Most presentations on the structure of the BCT did not anticipate the inclusion of modular elements with much relevance to stability operations.[84] Indeed, commenting upon the Army's conceptualization of modularization, one analyst framed its relevance to stability operations as "unclear" or "minimal."[85] A senior Army officer involved in the debate was starker yet: "The BCT does not increase our SSTR capability. . . . If you look across the structure of the BCT, it is well configured for executing lethal missions, not non-lethal ones."[86]

These arguments were captured in a paper by U.S. Army Col. Brian W. Watson on modularization and its links to stability operations. While acknowledging that "the modular BCT does feature some organic military police, intelligence collection, signal, and combat engineer assets that were not previously organic to combat brigades," he also noted that "the current design of these units represents a minimalist approach, barely capable of accomplished the tasks necessary to support combat operations—let alone the additional tasks required for stabilization."[87] He therefore concluded that modularization "does little to improve the Army's stabilization capability." In particular:

1. It has not focused on providing the modular and scalable force pool of stabilization capabilities that can augment brigade combat teams;

2. It does not provide the land force with a multifunctional brigade capable of exercising mission command for area-wide stabilization efforts to free forward BCTs for maneuver; and

3. It does not generate an adequate mix of modular brigades within the active and reserve components given the characteristics of future land campaigns.[88]

The Army was reportedly receptive to Watson's criticism yet stuck to its original argument that BCTs were designed as "full-spectrum forces, equally capable of performing traditional combat, counterinsurgency, and stability operations," a claim predicated on its "vastly improved communications infrastructure."[89] This assertion by the Army may have some merit, but it requires closer scrutiny. First, the Army had peddled the notion of a "full-spectrum" and "full-dimensional" force since at least the mid-1990s, yet it has nonetheless struggled to prioritize stability and counterinsurgency operations as a critical part of that spectrum.[90] Second, given the Army's overmatch in conventional war-fighting, any sincere attempt to become a truly full-spectrum force would have had to involve a discernable reinvestment and the elevation of stability operations in particular. For example, rather than train and educate conventionally minded soldiers to conduct stability operations tasks as they come up, a basic shift in force structure to meet the requirements of such missions would have gone a long way toward consolidating and institutionalizing the Army's ability to conduct operations across the spectrum. Nonetheless, no such move was seen when the Army rolled out the BCT.

Rebalancing the Active and Reserve Corps

Beyond modularization, a second means by which the U.S. Army sought to adapt its force structure to meet the demands of stability operations was by rebalancing its Active Corps and Reserve Corps. Most of the Army's combat support (CS) and combat service support (CSS) military occupational specialties (MOS) have typically resided in the RC. This organizational setup stemmed from the Total Force Concept (also known as the Abrams doctrine after its main proponent, Gen. Creighton Abrams), which was elaborated after Vietnam to delineate resources and capabilities between the AC and RC. One imputed intention behind the Abrams Doctrine was to ensure that no president would be able to take the Army to war for a prolonged period without drawing on reserves, something that would in theory engage the entire country in a public debate as to the necessity and judiciousness of the military action.[91] Regardless of whether this safeguard was indeed the intent, one side effect of the resultant AC/RC setup was that the MOS most relevant to stabilization and reconstruction operations were placed within the RC, where they are less accessible and deployable. In Iraq and other stability operations conducted by the U.S. Army, this has resulted in severe strain on certain "high-demand low-density" units within the RC, such as military police and civil affairs, for which demand has consistently exceeded supply.

Partly in recognition of the Army's role in stability operations, the Army leadership decided in 2003 to shift more than 100,000 positions from the RC to the AC and vice versa, thus adapting the force for the types of operations that it was increasingly facing. The rebalancing would be conducted in a three-phase process spanning from fiscal year 2004 to fiscal year 2011 and result in decreases in field artillery, air defense, engineers, armor, and logistics within the AC, with attendant increases in military police, transportation, petroleum/water distribution units, civil affairs, PSYOPS, and biological integrated defense companies.[92] By the end of fiscal year 2006, a total of 57,000 slots had been moved.[93]

It is clear that the AC/RC rebalancing could very well improve the Army's capability to conduct stability operations. However, some critics have suggested that the effect was incidental rather than intended and that the shifts in MOS related instead to the building of a more deployable military, able to conduct combat operations with greater agility and with less strain on the force—all valid and important objectives, but none that relate directly to stability operations. It is true that the initial language surrounding the AC/RC rebalancing referred not to stability operations but to reducing "reliance on the reserve component during the first 15 days of a 'rapid response operation' and to limit reserve mobilization, especially for high demand units, to once every six years."[94]

Given the origins of the AC/RC rebalancing, it is doubtful whether it will be sufficiently targeted to overcome the shortfall in U.S. Army capabilities for stability operations. "While some criticize the reforms as short-term measures primarily geared to deal with the demands of several more years in Iraq rather than with the combat realities of future battlefields, others might look at them as insufficient if the Army is to possess the types of forces necessary to carry out peacekeeping and related stability operations as an inevitable component of its future missions."[95] Other analysts worry that shifting RC personnel into the active corps will result in the depletion of the knowledge and expertise that these forces would normally derive from their civilian professions. Because many of these civilian skills are also highly relevant to stability operations, there is a risk that rebalancing, unless done very carefully, will weaken rather than strengthen the U.S. military's capability for stability operations.

In a similar vein, it is uncertain whether units of apparent relevance in stability operations would be trained accordingly. The authors of a 2007 report on U.S. force structure elaborate on this point: "Is civil affairs organized, trained, equipped, and educated adequately for future missions, or is it still geared for dealing with civilians in a more traditional fight? Are medical personnel trained for family medicine or combat triage and emergencies? Are engineers prepared for tasks such as reconstruction, economic development, and reestablishing (or in some cases, creating) essential services, or are they primarily combat engineers who build under fire the facilities needed for conventional military engagements? Even more fundamentally, given the complexity of the task, it may be possible that new specialties need to be created."[96]

This last point is critical and underscores the specific skills needed for stability operations and the attendant need to rethink entirely how a military dedicated to both stability operations and conventional combat ought to shape and size its ground forces to fulfill these different types of missions.

An Increase in Ground Forces

The third element of the Army's reforms to adapt its force structure for counterinsurgency and stability operations related to the growing of the ground forces announced in late December 2006 by President Bush. According to these plans the Army was to grow by 65,000 personnel to 547,000 and the Marine Corps by 27,000 to 202,000. Although this move did not relate immediately to Iraq—any change in the total size of these services would require years to take effect—the move suggested a new willingness to consider manpower-intensive, heavy-footprint operations.

The decision to boost the size of the Army and Marine Corps broke radically with prior DoD policy. Since the Cold War, in particular during the Rumsfeld era, DoD had sought to downsize the Army, first to cash in on the expected peace dividend to flow from the fall of the Soviet Union, and then to cut personnel costs in order to finance investment in high-tech combat capabilities. Given the operational tempo of the War on Terror—and the demands of the Iraq campaign in particular—DoD faced mounting pressure to adjust the size of the Army and Marine Corps, which many critics felt were too thinly stretched to operate effectively not only in Iraq but also to respond to unforeseen crises elsewhere.[97]

Despite this pressure Rumsfeld consistently argued against a permanent increase in ground forces, which he perceived as an unwise investment of finite resources given the rising costs of sustaining U.S. uniformed personnel. A permanent increase in manpower, he explained, "required cuts elsewhere in the Defense budget . . . crowding out funding for various types of transformational capabilities that can allow us to do more with the forces that we currently have."[98] In other words, advanced information and technological capabilities would reduce the need for boots on the ground; in line with the central promise of transformation, mass would be replaced with information. This position reflected Rumsfeld's understanding of combat effectiveness; as he put it, "in the 21st century, what is critical to success in military conflict is not necessarily mass as much as capability."[99]

DoD had therefore experimented with a variety of means to boost the combat capability of the Army and Marine Corps without increasing overall size. High-tech capabilities were one "force multiplier"; another was modularization, which was to increase combat capability by restructuring rather than resizing.[100] With the pressure of the War on Terror—and the Iraq War in particular—the Pentagon did acquire the authority to increase provisionally the size of the Army by a maximum of 36,000 troops. This boost was, however, a temporary expedient to meet the demands of what Donald Rumsfeld called a "spike period" rather than an attempt to prepare for future counterinsurgency and stability operations.[101] In other words, basic DoD orthodoxy on the size of ground forces remained unmitigated.

It was only under the leadership of Secretary of Defense Robert Gates that the Pentagon broke with this long-standing policy, announcing in late 2006 a permanent increase in both the Army and the Marine Corps. The sudden shift indicated recognition that, beyond restructuring and new technology, a simple boost in numbers would in fact be needed to fill the shortfall in manpower exposed through the ground services' engagement in stability operations. As President Bush put it, "we're going to need a military that's . . . able to sustain our efforts and to help us achieve peace."[102] Nonetheless, even though the increases in end strength did respond to those who had demanded larger U.S. ground forces, it is unclear whether the "plus-up" would have a significant effect on the abilities of the Marine Corps or the Army to conduct stability operations. There are three main reasons for this.

First, counterinsurgency is notoriously difficult—"like eating soup with a knife"—requiring not only a large force but also one that is capable, disciplined, and intelligent—soldiers and Marines who have the education, maturity, and resilience to manage its complexity and act accordingly, even under pressure.[103] The Army and the Marine Corps recognize this feature of modern warfare. The Army has introduced the concept of the "pentathlete soldier"—"a multiskilled leader who personifies the warrior ethos in all aspects, from war fighting to statesmanship to enterprise management."[104] Similarly the Marine Corps has for some years advanced the idea of the "strategic corporal," a Marine "firmly grounded in our ethos, thoroughly schooled and trained, outfitted with the finest equipment obtainable, infinitely agile, and above all else, a leader in the tradition of the Marines of old."[105] Strategic corporals and pentathlete soldiers are certainly needed, yet acknowledging this fact is far easier than attracting and retaining the required personnel.

Indeed, the Army and Marine Corps were, even before the troop increase, struggling to meet recruitment and retention quotas: "In 2005, the active Army missed its recruitment goal by 8 percent, or 6,600 personnel. Worse, the Army Reserve fell short of its recruitment goal by 16 percent, or 4,600 personnel, while the Army National Guard's recruitment efforts fell short by 20 percent, or 12,800 personnel."[106] The situation forced the Army to lower its acceptance standards, resulting in a drop of recruits deemed "high-quality" from 61 percent in 2004 to 47 percent in 2006.[107] As Andrew Krepinevich noted in his April 2007 testimony to the Senate Armed Services Committee, the Army also "granted some 8,500 moral waivers for recruits in 2006, more than triple the 2,260 granted a decade ago" and "up 30 percent" from the previous year.[108] Krepinevich also observed that only 82 percent of Army recruits in 2006, compared to a benchmark of 90 percent, had high school diplomas—"the lowest rate since 1981, when the Army was beginning to come out of the depths of the 'hollow force' of the immediate post-Vietnam era."[109] Although the Marine Corps faced less cumbersome problems with recruitment and retention, similar pressures would most likely be felt, especially as the Army and Marine Corps depend on the same recruitment pool.[110] With DoD already struggling to fill existing positions, concern mounted that reaching higher end-strength targets would necessarily demand further relaxations in recruitment standards. "The United States may, ultimately, end up with larger but, unit-for-unit, somewhat less capable ground forces."[111]

The quality of recruits is foundational to the construction of an effective counterinsurgency force. However, this problem was extrinsic to the troop increase and could plausibly be corrected over time. A more critical issue—relating specifically to the appropriateness of the U.S. force structure for counterinsurgency operations—is how the Army and Marine Corps intended to incorporate the additional troops within the existing force. Increasing the force pool of the Army and USMC would in itself improve their abilities to sustain a large presence abroad. The question, however, is whether the U.S. military was merely creating a larger conventional force or whether its planned expansion would also help it face the likely threats of tomorrow.

Although it will be years before the additional positions are filled, plans for the expansion presented by the Army and Marine Corps provide insight into how each service would use the opportunity to grow. A preliminary assessment reveals that both services did take steps to develop capabilities for stability operations. Citing an Army briefing of May 2007, Michèle Flournoy and Tammy Schultz revealed that 16,000 of the new Army positions would go into the building of greater CS/CSS capabilities, including military police, linguists, and engineers along with specialists in medicine, ordnance disposal, and PSYOPS.[112] The Marine Corps, meanwhile, planned to focus specifically on those types of units that have been in highest demand through its engagement in Iraq and Afghanistan: infantry battalions, military police, civil affairs, and intelligence units.[113]

These steps addressed longstanding capability gaps in the force structure of both services. Beyond these measures, however, the Army and Marine Corps displayed a continuing and some would say unwavering preoccupation with high-intensity operations.[114] On the Army side, 20,600 of the additional 65,000 Army personnel were allocated to the construction of additional BCTs—bringing the total number from forty-two to forty-eight—yet as envisioned these units were not structured to conduct counterinsurgency or stability operations.[115] Similarly, "the Marine Corps proposal includes some laudable steps to strengthen the Corps's capabilities for irregular operations, but the bulk of additional end strength is currently allocated to building more conventional combat capabilities," such as artillery batteries, tank units, fighter squadrons, and an additional regimental combat team.[116] Commenting on the inadequacy of Marine Corps' force structure for irregular war, USMC Capt. Scott Cuomo noted that "at the company level, we have no organic intelligence capability, information specialist(s), media (television, radio, and Internet) liaisons, non-lethal units, money handlers, general engineers, human terrain experts, or linguists and possess limited communications expertise."[117] There were few indications that the USMC's expansion plan would adequately address these shortfalls. In the end both the Army and Marine Corps demonstrated far too much continuity with traditional priorities, particularly given each service's shortfall in skill sets and MOS relevant to stability operations; "absent are the sorts of organizational innovations that would signal that a more fundamental shift was afoot."[118]

The half-hearted reform effort can be explained by the motivating factors behind the increase. Rather than to prepare for stability operations, the decision to grow the ground services related to a range of unrelated factors, chief among which was the need to alleviate the personnel tempo of each service, which had increased substantially due to the frequent rotations into and out of Iraq. More tangentially, the expansion was also to take some pressure off the National Guard, which had been strained as a result of the Iraq War, and to decrease risk by boosting the U.S. military's ability to respond to crises unrelated to ongoing operations.[119] Although necessary, these factors do not affect the Army and Marine Corps' basic preparedness and suitability for stability operations—their understanding of counterinsurgency, their ability to gather and process human intelligence, their language and cultural skills, their understanding of the "battlefield," and skills for civil-military operations in urban environments. The distinction is critical: As Frank Hoffman has argued, although "some point to Iraq and strenuously argue that Operation Iraqi Freedom or the subsequent insurgency 'proves' we need more ground forces . . . just having more forces, without the right operating framework, would not have materially improved events in Iraq in 2003 or 2004."[120] Assessing the planned increase, Hoffman therefore concluded that with regard to the Army and Marine Corps "neither institutional vision shapes unique capabilities for dealing with asymmetric and protean adversaries."[121]

Needless to say, given this backdrop the Army and Marine Corps rejected more radical suggestions to restructure ground forces for stability operations. One of the more high-profile proposals was to bifurcate the force. In late 2006 and early 2007 Andrew Krepinevich briefed OSD and the Joint Staff on one proposal to create a high-intensity force of fifteen BCTs, which would be centered on the FCS, and another twenty-seven brigades optimized for irregular warfare, including advisory missions, SSTR operations, and pacification.[122] Lt. Col. John Nagl suggested creating a permanent advisory corps within the Army to standardize and systematize training programs; a similar suggestion came out of a CSBA wargame on the force requirements for irregular operations, commissioned by OSD.[123] These and other proposals did not gain much traction with the Army leadership. Similarly, an early proposal to stand up/establish a Marine Corps Advisor Group was soon rejected.[124] In all cases the notion of singling out specialized forces for stability operations cut against the ground services' culture and self-perception. Meanwhile, the elevation of a standing advisory unit clashed with the low priority placed on this type of work. Indeed, until mid-2008 the U.S. Army did not recognize advisory positions as command experience, meaning that a soldier's involvement in transition teams would not appear on career records.[125] While service on transition teams has since then been included in official records, promotion boards do not tend to value the experience and the field is therefore still not perceived as career-enhancing.

Ad Hoc Structural Innovations

In the absence of fundamental reforms in force structure, the United States underwent incremental adjustments to equip deployed units with some of the capabilities and skill sets needed for counterinsurgency and stability operations. These developments responded to immediate operational demands but did not inform the U.S. military's basic force structure. In that sense the adjustments belied the military's perception of counterinsurgency as an afterthought: a temporary mission that might prompt adaptation occasionally but would not in the long run affect fundamental structure, resources allocation, and priorities.

Perhaps the most groundbreaking innovation was the Provincial Reconstruction Team. As noted in chapter 3, the first PRTs appeared in
Afghanistan in early 2003 and were the culmination of attempts to integrate military and civilian stabilization and reconstruction efforts on the
ground. In subsequent years the number of PRTs in Afghanistan multiplied;
by 2008 there were twenty-five PRTs working in country, of which twelve
were led by the United States. The structure varied, but the teams tended
to consist of fifty to one hundred personnel, including a handful of civilians
or contractors and representation from the Afghan interior ministry, along
with military police, PSYOPS, explosive ordinance/demining, intelligence,
medics, force protection, and administrative and support personnel.[126] Regardless of the PRT's structure, the idea was always to bring civilian and military counterinsurgency efforts closer together and thereby to extend the
reach of civilian workers to unstable areas.

The PRT format was not replicated in Iraq until October 2005, when
three teams—substantially reworked from the Afghan prototype—were
created in Mosul, Kirkuk, and Hillah. Staffed by civilians and soldiers, these
PRTs were to "assist Iraq's provincial governments in developing a trans-
parent and sustained capability to govern, to promote increased security
and rule of law, to promote political and economic development, and to
provide the provincial administration necessary to meet the basic needs of
the population."[127] By 2007 there were twenty-five PRTs in Iraq. As part of
the shift in strategy announced that year, fifteen PRTs were "embedded"
within combat brigades and given the mission to "support counterinsurgency operations." Due to their placement within military units, these PRTs
were better able to operate in volatile areas.[128]

The PRT concept was inspired by the interagency CORDS teams (Civil
Operations and Revolutionary Development Support) created in May 1967
and used to good effect during the Vietnam War. Much like their conceptual predecessors, PRTs were able to contribute effectively to the U.S. government's counterinsurgency campaigns in Afghanistan and Iraq, mostly
because no other structure brought civilians and military staff together to
operate in unison. It was plausibly for this reason that Gen. David Petraeus
included PRTs as one of ten points in his June 2007 *Iraq Counterinsurgency
Guidance*.[129] Indeed, as a House Armed Services Committee report on
PRTs was quick to point out, they "exemplify the type of interagency stability operations units deemed by the Administration to be essential to reconstruction and counterinsurgency."[130]

However, the development and fielding of PRTs also reflected underlying problems in the U.S. military and civilian departments' suitability for
and investment in counterinsurgency. First, the parallel made between PRTs
and CORDS can be misleading, particularly given the scale of each structure. More than 8,000 U.S. soldiers and civilians were committed to the

CORDS program in Vietnam, working on developmental, training, and security missions as well as several smaller projects. As Richard Stewart put it, "if one counts up all of the Vietnamese elements involved in pacification, not including the conventional RVNAF, the number of personnel involved was nearly 850,000."[131] By contrast, the entire PRT effort in Afghanistan amounted to no more than 3,000 personnel. The $7.8 billion (adjusted) per year spent on CORDS at its peak also outstrips the $2 billion devoted annually to PRTs in Iraq. In the words of Ginger Cruz, DoD's deputy special inspector general for Iraq reconstruction, "PRTs, like so many efforts in Iraq, tend to program to budgets, rather than budgeting to programs."[132]

Compounding such resource constraints, PRTs were further undercut by their ad hoc evolution and improvised mandates. There was very little, if any, coordination or coherent direction among PRTs deployed in Afghanistan and Iraq. Instead each tended to work separately in its own region and according to its own means and vision, even more so when each PRT was commanded by a different country—as with NATO operations in Afghanistan. Absent was any meaningful unity of effort: PRTs are "often free to pursue their interests as they determine them, in their own ways, and with varying levels of resources with only a modicum of coordination."[133] Although devolution of responsibility to the greatest degree can often translate into agility and responsiveness to local conditions, in this case the lack of any framework to tie together the efforts of the PRTs threatened to jeopardize missions. As a congressional report on the PRTs noted in 2008, "the heroic tactical work being done by PRTs will go for naught without more coherent strategic and operational level guidance and oversight. In the absence of such guidance and oversight, resources, instead of supporting strategic agility, may be poorly prioritized and coordinated and, in some cases, squandered."[134]

Finally, PRTs highlighted the broader difficulties of getting civilians deployed to the field as part of the counterinsurgency effort, with U.S. civilian government departments having struggled to fill their allocated PRT positions. The result, as detailed in a status report by the Office of the Inspector General on Iraq Reconstruction, was that DoD personnel were forced to "compensate for the lack of civilians" by providing "civil affairs personnel to fill the void for many of the vacant PRT Program positions . . . such as local government, economic, and agriculture adviser."[135] Again this highlights the common practice of DoD counterbalancing civilian shortfalls in stabilization and reconstruction—and the ensuing need for the U.S. military to prepare accordingly. Indeed, as a result of the underdevelopment of its own reconstruction and stabilization capabilities the U.S. military often struggled to find suitably trained and skilled personnel to fill the PRT capability gaps. Ultimately, therefore, and as explained by Ginger Cruz, "PRTs, on the whole, were short of personnel that could best assist Iraqis in developing their own capacity to administer the economy, establish the rule of law, and implement good governance."[136] Although Cruz also identified some measures to address this shortfall, the overall problem well illustrated the hazards of failing to shape force structure with stability operations in mind and the consequent risks of relying on hurried "fixes" to fill the ensuing shortfall in skill sets and capabilities.[137]

Another "fix" was the Human Terrain Team (HTT), groups of social scientists, anthropologists, and other experts with area, linguistic, or research skills relevant to the country or context in which they were operating. Forming part of the brigade staff, HTTs were supposed to provide units in theater cultural knowledge and awareness of the local population and society, along with social-scientific research tools to aid operational analysis and planning. Following the deployment of the first HTT to Afghanistan in 2006, several commanders testified to their disproportionately positive impact.[138] In recognition of this contribution, Robert Gates added $40 million to the funding of the human terrain program in September 2007. During the next two months five additional HTTs were assigned to the Baghdad area, bringing the total number there to six. Plans suggested that during the following year that number was to increase to twenty-six, with one HTT for each combat brigade.

Again the value of this addition to the U.S. military units lay in the absence of an equivalent capability within the existing force structure: the know-how necessary to understand the local population, to speak their language, and to find culturally acceptable and conciliatory means of interacting. As one paper on HTTs noted, "commanders arriving in their areas of operation are routinely left to fend for themselves in inventing their own systems and methodologies for researching and analyzing such data" and "the resulting database is generally accomplished through ad hoc rearrangement of the staff."[139] Seeking to address this weakness, units in theater issued a Joint Urgent Operational Needs Statement calling for something akin to HTTs to be established and deployed.

It remains a point of contention as to whether HTTs were ultimately sufficient or even adequate. Regardless, insofar as the teams answered to a need felt by troops in theater, they also pointed to enduring capability gaps within the military itself. The question may legitimately be asked why the needed skill sets were not already present within civil affairs, PSYOPS, intelligence, and other units dedicated to the relevant fields of knowledge. The natural follow-on question is whether improvised organizational fixes such as HTTs can compensate for the lack of preexisting institutionalized capabilities within the military force structure or whether the latter should in fact be more closely aligned with the requirements of modern operations.

Although HTTs often contributed meaningfully, their short history reveals some of the hazards of improvised outsourcing: The deployment of HTTs faced delays due to the shortage of qualified civilian volunteers; the available teams were therefore by force placed at the brigade level rather than at the battalion or company level, where they might have had a greater impact; team members were not always adequately trained for deployment; contributions were of varied quality; and the managerial practices and protocols governing their use and activity in a war zone were at times undefined.[140] Finally it seems clear that whatever the contribution of HTTs they would have been more effective had they been at hand during the early phases of the Afghanistan and Iraq campaigns. All of this points to the costs of relying on midcourse adaptation to unanticipated operational challenges and provides further evidence of the need to institutionalize needed capabilities within the military's own force structure.

CONCLUSION

The prosecution of counterinsurgency in Iraq sparked a debate within the Pentagon as to how to balance its traditional pursuit of conventional combat capabilities and its newfound interest in irregular operations. This debate would be necessary, yet in 2007–2008 it was arguably premature. Indeed, in terms of resource allocation and force structure the U.S. military behaved, even during the surge, as an institution predominantly committed to major combat operations and with little apparent interest in reforming itself to better deal with counterinsurgency.

The armed services remained firmly anchored to conventional priorities and programs. For the Army the pursuit of FCS seemed to suggest that the implicit assumptions behind transformation remained in force: Total battlespace awareness can be achieved, that superior communications can substitute for boots on the ground, and that the ability to locate and strike targets will achieve strategic victory. For the Marine Corps the continued and virtually exclusive investment in capabilities that were intended to take Marines from the sea onto land revealed a continued self-identification as an amphibious assault force—"shock troops"—rather than one optimized for protracted occupational duties.

Ongoing changes in force structure may offer some benefits for the U.S. military's next engagement with counterinsurgency: Ground forces will be larger, the Active Corps will host a larger proportion of stability operations–relevant MOS, and modular units will be more self-contained and cohesive. More fundamentally, however, the U.S. military continued to structure itself for major combat operations, with stability operations remaining very much a secondary concern—a prioritization evident in the design of the new BCT and in the Army's and Marine Corps' plans for the increase in ground forces.

Ultimately the many achievements of the COIN community and the shift to a counterinsurgency strategy in Iraq were, much like previous developments, events conducted on the sidelines of an institution unwilling or unable to displace its established priorities. From this incongruence between priorities in Baghdad and in Washington, one must draw the conclusion that the operational engagement with counterinsurgency in Iraq was not informing DoD policy, at least not where it really mattered.

CONCLUSION: KICKING THE COUNTERINSURGENCY SYNDROME?

The U.S. military's learning of counterinsurgency has in many ways been remarkable, particularly in light of the institution's prior marginalization of such operations.[1] The reorientation can be said to have started in early 2004, with subsequent innovation occurring on three levels. *Conceptually*, the U.S. military gradually gained a clearer understanding of counterinsurgency, a process fueled by the Iraq War and driven by a community of officers and civilians versed in these types of campaigns. *Institutionally*, counterinsurgency came to be better integrated within military training, education, and planning. *Operationally*, the U.S. military radically changed its mode of engagement, launching in early 2007 Operation Fardh al-Qanoon—the first time since at least the Vietnam War that it was officially directed to prosecute a community-oriented, population-centered counterinsurgency campaign.

Of course the learning process was gradual. The conceptual engagement with counterinsurgency was initially marked by questionable assumptions. Confusion was, for example, evident in the Army's 2004 interim field manual on counterinsurgency as to the division of labor between military and civilian agencies involved in such campaigns. The Army recognized that counterinsurgencies cannot be solved by military means alone and therefore assumed that the burden of running a counterinsurgency campaign would be shared with civilian government departments. Seemingly logical, this calculation grossly exaggerated the ability of civilian agencies and departments to deploy to the field in sufficient numbers and to operate in a nonpermissive environment. The wholesale delegation of the developmental, reconstruction, and governance aspects of such campaigns to unable or ill-suited civilian agencies creates a capability gap, which the military has and will be asked to fill. The failure to consider this conundrum in the early conceptual treatment of counterinsurgency and stability operations was therefore a serious shortcoming.

However, these types of missteps were quickly addressed in large part due to the tenacity and intellectual openness of the soldiers and academics driving the learning process. Members of this informal network tended to be educated in the finer points of counterinsurgency, often having earned a doctoral degree on the subject or had relevant operational experience in previous "peace operations." Others were simply of the conviction that these types of challenges would be more common in the future and that the U.S. military therefore needed to get up to speed. Between tours in Iraq, or from within the military's war colleges and research centers, this "COIN community" would disseminate its understanding of the operational environment in Iraq, sustaining a process of conceptual learning and refinement.

The COIN community's desire to learn was marked by an uncommon level of humility and lack of chauvinism. Its members challenged the orthodoxy of their own services and even listened carefully to critics of the military and its operations in Iraq. Gaining speed in 2005 this effort to learn translated into a number of high-profile conferences devoted to counterinsurgency, and a significant increase in articles and monographs published on the topic by military authors. In this manner the U.S. military developed a clear and realistic understanding of counterinsurgency—one laid out in several works on the topic produced in 2006. The flagship publication was undoubtedly U.S. Army/Marine Corps FM 3-24/MCWP 3-33.5, *Counterinsurgency*—a doctrinal field manual devoted exclusively to the subject. This new field manual focused on the implications of committing U.S. ground troops to counterinsurgency operations and of undertaking, when necessary, strictly civilian as well as military tasks. Previous doctrine had assumed that U.S. troops would not play an active role in such missions, which—although laudable in theory—has neither prevented deployments from taking place nor prepared U.S. troops for when they do. By addressing this issue directly FM 3-24 gave proof of an unprecedented understanding of what counterinsurgency can and often has required.

Alongside the conceptual learning of counterinsurgency the Pentagon also sought to integrate counterinsurgency and stability operations into its planning and priorities. Soon after the Iraq invasion counterinsurgency began to feature more heavily in the military's training exercises and curricula. Beginning in 2004 new centers were established and new programs announced dedicated to improving the ability of the force to conduct stability operations. While many of these initiatives were small in scale and slow to come to fruition, there was nonetheless a sense that new priorities were being taken on board. The overall effort was also helped in November 2005 by Directive 3000.05, which instructed the military to view stability operations on the same level of importance as major combat operations, to prepare accordingly, and to conduct such missions—including, as and when needed, its civilian components. In subsequent years activity within DoD relating directly or indirectly to counterinsurgency and stability operations was of such a magnitude as to complicate seriously any attempt to trace or enumerate all related efforts.

Operationally, too, the U.S. military underwent a gradual process of learning. During the peace operations of the 1990s and during the early years of the War on Terror the U.S. military tended to emphasize force protection over mission objectives. Concerned above all with minimizing the risk of casualties, U.S. soldiers were unable to provide sustained security, to gather human intelligence through foot patrols, or to project a presence— tasks deemed critical to the prosecution of a counterinsurgency campaign. When it came to the use of force the U.S. military tended to focus on combating the enemy rather than protecting the population, and to make matters worse these operations were often conducted with insufficient awareness of the potentially counterproductive effects of projecting force indiscriminately or excessively. With few exceptions this mode of operations characterized the U.S. military's early experiment with counterinsurgency in Iraq. In broad terms the U.S. military was as an institution either unaware or unswayed by the logic of counterinsurgency and stability operations—endeavors that differ in important ways from those conducted to defeat a specific adversary.

In contrast, the planning and implementation of Operation Fardh al-Qanoon in February 2007 emphasized several of the principles laid out in the new counterinsurgency field manual. The continuity between the conceptual learning of counterinsurgency and its operationalization in Iraq was personified in Gen. David Petraeus, who as commanding general at Fort Leavenworth had helped author the counterinsurgency field manual and who was subsequently appointed commander of Multinational Force Iraq (MNF-I), putting him in charge of all U.S. forces in Iraq. Soldiers participating in the Baghdad Security Plan were instructed to operate extensively on city streets rather than occupy fortified isolated bases; to provide security rather than strike individual targets; and to deploy in mass with an increased risk of U.S. casualties but with a higher likelihood of gaining the support of a better-protected population. For various reasons the adoption of counterinsurgency principles was problematic: The shift in strategy may have been too tardy, applied on too limited a scale, and with insufficient domestic support to be sustained for the necessary period of time. The notion of U.S. combat troops conducting these operations was, nonetheless, testament to a remarkable learning curve.

There is thus clear evidence that the U.S. military is learning counterinsurgency. If the 9/11 attacks and the invasion of Afghanistan did not prompt a realignment of U.S. military priorities, its encounter with insurgency in Iraq triggered a learning process that in the span of a few years generated promising results. In 2007 and 2008 the synergy of simultaneous conceptual, institutional, and operational learning processes gave the appearance of an institution seriously concerned and increasingly able to understand and conduct counterinsurgency. To many it seemed implausible that the U.S. military would again fail to plan properly for stability operations, as it had in 2003 with the invasion of Iraq, or be caught flatfooted by a nascent insurgency. In that sense it is possible to argue that the U.S. military had in fact learned counterinsurgency, at least to the degree possible in this short time period.

At the same time, the learning process was neither unproblematic nor incontrovertible. Indeed, we must go beyond the mere recital of counterinsurgency-related initiatives and place this narrative within the wider institutional context of the Department of Defense. In so doing it becomes clear that although the learning was in many ways impressive its manifestations have often been peripheral to DoD as a whole. As a result the learning has not to date compelled a genuine acceptance of counterinsurgency as a U.S. military mission or a related reorientation of priorities and culture.

This lag was primarily due to the fact that the people driving the learning process have so far lacked the influence necessary to sway DoD. The COIN community framed the Iraq operation as the latest in a string of campaigns in which the U.S. military has had to conduct community-oriented operations in a nonpermissive environment. Perceiving signs of a future marked by increasingly frequent and complex irregular campaigns—in the rise of al-Qaeda, the conventional supremacy of the United States, and the growing potential and sophistication of nonstate armed groups—those interested in counterinsurgency insisted that the U.S. military must innovate by developing a capability to conduct such missions.

While rarely outright rejected, this logic was not widely shared inside the Pentagon. DoD's 2006 Quadrennial Defense Review offered little beyond vague rhetoric to fulfill the vision of the stability operations directive released only three months earlier. Other major Pentagon policy papers were similarly silent on the topic of counterinsurgency—strikingly so given that the U.S. military was then engaged in two such campaigns. At most these institution-wide documents would acknowledge the importance of irregular war but prioritize counterterrorism strikes or vicarious advisory efforts over the population-centered and manpower-intensive operations included in the same category. Those interested in counterinsurgency and stability operations were going against the grain of the wider organization, so much so that their cause was likened by some to an "institutional insurgency."[2]

Opposition to learning counterinsurgency sprang from a combination of old, flawed, and wishful thinking. In the first instance the COIN community faced resistance from the old guard that clung to the conventional priorities, "tribal" equities, and culture typical of the U.S. military. Whether through inertia or conviction, large swathes of DoD continued to view all "operations other than war" as an afterthought to the U.S. military's primary mission—major combat operations—despite the threat of terrorism, the U.S. military's involvement in Afghanistan and Iraq, and the significant difficulties faced in these campaigns. This continuity expressed itself most clearly in the Pentagon's budgetary allocations and decisions over force structure, which throughout this period remained predominantly oriented toward high-intensity combat.

In its budget requests DoD continued to pour money into costly programs with questionable value in today's and tomorrow's likely campaigns. Although the extrabudgetary supplemental appropriations did help to cover the costs of ongoing operations, such funds were never intended to develop a general capability to conduct counterinsurgency. Most disturbingly, even these supplementals were at times used to fund conventional weapons systems unrelated to the wars in Afghanistan and Iraq. Clearly, the changed strategic environment had done little to erode the armed services' awe for big-ticket weapons systems.[3]

The military's force structure also remained optimized for high-intensity combat. Even though a number of steps taken by DoD improved the ground forces' suitability for counterinsurgency, their primary aim was to improve the military's *usability*—and its anticipated "use" remained major combat operations. Despite all the benefits inherent to modularization, for example, the Army's new unit, the brigade combat team, was designed primarily for conventional combat. Although the Army does plan to place more stability operations–relevant forces in various "functional" and "multifunctional brigades," it is telling that the Army's plans for the increase in forces focused so heavily on the construction of more combat-oriented BCT units. Similarly, although the Marine Corps' plans for the increase in ground forces did include boosts to some stability operations–relevant units, the bulk of the increase was allocated toward war-fighting. The rebalancing of the Army's Reserve Corps and Active Corps represented a more promising initiative, but it must also be asked whether this action related primarily to stability operations and whether the units characterized as relevant to such operations were to be trained accordingly.

A total disinvestment in conventional capabilities would be unwarranted and undesirable. Given the advantage in combat power and relative weakness in counterinsurgency and stability operations, however, it is telling that the U.S. military did not undergo more of a rebalancing—particularly given the nature of ongoing operations. So far the COIN community has struggled to displace traditional preoccupations and entrenched interests; to a large extent old think has prevailed.

Importantly, this outlook has persisted despite the absence of a near-peer competitor who might challenge the U.S. military in high-intensity warfare. During the Cold War the focus on counterinsurgency had to be balanced against the need to defend against an armored attack by the Soviet Union across the European plains. After the Cold War no likely conventional adversary presented itself, yet there is little evidence to suggest that this affected the learning process under way. Instead, the mere possibility of future high-intensity wars provided ample ammunition to those opposing the learning of counterinsurgency, who would decry each step of that process as unforgivably compromising U.S. combat power and urge a quick return to traditional priorities. All too often missing in this polemic, inevitably one of striking a balance, was any clear-eyed assessment of how little had in fact changed. Certainly, U.S. ground troops were overwhelmingly committed to counterinsurgency *operationally* by virtue of ongoing campaigns, yet *institutionally* old orthodoxies had prevailed.

It did not help, of course, that the COIN community advanced a cause that was *anathematic* to the "American way of war," significantly raising the barrier against its entry into the DoD mainstream. Convinced of the need for the U.S. military to learn counterinsurgency, the group broke with the traditional mind-set of the old guard and with the transformational priorities of the Rumsfeld era. The use of force could not be overwhelming; victory—if achieved—was ambiguous rather than decisive; the winning formula was low-tech and high-risk; and casualties must be expected as part of a long-haul effort likely to span years if not decades. Through its culture and history the U.S. military was from the outset averse to these types of operations. This predisposition intensified with the Iraq campaign, which showcased the complexity and apparent intractability of counterinsurgency.

In addition to the "old guard" at DoD, the COIN community faced competition from those who acknowledged the ascendance of irregular war but who sought to combat the new threats of this era without deploying U.S. troops. Rather than repeat the errors of Iraq, it was argued, the U.S. military would henceforth confront its irregular adversaries indirectly and avoid the large-scale and lengthy troop deployments typical of counterinsurgency campaigns. As laid out in the 2006 QDR the "indirect approach" envisaged that terrorists and insurgents would be combated by local security forces trained, equipped, and otherwise assisted by the U.S. military (often SOF). Not only would this approach protect U.S. soldiers and Marines from the dangers inherent to protracted counterinsurgency campaigns; it was also argued—with good cause—that there were distinct limits to what U.S. forces could by themselves achieve in terms of stabilizing a foreign country or rooting out a local insurgency. These tasks were seen as requiring a local understanding and a homegrown solution that the United States could certainly influence but whose sustenance it would not be directly responsible for upholding, particularly not at the expense of its own troops.

Although the indirect approach is compelling, its applicability is limited. First, there is only so much that can be achieved through the deployment of SOF: Their numbers and—in the case of the U.S. military—markedly combat-oriented disposition render these elite forces ill suited to the sustained provision of security in contested areas and to engagement in "softer" advisory and nonmilitary tasks, particularly if on a large scale. Second, the employment of local security forces as surrogates clearly relies on such forces' existence and their ability to conduct operations as wanted. As in Afghanistan and Iraq, circumstances have and will arise in which U.S. soldiers and Marines constitute the only force available to establish order and protect an insurgency-threatened country. This is particularly so during and in the aftermath of a major combat operation.

Given the indirect approach's limited applicability, then, it must complement—not supplant—the ability to intervene directly as needed. In this instance, however, the indirect approach emerged not alongside but to obviate the direct types of engagements typified by Iraq. Because the indirect approach appeared so uncomplicated when compared to the situation in Iraq, DoD policymakers deduced that irregular operations should simply be conducted indirectly by SOF, or by regular forces taking on SOF missions, so as to maintain a low profile and assume fewer risks. Within this particular logic, learning how to engage directly in counterinsurgency came to be seen as not so urgent, if at all necessary. At worst this endeavor was regarded as potentially misguided, for it implied a future of repeated involvement in the problematic types of operations seen in Iraq.

In this manner, DoD once again submitted to the alluring notion that it could choose how it would and would not engage its irregular adversaries. In that sense the learning process was reminiscent of those seen in the 1960s and 1980s, when DoD's attempts to learn counterinsurgency were similarly hampered by its overriding assumption that the commitment of general-purpose troops would not be required. Then as now, history has shown that DoD's preference for indirect engagement in irregular operations has not precluded the eventual deployment of U.S. troops, by the president, for stability and counterinsurgency operations. A failure to internalize this historically consistent fact has contributed to the U.S. military being less than ready for such missions. Despite or perhaps because of the backdrop of the Iraq campaign, there is a danger of history once again repeating itself.

This time around such an outcome would be especially disconcerting, as the trend toward direct engagement in irregular operations appears to be growing. Given the persistent attraction and apparent effectiveness of asymmetric tactics to militarily inferior adversaries; the increased frequency of operations aimed at building local capacity; and the continued threat of ungoverned spaces acting as potential havens for terrorist groups, the U.S. military is likely to confront insurgents, militia, and other irregular threats in most if not all future operations. Such endeavors may not always take the form of a "counterinsurgency campaign" or "stability operation." Nevertheless global urbanization, the need to secure conquered territory, and the inevitability of dealing with local cultures and populations with whom the foreign forces will enjoy transient legitimacy at best will force upon any expeditionary military tasks and responsibilities that closely resemble those called for in Iraq, Afghanistan, and other "irregular" battlefields.

Iraq is therefore representative of the future not because the U.S. military will necessarily engage in ambitious (and often ill-advised) exercises in state-building but because the skills and capabilities required in such endeavors are also increasingly relevant to modern wars: the ability to "apply soft power as well as hard; work in partnership with multinational, multiagency organizations, civilian as well as military . . . ; master information operations and engage successfully with the media; conduct persuasive dialogue with local leaders . . . ; mentally out-manoeuvre a wily and ruthless enemy; and, perhaps most often overlooked, measure progress appropriately."[4] These are competencies that, as Gen. John Kiszely perceptively notes, will require a high level of understanding of "the political context; the legal, moral and ethical complexities; culture and religion; how societies work; what constitutes good governance; the relationship between one's own armed forces and society; the notion of human security; the concept of legitimacy; the limitations on the utility of force; the psychology of one's opponents and the rest of the population."[5] To cite, once again, Michael Howard, "The military may protest that this is not the kind of war that they joined up to fight. [Yet] this is the only war we are likely to get: it is also the only kind of peace. So let us have no illusions about it."[6]

THE WAY AHEAD

Thus far Michael Howard's injunction has not fallen on fertile soil. One might have imagined that the costly campaign in Iraq would have provided ample evidence for the need to reform. In one sense it did allow for greater learning than seen in either the 1960s or the 1980s, in that it provided a platform for those advocating the learning of counterinsurgency from which to spread their ideas. Even so their interpretation of this campaign as signifying a need for permanent change clashed with that of other DoD components, which viewed it as a temporary aberration that will not be repeated.

All too often Iraq was cast as an exception to the rule: The specific political circumstances leading to the invasion were so peculiar, the international isolation of the United States so inauspicious, and the initial occupation so bungled that it was thought unlikely that a similar scenario would ever occur. At best, therefore, the learning of counterinsurgency was understood as an Iraq exit strategy, after which time the topic would lose relevance. More often the learning of counterinsurgency was dismissed as an unimaginative attempt to "prepare to fight the last war," a fallacy typical of military institutions undergoing change. These arguments were supported—if not rationally then emotively—by the troubled nature of the Iraq campaign: There was no enthusiasm to consider a future marked by similar engagements. In this sense, then, having provided the initial impetus for the learning of counterinsurgency the Iraq campaign could also sound the death knell for the entire enterprise.

It should be added in this context that the Pentagon's leadership had for the most part opposed the application of counterinsurgency methods in Iraq in the first place. This change in strategy was instead driven by the White House and forced on the Pentagon. DoD papers were paying scant attention to counterinsurgency in October 2005 when Secretary of State Condoleezza Rice announced a "clear-hold-build" strategy for Iraq steeped in classical counterinsurgency theory. The commanders of CENTCOM and MNF-I opposed this change in strategy, pushing instead for a *reduction* in the presence and visibility of U.S. troops in Iraq. Thereafter the split between the Pentagon and White House widened: President Bush's request that Donald Rumsfeld resign in late 2006 was a clear sign that the Pentagon's approach to operations in Iraq was no longer *de rigueur*. When it came to changing course in Iraq, Bush set out an escalation rather than a reduction of the U.S. commitment of troops, thereby heeding the advice of the COIN community ahead of the Chairman of the Joint Chiefs of Staff and the military brass.

Against this backdrop, and given the tentative manner in which the Pentagon had engaged with counterinsurgency to that point, questions must be asked regarding the sustainability of the innovative measures seen in the 2004–2008 period, to wit, the rapid, if limited, integration of counterinsurgency in the training, doctrine, and education of the U.S. military. The previous attempts at DoD to develop a counterinsurgency capability also featured a range of associated innovations in doctrine and training but in the end failed to change the U.S. military's prioritization and ability to conduct such missions. It is also historically typical for the U.S. military to adapt to ongoing counterinsurgency campaigns, sometimes successfully, only then to discard the lessons learned at the close of the operation. In light of these tendencies, do the most recent initiatives represent learning counterinsurgency anew, or are they simply a logical reaction to the unanticipated encounter with insurgents in Iraq? With the eventual close of the Iraq campaign, will counterinsurgency again be pushed off the table, leaving the military just as unprepared for these contingencies as it was when it invaded Iraq in 2003?

The answer depends in part on the outcome in Iraq and in part on the manner in which this campaign is interpreted within DoD. If the surge is judged to have heralded a new era of stability in Iraq, this may help their message, gain positions of influence, and continue to affect the institution's orientation. No doubt the tentative yet undeniably positive results of the surge in Iraq in 2007 influenced the decision to have General Petraeus chair the Army board selecting promotions to brigadier general and his subsequent promotion to commander of CENTCOM in spring 2008. These developments, and others like them, were signs of the increased power and influence available to the proponents of counterinsurgency as a result of the improved security situation in Iraq. If DoD was to move farther in this direction, the learning of counterinsurgency would be aided by the fact that the majority of low- to middle-ranking soldiers and Marines have conducted several tours in Iraq and gained a hard-won familiarity with counterinsurgency. The problem is that sustaining a "good-news story" in Iraq, never mind Afghanistan, will be costly, requiring a sustained effort for which there appears to be no real appetite.

Should the gains of the surge be reversed and Iraq slide back into civil war, the fate of the COIN community and of counterinsurgency as a topic would appear bleak. Given the opportunity to employ its new doctrine in Fardh al-Qanoon, which at first glance appeared congruent enough with the wisdom of FM 3-24, any failure to achieve results might tarnish not only the counterinsurgency manual but also those associated with it. Many may deduce that counterinsurgency simply does not work.[7] Of course, such a conclusion would be unfair, as the implementation of FM 3-24 in Iraq was not only extremely limited both in breadth and in depth, but also tardy and undercut by declining domestic support. This level of nuance may, however, be lost in the search to apportion blame, an endeavor in which problems with implementation may very well be confused with poor theory—particularly as the senior brass of the military opposed the surge from the very outset.

Whatever the outcome in Iraq, the experience of the campaign as a whole is likely to reinforce the notion that future counterinsurgencies must be avoided. Already in 2006 some defense analysts were arguing that the U.S. military should adopt a policy of abstention from small wars of choice."[8] Although the costs, complexity, and duration of counterinsurgency would certainly support such a course of action, it must be recalled that this was precisely the policy followed by the U.S. military as it invaded Afghanistan and Iraq. Throughout the history of the U.S. military, the hope of avoiding counterinsurgency has all too often been confused with an ability to do so and justified the marginalization of counterinsurgency in training, education, and doctrine. Not only has this mind-set unnecessarily complicated the U.S. military's eventual involvements in counterinsurgency, it has also encouraged its adversaries to attack it asymmetrically where it is weak.

Despite this historical trend, there are already signs within DoD that the learning of counterinsurgency has run its course, as an increasing number of senior officers in the Marine Corps and Army argue for a return to conventional priorities in training and education. Certainly there are good reasons to retain the ability to conduct conventional combat—and it is true that the Iraq War has strained both services' combat capability. Yet given the U.S. military's enduring superiority in conventional combat, its comparative weakness in stability operations and counterinsurgency, and the lack of a near-peer competitor that might engage the United States conventionally in the foreseeable future, the demands for a return to conventional priorities appear more emotive than rational, more doctrinaire than reasoned.

It is imperative that the U.S. military engage with rather than seek to forget the many lessons from Iraq. "Reform," James Dobbins notes, "comes in the wake of disaster [and] sadly, Iraq represents an opportunity in this regard, one too good to be passed up."[9] Yet, the military's effort to "get things right" will depend heavily on the analysis of what went wrong. After the Vietnam War the U.S. military was able to disassociate itself from the American defeat by blaming the politicians who had embroiled the nation in war and then forced the military to fight with "one hand tied behind its back." With regard to Iraq several such narratives could be construed to shield the military from closer self-scrutiny and reform.

First, much blame could be placed on the shoulders of politicians and ideologues deemed responsible for the initial invasion. President George W. Bush, but even more so the neoconservative quorum of policymakers and advisers thought in large part to have determined the administration's foreign policy, may—due to their presumed influence—carry the brunt for having dragged the U.S. military into a counterinsurgency campaign in Iraq and for the blowback that this war has and may yet cause. Although justifiable such a critique can easily obscure the flaws in the military's own approach to the mission, its one-sided investment in conventional weapons capabilities, and its wholesale faith in the ability of transformational capabilities and precision-strike munitions to win wars.

On that note it is similarly plausible that the uniformed military will look back upon and condemn the transformation enthusiasts—including Donald Rumsfeld—who were so influential in setting the U.S. military's strategy in Iraq.[10] Such a narrative would likely invoke Gen. Eric Shinseki's February 2003 Senate testimony, in which he recommended a force of "several hundred thousands" to stabilize Iraq, and claim that his view was widely representative of the uniformed military but quashed by civilian ideologues whose limited combat experience did little to temper their trust in transformational gadgets and capabilities.[11] For many in the military this assessment would resonate—but it must be recalled that the Army and the Marine Corps had dismissed stability operations and small wars as very distant priorities.[12] More generally, whereas a larger occupying force might very well have helped, the Army and Marine Corps would nonetheless, through their own narrow pursuit of conventional dominance, have been ill prepared to undertake the tasks required to stabilize postwar Iraq. If momentum is to amass behind the need to learn counterinsurgency, it is critical that the Army and Marine Corps leadership recognize their own inadequacies in preparing for and conducting full-spectrum operations.

Finally, it is also far from implausible that the military will want to blame its interagency partners rather than recognize its own faults. Whatever may be said about the U.S. military's learning of counterinsurgency, it remains the case that "the greatest challenge to the U.S. Government's ability to conduct SSTR operations is the lack of integrated capability and capacity of civilian agencies with which the military must partner to achieve success."[13] Although the military can be faulted for not having studied or prepared for counterinsurgency, these operations do require the expertise and resources of several civilian departments and agencies, all of whom have—with few exceptions—struggled to deploy and operate effectively in Iraq and other conflict zones. To a large extent this relates to the lack of security in theater, but it is also true that within several civilian agencies participation in foreign campaigns and cooperation with DoD have not been cast as career-advancing experiences.[14]

The military can be justified in criticizing its civilian counterparts for not playing a more active role in what should ideally be interagency campaigns. However, it is important that this critique not be accompanied by any undue complacency within the military as to its own readiness and ability to conduct counterinsurgency—or about its role in such campaigns. It is not only the prescribed responsibility of the military to administer military occupation abroad but also—subsequent to Directive 3000.05—its policy.[15] In the haste to blame civilian agencies and departments, this critical injunction must not be forgotten—indeed it must prompt greater learning and coordination between the military and the civilian agencies so as to create a veritable national counterinsurgency capability.

With so many means of shielding itself from criticism arising from any suboptimal outcome in Iraq, it nonetheless seems uncertain whether the military will engage in the type of self-critical assessment needed to pursue its learning of counterinsurgency. Perhaps the greatest source of hope is the accumulated experience of the soldiers and Marines who deployed to Iraq and gained first-hand experience with counterinsurgency.[16] For these service members Iraq has been a punishing experience. If they conclude that the U.S. military cannot simply ignore counterinsurgency but must instead prepare for an increasingly irregular world, the U.S. military may move in the direction of learning counterinsurgency. Indeed, it is difficult to imagine the circumstances in which the collective familiarity with counterinsurgency gained through the campaign in Iraq would disappear or be displaced by strictly conventional war-fighting priorities.

At the same time the process of turning individual operational experience into institutional memory is far from straightforward. The British Army, despite repeated engagement in counterinsurgency, has historically found it difficult to internalize the lessons drawn from such campaigns, necessitating quick adaptation on the ground with each new engagement. There the individual memory of previous notionally similar operations has sometimes flattened the learning curve, but to institutionalize this wisdom has proved to be an altogether more difficult proposition.[17] During the Cold War the continued fixation with major combat operations could in part be explained by the pressing need to counter a possible Soviet advance across the Central Front. Even though the Soviet Union is no more, the question for the U.S. military may now be whether anticipated threats from China or other rising powers are seen as justifying—or requiring, even—a return to conventional priorities. If these arguments gain momentum, the institutional reaffirmation of decades-old priorities risks smothering the limited learning of counterinsurgency that has occurred in recent years.

It should be added that DoD is a highly conformist institution, which greatly complicates efforts to introduce new ways of thinking, particularly if it goes against the organization's prevailing logic. The U.S. military's leadership has been raised with conventional priorities and represents institutional orthodoxy. Any attempt to displace this orthodoxy from within has to occur with the consent of the senior brass, who would thereby devalue their own experience and standing.[18] In this manner, and with few exceptions, the self-identification of the organization is perpetuated. Indeed, writing in 2007 Fred Kaplan noted that "six years into this war, the armed forces—not just the Army, but also the Air Force, Navy and Marines—have changed almost nothing about the way their promotional systems and their entire bureaucracies operate."[19] The critical question is whether General Petraeus and his quorum of counterinsurgency experts within the military will be given sufficient power to change this state of affairs.

Any effort to displace the existing institutional orthodoxy will be further complicated by the resource constraints that will affect the U.S. military in the near future. For DoD to maintain its conventional primacy while developing additive capabilities for counterinsurgency, its budget would most probably need to grow. Yet as Steven Kosiak has argued, "such increases may be unlikely given growing concerns about the size of the deficit and budgetary pressures associated with the pending retirement of the baby boomer generation."[20] A 2007 Office of Management and Budget report detailed how the combined spending on Medicare, Social Security, and Medicaid—three major federal entitlement programs—is likely to increase from 43 percent of noninterest federal spending to as much as 66 percent in 2035, when many baby boomers will be in their seventies and eighties, to around 75 percent by 2080: "In other words, almost all of the budget, aside from interest, would go to these three programs alone [which] would severely reduce the flexibility of the budget."[21] Covering these costs, Steven Kosiak further explains, "will become ever more difficult as the ratio of working-to-retired Americans declines" and because of the "continued growth in per capita health care costs."[22] The result will be a larger federal deficit and additional funding constraints imposed on DoD.

This squeeze on the defense budget will be further tightened as the military draws down in Iraq. Since roughly 2005 the U.S. military has been able to fund some counterinsurgency initiatives through extrabudgetary supplementals whose primary function has been to cover unexpected war costs. At the very least supplementals have granted DoD a larger pool of funds and greater flexibility in budgetary allocations. However, this state of affairs will not persist. Already in 2007 Congress with good reason clamped down on DoD's use of supplemental requests—measures that, in theory, ought only to be employed when the related costs are of an emergency nature.[23] Whatever the duration of the Iraq campaign it is likely that DoD will increasingly be forced to integrate the extraordinary costs of ongoing operations into its baseline budget. In the face of such a squeeze the Pentagon will have to make a series of tough choices as to what priorities to pursue and which ones to drop. It is highly uncertain whether counterinsurgency will make the cut.

It is therefore too early to predict whether counterinsurgency will become and remain a priority for the U.S. military. The evidence emerging from its initial encounter with counterinsurgency in 2003 presents a mixed picture: On the one hand a group within DoD has driven an impressive learning process featuring the rapid integration of counterinsurgency across the doctrine, education, and training of the armed services. On the other hand the U.S. military has remained structured for conventional war, and emerging opportunities to change force structure or budgetary priorities have not been seized. To the extent that the U.S. military has innovated to face irregular threats it has concentrated predominantly on various *indirect* means of exerting influence, which do not involve the direct deployment or appropriate training of regular U.S. ground troops for counterinsurgency. The future of counterinsurgency within the U.S. military thus seems to hang in the balance and depends on whether the message and cause of the COIN community are accepted and gain momentum or whether they are rejected and lose steam. The outcome of the Iraq War, and even more so the lessons drawn from this campaign within DoD and the country at large, will most likely be the difference between failure and success.

NOTES

INTRODUCTION

1. This section draws in part on Ucko, "Innovation or Inertia," this volume.
2. Hoffman, "Small Wars Revisited."
3. Examples might include: the reconstruction of Germany and Japan following World War II, the advisory phase that preceded the Vietnam War, the stabilization of Panama following Operation Just Cause, and the commitment of troops for peacekeeping duties in the Balkans following the interventions there in 1995 and 1999.
4. Kagan, *Finding the Target*.
5. Peters, "Heavy Peace."
6. See Ricks, *Fiasco;* Aylwin-Foster, "Changing the Army," pp. 2–15; Packer, *Assassins' Gate*, pp. 210–250, 305.
7. See Blaufarb, *Counterinsurgency Era;* and Downie, *Learning from Conflict*.

CHAPTER 1

1. Krepinevich, *Army and Vietnam*, p. 5.
2. In 2006, the Joint Chiefs of Staff defined stability operations as "missions, tasks, and activities [that] seek to maintain or reestablish a safe and secure environment and provide essential governmental services, emergency infrastructure reconstruction, or humanitarian relief." JCS, *Joint Operations*, p. V-1. Counterinsurgency operations, meanwhile, are defined as "those military, paramilitary, political, economic, psychological, and civic actions taken by a government to defeat insurgency," itself defined as "an organized movement aimed at the overthrow of a constituted government through use of subversion and armed conflict." See JCS, *Department of Defense Dictionary* (2001 update); Department of the Army, *Stability Operations* (2003).
3. It would not be entirely unfair to suggest that for every two defense analysts, there will be three opinions on how stability operations relate to counterinsurgency.
4. For an in-depth articulation of this point, see Berdal, "Consolidating Peace," pp. 120–125.

5. Definition drawn from OUSD(P), *Interim Progress Report on DoD Directive 3000.05*, p. 4.

6. Ibid. Notably, we are not here concerned with the purely enemy-centered approach to counterinsurgency, described in some detail by Martin van Creveld with reference to the efforts by the late President Hafez Assad of Syria to put down the attempted uprising of the Muslim Brotherhood in 1982. See van Creveld, *Changing Face of War.*

7. Interview with Thomas A. Marks. See also Ucko, "Countering Insurgents."

8. For what is probably the most influential listings of counterinsurgency principles, see Robert Thompson, *Defeating Communist Insurgency.* Other takes on these principles can be found in Kitson, *Bunch of Five*, pp. 284–290, and, more recently, in Eliot Cohen et al., "Principles, Imperatives, and Paradoxes."

9. See, e.g., Hoffman, "Neo-Classical Counterinsurgency?"; Kilcullen, "Counterinsurgency. *Redux.*"

10. In the words of Brig. Gen. H. R. McMaster, correctly described by many as a counterinsurgency expert, "The fundamentals of counterinsurgency apply to the situation in Iraq [and] it applied as the conflict in Iraq evolved over time." Interview on *Charlie Rose*, broadcast May 30, 2008.

11. Many of these arguments, and several others, against the U.S. military prioritizing counterinsurgency can be found in Mazarr, "Folly of 'Asymmetric War.'"

12. Luttwak, "Give War a Chance."

13. See James Dobbins et al., *America's Role in Nation-building*, p. xv.

14. McMaster, "On War," p. 27.

15. Schmidle and Hoffman, "Commanding the Contested Zones."

16. Urbanization is today, as it has been for some time, a global phenomenon. For relevant statistics, see the yearly reports *World Population Prospects*, released by the Population Division of the Department of Economic and Social Affairs of the United Nations Secretariat.

17. Berdal, "Consolidating Peace," p. 104.

18. Howard, "Long War?" Lt. Gen. Sir John Kiszely provides a valuable and comprehensive elaboration on the complexity and requirements of what he calls "post-modern operations." See Kiszely, *Post-Modern Challenges*, p. 8.

19. DoD, *Directive 5100.1: Functions of the Department*, pp. 1–2.

20. Allison and Zelikow, *Essence of Decision*, pp. 143, 255–257. For a convincing critique of this framework, see Freedman, "Logic, Politics, and Foreign Policy."

21. For an informative study of apparent government idiosyncrasy in policymaking, see Halperin, *Bureaucratic Politics and Foreign Policy.*

22. Wilson, *Bureaucracy*, p. 91. See also Terriff, "Warriors and Innovators."

23. Allison and Zelikow, pp. 144, 255.

24. Some leading works dealing with this topic are Posen, *Sources of Military Doctrine*; Rosen, *Winning the Next War*; Avant, *Political Institutions*; and Farrell and Terriff, eds., *Sources of Military Change.*

25. For a summary of these different schools of thought, see Grissom, "Future of Military Innovation."

26. Downie, *Learning from Conflict*, p. 5.

27. Ibid.

28. Though "consensus" is the term used, it is somewhat inaccurate. The key lies not in consensus but in achieving a *sufficiently large* consensus.

29. Grissom, "Future of Military Innovation," p. 920.

30. Ibid., pp. 920–925.

31. See Nagl, *Learning to Eat Soup with a Knife*, pp. 87–111, and Ucko, "Countering Insurgents," pp. 57–58.

32. Notable cases of comparative success are recounted by Atkinson, *In the Company of Soldiers*, pp. 294–303, with regard to the 101st Airborne in Mosul, and Ricks, *Fiasco*, pp. 419–424, with regard to the 3rd Armored Cavalry in Tal Afar.

33. Rose interview with Brig. Gen McMaster.

34. Ambassador Eric Edelman, remarks at the DoS and DoD Counterinsurgent Conference, September 2006, Washington, DC.

35. This is the metric employed in Cassidy, *Peacekeeping in the Abyss;* see also Downie, *Learning from Conflict*, and Avant, *Political Institutions*.

36. Downie, *Learning from Conflict*, p. 23; Cassidy, *Peacekeeping in the Abyss*, p. 3.

37. Several authors have sought to comment on the prioritization of the U.S. military by quantifying the number of course hours devoted by various PME institutions to the specific topic of stability or counterinsurgency operations; see, e.g., Downie, *Learning from Conflict;* Cassidy, "Prophets or Praetorians?"; Cassidy, *Peacekeeping in the Abyss;* Caraher, "Broadening Military Culture," pp. 87–96. Though the quantitative metric of course hours can indicate institutional priorities, such analysis must also consider the curricula's true *content*. Andrew Krepinevich has, for example, revealed some very "creative labeling of conventional topics as counterinsurgency-related" throughout the 1960s, severely skewing quantitative measures of how devoted the institution was to the topic of counterinsurgency. See Krepinevich, *Army and Vietnam*, pp. 49–53.

38. Dobbins, "Next Steps," p. 1.

39. These categories are borrowed from Binnendijk, "Transforming Stabilization."

40. Shafer, *Deadly Paradigms*, p. 281.

41. For an exhaustive list of stability operations–relevant technology, see Eash, "Supporting Technologies," pp. 98–105.

42. International Institute for Strategic Studies, *Military Balance 2005·2006*, p. 413.

43. Center for Advanced Command Concepts and Technology, *Operations Other Than War*, p. 7.

44. Sewall, "Radical Field Manual," p. xxxv.

45. Adapted from Caraher, "Broadening Military Culture," pp. 90–91. List based on a USIP study of the U.S. military in Bosnia; see Olsen and Davis, *Training U.S. Army Officers*, pp. 5–7.

46. As cited in Gordon, "2000 Campaign."

47. A list of capabilities relevant to stability operations and a description of each unit's abilities is provided in Flournoy and Schultz, *Shaping U.S. Ground Forces*, p. 22.

48. Barry, "Rebalancing the Active/Reserve Mix," p. 79.

49. The percentages of the 37,350 troops drawn from the Reserve Corps ranged from 35 percent for the medical staff to 98 percent for both civil affairs and PSYOPS. See ibid., p. 79.

50. Ibid., p. 78.

51. Ibid.

52. Binnendijk, Gompert, and Kugler, "New Military Framework," p. 10. A similar point is made by Janine Davidson, then the director of DoD stability operations capabilities at OSD, in a paper published by the Center for a New American Security. See Flournoy and Schultz, *Shaping U.S. Ground Forces*, p. 20.

53. Bingham, Rubini, and Cleary, *U.S. Army Civil Affairs*, p. 4.

54. It remains a moot point whether the U.S. public's Vietnam syndrome will be similarly affected.

55. Freedman, "Rumsfeld's Legacy?" The implications of a possible Iraq syndrome are also touched upon in Mueller, "Iraq Syndrome."

CHAPTER 2

1. Weigley, "American Strategy," p. 408. See also Nagl, *Learning to Eat Soup with a Knife*, pp. 43–44.

2. Cassidy, *Peacekeeping in the Abyss*, p. 88.

3. Linn, "Impact of the Imperial Wars," p. 2.

4. Ibid., p. 5. Ironically, Root oversaw protracted occupations in both Cuba and the Philippines.

5. JCS, *National Military Strategy* (1995).

6. Lovell, "Vietnam and the U.S. Army," p. 133. See also Serafino, *Peacekeeping and Related Stability Operations*, pp. 8–9.

7. Cassidy, *Peacekeeping in the Abyss*, p. 93.

8. Boot, *Savage Wars of Peace*, pp. xix, 129–181, 231–252.

9. Maechling, "Counterinsurgency," p. 21.

10. This taxonomy is used by Eliot Cohen and John Gooch in their study, *Military Misfortunes*. This "counterinsurgency syndrome" is not unique to the U.S. military. Writing in 1966, Richard L. Clutterbuck observed that "the British have been learning the same lessons about counterinsurgency for nearly 200 years." See Clutterbuck, *Long, Long War.* A later study of the UK military's approach to low-intensity operations drew a similar conclusion. See Eaton et al., *British Approach to Low-Intensity Operations.*

11. Waghelstein, "What's Wrong in Iraq?," p. 112.

12. I am grateful to Col. Michael S. Bell, U.S. Army, for this insight.

13. Weigley, *American Way of War*, p. 36.

14. Max Boot makes the point that "out of 30 U.S. generals who served in the Philippines from 1898 to 1902, 26 had fought in the Indian Wars." See Boot, *Savage Wars of Peace*, p. 127.

15. This point remains valid even though these programs constituted mere sideshows to the U.S. military's larger and much more conventionally oriented effort in Vietnam. For a discussion of the value of CORDS as an approach to counterinsurgency, see Stewart, "CORDS and the Vietnam Experience."

16. Mahon, *History of the Second Seminole War,* p. 209.

17. Collette, "Countering Irregular Activity," pp. 10–11. See also Mackey, *Uncivil War,* chaps. 1–2.

18. Boot, *Savage Wars of Peace,* p. 127.

19. Weigley, *American Way of War,* p. xxii.

20. As quoted in Summers, *On Strategy,* p. 25.

21. Letter from Maj. Gen. William T. Sherman to the mayor and city council of Atlanta, September 12, 1864.

22. Metz and Millen, *Insurgency and Counterinsurgency,* pp. 21–22.

23. See USMC, *Small Wars Manual.* The influence of the Manual was to be short-lived. As Max Boot explains, "The final edition of the *Small Wars Manual* was published at the most inopportune of times, 1940. It seemed to have little application to World War II. . . . By the time America found itself embroiled in a small war in a place called Vietnam . . . the *Small Wars Manual* and its lessons had been all but forgotten." Boot, *Savage Wars of Peace,* p. 285.

24. White, "American Military Strategy."

25. Deady, "Lessons from a Successful Counterinsurgency," p. 53.

26. Linn, "Impact of the Imperial Wars," p. 9.

27. For more information on these motivations, see Herbert, "Deciding What Has to Be Done." See also Lovell, "Vietnam and the U.S. Army," p. 133. U.S. military personnel in the European Command (EUCOM) dropped from 416,000 in 1962 to 300,000 in 1973. For a 1950–1982 yearly breakdown of U.S. personnel in EUCOM, see Record, *Revising U.S. Military Strategy,* p. 104. Writing in 1983, Fred Halliday notes that "NATO has 17,000 main battle tanks in Europe, as opposed to 26,300 WTO [Warsaw Treaty Organization] tanks in eastern Europe and another 19,200 in the western parts of the USSR." See Halliday, *Making of the Second Cold War,* p. 60.

28. Herbert, "Deciding What Has to Be Done."

29. Quoted in Hennessy, *Strategy in Vietnam.* For an elaboration of the USMC's "forget Vietnam syndrome," see also Dalton, "Village." Finally, for more detail on the Corps' maneuverings post-Vietnam, see Terriff, "'Innovate or Die,'" pp. 485–493.

30. Thompson, ed., *Low Intensity Conflict,* p. 8. The subsequent edition of the U.S. Army capstone field manual FM 100-5, *Operations,* published in 1976, did not once mention counterinsurgency. Similarly, the 1972 and 1974 editions of FM 100-20, *Internal Defense and Development,* and the 1972 version of FM 31-23, *Stability Operations,* all emphasized the need to distance the U.S. Army from anything but conventional scenarios. See Downie, *Learning from Conflict,* p. 57.

31. McClintock, *Instruments of Statecraft.*

32. Maechling, "Counterinsurgency," p. 22. A cogent analysis of how Khrushchev's speech was received within the White House is offered in Blaufarb, *Counterinsurgency Era*, pp. 52–55.

33. President John F. Kennedy, address to the American Newspaper Publishers Association.

34. Klare and Kornbluh, "New Interventionism," pp. 7–8.

35. See Kirkpatrick, "Role of the Soviet Union."

36. See Gorman, "Low Intensity Conflict." See also Kirkpatrick, "Role of the Soviet Union," and, for a critique of this monolithic worldview, Shafer, *Deadly Paradigms*, pp. 276–290.

37. NSAM 2, February 3, 1961. See Krepinevich, *Army and Vietnam*, pp. 27–33, for a more in-depth account of this "revolution from above."

38. NSAM 124, January 18, 1962.

39. NSAM 182, August 24, 1964.

40. Krepinevich, *Army and Vietnam*, p. 31. For Krulak's own account of this period, see *First to Fight*, chap. 12.

41. See USMC, FMFM 8-2, *Operations against Guerrilla Forces* (1962), and Department of the Army, FM 100-5, *Field Service Regulations: Operations* (1962), chaps. 11, 12. Krepinevich, *Army and Vietnam*, pp. 38–41, provides a more comprehensive account of the development of counterinsurgency doctrine in the 1960s.

42. JCS Chairman, *Military Counter-Insurgency Accomplishments*. Extracts of the report can be found in Blaufarb, *Counterinsurgency Era*, pp. 70–71, and McClintock, *Instruments of Statecraft*, chap. 7.

43. JCS Chairman, *Military Counter-Insurgency Accomplishments*.

44. Blaufarb, *Counterinsurgency Era*, p. 71.

45. Lovell, "Vietnam and the U.S. Army," p. 143.

46. Department of the Army, FM 100-5, *Operations* (1962).

47. Sarkesian, "Commentary on 'Low Intensity Warfare,'" p. 38.

48. CLIC Activation Plan, cited in Klare and Kornbluh, "New Interventionism," pp. 4–5.

49. Army-Air Force Center for Low-Intensity Conflict, *Joint Low-Intensity Conflict Final Report*, p. 4.

50. The conference "Proceedings of the Low-Intensity Warfare" took place during January 14–15, 1986. See Shafer, *Deadly Paradigms*, pp. 283–290, for more details on attendance and topics covered.

51. U.S. Code of Federal Regulations, Title 50, chap. 15, subchap. I, sec. 402(g) "National Security Council."

52. As quoted in Klare and Kornbluh, "New Interventionism," p. 4.

53. *Military Counter-Insurgency Accomplishments*. As quoted in Blaufarb, *Counterinsurgency Era*, p. 71.

54. Maechling, "Counterinsurgency," p. 26.

55. Blaufarb, *Counterinsurgency Era*, p. 87.

56. Doughty, *Evolution of U.S. Army Tactical Doctrine*.

57. Blaufarb, *Counterinsurgency Era*, p. 318, n. 50.

58. McClintock, *Instruments of Statecraft*, chap. 6.

59. Harmon, "Illustrations of 'Learning,'" p. 46, n. 19.

60. Collins, "Vietnam Postmortem," pp. 46–55.

61. Harmon, "Illustrations of 'Learning,'" p. 40.

62. See Krepinevich, *Army and Vietnam*, p. 41; Department of the Army, FM 31-16, *Counterguerrilla Operations* (1967).

63. See Krepinevich, *Army and Vietnam*, p. 41.

64. See JCS, amended *Publication 1* (1984). A subsequent Army Field Circular offered a similar definition; see Department of the Army, FC 100–20, *Low-Intensity Conflict* (1986), p. v.

65. Downie, *Learning from Conflict*, p. 119.

66. Department of the Army, *Operations* (1986), p. 6.

67. Cohen, *Commandos and Politicians*, p. 40; McClintock, *Instruments of Statecraft*, chap. 7; Blaufarb, *Counterinsurgency Era*, p. 76.

68. With regard to the 1960s, Krepinevich notes that "it was a case of the Army satisfying a requirement using the 'parts on hand' in such a way as to disrupt as little as possible the essence of the organization: the heavy (armor and mechanized) division." See Krepinevich, *Army and Vietnam*, p. 103. As will be illustrated, there is reason to believe a similar logic underlay the decision to delegate counterinsurgency to SOF in the 1980s.

69. McClintock, *Instruments of Statecraft*, chap. 7.

70. Ibid.

71. Weinberger, *Annual Report to Congress*, fiscal year 1988, pp. 293–296.

72. Holzworth, "Operation Eagle Claw."

73. For a more detailed account of the emerging SOF capabilities and units, see Thompson, ed., *Low Intensity Conflict*, pp. 10–15; McClintock, *Instruments of Statecraft*, chap. 16. A narrative of the resistance among the U.S. regular services to these changes can be found in Koch, "Objecting to Reality," pp. 51–75.

74. As cited in Nagl, *Learning to Eat Soup with a Knife*, p. 120. The process and decisions involved in shaping the ARVN like the U.S. Army are covered in some detail in Krepinevich, *Army and Vietnam*, pp. 21–26.

75. Maechling, "Counterinsurgency."

76. Blaufarb, *Counterinsurgency Era*, p. 86.

77. Bacevich et al., *American Military Policy*, p. 12.

78. For an overview of some of the specialized counterinsurgency units in El Salvador, see Jurado and Thomas, *Central American Wars*, pp. 13–16.

79. Manwaring and Prisk, *Strategic View*, p. 20; Ramsey, *Advising Indigenous Forces*, p. 103. To Richard Shultz a similar phenomenon occurred in the simultaneous U.S. advisory effort in the Philippines: "Weapons and training have not been tailored to meet the CPP/NPA [guerrilla] challenge. The Americanization of the AFP continues, with emphasis on technology and fire-power." See Shultz, "Low-Intensity Conflict," p. 362.

80. Downie, *Learning from Conflict*, p. 132. By 1987, this limit had through various means been exceeded by a factor of three. Additional advisers were also involved in the effort, but based outside El Salvador. The point remains, however, that the deployment was comparatively minimal and that the U.S. never officially partook in combat operations.

81. The adviser goes on to say: "Neither of these conditions existed for me and so during almost my entire tour, I was strictly an observer." See "After Action Report," as cited in Ramsey, *Advising Indigenous Forces*, p. 89.

82. Bacevich et al., *American Military Policy*, pp. 29–30.

83. Downie, *Learning from Conflict*, p. 152.

84. Ramsey, *Advising Indigenous Forces*, pp. 86–87.

85. Bacevich et al., *American Military Policy*, p. vii. See also Manwaring and Prisk, *Strategic View*.

86. Bacevich et al., *American Military Policy*, p. 37. See also Stringham, "Military Situation," pp. 148–151.

87. Ramsey, *Advising Indigenous Forces*, p. 87.

88. McClintock, *Instruments of Statecraft*. See also Blaufarb, *Counterinsurgency Era*, p. 79.

89. Richard Nixon, "Address to the Nation." This policy was later included in military doctrine: The 1972 edition of FM 100-20, *Internal Defense and Development*, states that an insurgency-threatened country should "assume primary responsibility for providing the manpower needed for its own defense . . . the U.S. role is to: assist countries to devise effective internal defense and development programs . . . to make unnecessary the future need for employment of U.S. combat troops." See Department of the Army, FM 100-20, *Internal Defense and Development* (1972), p. 4.1.

90. Blaufarb, *Counterinsurgency Era*, p. 80.

91. McClintock, *Instruments of Statecraft*.

92. Krepinevich, *Army and Vietnam*, pp. 36–37.

93. Shafer, *Deadly Paradigms*, p. 23.

94. Norman and Spore, "Big Push in Guerilla Warfare," p. 36.

95. Heymann and Whitson, *Can and Should?*, p. 37.

96. Norman and Spore, "Big Push in Guerilla Warfare," p. 36.

97. Blaufarb, *Counterinsurgency Era*, p. 288.

98. Downie, *Learning from Conflict*, p. 178. See pp. 178–180 for more evidence of this bias within the Army.

99. See DoD, *Restricted Engagement Options*. The point is also well illustrated in relation to Vietnam in Dunn, "American Army."

100. See Cole, "Grenada, Panama, Haiti," p. 58; Holzworth, "Operation Eagle Claw."

101. Robert H. Kupperman and Associates, *Low Intensity Conflict*.

102. Downie, *Learning from Conflict*, p. 77.

103. Mazarr, *Light Forces*, p. 12. Romjue, "Evolution of the AirLand," p. 26. Chief of Staff Gen. John A. Wickham Jr.'s 1984 *White Paper* on LIDs as quoted in Mazarr, *Light Forces*, p. 34.

104. Gorman, "Low Intensity Conflict," p. 21.

105. Terriff, "Innovate," pp. 484–489.

106. See esp. Lind, "Proposing Some New Models"; and Miller, "Winning through Maneuver."

107. See Terriff, "Innovate," pp. 495–497. "What Miller was proposing was that the concept of maneuver warfare furnished a way for the Marine Corps to improve its combat effectiveness while retaining its distinctive amphibious warfare role, and it could do so without having to become overburdened with 'heavy metal' and thereby being transformed into little more than a second army," p. 497.

108. Cassidy, "Prophets or Praetorians?," p. 131.

109. Weinberger, "Uses of Military Power."

110. Doughty, *Evolution of U.S. Army Tactical Doctrine.*

111. Blaufarb, *Counterinsurgency Era*, p. 81.

112. As cited in Jenkins, *Unchangeable War*, p. 3.

113. General Westmoreland's decision to launch conventional operations during the initial years of the Vietnam War can in many ways be justified. These operations forced Hanoi to disperse its troops and to refrain from main-force attacks. As Dale Andrade explains, the U.S. military's problem was partly that it failed to respond to the North Vietnamese change in strategy. See Andrade, "Westmoreland Was Right," pp. 145–181.

114. Cited in Ellsberg, *Papers on the War*, p. 234. Depuy served first as assistant chief of staff for operations to Westmoreland and later as the commander of the First Infantry Division.

115. Maechling, "Counterinsurgency," pp. 42–43. See also Dunn, "The American Army," pp. 85–92.

116. Maechling, "Counterinsurgency," pp. 46.

117. DSB, *2004 Summer Study*, p. 18. See Flanagan, *Battle for Panama*, p. 232, for a typical example of the type of adulation heaped upon the military in the aftermath of the Panamanian invasion.

118. Crowell, "Anatomy of *Just Cause*," p. 96.

119. See Taw, *Operation Just Cause*, pp. 26–29; von Hippel, *Democracy by Force*, p. 42; DSB, *2004 Summer Study*, pp. 14–15.

120. As quoted in Shultz, *In the Aftermath of War*, p. 16. See also Fishel, *Fog of Peace*.

121. Shultz, *In the Aftermath of War*, p. 3.

122. Defense Science Board, *2004 Summer Study, Supporting Papers*, p. 19.

123. Defense Science Board, *2004 Summer Study*, p. 20. Emphasis in original.

124. Blaufarb, *Counterinsurgency Era*, p. 86.

125. Downie, *Learning from Conflict*, p. 10.

CHAPTER 3

1. See DoD, *Directive 3000.05.*
2. See Department of the Army, *Peace Operations* (1994); JCS, *Joint Doctrine* (1995).
3. See JCS, *Joint Doctrine* (1995), p. I-2. See also Department of the Army, *Peace Operations* (1994), p. 7.
4. For a more detailed account of how this occurred, see Berdal, "Lessons Not Learned," pp. 59–62.
5. Bowden, *Black Hawk Down*, provides a blow-by-blow account of this episode.
6. MacFarlane, *Intervention in Contemporary World Politics*, p. 61. For an overview of some of the lessons learned from Somalia, see Allard, *Somalia Operations*. Despite the value of some of these lessons, they do not appear to have informed subsequent U.S. defense policy.
7. Cassidy, *Peacekeeping in the Abyss*, pp. 238–239. The PDD itself is classified.
8. Daalder, "Knowing When to Say No," p. 36. Daalder also provides a compelling account of how the peacekeeping experiences of the early 1990s informed the Clinton administration's stance on U.S. participation in such endeavors.
9. Fishel and Baumann, "Operation Uphold Democracy," p. 106. Typical of the risk-aversion was an event on September 20, 1994, when U.S. troops failed to intervene to stop the Armed Forces of Haiti (FAd'H) beating down on a civilian demonstration at the Port-au-Prince Harbor.
10. "Kevlar zone" was the name given by U.S. Special Forces to the Army-controlled area in Port-au-Prince. The Special Forces, out in the countryside, were operating under less restrictive force protection regulations. See Fishel and Baumann, "Operation Uphold Democracy," pp. 110, 120.
11. Mandelbaum, "Foreign Policy as Social Work," p. 25.
12. Fishel and Baumann, "Operation Uphold Democracy," pp. 145–146.
13. Traub, "Making Sense."
14. Clinton, "Statement by the President," March 24, 1999.
15. The notion of the "strategic luxury" of the 1990s is dealt with in more detail in Freedman, *Revolution in Strategic Affairs.*
16. The lack of training within the U.S. Army in skills relevant to peace operations is one of the many points brought out in Olson and Davis's analysis of the U.S. military in Bosnia. See Olsen and Davis, *Training U.S. Army Officers.*
17. Department of the Army, FM 100-5 (1993), *Operations*, pp. 1–4.
18. Ibid., pp. 1–5. See also Cassidy, *Peacekeeping in the Abyss*, p. 215.
19. For material advancing these arguments, see GAO, *Peace Operations: Heavy Use;* GAO, *Peace Operations: Effect;* as well as Rice, "Campaign 2000."
20. Gordon, "2000 Campaign."
21. The JCS produced futuristic policy papers with titles like "Joint Vision 2010" and "Joint Vision 2020," the Air Force went with "Air Force 2025," the Navy experimented with "network-centric warfare," and the Army sought to build "Force XXI" and even "the Army after Next." See Donnelly and Kagan, *Ground Truth*, pp. 7–8.

22. Owens, *Lifting the Fog*, p. 69. For a similar take, see Levite and Sherwood-Randall, "Case for Discriminate Force," pp. 81–98.

23. Jablonsky, "Army Transformation"; Owens, *Lifting the Fog*, p. 5.

24. The second Gore-Bush presidential debate of October 11, 2000, can be retrieved at Commission on Presidential Debates (www.debates.org).

25. Rice, "Campaign 2000," p. 54.

26. White House, "Period of Consequences," Address given at the Citadel, South Carolina, September 23, 2003.

27. Official Welcoming Ceremony to Secretary of Defense Rumsfeld, January 26, 2001.

28. Ucko, "U.S. Counterinsurgency," p. 7. See DoD, *Quadrennial Defense Review* (2001).

29. Weinberger, "Uses of Military Power," Remarks to the National Press Club, November 28, 1984.

30. Buley, *The New American Way of War.*

31. Powell, "U.S. Forces," p. 40. During his time as Chairman of the JCS, Colin Powell adapted and popularized the Weinberger doctrine into what others have since renamed the Powell doctrine.

32. Bush's support of the transformation agenda was clear in several addresses made during his election campaign and while in office. In a speech in May 2001, Bush, for example, announced his commitment to "building a future force that is defined less by size and more by mobility and swiftness, one that is easier to deploy and sustain, one that relies more heavily on stealth, precision weaponry and information technologies." See White House, "Remarks by the President at U.S. Naval Academy Commencement."

33. This schism is well documented in Gordon and Trainer, *Cobra II*, pp. 3–54. See Buley, *The New American Way of War*, for a compelling analysis of the historical interaction between these two camps and their respective visions for the U.S. military and its use of force.

34. DoD, *Transformation Planning Guidance* (2003).

35. References to counterinsurgency and similar types of operations are, for example, absent from some of the more influential works on transformation: Owens, *Lifting the Fog*; MacGregor, *Transformation under Fire*; and Alberts, *Information Age Transformation*. Berkowitz, *New Face of War*; Ullman and Wade, *Shock and Awe*, chap. 3; Alberts, Garstka, and Stein, *Network Centric Warfare*, pp. 7–8.

36. Kagan, *Finding the Target*, p. 265.

37. Krulak, "Operational Maneuver from the Sea," p. 79.

38. Terriff, "Of Romans and Dragons," p. 156; for more detail on this period of USMC innovation, see esp. pp. 148–150. See also Hoffman, "Complex Irregular Warfare," p. 404.

39. "During the first 16 months of his Administration, Bush sought and achieved a reduction of over 50% of U.S. forces in the Balkans." See Serafino, *Peacekeeping*, p. 3.

40. According to one of the many polls taken throughout the autumn of 2001, "90 percent of [Americans] supported bombing the Taliban and al-Qaeda"; see Hanson, *Autumn of War,* p. xvii. For similar statistics, see Americans and the World: Public Opinions, www.americans-world.org/digest/global_issues/terrorism/terrorism_milAct.cfm.

41. DoD, *Quadrennial Defense Review* (2001), p. 5.

42. Ibid., p. 21.

43. Ibid., p. 5. As Kagan puts it, while the QDR was "one of the first documents to state directly that the U.S. military must be capable of unseating an enemy government and occupying an enemy country . . . it did not consider the consequences of the policy of regime change that it openly accepted as a possible military mission." See Kagan, *Finding the Target,* pp. 285–286.

44. DoD, *Quadrennial Defense Review* (2001), p. 30.

45. Ibid.

46. Ibid., p. v.

47. Ibid.

48. Scarborough, *Rumsfeld's War,* p. 127.

49. Ucko, "U.S. Counterinsurgency," p. 7.

50. For a detailed analysis of the use of precision-guided munitions in urban operations, see Conetta, *Disappearing the Dead,* pp. 15–26. Of particular interest is the circular error probable (CEP)—the technical definition of what constitutes a precise or "smart" munition.

51. See Ucko, "U.S. Counterinsurgency," p. 8, for a lengthier discussion of the many incompatibilities separating the type of warfare anticipated through transformation and those faced in Iraq and Afghanistan.

52. DoD, "Rumsfeld and Myers Briefing on Enduring Freedom," October 7, 2001.

53. See "Go after Them and Destroy Them."

54. Ibid.

55. Ibid.

56. For a summary of the criticism leveled against the administration over the issue of Afghan stabilization, see Perito, *Where Is the Lone Ranger?,* pp. 293–295.

57. See Fallows, "Blind into Baghdad," p. 64; Roy, "Development and Political Legitimacy," p. 172; and Hersh, "Other War," p. 3.

58. Rumsfeld, "Special Briefing on the Unified Command Plan."

59. Rumsfeld, "Beyond Nation Building."

60. Ibid.

61. Graham, "Pentagon Plans."

62. White House, "President Speaks . . . to Citadel Cadets." The enthusiasm of what transformation could do in the global war on terror was such that the OFT felt compelled to remind its readers in one of its pamphlets that "defense transformation is not simply a response to global terrorism." See Office of Force Transformation, *Elements of Defense Transformation,* p. i.

63. See Department of the Army, FM 3-0, *Operations* (2001), chaps. 9–10.

64. Gordon and Trainer, *Cobra II*, pp. 3–54; Woodward, *Plan of Attack*, p. 80; Ricks, *Fiasco*, pp. 120–123.

65. The document listed sought-after capabilities, which focused on "effects-based, adaptive planning"; "defeating enemy threats using networked modular forces"; "defeat the most potent of enemy anti-access and area denial capabilities"; "unparalleled [C4ISR] capabilities"; "joint common relevant operational situational awareness of the battlespace, rapid and robust sensor-to-shooter targeting"; "combined arms forces armed with superior situational awareness"; and "precision engagement capabilities." DoD, *Transformation Planning Guidance*, p. 10.

66. Graham, "Pentagon Plans."

67. Spc. Jim Wagner, "Gardez Office Opening," *DefendAmerica.com*, February 4, 2003. The PRT were the end-product of various attempts to coordinate civilian and military efforts beyond Kabul. As Richard Stewart explains, "U.S. Army Civil Affairs (CA) personnel had arrived in the theater of operations in Afghanistan in late November 2001 to conduct surveys as part of Joint Special Operations Task Force Dagger. They were followed by a Combined Joint Civil Military Operations Task Force (CJMOTF) and reserve Civil Affairs personnel that created Coalition Humanitarian Liaison Cells (CHLCs) and Civil Affairs Teams-Afghanistan (CAT-As) throughout the country. After a renewed U.S. commitment to provide reconstruction aid, USAID and U.S. Central Command (USCENTCOM) devised and implemented a plan to provide interagency 'civil-military field teams,' initially called Joint Regional Teams, but renamed Provincial Reconstruction Teams at the request of interim President of Afghanistan Hamid Karzai." See Stewart, "CORDS and the Vietnam Experience."

68. See Rothstein, *Afghanistan and the Troubled Future*, pp. 115–117.

69. See Dodge, "Written Testimony of Dr. Toby Dodge," January 25, 2007.

70. These "key tasks" of post-conflict planning are listed in a slide of the U.S. Central Command's "Phase IV OPlan," a secret plan partially reproduced in Scarborough, *Rumsfeld's War*, p. 181.

71. CENTCOM PowerPoint Polo Step Planning Slides Briefed to White House and Rumsfeld in 2002, Obtained by National Security Archive through Freedom of Information Act.

72. As Lt. Col. John D. Nelson has argued, with one organization built for peace and the other for war, "neither organization planned for the transition." Nelson, "Swiftly Defeat the Efforts," p. 60.

73. Ricks, *Fiasco*, pp. 203–206. Indeed, the original mandate of the OHRA was to *plan*, not to execute, post-conflict humanitarian assistance operations.

74. See, e.g., Atkinson, *In the Company of Soldiers*, pp. 294–303, for an account of then Maj. Gen. David Petraeus's comparatively successful experience in Mosul in 2003.

75. See International Institute for Strategic Studies, *Strategic Survey 2003/4*, p. 45; and Packer, "Lessons of Tal Afar," p. 51.

76. "Secretary Rumsfeld Media Availability with Jay Garner," June 18, 2003. As T. X. Hammes noted in 2004: "The United States had not answered the key

question of 'Who are these anti-coalition forces?' To date, the administration has clung to the idea that they are only 'bitter-enders' or, more formally, former regime loyalists (FRLs). . . . Given that the resistance has continued despite the capture of Saddam and the death of his sons, the concept that it is only regime loyalists who are fighting the United States is becoming a bit absurd." Hammes, *The Sling and the Stone*, p. 177.

77. DoD, "DoD News Briefing—Secretary Rumsfeld and Gen. Myers," April 11, 2003.

78. Ibid.

CHAPTER 4

1. The lagging realization on the part of top DoD officials as to the nature of the insurgency in Iraq is clearly demonstrated in Packer, *Assassins' Gate*, pp. 300–305. Frederick W. Kagan also notes that "the process of preparing for future [conventional] threats continued and even gained emphasis despite the rapid emergence of chaos in Afghanistan and a major insurgency in Iraq." See Kagan, *Finding the Target*, p. 288.

2. Terms of Reference, in Defense Science Board, *Transition*, app. A.

3. Defense Science Board, *Transition*, pp. 1–26, chap. 7.

4. Ibid., pp. 48–49.

5. DoD, Strategic Planning Guidance 2006–11 (classified).

6. Tyson, "U.S. Tests New Tactics," November 9, 2004.

7. Cone, "Changing National Training Center." See also Tiron, "Real-World Missions"; Mueller, "Counterinsurgency Training."

8. Press Enterprise, "Taking Shock Out of Culture."

9. JFCOM, *Stability Operations JOC* (2004), p. 55.

10. Department of the Army, FMI 3-07-22, *Counterinsurgency Operations* (2004), p. 2-1.

11. Ibid., p. 2-13.

12. Army Strategic Policy Guidance, January 14, 2005, www.army.mil/references/APSG14Jan05.doc.

13. Commandant Gen. Mike Hagee, All Marine Message 018/05, April 18, 2005.

14. Commandant Gen. Mike Hagee, All Marine Message 008/03, January 28, 2003.

15. Department of the Army, *Counterinsurgency Operation* (2004), p. vii.

16. Ibid., p. 1-10.

17. Ibid., p. 3-2.

18. JFCOM, *Stability Operations JOC* (2004), p. iii.

19. This conflation is noted, but not explained, in a footnote to the introduction of the concept paper: "For brevity's sake, 'joint' in the context of this concept refers to a joint, multiagency, and multinational force and includes the integration and appropriate balance of conventional and special operations forces," JFCOM, *Stability Operations JOC* (2004), p. iii.

20. Ibid., p. v.

21. Ibid., p. 7.

22. International Institute for Strategic Studies, *Strategic Survey 2003/4*, p. 45; Packer, "Lessons of Tal Afar," p. 51.

23. Observation based on interviews and interaction with U.S. military service members, 2005–2007.

24. See Department of the Army, FM 3-0, *Operations* (2001), and Department of the Army, FM 3-07, *Stability Operations and Support Operations* (2003).

25. As Thomas A. Marks puts it, "I have been struck . . . by how little we learned even when we got systems in place to capture the lessons: we do take those lessons, we translate them into doctrine, and it doesn't take." Interview with Marks.

26. JCS, *National Military Strategy* (2004), p. 14.

27. Ibid., p. viii.

28. Ibid.

29. Interview with officer involved in writing the *National Military Strategy* (2004).

30. DoD, *National Defense Strategy* (2005), p. 3.

31. Ibid., p. 7.

32. Ibid., p. 9.

33. JCS, *Capstone Concept for Joint Operations* (2005), p. 9.

34. Ibid., p. 25.

35. Ibid., pp. 20–23.

36. Donnelly, "Mind the Gap."

37. DoD, *Defense Language Transformation Roadmap*, p. 3.

38. Ibid., p. 4.

39. Kipp et al., "Human Terrain System," p. 9.

40. Salmoni, "Advances in Pre-Deployment," p. 80. Mattis has since been promoted to full general.

41. See U.S. Marine Corps., *Center of Excellence Charter*, January 14, 2006, www.tecom.usmc.mil/caocl/Includes/CAOCL%20COE.pdf.

42. Agg, "Small Arms."

43. See Marine Corps Warfighting Laboratory, "Joint Urban Warrior 05 Fact Sheet," www.mcwl.usmc.mil/factsheets/JUW05.pdf, and, for the original elaboration of the Three-Block War concept, Krulak, "Strategic Corporal."

44. Salmoni, "Advances in Pre-Deployment," p. 80.

45. Correspondence with CAOCL employee, March 16, 2007. See also Max Boot, "Navigating the 'Human Terrain.'"

46. The aim of organizing crash language courses for deploying forces did not need to be met until September 2007, more than two years after the issuing of the roadmap. And, as Kaplan notes, "all of these tasks are simply to set up a management system for improving the military's language skills—not actually to begin improving the skills." See Kaplan, "How Many Government Agencies Does It Take?"

47. Terms of Reference, in DSB, *Institutionalizing Stability Operations within DoD,* app. A.
48. Defense Science Board, *Institutionalizing Stability Operations,* p. 3.
49. DoD, *Directive 3000.05,* p. 1.
50. Ibid., p. 2.
51. Ibid., p. 4.
52. Rice, "Iraq and U.S. Policy."
53. Ibid.
54. Krepinevich, "How to Win in Iraq," p. 89.
55. Ibid.
56. Packer, "Lessons of Tal Afar," p. 52.
57. White House, "President Discusses War on Terror," March 20, 2006.
58. Atkinson, *In the Company of Soldiers,* pp. 294–303.
59. Warner and Willbanks, "Preparing Field Grade Leaders," p. 108.
60. Ibid.
61. See Schoomaker, "Foreword," pp. ix–x.
62. Ricks, "U.S. Counterinsurgency Academy." See also Schmitt, "U.S. to Intensify Its Training."
63. Sepp, "Best Practices in Counterinsurgency." See in particular the principles for counterinsurgency warfare enumerated in the text, and the listing of successful and unsuccessful counterinsurgency strategies.
64. Chiarelli and Michaelis, "Winning the Peace," p. 7. Encompassing these five lines of operations were "full-spectrum information operations" designed to shape and communicate the message of the campaign to its various audiences.
65. See Department of the Army and USMC, FM 3-24/MCWP 3-33.5, *Counterinsurgency* (2006), p. 5-5, and OUSD(P), *Interim Progress Report on DoD Directive 3000.05,* p. 6.
66. McFate, "Iraq."
67. See McFate, "Anthropology and Counterinsurgency"; McFate and Jackson, "Organizational Solution."
68. Interview with Montgomery McFate.
69. Packer, "Knowing the Enemy," pp. 60–62.
70. Kilcullen, "Countering Global Insurgency."
71. Aylwin-Foster, "Changing the Army."
72. Ibid., p. 3.

CHAPTER 5

1. United States Code (2001), Title 10 (Armed Forces), p. 29, sec. 118 as amended through December 31, 2000.
2. Henry, "Defense Transformation," p. 5.
3. JCS, *Joint Vision 2010,* p. 1.
4. Ibid., p. 2.

5. See DoD, *Quadrennial Defense Review* (1997), sec. V. Kagan provides a compelling analysis of the 1997 QDR and of other contemporaneous policy papers. See Kagan, *Finding the Target*, pp. 227–253.

6. Kagan, *Finding the Target*, p. 286.

7. DoD, *Quadrennial Defense Review* (2006), p. 36.

8. Ibid., p. 42.

9. Ibid., p. 5.

10. Ibid., p. 77.

11. Ibid., p. 15.

12. Ibid., p. 79.

13. Ibid., p. 38.

14. Ibid.

15. Ibid.

16. Ibid., p. 43.

17. On this point, see, e.g., Malkasian, "Did the United States Need More Forces in Iraq?" pp. 78–104.

18. Flournoy, "Did the Pentagon Get the Quadrennial Review Right?" p. 75.

19. Ibid.

20. Office of the Undersecretary of Defense (Comptroller), *National Defense Budget Estimates for FY 2006*, p. 81.

21. Flournoy, "Did the Pentagon Get the Quadrennial Review Right?" p. 69.

22. The defense budget in FY06 was $441.8 billion of a total federal unified budget of $2,122.5 billion. See OUSD (Comptroller), *National Defense Budget Estimates for FY 2006*, pp. 10–11.

23. DoD, *Quadrennial Defense Review* (2006), p. 42.

24. The relevance of force-structure modularization to the Army's learning of counterinsurgency is examined in more detail in chapter 7.

25. For an instructive analysis of how modularization could be rethought to suit the demands of stability operations, see Watson, *Reshaping the Expeditionary Army*.

26. As presented in 2005 and 2006, the modularization concept included no significant organizational reworking that would be of particular relevance to counterinsurgency.

27. Indeed, a congressional report cited concern that FCS "will be a more efficient way to fight the kind of armored warfare at which U.S. forces already excel while offering no clear advantage in fighting the sort of counterinsurgency operations that may be a major focus of U.S. ground operations for some time to come." See Towell, Daggett, and Belasco, *Defense: FY2008*, p. 21.

28. DoD, *Quadrennial Defense Review* (2006), p. 42.

29. Roosevelt, "FCS."

30. Isenberg, *Budgeting for Empire*.

31. Davidson, "Air Force Tactical."

32. Boot, "Wrong Weapons."

33. Ibid. The QDR asked for increased production from one to two *Virginia* class submarines per year; each was expected to cost $2.4 billion.

34. "In 2003, FCS's anticipated cost to develop and field the first 15 (out of 42, possibly 48) army Units of Action (brigades) was 92 billion dollars. By 2005 GAO estimated the cost at approximately 108 billion dollars and by 2006 the Congressional Budget Office estimated the cost for the first 15 units to be nearly 165 billion dollars." See Reynolds, "Insurgency/Counterinsurgency'" p. 30.

35. Woodward, *State of Denial*, p. 432.

36. von Drehle, "Rumsfeld's Transformation."

37. DoD, *Quadrennial Defense Review* (2006), pp. 11, 4.

38. This point was picked up upon in a JFCOM special report on irregular warfare dated August 2006: "There is no doctrinal value to arbitrarily grouping activities that are loosely related. Unless there are underlying principles common to all activities, grouping them serves no purpose." See JFC, *Irregular Warfare*, p. III-2. Unsurprisingly, this analysis did not gain much traction within the DoD, which had already publicly embraced the irregular warfare concept.

39. In several policy papers, counterterrorism was framed as predominantly geared toward the hunting down and killing of terrorists abroad. See White House, *National Security Strategy of the United States of America* (2006); White House, *National Strategy for Combating Terrorism* (2006). For an alternative conceptualization of the War on Terror as a global counterinsurgency campaign, see Kilcullen, "Countering Global Insurgency."

40. JCS, JP 1–02, *Department of Defense Dictionary* (2001), p. 212.

41. DoD, *Quadrennial Defense Review* (2006), p. 20.

42. Ibid., p. 11.

43. Ibid., p. 2.

44. Ibid., p. 44. The U.S. military defines direct action as "short-duration strikes and other small-scale offensive actions conducted as a special operation in hostile, denied, or politically sensitive environments and which employ specialized military capabilities to seize, destroy, capture, exploit, recover, or damage designated targets." See JCS, *Dictionary* (2001), p. 158.

45. DoD, *Quadrennial Defense Review* (2006), pp. 44–45.

46. Tyson, "Pentagon Adds Initiatives."

47. The exact effect of the UCP was to make SOCOM the "lead combatant commander for planning, synchronizing, and as directed, executing global operations against terrorist networks in coordination with other combatant commanders." See testimony of Vice Admiral Olson before the Senate Armed Services Committee, Subcommittee on Emerging Threats and Capabilities, April 5, 2006.

48. de la Garza, "Special Ops' Expanding Role."

49. DoD, *Quadrennial Defense Review* (2006), p. 44.

50. Ibid., p. 12.

51. Ibid. For a less unambiguously positive account of the CJTF-HOA, see Lischer, "Winning Hearts and Minds."

52. DoD, *Quadrennial Defense Review* (2006), p. 12.

53. Kaplan, "Imperial Grunts," p. 86.

54. Donnelly and Kagan, *Ground Truth*, pp. 80–86.

55. See, e.g., Kaplan, "Imperial Grunts": "Iraq and Afghanistan are rare examples where restrictive rules of engagement do not apply. But in most other cases U.S. troops will be deployed to bolster democratic governments rather than to topple authoritarian ones. Therefore unconventional warfare in the Philippines provides a better guidepost for our military than direct action in Iraq and Afghanistan." For a variation on this argument, see Laird, "Iraq," pp. 28–29, and Dunlap, "America's Asymmetric Advantage," the latter of which advocates the use of precision-guided munitions rather than ground troops to conduct counterinsurgency.

56. See chapter 2.

57. DoD, *Quadrennial Defense Review* (2006), p. 23.

58. Interview with Richard Downie.

59. See Rothstein, *Afghanistan and the Troubled Future*. DoD defines unconventional warfare as "a broad spectrum of military and paramilitary operations, normally of long duration, predominantly conducted through, with, or by indigenous or surrogate forces who are organized, trained, equipped, supported, and directed in varying degrees by an external source." See JCS, *Dictionary* (2001), p. 560.

60. Statement of Max Boot before the House Armed Services Subcommittee on Terrorism, June 29, 2006.

61. Ibid. A similar worry is expressed by Mark Haselton, a retired Special Forces lieutenant colonel, in Naylor, "More Than Door-Kickers."

62. Rothstein, *Afghanistan and the Troubled Future*, p. 19.

63. Ibid., p. 18.

64. Collins, *Special Operations Forces*, p. 123.

65. Flournoy and Schultz, *Shaping U.S. Ground Forces*, p. 30.

66. Interview with Thomas A. Marks.

67. Rothstein, *Afghanistan and the Troubled Future*, p. xiii.

68. DoD, *Quadrennial Defense Review* (2006), pp. 3–4 (emphasis added).

69. Ibid., pp. 83–92.

70. This is also recognized in the QDR: "Although many U.S. Government organizations possess knowledge and skills needed to perform tasks critical to complex operations, they are often not chartered or resourced to maintain deployable capabilities." See DoD, *Quadrennial Defense Review* (2006), p. 86. It should be added that, technically, the foreign-service officers of the Department of State are "world-wide available" and can be directed to serve. However, with regard to the FSO, the larger problem concerns the lack of numbers—indeed it is frequently said that "more people play in Army bands than serve in the U.S. foreign service." Sewall, "Radical Field Manual," p. xxx. The exact figures have been contested, but the point remains.

71. Galula, *Counterinsurgency Warfare*, p. 88. See Cooling and Gropman, "Resourcing Stability Operations," for a historical perspective on the need for the military to accept civilian tasks during and following conventional conflict.

72. OUSD(P), *Interim Progress Report on DoD Directive 3000.05*, p. 2.

73. See U.S. Code of Federal Regulations, Title 32, vol. 2, sec. 368.6. I am grateful to Col. Michael S. Bell, U.S. Army, for having drawn my attention to this section of the CFR.

74. See "About S/CRS," U.S. Department of State, www.state.gov/s/crs /c12936.htm, May 18, 2006.

75. See U.S. Senate, "Foreign Affairs Authorization Act, Fiscal Years 2006 and 2007," U.S. Senate Report 109–035, 109th Cong., 1st sess., March 10, 2005, pp. 20–22.

76. Interview with Lt. Col. Richard A. Laquement.

77. Prepared statement of Principal Deputy Ryan Henry to the Committee on Foreign Relations, June 16, 2005.

78. Interview with Hans Binnendijk.

79. Nash and Knudsen, "Reform and Innovation," p. 7; Oleszycki, "Update on Department of State and Department of Defense."

80. Interview with Robert M. Perito.

81. Interview with Ambassador James Dobbins.

82. Interview with Robert M. Perito.

83. See Department of State, "State Department Stands Up."

84. This measure formed part of a wider initiative to use the incomparable DoD budget and resources to boost the starved S/CRS; along with the detailing of several members of its staff to S/CRS, DoD also organized joint conferences, training classes, advisory assistance and sponsored legislation to enable DoD to fund the S/CRS directly. Prepared statement of Principal Deputy Ryan Henry, June 16, 2005.

85. Incidentally, "the State Department didn't spend the money. Whether it was lack of personnel, interest or capacity, its inaction has further exacerbated the frustration among the military services which are then forced to assume ever more national security responsibilities." See Kelly, *Unbalanced Security*.

86. Interview with Col. T. X. Hammes (ret.).

87. Interviews with Dayton L. Maxwell and Col. Michael Bell. See also Metz, *Learning from Iraq*, p. 66, and Ekbladh, "From Consensus to Crisis," in Fukuyama, ed., *Nation-Building*. As Ekbladh notes at page 32: "the effects [of Vietnam] on USAID were immediate and dramatic: worldwide staff declined from a high of 18,030 in 1968 to just 8,489 in 1975."

88. Hegland, "Pentagon."

89. Indicative of this tendency were the bureaucratic maneuverings necessary for the creation of the Office of Military Affairs within USAID.

90. Interview with Hans Binnendijk.

91. Interview with former OSD official involved in the implementation of Directive 3000.05.

92. White House, "Management of Interagency Efforts," p. 1.

93. Ibid., p. 2.
94. Ibid.
95. DoD, *Quadrennial Defense Review* (2006), pp. 85–86.
96. Ibid., p. 38 (emphasis added).
97. OUSD(P), *Interim Progress Report on DoD Directive 3000.05*, p. 7.
98. DoD, *Quadrennial Defense Review* (2006), pp. 85–86.
99. OUSD(P), *Interim Progress Report on DoD Directive 3000.05*, p. 7.

CHAPTER 6

1. International Institute for Strategic Studies, "Iraq under the Surge," p. 1.
2. Interview with Stephen Biddle. See also Biddle, "Seeing Baghdad."
3. Interview with Lt. Col. John Nagl. See also Aylwin-Foster, "Changing the Army."
4. Interview with Lt. Col. John Nagl.
5. Presentation by Janine Davidson to National Defense University, March 14, 2007.
6. USMC, "Marine Corps Operating Concepts," p. 60.
7. Ibid., p. 61.
8. Ibid. In a similar vein, the concept paper also stated that "it is highly likely that Naval forces will either support other agencies in, or perhaps even be directly responsible for, the provision of essential services such as food, power, potable water, the handling of waste, and basic medical care," p. 66.
9. See Chiarelli and Michaelis, "Winning the Peace."
10. In the words of the Progress Report on DoD Directive 3000.05, "In Iraq, Major General Peter Chiarelli was among the first to identify the non-kinetic lines of operation critical to success." See OUSD(P), *Interim Progress Report on DoD Directive 3000.05*, p. 6.
11. U.S. Marine Corps, *Tentative Manual*. Around the same time, the USMC also released another quasi-doctrinal manual dealing with counterinsurgency: MCCDC, *Small-Unit Leaders' Guide.*
12. ———., *Tentative Manual*, p. 79.
13. Ibid., p. 80.
14. Ibid.
15. Ibid., p. 93.
16. Ibid., p. 99.
17. Ibid., pp. 94, 95, 101.
18. Ibid., p. 116.
19. Ibid., pp. 129–130.
20. JCS, JP 3-0, *Joint Operations* (2006), p. xxii (emphasis in original).
21. Ibid., p. IV-26.
22. Ibid., pp. iii–iv.
23. Ibid.

24. Hajjar, "Army's New TRADOC," pp. 89–92.

25. Hilburn, "Rethinking the Enemy," p. 26.

26. Association of the United States Army, *U.S. Army's Role*, p. 19.

27. Conference Report, "Counterinsurgency," September 28–29, 2006.

28. Interview with Donna L. Hopkins. Following the release of a draft version in October 2007, a final U.S. government counterinsurgency manual was published in January 2009. See Department of State, *U.S. Government Counterinsurgency Guide*.

29. Department of the Army and USMC, FM 3-24/MCWP 3-33.5, *Counterinsurgency* (2006).

30. Sewall, "Radical Field Manual," p. xxi.

31. See Department of the Army, FM 100-5, *Operations* (1993), p. 13–7; JCS, JP 3-07, *Joint Doctrine* (1995), p. III-9; Department of the Army, FM 3-07, *Stability Operations and Support Operations* (2003), p. 4-12.

32. Department of the Army and USMC, FM 3-24/MCWP 3-33.5, *Counterinsurgency* (2003), p. 1-20.

33. Ibid., p. 5-25.

34. Ibid., p. 1-19.

35. Ibid.

36. FM 3-24 stated, for example, that "soldiers and Marines should prepare to execute many nonmilitary missions to support COIN efforts"; that "everyone has a role in nation building, not just Department of State and civil affairs personnel"; that military forces "can and should use their capabilities to meet the local populace's fundamental needs" as well as conduct security operations; and that "military planning includes preparing to perform these services [provision of basic services and infrastructural development] for an extended period." Ibid., pp. 1–27; 2–1-2; 5–14.

37. Ibid., p. 2-9.

38. Ibid., p. 2-5.

39. Ibid., pp. 1-21 to 1-24.

40. Ibid., pp. 1-24 to 1-26.

41. Ibid., pp. 1-26 to 1-28.

42. Foreword by Lt. Gen. David H. Petraeus, U.S. Army, and Lt. Gen. James F. Amos, U.S. Marine Corps, to FM 3-24/MCWP 3-33.5 (2006).

43. A handful of defense analysts did criticize the manual for restating the 1960s' wisdom on counterinsurgency without integrating new challenges such as the role of media, of religiously inspired violence, and of globalization in general. Interview with Lt. Col. Frank G. Hoffman (ret.). See also Hoffman, "Small Wars Revisited"; Kilcullen, "Counter-insurgency. *Redux*"; Metz, *Rethinking Insurgency*.

44. Some units in the field were already employing the principles and methods described in FM 3-24, even before it was produced. However, the senior military command in Iraq persisted with an approach based on self-imposed con-

finement in forward operating bases and that often favored quick strikes and "clearing" operations over the indispensable "holding" and "building" phases.

45. Department of the Army and USMC, FM 3-24/MCWP 3-33.5, *Counterinsurgency* (2006), p. 1-29.

46. See White House, "Press Conference by the President," November 8, 2006; Ricks and Abramowitz, "Meek Departure."

47. At his nomination hearing, Gates repeatedly asserted that "all options are on the table in terms of how we address this problem in Iraq." Robert Gates, hearing before the Senate Armed Services Committee, December 5, 2006.

48. In January 2007, announcing the new strategy, Bush clearly articulated his administration's reasoning that "to step back now would force a collapse of the Iraqi government, tear the country apart, and result in mass killings on an unimaginable scale." See White House, "President's Address to the Nation," January 10, 2007. Elsewhere the consequences of withdrawing were cast as a threat to U.S. national security: "if we're not steadfast in our determination to help the Iraqi government succeed, we will be handing Iraq over to an enemy that would do us harm, the consequences of which—of leaving Iraq before the job is done, for example, would be grave for the American citizens." See DoD, "President Bush Meets with Senior U.S. Defense Officials," December 13, 2006.

49. "President Bush on Iraq, Elections and Immigration."

50. Ibid.

51. "The United States should significantly increase the number of U.S. military personnel, including combat troops, imbedded in and supporting Iraqi Army units. As these actions proceed, we could begin to move combat forces out of Iraq. The primary mission of U.S. forces in Iraq should evolve to one of supporting the Iraqi army, which would take over primary responsibility for combat operations." See Baker and Hamilton et al., *Iraq Study Group Report*, p. 48.

52. Basing himself on a "little-noted passage, buried on Page 73" of the ISG report that advocated a "short-term redeployment or surge of American combat forces to stabilize Baghdad," and on alleged splits within the ISG, Fred Kaplan makes the argument that Robert Gates did in fact favor an increase in the number of troops deployed to Iraq (Kaplan, "The Professional"). Even if this is the case, the prosurge quorum within the ISG failed to affect the report's main recommendations in any meaningful way. The surge alluded to on page 73 would also appear to be much more limited in time—a feint allowing for full withdrawal—than the strategy eventually put in place by General Petraeus. Indeed, in the summer of 2007, Gates seemed to hold very different expectations to Petraeus as to the duration of the surge, which the Secretary of Defense sought to have reevaluated just as it got under way. See Spiegel, "Gates."

53. DoD, "Defense Secretary Gates Announces Recommendations," January 5, 2007.

54. White House, "President's Address to the Nation," January 10, 2007.

55. The nonmilitary measures touched upon "legislation to share oil revenues among all Iraqis," increased funding for "reconstruction and infrastructure pro-

jects that will create new jobs," "provincial elections," a reform of the de-Baathification laws and a "fair process for considering amendments to Iraq's constitution." See White House, "President's Address to the Nation," January 10, 2007.

56. *Iraq Study Group Report*, p. 15.

57. White House, "President's Address to the Nation," January 10, 2007.

58. *Iraq Study Group Report*, p. 15.

59. Notable examples include the experiences of Dagger Brigade (2nd Brigade, 1st Infantry Division) in northwest Baghdad and that of 1st Brigade, 1st Armored Division, the Ready First Combat Team (RFTC) in al-Anbar province. See, respectively, Kagan, "ISW Interview with COL J.B. Burton"; and Smith and MacFarland, "Anbar Awakens."

60. Boot, "Can Petraeus Pull It Off?"

61. Petraeus, Opening Statement at Hearing on Nomination, Senate Armed Services Committee, January 23, 2007.

62. Ibid.

63. Department of the Army and USMC, FM 3-24/MCWP 3-33.5, *Counterinsurgency* (2006), p. 1-29.

64. See Press Conference with Maj. Gen. Joseph Fil Jr., Commanding General, Multinational Division, Baghdad and 1st Cavalry Division, February 16, 2007. The clear-build-hold, or what General Fil referred to as "clear, control, retain" approach, correlates with that set out in FM 3-24. See Department of the Army and USMC, FM 3-24/MCWP 3-33.5, *Counterinsurgency* (2006), pp. 5-18 to 5-19.

65. Both Mansoor and McMaster had sat on a CJCS-commissioned study on policy alternatives in Iraq, whose final report advocated a surge strategy similar to the one later adopted by President Bush. Ricks, "Officers with PhDs Advising War Effort."

CHAPTER 7

1. Wright and Tyson, "Joint Chiefs."

2. Vanden Brook, "Redeploy Troops."

3. "I met with every divisional commander, General Casey, the core commander, General Dempsey, we all talked together. And I said, in your professional opinion, if we were to bring in more American troops now, does it add considerably to our ability to achieve success in Iraq? And they all said no." Gen. John Abizaid, Hearing before the Senate Armed Services Committee, November 15, 2006.

4. See, e.g., Statement by Schoomaker before the Commission on National Guard and Reserves. See also Shanker, "Army Is Worried."

5. For an account of some of the problems facing the Army at this time, see Tilghman, "The Army's Other Crisis." See also Thompson, "Why Our Army."

6. "If you look at the front page of the *Washington Post* each day of the week the plus-up in ground forces was announced, you see several references to the

meeting between the President and the Chiefs, with leaks that they disagreed with the President. Then we have the meeting, where the President undoes four years of policy [regarding the size of the Army and Marine Corps] and gives the ground services $100 billion. Hard not to draw the conclusion." Interview and written correspondence with U.S. defense analyst, March 2007. See also Barnes, "How Bush Decided"; and Simon, "Price of the Surge," p. 59.

7. Department of the Army and USMC, FM 3-24/MCWP 3-33.5, *Counterinsurgency* (2006), p. 1-24.

8. Blanton, "FOX News Poll." Braiker, "Dirge for a 'Surge.'"

9. Department of the Army and USMC, FM 3-24/MCWP 3-33.5, *Counterinsurgency* (2006), p. 1-24.

10. H. Con. Res. 63, 110th Cong., 1st sess., February 16, 2007.

11. "Senate Passes Iraq Withdrawal Bill."

12. H. R. 2206, 110th Cong., 1st sess., May 8, 2007.

13. Ibid., pp. 12–13.

14. Ibid.

15. Gen. David Petraeus on "FOX News Sunday," June 17, 2007.

16. "Petraeus Cites Areas of Improvement."

17. Less charitable critics would also characterize him as sectarian, indecisive, incompetent, or corrupt.

18. "DoD News Briefing with Gen. Petraeus."

19. Raghavan and Brulliard, "April Toll."

20. "DoD Media Roundtable."

21. The yearly U.S. casualty figures had been in the lower 800s from 2004 to 2006 but jumped to 902 in 2007, despite a radical decrease in casualties in the later months of that year. See Iraq Coalition Casualties, icasualties.org/oif, for statistics on casualties in Iraq.

22. See "USA TODAY/Gallup Poll on Iraq."

23. Department of the Army and USMC, FM 3-24/MCWP 3-33.5, *Counterinsurgency* (2006), p. 1-24.

24. Ibid., p. 2-3.

25. Ibid., pp. 1-22, 5-1. Krepinevich, "'New' Counterinsurgency Doctrine."

26. Hearing at U.S. Senate Armed Services Committee to consider nomination of Lt. Gen. David H. Petraeus to be General and Commander, Multi-National Forces-Iraq, January 23, 2007. Transcript: armed-services.senate.gov/statemnt /2007/January/Petraeus%2001-23-07.pdf. See Department of the Army and USMC, FM 3-24/MCWP 3-33.5, *Counterinsurgency* (2006), p. 1-13, for FM 3-24's proposed troop ratios.

27. Department of the Army and USMC, FM 3-24/MCWP 3-33.5, *Counterinsurgency* (2006), p. 6-19.

28. Ibid., pp. 5-5, 5-10.

29. International Institute for Strategic Studies, "Iraq under the Surge," p. 1. This was one finding of the UN Secretary-General Ban Ki-moon in his June 2007

report on Iraq to the Security Council. See United Nations, "Report of the Sec-retary-General," June 5, 2007.

30. This section draws heavily on Ucko, "Militias, Tribes and Insurgents," and Ucko, "Upcoming Iraqi Elections."

31. McCaffrey, "After Action Report," p. 5.

32. Boot, "Can Petraeus Pull It Off?" An article published by the IISS was simi-larly positive about the surge: "Initial indications suggested that it had a sig-nificant effect on the levels of violence in Baghdad. Economic activity increased as people felt able to return to work. There was limited evidence that small numbers of people displaced by sectarian violence had returned to their homes"; see International Institute for Strategic Studies, "Iraq," p. 1.

33. Boot, "Can Petraeus Pull It Off?"

34. See Iraq Coalition Casualties, icasualties.org/oif, for statistics on casualties in Iraq.

35. O'Hanlon and Campbell, *Iraq Index Tracking Variables*, pp. 4–5.

36. MNF-I, "Charts to Accompany Testimony of Gen. David H. Petraeus," slide 2.

37. Ibid., slide 7.

38. See International Crisis Group, *Iraq after the Surge I*, pp. 12–19. See also Kil-cullen, "Anatomy of a Tribal Revolt."

39. As the ICG put it, "The surge in some cases benefited from, in others en-couraged, and in the remainder produced, a series of politico-military shifts affecting the Sunni and Shiite communities." See International Crisis Group, *Iraq after the Surge I*, p. i.

40. Ricks, "Situation Called Dire." See also Smith and MacFarland, "Anbar Awak-ens."

41. Correspondence with senior officer, RFTC, March 2008.

42. Interview with Col. J. B. Burton, commander of Dagger Brigade, Washington, DC, March 2008.

43. Kagan, "ISW Interview with COL J.B. Burton."

44. The value of this approach is highlighted when one compares the success of the RFCT with previous efforts by the U.S. military to support the tribes using air-strikes alone, such as its support of the Albu Mahal tribe in August 2005. See Long, "Anbar Awakening," pp. 78–79.

45. Kagan, "ISW Interview with COL J.B. Burton."

46. Smith and MacFarland, "Anbar Awakens," p. 44; Long, "Anbar Awakening," p. 80.

47. International Institute for Strategic Studies, "Iraq," pp. 1–2.

48. Ibid., p. 1.

49. Boot, "Can Petraeus Pull It Off?"

50. As one commander, interviewed by the ICG, explained, "Improvement in se-curity happened because increased forces allowed our division to focus on smaller areas so we could come in and stay. . . . We came, we secured the area and we stayed, thus projecting a sense of security. . . . We had a very hard fight in September as we arrived. Al-Qaeda launched several vicious counteroffen-sives, but these attacks proved unsuccessful. We'd still be around, shops would

reopen the next day, and the city would continue to thrive." See International Crisis Group, *Iraq after the Surge I*, p. 7.

51. By March 2008 nearly 80,000 forces were on the U.S. payroll. See Dehghan-pisheh and Thomas, "Scions of the Surge."

52. For more detail on the workings of the Sons of Iraq units, see Dale, *Operation Iraqi Freedom*, pp. 86–91.

53. International Crisis Group, *Iraq after the Surge I*, p. 13.

54. The renegade Mahdi Army units would clear neighborhoods of their Sunni population, take control of their common resources, seize and/or sell individual property and possessions, and engage in kidnapping to extort ransoms. See International Crisis Group, *Iraq's Civil War*, pp. 6–10. See also Dehghan-pisheh, "Great Moqtada Makeover."

55. International Crisis Group, *Iraq's Civil War*, p. 8.

56. Ibid., p. i.

57. Nordland, "Radical Cleric."

58. Dehghanpisheh, "Great Moqtada Makeover."

59. See Nordland, "Radical Cleric"; Dehghanpisheh, "Great Moqtada Makeover."

60. Petraeus, as cited in Haynes, "Transcript of *The Times* interview with David Petraeus."

61. Dehghanpisheh, "Great Moqtada Makeover." See also Paley, "U.S. Deploys."

62. Senanayake, "Iraq."

63. See the late August 2008 interview with General Petraeus in Rod Nordland, "Avoiding the V Word," *Newsweek*, September 1, 2008.

64. The problem was not merely one of Baghdad intransigence: while seeking the legitimacy of national service, some tribal elements resisted foreswearing the benefits of their isolation, which ranged from control over local jobs and business opportunities to the significant pay-off provided through the extra-governmental deals made with the U.S. military. See Westervelt, "Iraqi Tribal Leaders." See also Simon, "Price of the Surge," p. 65.

65. International Crisis Group, *Iraq's Civil War*, p. 19.

66. See International Crisis Group, *Iraq after the Surge I*, p. i.

67. Ibid.

68. Gates's earlier position is reflected in Barnes and Spiegel, "Gates May Not Be Following"; Sanger, "In White House." Gates also told the Senate in January 2007 that the surge would most likely last "a matter of months, not 18 months or two years." See Pleming and Mohammed, "Bush Team Grilled." In contrast, Gates told the audience at a press conference in 2008 that "I'll leave it to General Petraeus to make recommendations in terms of what the sequencing and the timing would be." See DoD, "DoD News Briefing with Secretary of Defense Robert Gates and Adm. Mullen," July 31, 2008. For the Bush quotation, see White House, "President Bush Discusses Iraq," April 10, 2008.

69. See Petraeus, "Report to Congress on the Situation in Iraq," September 10–11, 2007. See also Cloud and Shanker, "Petraeus Warns."

70. Tyson, "Petraeus Helping Pick New Generals."

71. Kaplan, "Petraeus Wins"; Arkin, "Petraeus Wins in Iraq Battle"; Shanker, "Mideast Commander Retires."

72. As cited in Miles, "Petraeus-Odierno Team Nominated."

73. See Chiarelli and Michaelis, "Winning the Peace."

74. Department of the Army, *Army Action Plan for Stability Operations*, p. 4.

75. Ibid., p. 5.

76. While guidelines for FID already existed, other types of irregular operations had received scant attention in USAF doctrine. Haendschke, "Adding Less-Lethal Arrows to the Quiver."

77. Harrison, "Doctrine Center."

78. Bergquist, "Air University Hosts Counterinsurgency Symposium."

79. For a more thorough account of possible and extant USAF contributions to irregular warfare, see Peck, "Airpower's Crucial Role."

80. Department of the Air Force, Air Force Doctrine Document 2–3, *Irregular Warfare* (2007), pp. 3, 10, and 48.

81. Dunlap, "Making Revolutionary Change," p. 60.

82. DoD, *Quadrennial Defense Review* (2006), p. 11.

83. DoD, *Irregular Warfare Joint Operations Concept* (2007), p. 1.

84. "The current edition describes stability operations as tactical tasks applicable at all echelons of Army forces deployed outside the United States." Department of the Army, FM 3-0, *Operations* (2008), p. viii.

85. Ibid., pp. 1–4, viii.

86. Ibid., pp. viii, chap. 3.

87. See Kaplan, "The Professional." The article was eventually published in *Military Review*. See Chiarelli with Smith, "Learning from Our Modern Wars."

88. Gates, "Secretary Gates Addresses the Marine Corps Association," July 18, 2007.

89. Gates, Remarks at the AUSA, October 10, 2007.

90. Kaplan, "Secretary Gates Declares War."

91. Gates, "Landon Lecture," November 26, 2007.

92. MacGregor, "Reforming the Army and Marine Corps."

93. As cited in Malenic, "Hard Skills Going Soft." The comment is ironic in that it acknowledged the "long" duration of the irregular campaign against terrorism and insurgency but nonetheless insists that the ability to conduct major combat operations remain the "core" capability of the U.S. military.

94. "Army Prepares to Keep Troop Levels Steady."

95. Malenic, "Hard Skills Going Soft."

96. Munoz, "JFCOM Chief."

97. As quoted in Raz, "Army Focus." See also Lt. Col. Gian P. Gentile, "Our COIN Doctrine."

98. Conway, "Commandant's Planning Guidance," p. 3 (emphasis in original).

99. Conway, "Remarks by General James T. Conway," October 16, 2007.

100. Gates, Remarks to the Heritage Foundation, May 13, 2008.

101. Ibid.
102. Interview with senior OUSD(P) staff, Department of Defense, Arlington, VA, April 2007.
103. Sherman, "New Blueprint." The Irregular Warfare Roadmap is classified.
104. Ibid.
105. Interview with Thomas Mahnken.
106. This process grew out of the QDR, which in one sentence asserted that "to defeat terrorist networks . . . multipurpose Army and Marine Corps ground forces will increase their capabilities and capacity to conduct irregular warfare missions." See DoD, *Quadrennial Defense Review* (2006), p. 5.
107. Mancuso, "Irregular Warfare Roadmap."
108. Statement by Brig. Gen. Otis G. Mannon (USAF), Deputy Director, Special Operations, J-3 Joint Staff, before the Committee on Armed Services Subcommittee on Terrorism, Unconventional Threats, and Capabilities, U.S. House of Representatives, September 27, 2006.
109. Mancuso, "Irregular Warfare Roadmap." See also statement by Mannon.
110. Mancuso, "Irregular Warfare Roadmap."
111. See OUSD(P), *Interim Progress Report on DoD Directive 3000.05*, p. 5.
112. Of course, the proponents of the indirect approach also struggled, much like the COIN community, to shift the entrenched interests and priorities of DoD. This resistance to change led Deputy Defense Secretary Gordon England to issue a memorandum to the armed services, the CJCS, and combatant commands emphasizing the many "'shortfalls' in doctrine, training and institutions" that had to be fixed "before general-purpose forces can train, equip and advise large numbers of foreign security forces in key irregular warfare missions." See Castelli, "Pentagon Must Fix 'Shortfalls.'"

CHAPTER 8

1. This section draws in part on Ucko, "Innovation or Inertia."
2. OUSD(P), *Interim Progress Report on DoD Directive 3000.05*, p. 12.
3. Ibid.
4. Ibid.
5. Ibid., pp. 14–15.
6. Ibid., p. 5.
7. Government Accountability Office, *Stabilization and Reconstruction*, p. 10.
8. Ibid., p. 15.
9. Ibid., pp. 10, 15.
10. Ibid., p. 10.
11. Cuomo, "Will We Be Prepared for What's Next?"
12. Kaplan, "Challenging the Generals."
13. Burke, "Sorry," p. 1.
14. Reynolds, "Insurgency/Counterinsurgency," p. 7.

15. Ibid., pp. 7–8.

16. Correspondence with Col. Kevin Reynolds (ret.), U.S. Army, July 25, 2008.

17. Reynolds, "Insurgency/Counterinsurgency," p. 9.

18. See Cuomo, "Will We Be Prepared for What's Next?"

19. OUSD(P), *Interim Progress Report on DoD Directive 3000.05*, p. 14.

20. Within one year into the Korean War, and within three years of the Vietnam War, 86 to 90 percent of total funding was to be found in the regular annual budget. See Kosiak, "Cost and Funding."

21. As Lt. Gen. Peter W. Chiarelli and Maj. Stephen M. Smith argue, "one of the causes of our industrial inertia was a series of incorrect assumptions about how long U.S. forces would be committed in Iraq. In the early years of the war, civilian and military leaders repeatedly assumed that force levels would steadily decrease over time, and they made many resourcing decisions accordingly." See Chiarelli with Smith, "Learning from Our Modern Wars," p. 4.

22. Capaccio, "Bush Seeks Big Boost."

23. Kosiak, *FY 2008 Defense Budget Request*, p. 20.

24. DoD, *Fiscal Year 2009 Budget Request*, pp. 18, 153.

25. Towell, Daggett, and Amy, *Defense: FY2008*, p. 13.

26. Ibid., p. 16.

27. Ibid.

28. Miles, "Gates Asks Congress"; Osborn, "Gates Urges Ramping Up."

29. See Krepinevich and Wood, *Of IEDs and MRAPs*, p. 53. The study offers an in-depth look at the MRAP and the merits of a surged production of these vehicles to counter IEDs in Iraq.

30. Conway, "Remarks by General James T. Conway," October 16, 2007.

31. Ibid.

32. Gayl, *Mine Resistant Ambush Protected Vehicles*, pp. vii–viii.

33. See DoD, "DoD News Briefing with Secretary Gates and Under Secretary Jonas," February 5, 2007. See also de Rugy, "Today's Bipartisan Issue."

34. Towell, Daggett, and Belasco, *Defense: FY2008*, p. 15.

35. Fabey, "JSFs."

36. Karp, "Pentagon Redefines 'Emergency.'"

37. Towell, Daggett, and Belasco, *Defense: FY2008*, p. 14.

38. Kosiak, *FY 2009 Defense Budget Request*, pp. 3–4.

39. Towell, Daggett, and Belasco, *Defense: FY2008*, p. 2.

40. Jaffe, "Despite $168B Budget."

41. Reynolds, "Insurgency/Counterinsurgency," pp. 26–27.

42. Kosiak, *FY 2008 Defense Budget Request*, p. 9.

43. Department of the Army, *2007 Army Posture Statement*, p. 3.

44. In FY08, the Army, Air Force, and Navy were allocated $128,564 million, $136,561 million, and $139,810 million, respectively. In FY09, the figures were $140.7 million, $143.9 million, and $149.3 million. See Office of the Undersecretary of Defense (Comptroller), *National Defense Budget Estimates*

for FY 2008, p. 79; Department of Defense, *Fiscal Year 2009 Budget Request*, p. 19.

45. Kaplan, "What's Really in the U.S. Military Budget?"
46. Kagan, *Finding the Target*, p. 386.
47. Putrich, "U.S. House Panel."
48. Ibid.
49. Towell, Daggett, and Belasco, *Defense: FY2008*, p. 29. See also Hodge and Harrington, "FCS Project."
50. Towell and Daggett, *Defense: FY2009 Authorization and Appropriations*, pp. 1–2.
51. Jaffe, "Despite $168B Budget."
52. Hoffman, "Complex Irregular Warfare," p. 404.
53. DoD, *Fiscal Year 2009 Budget Request*, pp. 164–165, 187; Boot, "Corps Should Look to Its Small-Wars Past."
54. See Transcript, "Future of the United States Marine Corps," conference held at the American Enterprise Institute, Washington, DC, August 18, 2005.
55. Kosiak, *FY 2008 Defense Budget Request*, p. 28.
56. DoD, *Fiscal Year 2009 Budget Request*, p. 165.
57. Terriff, "Of Romans and Dragons," p. 151.
58. Boot, "Corps Should Look to Its Small-Wars Past."
59. "If you discount smaller operations that took place against little or no opposition in the Dominican Republic (1965) and Grenada (1983), you really have to go back to the 1950 landing at Inchon for a full-scale amphibious assault against a defended shoreline," Boot, "Corps Should Look to Its Small-Wars Past." Elsewhere, Boot argues that "the costs [of amphibious operations] are simply too high and given the capabilities of our air power, the needs are not likely to be as pressing. I suspect it will be judged more expedient to secure a contested shoreline with aerial assault so that Marines will not have to swim ashore under fire and suffer the devastating casualties of wars past." See statements made by Max Boot, "Future of the United States Marine Corps," proceedings of conference held at the American Enterprise Institute, Washington, DC, August 18, 2005.
60. Gates, Remarks at the AUSA, October 10, 2007.
61. Gates, Remarks to the Heritage Foundation, May 13, 2008.
62. Scully, "Changes to Army's Modernization Program."
63. DoD, "DoD News Briefing with Secretary of Defense Robert Gates and Adm. Mullen," July 31, 2008.
64. JCS, *Dictionary* (2001 update), p. 338.
65. Graham, "Pentagon Considers."
66. Telephone interview with Hans Binnendijk. See Binnendijk and Johnson, eds., *Transforming for Stabilization*, for his proposal for specialized stability and reconstruction forces. Ralph Peters provides a summation of the arguments against such forces: "Apart from the impossibility of recruiting international garbage collectors, the argument [for a bifurcated force] founders on cost

analysis (it would not, in fact, be cheaper), inevitable jealousies, and the damage that consequent reductions in the number of combat units would do to our forces." See Peters, "Heavy Peace."

67. Telephone interview with Maj. Gen. David Fastabend.

68. DoD, *Quadrennial Defense Review* (2006), pp. 42–43.

69. Association of the United States Army, *U.S. Army*, p. 4. For the anticipated benefits of modularization, see U.S. Dept. of Army, TRADOC, *Army Comprehensive Guide to Modularity*, pp. 1–6, 1–15; and Feickert, *U.S. Army's Modular Redesign*, p. 2.

70. U.S. Dept. of Army, TRADOC, *Army Comprehensive Guide to Modularity*, p. 1-6.

71. DoD, *Quadrennial Defense Review* (2006), p. 42.

72. Ibid.

73. AUSA, *U.S. Army's Role*, p. 15.

74. DoD Strategic Planning Guidance 2006–11 (classified).

75. See MacGregor, *Breaking the Phalanx*, and Feickert, *U.S. Army's Modular Redesign*, pp. 3–4.

76. Defense Science Board, *Transition to and from Hostilities, DSB 2004 Summer Study*, pp. 48–49.

77. IDA Working Paper, "Army QDR Issue," cited in Feickert, *U.S. Army's Modular Redesign*, p. 3.

78. Grossman, "Study Finds Army Transformation."

79. Ibid.

80. See Feickert, *U.S. Army's Modular Redesign*, p. 4, for an elucidation of the Army's critique of the IDA study.

81. The Army Strategic Planning Guidance of 2005 states that the Army will "resource up to 48 Active Component BCT." See "Army Strategic Planning Guidance 2005," p. 9. For the QDR reference, see DoD, *Quadrennial Defense Review* (2006), p. 43.

82. Jaffe and Karp, "Pentagon Girds." See Feickert, *U.S. Army's Modular Redesign*, p. 11.

83. Feickert, *U.S. Army's Modular Redesign*, p. 11.

84. Observation based on personal attendance at U.S. Army presentations on modularization and BCTs, 2003–2007.

85. Telephone interview with Hans Binnendijk.

86. Interview with senior Army officer working on stability operations, 2006.

87. Watson, *Reshaping the Expeditionary Army*, pp. 12–13.

88. Ibid., pp. 1, 12.

89. Feickert, *U.S. Army's Modular Redesign*, p. 6.

90. See Department of the Army, FM 100-5, *Operations* (1993), pp. 1–4.

91. For more information on the Abrams doctrine, see Carafano, "Army Reserves."

92. Feickert, *U.S. Army's Modular Redesign*, p. 19.

93. Flournoy and Schultz, *Shaping U.S. Ground Forces*, p. 25.

94. Serafino, *Peacekeeping and Related Stability Operations,* p. 11.

95. Ibid.

96. Flournoy and Schultz, *Shaping U.S. Ground Forces,* p. 20. A similar argument was made in Binnendijk, Gompert, and Kugler, "New Military Framework," p. 10.

97. See O'Hanlon, "Need to Increase"; Boot, "Struggle to Transform the Military." See also Landay, "Congress, Rumsfeld at Odds."

98. DoD, "Defense Department Operational Briefing: Rumsfeld," January 13, 2004.

99. Ibid.

100. Office of Management and Budget, Executive Office of the President, "Statement of Administration Policy," June 14, 2006.

101. DoD, "Defense Department Operational Briefing: Rumsfeld."

102. "President Bush on Iraq, Elections, and Immigration."

103. Lawrence, *Seven Pillars of Wisdom,* p. 132.

104. Harvey, "Building the Future Force," p. 19.

105. Krulak, "Strategic Corporal."

106. Kosiak, *FY 2008 Defense Budget Request,* p. 15.

107. "A 'high quality' recruit is defined by the DoD as one with a regular high school diploma AND who scores in the 50th percentile or greater on the Armed Forces Qualification Test (AFQT)." See National Priorities Project, *Military Recruitment 2006,* December 200622; www.nationalpriorities.org/index.php?option=com_contentandtask=viewandid=263andItemid=61.

108. Krepinevich, "Future of U.S. Ground Forces," p. 2.

109. Ibid.

110. For some of the challenges facing the Marine Corps, see Megan Scully, "Conway."

111. Kosiak, *FY 2008 Defense Budget Request,* p. 18.

112. Flournoy and Schultz, *Shaping U.S. Ground Forces,* pp. 25–26.

113. Ibid.

114. This is one of the central points brought out in Krepinevich, "Future of U.S. Ground Forces," p. 5.

115. Flournoy and Schultz, *Shaping U.S. Ground Forces,* pp. 25–26. See also "DoD News Briefing with Under Secretary of Defense David Chu [and others]," January 19, 2007.

116. Flournoy and Schultz, *Shaping U.S. Ground Forces,* p. 28.

117. Cuomo, "Will We Be Prepared for What's Next?"

118. Flournoy and Schultz, *Shaping U.S. Ground Forces,* p. 31.

119. See Hoffman, "Strategic Rationale."

120. Hoffman, "Troop Level Increases."

121. Ibid.

122. Interview with Andrew F. Krepinevich.

123. Personal recollection from event. For more details on Nagl's proposal, see Nagl, *Institutionalizing Adaptation.*

124. See "Army Opposes Permanent Adviser Corps." Flournoy and Schultz, *Shaping U.S. Ground Forces,* p. 31. The authors specify that "the Marines argue that this advisory role can be picked up by the Corps's Security Cooperation Education and Training Center (SCETC)," but add that "training and advising foreign forces are not necessarily interchangeable skills" (p. 31).

125. Interview with Col. Michael Bell. In a briefing on "The 'New' Counterinsurgency Doctrine and the Baghdad Surge," Krepinevich also notes that there is "little incentive for officers and NCOs to serve with HN [host-nation] forces" and that "commanders [are] reluctant to give up their 'star' players to the advisory effort"; see www.csbaonline.org/4Publications/PubLibrary/S.20070228.New_Counterinsurge/S.20070228.New_Counterinsurge.pdf. There were signs in mid-2008 that this was changing, at least for those soldiers operating in transition teams. See Cavallaro, "War Zone Training."

126. House Armed Services Committee, *Agency Stovepipes,* pp. 13–14.

127. Joint Cable 4045, as cited in armedservices.house.gov/pdfs/OI090507/Cruz%20_Testimony090507.pdf.

128. See HASC, *Agency Stovepipes,* p. 15, for more details.

129. Petraeus, "Multi-National Force—Iraq Counterinsurgency Guidance," released in June 2007 as unclassified guidance to be circulated to MNF-I for counterinsurgency operations in Iraq.

130. See HASC, *Agency Stovepipes,* p. 16.

131. Stewart, "CORDS and the Vietnam Experience," p. 131.

132. Testimony of Ginger Cruz, "Role of the Department of Defense."

133. Stewart, "CORDS and the Vietnam Experience," p. 130: "There is no unified concept or guidance on how to measure success, with only the broadest sense of color codes (Red, Green, Amber) assigned locally to indicate degree of progress with no agreed upon criteria or data for what those colors mean."

134. See HASC, *Agency Stovepipes,* p. 28.

135. Office of the Special Inspector General for Iraq Reconstruction, *Status of the Provincial Reconstruction Team Program in Iraq.*

136. Testimony of Ginger Cruz.

137. This point gains further salience when considering the fact that, no matter the levels of staffing, a PRT will necessarily have a much lesser capacity to conduct stability operations than the military's BCTs, whose manpower, resources, equipment, and deployability render it a much more effective actor on the ground.

138. See, e.g., Rohde, "Army Enlists Anthropology"; Mulrine, "Culture Warriors."

139. Kipp et al., "Human Terrain System," p. 12.

140. For some of these arguments, see Stanton, "US Army Human Terrain System," and Stanton, "US Army's Human Terrain System."

CONCLUSION

1. This chapter draws in part on Ucko, "Innovation or Inertia."

2. Interview with Lt. Col. John Nagl.

3. This trend is even growing within the Marine Corps, which has throughout history been less interested in pursuing sophisticated and high-cost weapons platforms. By 2008, its most "transformational" programs—"the new ships, the V-22, a host of upgrades to conventional helicopters, and a kind of tank that swims" [the EFV]—came to a combined $100 billion, a total that did not include the USMC's share in the F-35. That bill was "close to the $129 billion estimate for the Army Future Combat System and well above the cost of the media's favorite poster child for overpriced weapons systems, the $63 billion F-22 Raptor fighter jet." See Freedberg, "Marine Corps."

4. Kiszely, *Post-Modern Challenges*, p. 8.

5. Ibid.

6. Howard, "Long War?" p. 14.

7. Some of the early proponents of this view include Maj. Gen. Charles J. Dunlap, the deputy judge advocate general of the U.S. Air Force, who has written a number of articles arguing against the logic of FM 3-24 and of the boots-on-the-ground zealots (BOTGZ; pronounced BOW-togs). See Dunlap, "America's Asymmetric Advantage." Edward N. Luttwak provides another critique of counterinsurgency theory as defunct, arguing that the prescriptions of FM 3-24 "are in the end of little use or none." To Luttwak, "the easy and reliable way of defeating all insurgencies everywhere" involves, instead, a willingness to "out-terrorize the insurgents"—the "necessary and sufficient condition of a tranquil occupation." See Luttwak, "Dead End." For a convincing critique of Luttwak's argument, see "Edward Luttwak's 'Counterinsurgency Malpractice,'" by Kilcullen and "Luttwak's Lament," by Hoffman.

8. Record, "American Way of War," p. 17.

9. Dobbins, "Who Lost Iraq?" p. 64.

10. Bumiller, "At an Army School for Officers."

11. Shinseki's statement, in full, reads as follows: "I would say that what's been mobilized to this point—something on the order of several hundred thousand soldiers are probably, you know, a figure that would be required. We're talking about post-hostilities control over a piece of geography that's fairly significant, with the kinds of ethnic tensions that could lead to other problems. And so it takes a significant ground-force presence to maintain a safe and secure environment, to ensure that people are fed, that water is distributed, all the normal responsibilities that go along with administering a situation like this." See "Hearing of the Senate Armed Services Committee," February 25, 2003.

12. See Kagan, *Finding the Target*; Hoffman, "Complex Irregular Warfare," pp. 404–405.

13. Gates, "Report to Congress," p. i.

14. Interview with Col. T. X. Hammes (ret.).

15. See U.S. Code of Federal Regulations, Title 32, vol. 2, sec. 368.6.

16. Fred Kaplan noted in August 2007 that "of the 127 captains taking the five-week [Captains Career] course, 119 had served one or two tours of duty in Iraq or Afghanistan, mainly as lieutenants. Nearly all would soon be going back as company commander." See Kaplan, "Challenging the Generals."

17. This was one of the central findings of an OSD-sponsored study of the UK approach to low-intensity conflicts, to which this author was a contributor. See Eaton et al., *British Approach to Low-Intensity Operations.*

18. Interview with Richard Downie. Lt. Col. Paul Yingling makes a similar point in an influential article on the failure of the general officer corps to adapt. "It is unreasonable to expect," he writes, "that an officer who spends 25 years conforming to institutional expectations will emerge as an innovator in his late forties." See Yingling, "Failure in Generalship."

19. Kaplan, "Challenging the Generals."

20. Kosiak, *FY 2009 Defense Budget Request*, p. 22.

21. Office of Management and Budget, *Fiscal Year 2008*, p. 183.

22. Kosiak, *FY 2008 Defense Budget Request*, p. 20; and Kosiak, *FY 2009 Defense Budget Request*, p. 9.

23. Towell, Daggett, and Belasco, *Defense: FY2008*, p. 2.

BIBLIOGRAPHY

INTERVIEWS

(Affiliation and rank as at time of interview.)

Agoglia, Col. John. U.S. Army, Director, U.S. Army Peace Keeping and Stability Operations Institute, Arlington, VA, February 20, 2007.

Anderson, Col. Joseph. U.S. Army, Executive Officer to the Secretary of the Army, Department of the Army, Department of Defense, Arlington, VA, March 29, 2006.

Bell, Col. Michael. U.S. Army, Senior Military Fellow, Institute for National Strategic Studies, National Defense University, Washington, DC, March 28, 2007.

Biddle, Stephen. Senior Fellow in Defense Policy, Council of Foreign Relations, Washington, DC, March 27, 2006.

Binnendijk, Hans. Director, Center for Technology and National Security Policy, National Defense University, Washington, DC, August 30, 2005 (telephone) / October 11, 2006 (telephone) / March 29, 2006 / March 1, 2007.

Boozell, Lt. Col. James. U.S. Army, Strategy and Policy Branch Chief, SSTR Division, Department of Defense, December 7, 2006 (telephone).

Burton, Col. J. B. U.S. Army, former commander of Dagger Brigade (2nd Brigade, 1st Infantry Division), March 19, 2008 (telephone).

Collins, Joseph J. former Deputy Assistant Secretary of Defense for Stability Operations, National War College, Washington, DC, March 30, 2006.

Dobbins, Amb. James. Director, International Security and Defense Policy Center, RAND National Security Research Division, Arlington, VA, March 29, 2006.

Downie, Richard. Director, Center for Hemispheric Defense Studies, National Defense University, Washington, DC, March 30, 2006.

Fastabend, Brig. Gen. David. U.S. Army, Deputy Director, Futures Center, Army Training and Doctrine Command, March 25, 2005 (telephone) / September 16, 2005 (telephone).

Fischel, John T. Professor and Research Director, Center for Hemispheric Defense Studies, National Defense University, Washington DC, March 30, 2006.

Hammes, Col. T. X. (ret.). USMC, Washington, DC, May 17, 2007.

Hoffman, Lt. Col. Frank G. (ret.) USMC, Center for Emerging Threats and Opportunities, U.S. Marine Corps Warfighting Laboratory, Quantico, VA, February 27, 2007 (telephone) / March 7, 2007.

Hopkins, Donna L. Political Military Plans and Policy, Bureau of Political-Military Affairs, Department of State, Washington, DC, February 21, 2007.

Krepinevich Jr., Andrew F. Executive Director, Center for Strategic and Budgetary Assessments, Washington, DC, February 28, 2007.

Laquement Jr., Lt. Col. Richard A. U.S. Army, Strategist, Stability Operations, Special Operations/Low Intensity Conflict, OSD (Policy), Arlington, VA, March 28, 2006.

Laughrey, Lt. Col. James. U.S. Army, Senior Military Fellow, Institute for National Strategic Studies, National Defense University, Washington, DC, April 5, 2007.

Mahnken, Thomas. Deputy Assistant Secretary of Defense for Policy Planning, Department of Defense, Arlington, VA, April 9, 2007.

Marks, Thomas A. Political Risk Consultant, Center for Hemispheric Defense Studies, National Defense University, Washington, DC, March 30, 2006.

Maxwell, Dayton L. Senior Adviser, Joint Staff, J-5/USAID, Department of Defense, Arlington, VA, August 9, 2007.

McFate, Montgomery. Senior Fellow, Post-Conflict Peace and Stability Operations, United States Institute of Peace, Washington, DC, February 1, 2007.

McMaster, Col. H. R. U.S. Army, Senior Research Associate, International Institute for Strategic Studies, London, UK, January 15, 2007.

Nagl, Lt. Col. John. U.S. Army, Military Assistant to the Deputy Secretary of Defense, Department of Defense, Arlington, VA, March 28, 2006.

Panitz, Heather C. Stability Operations Coordinator, Stability Operations, Special Operations/Low Intensity Conflict, OSD (Policy), Arlington, VA, March 28, 2006.

Perito, Robert M. Senior Program Officer, Center for Post-Conflict Peace and Stability Operations, United States Institute of Peace, Washington, DC, March 27, 2006.

Singh, Vikram. Stability Operations, Special Operations/Low Intensity Conflict, OSD (Policy), London, June 28, 2006; Washington DC, March 20, 2007.

Terriff, Terry. Reader, Department of Political Science and International Studies, University of Birmingham, July 11, 2007 (telephone).

Williamson, J. Clint. Director for Stability Operations, National Security Council, Washington, DC, March 28, 2006.

Sources

Agg, Cpl. J. "Small Arms COE Delivers Search Engine for the Information Age War Fighter." *Marine Corps News*, May 12, 2005.

Alberts, David S. *Information Age Transformation: Getting to a 21st Century Military.* Rpt. ed. Washington, DC: Department of Defense Command, and Control Research Program, 2003.

Alberts, David S., John J. Garstka, and Frederick P. Stein. *Network Centric Warfare: Developing and Leveraging Information Superiority.* Washington, DC: Department of Defense Command, and Control Research Program, 1999.

Allard, Kenneth. *Somalia Operations: Lessons Learned.* Washington, DC: National Defense University Press, 1995.

Allison, Graham, and Philip Zelikow. *Essence of Decision: Explaining the Cuban Missile Crisis.* 2nd ed. New York: Longman, 1999.

Andrade, Dale. "Westmoreland Was Right: Learning the Wrong Lessons from the Vietnam War." *Small Wars and Insurgencies* 19, no. 2 (2008).

Arkin, William M. "Petraeus Wins in Iraq Battle, Kills Iran War." *Washington Post*, March 13, 2008.

"Army Opposes Permanent Adviser Corps to Train Foreign Forces." *Inside the Pentagon*, September 13, 2007.

"Army Prepares to Keep Troop Levels Steady in Iraq." *AUSA News*, November 1, 2006.

Association of the United States Army. *The U.S. Army: A Modular Force for the 21st Century.* Torchbearer Issue March 2005. Arlington, VA: AUSA Institute of Land Warfare, 2005.

———. *The U.S. Army's Role in Stability Operations.* Torchbearer Issue October 2006. Arlington, VA: AUSA Institute of Land Warfare, 2006.

Atkinson, Rick. *In the Company of Soldiers: A Chronicle of Combat.* New York: Henry Holt, 2004.

Avant, Deborah D. *Political Institutions and Military Change.* Ithaca, NY: Cornell University Press, 1994.

Aylwin-Foster, Nigel. "Changing the Army for Counterinsurgency Operations." *Military Review* 85, no. 6 (November-December 2005).

Bacevich, A. J., James D. Hallums, Richard H. White, and Thomas F. Young. *American Military Policy in Small Wars: The Case of El Salvador* (Special Report). Cambridge, MA: Pergamon-Brassey's, 1988.

Baker, James A. III, and Lee H. Hamilton et al. *The Iraq Study Group Report.* Washington, DC: USIP, 2006.

Barnes, Fred. "How Bush Decided on the Surge." *Weekly Standard* 13, no. 20 (February 4, 2008).

Barnes, Julian E., and Peter Spiegel. "Gates May Not Be Following Bush's Playbook on Iraq." *Los Angeles Times*, May 6, 2007.

Barry, Charles L. "Rebalancing the Active/Reserve Mix." In Hans Binnendijk and Stuart E. Johnson, eds. *Transforming for Stabilization and Reconstruction Operations.* Washington, DC: National Defense University Press, 2004.

Berdal, Mats. "Consolidating Peace in the Aftermath of War—Reflections on 'Post-Conflict Peace-Building' from Bosnia to Iraq." In John Andreas Olsen, ed. *On New Wars.* Oslo: Norwegian Institute for Defence Studies, 2007.

———. "Lessons Not Learned: The Use of Force in 'Peace Operations' in the 1990s." *International Peacekeeping* 7, no. 4 (2000).

Bergquist, Carl. "Air University Hosts Counterinsurgency Symposium." *Air Force News*, April 30, 2007.

Berkowitz, Bruce. *The New Face of War: How War Will Be Fought in the 21st Century.* New York: The Free Press, 2003.

Biddle, Stephen. "Seeing Baghdad, Thinking Saigon." *Foreign Affairs* 85, no. 2 (March/April 2006).

Bingham, Bruce B., Daniel L. Rubini, and Michael J. Cleary, *U.S. Army Civil Affairs: The Army's "Ounce of Prevention."* Land Warfare Papers no. 41. Arlington, VA: Association of the United States Army, March 2003.

Binnendijk, Hans. "Transforming Stabilization and Reconstruction Operations." Paper presented at RUSI-JFCOM Conference on "Transformation of Military Operations on the Cusps." London, UK, July 14–15, 2005.

Binnendijk, Hans, David C. Gompert, and Richard L. Kugler. "A New Military Framework for NATO." *Defense Horizons*, 48 (May 2005).

Binnendijk, Hans, and Stuart E. Johnson, eds. *Transforming for Stabilization and Reconstruction Operations.* Washington, DC: National Defense University Press, 2004.

Blanton, Dana. "FOX News Poll: Most Think Troop Surge Is Bush's Last Chance in Iraq." *FoxsNews.com*, January 18, 2007.

Blaufarb, Douglas S. *The Counterinsurgency Era: U.S. Doctrine and Performance—1950 to Present.* New York: The Free Press, 1977.

Boot, Max. "Can Petraeus Pull It Off?" *Weekly Standard* 12, no. 31 (April 30, 2007).

———. "The Corps Should Look to Its Small-Wars Past." *Armed Forces Journal* (March 2006).

———. "Navigating the 'Human Terrain.'" *Los Angeles Times*, December 7, 2005.

———. *The Savage Wars of Peace: Small Wars and the Rise of American Power.* New York: Basic Books, 2002.

———. Statement before the House Armed Services Subcommittee on Terrorism, Unconventional Threats, and Capabilities. Washington, DC. June 29, 2006.

———. Statements made at "The Future of the United States Marine Corps." Proceedings of conference held at the American Enterprise Institute. Washington, DC. August 18, 2005.

———. "The Struggle to Transform the Military." *Foreign Affairs* 84, no. 2 (March/April 2005).

———. "The Wrong Weapons for the Long War." *Los Angeles Times*, February 8, 2006.

Bowden, Mark. *Black Hawk Down.* London: Bantam Press, 1999.

Braiker, Brian. "Dirge for a 'Surge,'" *Newsweek*, January 20, 2007.

Buley, Benjamin. *The New American Way of War: Military Culture and the Political Utility of Force.* New York: Routledge, 2007.

Bumiller, Elisabeth. "At an Army School for Officers, Blunt Talk about Iraq." *New York Times*, October 14, 2007.

Burke, Crispin. "Sorry, Pentathlete Wasn't on the Syllabus." *Small Wars Journal* (January 24, 2009). www.smallwarsjournal.com/mag/docs-temp/169-burke.pdf.

Capaccio, Tony. "Bush Seeks Big Boost for Plane, Ship, Space Programs." *Bloomberg.com*, February 5, 2007.

Carafano, James Jay. "The Army Reserves and the Abrams Doctrine: Unfulfilled Promise, Uncertain Future." *Heritage Lectures* no. 869, Heritage Foundation, Washington, DC, December 6, 2005.

Caraher, Leigh C. "Broadening Military Culture." In Hans Binnendijk and Stuart E. Johnson, eds. *Transforming for Stabilization and Reconstruction Operations.* Washington, DC: National Defense University Press, 2004.

Cassidy, Robert. *Peacekeeping in the Abyss: British, and American Peacekeeping Doctrine, and Practice after the Cold War.* Westport, CT: Praeger, 2004.

———. "Prophets or Praetorians? The Uptonian Paradox and the Powell Corollary." *Parameters: U.S. Army War College Quarterly* 33, no. 3 (Autumn 2003).

Castelli, Christopher J. "Pentagon Must Fix 'Shortfalls' in Key Irregular Warfare Missions." *Inside the Pentagon* 24, no. 21 (May 22, 2008).

Cavallaro, Gina. "War Zone Training Will Garner Command Credit." *Army Times,* June 19, 2008.

Center for Advanced Command Concepts and Technology. *Operations Other Than War (OOTW): The Technological Dimension.* Washington, DC: National Defense University Press, 1995.

Chiarelli, Maj. Gen. Peter, and Maj. Patrick Michaelis. "Winning the Peace: The Requirement for Full Spectrum Operations." *Military Review* 85, no. 4 (July-August 2005).

Chiarelli, Lt. Gen. Peter W., with Maj. Stephen M. Smith. "Learning from Our Modern Wars: The Imperatives of Preparing for a Dangerous Future." *Military Review* 87, no. 5 (September-October 2007).

Clinton, Bill. "Statement by the President to the Nation." Washington, DC. March 24, 1999. Available at www.thisnation.com/library/1999serbia.html.

Cloud, David S., and Thom Shanker. "Petraeus Warns against Quick Pullback in Iraq." *New York Times,* September 10, 2007.

Clutterbuck, Richard L. *The Long, Long War: The Emergency in Malaya 1948–1960.* London: Cassell, 1966.

Cohen, Eliot A. *Commandos and Politicians: Elite Military Units in Modern Democracies.* Cambridge, MS: Center for International Affairs, 1978.

Cohen, Eliot, Conrad Crane, Jan Horvath, and John Nagl. "Principles, Imperatives, and Paradoxes of Counterinsurgency." *Military Review* 86, no. 2 (2006).

Cohen, Eliot A., and John Gooch. *Military Misfortunes: The Anatomy of Failure in War.* New York: Vintage Books, Random House, 1991.

Cole, Robert H. "Grenada, Panama, Haiti: Joint Operational Reform." *Joint Force Quarterly* 20 (Autumn/Winter 1999).

Collette, Col. C., UK Army. "Countering Irregular Activity in Civil War Arkansas: A Case Study." U.S. Army War College Strategy Research Project, Carlisle Barracks, PA, March 30, 2007.

Collins, John M. *Special Operations Forces: An Assessment.* Washington, DC: National Defense University Press, 1996.

———. "Vietnam Postmortem: A Senseless Strategy." *Parameters: U.S. Army War College Quarterly* 8, no. 1 (March 1978).

Cone, Robert W. "The Changing National Training Center." *Military Review* 86, no. 3 (May-June 2006).

Conetta, Carl. *Disappearing the Dead: Iraq, Afghanistan and the Idea of "New Warfare."* Project on Defense Alternatives Research Monograph no. 9. Cambridge, MA: PDA, 2004.

Conway, General James T. "Remarks by General James T. Conway, Commandant of the Marine Corps," Center for a New American Security. Washington, DC. October 16, 2007.

Cooling, B. F., and Alan Gropman. "Resourcing Stability Operations and Reconstruction: A Historical Perspective." In *Resourcing Stability Operations and Reconstruction: Past, Present, and Future.* Washington, DC: Dwight D. Eisenhower National Security Series Symposium, 2006.

"Counterinsurgency in the 21st Century: Creating a National Framework." Conference Report. Washington, DC, September 28–29, 2006.

Creveld, Martin van. *The Changing Face of War: Lessons of Combat, from the Marne to Iraq.* New York: Presidio Press, 2007.

Crowell, Lorenzo. "The Anatomy of *Just Cause:* The Forces Involved, the Adequacy of Intelligence, and Its Success as a Joint Operation." In Bruce W. Watson and Peter G. Tsouras, eds., *Operation Just Cause: The U.S. Intervention in Panama.* Boulder, CO: Westview Press, 1991.

Cruz, Ginger. Deputy Special Inspector General for Iraq Reconstruction. Testimony on "The Role of the Department of Defense in Provincial Reconstruction Teams." House Committee on Armed Services, Subcommittee on Oversight, and Investigations. Washington, DC. September 5, 2007.

Cuomo, Scott A. "Will We Be Prepared for What's Next?" *Marine Corps Gazette* 91, no. 7 (July 2007).

Daalder, Ivo H. "Knowing When to Say No: The Development of U.S. Policy for Peacekeeping." In William Durch, ed., *UN Peacekeeping, American Politics, and the Uncivil Wars of the 1990s.* New York: St. Martin's Press, 1996.

Dale, Catherine Marie. *Operation Iraqi Freedom: Strategies, Approaches, Results, and Issues for Congress,* CRS Report for Congress, RL34387. Washington, DC: Congressional Research Service, March 28, 2008.

Dalton, Capt. R. J. "The Village." *Marine Corps Gazette* 56, no. 6 (June 1972).

Davidson, Janine. Director of DoD Stability Operations Capabilities. Presentation given at the National Defense University. Washington, DC. March 14, 2007.

Davidson, Sgt. Brian. "Air Force Tactical Air Control Party (TACP) in Afghanistan." *American Forces News Service,* January 25, 2004.

de la Garza, Paul. "Special Ops' Expanding Role." *St. Petersburg Times,* September 24, 2005.

de Rugy, Véronique. "Today's Bipartisan Issue: Sneaky Spending." *American.com,* March 22, 2007.

Deady, Timothy K. "Lessons from a Successful Counterinsurgency: The Philippines, 1899–1902." *Parameters: U.S. Army War College Quarterly* 35, no. 1 (Spring 2005).

Defense Science Board. *2004 Summer Study on Transition to, and from Hostilities— Supporting Papers.* Washington, DC: Office of the Under Secretary of Defense for Acquisition, Technology, and Logistics, 2005.

————. *Institutionalizing Stability Operations within DoD.* Washington, DC: Office of the Under Secretary of Defense for Acquisition, Technology, and Logistics, 2005.

————. *Transition to and from Hostilities.* Defense Science Board 2004 Summer Study. Washington, DC: Office of the Under Secretary of Defense for Acquisition, Technology, and Logistics, 2004.

Dehghanpisheh, Babak. "The Great Moqtada Makeover." *Newsweek*, January 19, 2008.

Dehghanpisheh, Babak, and Evan Thomas. "Scions of the Surge." *Newsweek*, March 24, 2008.

Dobbins, James. "Next Steps in Iraq and Beyond." Testimony presented before the Committee on Foreign Relations, United States Senate (Santa Monica, CA: RAND, September 23, 2003).

————. "Who Lost Iraq?" *Foreign Affairs* 86, no. 5 (September/October 2007).

Dobbins, James et al. *America's Role in Nation-building from Germany to Iraq*, Prepublication draft copy. Santa Monica, CA: RAND, 2003.

Dodge, Toby. "The Written Testimony of Dr. Toby Dodge, Consulting Senior Fellow for the Middle East." Senate Foreign Relations Committee, January 25, 2007.

Donnelly, Thomas. "Mind the Gap." *National Security Outlook*, American Enterprise Institute, June 10, 2004.

Donnelly, Thomas, and Frederick W. Kagan. *Ground Truth: The Future of U.S. Land Power.* Washington, DC: AEI Press, 2008.

Doughty, Robert A. *The Evolution of U.S. Army Tactical Doctrine, 1946–1976.* Ft. Leavenworth: KS: Combat Studies Institute, 1979.

Downie, Richard Duncan. *Learning from Conflict: The U.S. Military in Vietnam, El Salvador, and the Drug War.* Westport, CT: Praeger, 1998.

Dunlap, Maj. Gen. Charles J. Jr. "America's Asymmetric Advantage." *Armed Forces Journal* (September 2006).

————. "Making Revolutionary Change: Airpower in COIN Today." *Parameters: U.S. Army War College Quarterly* 38, no. 2 (Summer 2008).

Dunn, Peter. "The American Army: The Vietnam War, 1965–1973." In Ian Beckett and John Pimlott, eds., *Armed Forces and Modern Counterinsurgency.* New York: St. Martin's Press, 1985.

Eash, Joseph J. III. "Supporting Technologies." In Binnendijk and Johnson, eds. *Transforming for Stabilization and Reconstruction Operations.* Washington, DC: National Defense University Press, 2004.

Eaton, Hugh et al. *The British Approach to Low-Intensity Operations,* Technical Report, Network-Centric Operations (NCO) Case Study. Washington, DC: Office of Force Transformation, 2007.

Edelman, Eric. Ambassador and Under Secretary of Defense for Policy. Remarks at the DoS, and DoD Counterinsurgent Conference. Washington, DC. September 28, 2006.

Ekbladh, David. "From Consensus to Crisis: The Postwar Career of Nation-Building in U.S. Foreign Relations." In Francis Fukuyama, ed. *Nation-Building: Beyond Afghanistan and Iraq.* Baltimore, MD: Johns Hopkins University Press, 2006.

Ellsberg, Daniel. *Papers on the War.* New York: Simon, and Schuster, 1972.

Fabey, Michael. "JSFs, Strykers to Be Struck from Supplementals." *Aviation Week,* February 15, 2007.

Fallows, James. "Blind into Baghdad." *The Atlantic Monthly,* January/February 2004.

Farrell, Theo G., and Terry Terriff, eds. *The Sources of Military Change: Norms, Politics, Technology.* London: Lynne Rienner, 2002.

Feickert, Andrew. *U.S. Army's Modular Redesign: Issues for Congress,* CRS Report for Congress, RL32476. Washington, DC: Congressional Research Service, May 5, 2006.

Fil, Maj. Gen. Joseph Jr. Commanding General, Multinational Division, Baghdad, and 1st Cavalry Division, Press Conference, February 16, 2007.

Fishel, John T. *The Fog of Peace: Planning and Executing the Restoration of Panama.* Carlisle, PA: U.S. Army War College, Strategic Studies Institute, 1992.

Fishel, John, and Robert Baumann. "Operation Uphold Democracy: The Execution Phase." In Walter E. Kretchik, Baumann, and Fishel, eds. *A Concise History of the U.S. Army in Operation Uphold Democracy.* Ft. Leavenworth, KS: U.S. Army CGSC Press, 1998.

Flanagan, Edward M. Jr. *Battle for Panama: Inside Operation Just Cause.* Washington, DC: Brassey's, 1993.

Flournoy, Michèle. "Did the Pentagon Get the Quadrennial Review Right?" *The Washington Quarterly* 29, no. 2 (2006).

Flournoy, Michèle A., and Tammy S. Schultz. *Shaping U.S. Ground Forces for the Future: Getting Expansion Right.* Washington, DC: Center for a New American Security, 2007.

Freedberg, Sydney J. Jr. "Marine Corps Seeks Return to Its Role as a Naval Force." *National Journal,* May 14, 2008.

Freedman, Lawrence. "Logic, Politics and Foreign Policy Processes: A Critique of the Bureaucratic Politics Model." *International Affairs* 52, no. 3 (July 1976).

———. *Revolution in Strategic Affairs.* Adelphi Paper No. 318. Oxford: OUP for International Institute for Strategic Studies, 1998.

———. "Rumsfeld's Legacy: The Iraq Syndrome?" *Washington Post,* January 9, 2005.

"The Future of the United States Marine Corps." Conference held at the American Enterprise Institute. Washington, DC. August 18, 2005.

Galula, David. *Counterinsurgency Warfare: Theory and Practice.* Rpt. New York: Praeger, 2005 [1964].

Gates, Robert. Hearing before the SASC for the position of Secretary of Defense. Washington, DC. December 5, 2006. Transcript available at www.iht.com /articles/2006/12/06/america/web.1206gatestext.php.

———. Secretary of Defense. "Landon Lecture (Kansas State University)." November 26, 2007.

———. Secretary of Defense. Remarks at the AUSA. Arlington, VA, October 10, 2007.

———. Secretary of Defense. Remarks to the Heritage Foundation, Colorado Springs, CO, May 13, 2008.

———. "Report to Congress on the Implementation of DoD Directive 3000.05. *Military Support for Stability, Security, Transition and Reconstruction (SSTR) Operations.*" April 1, 2007.

Gayl, Franz J. *Mine Resistant Ambush Protected Vehicles,* Ground Combat Element Advocate Science, and Technology Advisor Case Study. Arlington, VA: U.S. Marine Corps. January 22, 2008.

Gentile, Lt. Col. Gian P. "Our COIN Doctrine Removes the Enemy from the Essence of War." *Armed Forces Journal* (January 2008).

"Go after Them and Destroy Them." *Washington Post,* December 16, 2001.

Gordon, Michael R. "The 2000 Campaign: The Military; Bush Would Stop U.S. Peacekeeping in Balkan Fights." *The New York Times,* October 21, 2000.

Gordon, Michael R., and Gen. Bernard E. Trainer. *Cobra II: The Inside Story of the Invasion and Occupation of Iraq.* New York: Pantheon Books, 2006.

Gorman, Gen. Paul F. "Low Intensity Conflict: American Dilemma." In *Proceedings of the Low-Intensity Conference.* Ft. McNair. Washington, DC: Department of Defense, January 14–15, 1986.

Graham, Bradley. "Pentagon Considers Creating Postwar Peacekeeping Forces." *Washington Post,* November 24, 2003.

———. "Pentagon Plans a Redirection in Afghanistan; Troops to Be Shifted into Rebuilding Country." *Washington Post,* November 20, 2002.

Grissom, Adam. "The Future of Military Innovation Studies." *The Journal of Strategic Studies* 29, no. 5 (2006).

Grossman, Elaine M. "Study Finds Army Transformation Plan Weakens Combat Capability." *Inside the Pentagon,* January 26, 2006.

Haendschke, Ernie. "Adding Less-Lethal Arrows to the Quiver for Counterinsurgency Air Operations." *Air and Space Power Journal* 22 (Summer 2008).

Hagee, Commandant Gen. Mike. All Marine Message 008/03, January 28, 2003. Available at www.marines.mil/cmc/33cmc.nsf/attachments/$FILE/33cpg.pd.

———. All Marine Message 018/05, April 18, 2005. Available at www.marines.mil/almars/almar2000.nsf/1babcf316f87f38c852569b8008017 e7/35a74723d7bcc61085256fe70061040a?OpenDocument.

Hajjar, Maj. Remi, U.S. Army. "The Army's New TRADOC Culture Center." *Military Review* 86, no. 6 (November-December 2006).

Halliday, Fred. *The Making of the Second Cold War.* 2nd ed. London: Verso, 1986.

Halperin, Morton H. *Bureaucratic Politics and Foreign Policy.* Washington, DC: Brookings Institution Press, 1974.

Hammes, Thomas X. *The Sling and the Stone: On War in the 21st Century.* St. Paul, MN: Zenith Press, 2004.

Hanson, Victor. *An Autumn of War: What America Learned from September 11 and the War on Terrorism.* New York: Anchor Books, 2002.

Harmon, Christopher C. "Illustrations of 'Learning' in Counterinsurgency." *Comparative Strategy,* 11 (1992).

Harrison, Christine. "Doctrine Center 'Jump Starts' Irregular Warfare Doctrine." *Air Force News,* March 1, 2007.

Harvey, Francis J. "Building the Future Force While Continuing to Fight the Global War on Terrorism." *Army* (October 2005).

"Hearing of the Senate Armed Services Committee—Subject: The Fiscal Year 2004 Defense Budget." *Federal News Service,* February 25, 2003.

Hegland, Corine. "Pentagon, State Struggle to Define Nation-Building Roles." *National Journal,* April 30, 2007.

Hennessy, Michael A. *Strategy in Vietnam: The Marines and Revolutionary Warfare in I Corps, 1965–1972.* Westport, CT, and London: Praeger, 1997.

Henry, Ryan. "Defense Transformation and the 2005 Quadrennial Defense Review." *Parameters: U.S. Army War College Quarterly* 35, no. 4 (Winter 2005).

———. Principal Deputy. Department of Defense. Prepared Statement for the Committee on Foreign relations, U.S. Senate, 109th Congress, 1st Session. Washington, DC. June 16, 2005.

Herbert, Paul. "Deciding What Has to Be Done: General William E. DePuy and the 1976 Edition of FM 100–5, *Operations.*" Leavenworth Papers, no. 16. Ft. Leavenworth, KS: U.S. Army Command and General Staff College, 1988.

Hersh, Seymour M. "The Other War: Why Bush's Afghanistan Problem Won't Go Away." *The New Yorker,* April 12, 2004.

Heymann, Hans Jr., and William W. Whitson. *Can and Should the United States Preserve a Military Capability for Revolutionary Conflict?* Santa Monica, CA: RAND, 1972.

Hilburn, Matt. "Rethinking the Enemy." *Sea Power,* April 2007.

Hippel, Karen von. *Democracy by Force: U.S. Military Intervention in the Post Cold War World.* Cambridge: Cambridge University Press, 2000.

Hodge, Nathan, and Caitlin Harrington. "FCS Project in the Frame for Major Funding Hit." *Jane's Defence Weekly,* May 9, 2007.

Hoffman, Frank G. "Complex Irregular Warfare: The Next Revolution in Military Affairs." *Orbis* 50, no. 3 (Summer 2006).

———. "Luttwak's Lament." April 22, 2007. Posted on the Small Wars Journal blog. Available at www.smallwarsjournal.com.

———. "Neo-Classical Counterinsurgency?" *Parameters: U.S. Army War College Quarterly* 37, no. 2 (2007).

———. "Small Wars Revisited: The United States and Nontraditional Wars." *Journal of Strategic Studies* 28, no. 6 (December 2005).

———. "A Strategic Rationale for Land Force Expansion." *E-Notes* (Foreign Policy Research Institute), March 2007. Available at www.fpri.org/200703.hoffman.landforceexpansion.html.

———. "Troop Level Increases: Pyrrhic Victory?" *Proceedings,* April 2007.

Holzworth, Maj. C. E. "Operation Eagle Claw: A Catalyst for Change in the American Military." Research Paper submitted to Marine Corps Command and Staff College, 1997.

Howard, Michael. "A Long War?" *Survival* 48, no. 4 (Winter 2006–2007).

IDA. "Army QDR Issue: Can the Overall Combat Output Potential of the Army Be Increased by Applying Existing Army Organizational Principles in a Different Way?" IDA Working Paper. September 2006.

International Crisis Group. *Iraq after the Surge I: The New Sunni Landscape,* Middle East Report 74 (Baghdad, Istanbul, Damascus, Brussels: ICG, April 2008).

———. *Iraq's Civil War: The Sadrists and the Surge,* Middle East Report 72 (Baghdad, Damascus, Brussels: ICG, February 2008).

International Institute for Strategic Studies. "Iraq under the Surge: Implementing Plan B." *Strategic Comments* 13, no. 2 (March 2007).

———. *Military Balance 2005·2006.* London: Routledge, 2005.

———. *Strategic Survey 2003/4.* Oxford: Oxford University Press for the International Institute for Strategic Studies, 2004.

Iraq Coalition Casualties. icasualties.org/oif.

Isenberg, David. *Budgeting for Empire: Ambitions Outweigh Strategy.* Silver City, NM, and Washington, DC: Foreign Policy in Focus, 2007.

Jablonsky, David. "Army Transformation: A Tale of Two Doctrines." *Parameters: U.S. Army War College Quarterly* 31, no. 3 (Autumn 2001).

Jaffe, Greg. "Despite a $168B Budget Army Faces Cash Crunch." *Wall Street Journal,* December 12, 2006.

Jaffe, Gregg, and Jonathan Karp. "Pentagon Girds for Big Spending Cuts." *Wall Street Journal,* November 4, 2005.

Jenkins, Brian M. *The Unchangeable War.* Santa Monica, CA: RAND, 1970.

Joint Chiefs of Staff. Chairman of the Joint Chiefs of Staff. *Military Counter-Insurgency Accomplishments since January 1961.* Report from the President's National Security Advisor, July 21, 1962.

Joint Chiefs of Staff. *Capstone Concept for Joint Operations,* vol. 2.0. Washington, DC: Joint Staff J-7/Director for Operational Plans, and Joint Force Development, 2005.

———. *JP 1-02. Department of Defense Dictionary of Military and Associated Terms.* Washington, DC: Joint Chiefs of Staff, April 12, 2001 (as amended through November 30, 2004).

———. *JP 3-07. Joint Doctrine for Military Operations Other than War.* Washington, DC: Office of the Joint Chiefs of Staff, 1995.

———. *JP 3-0. Joint Operations.* Washington, DC: Joint Chiefs of Staff, 2006.

———. *Joint Vision 2010.* Washington, DC: Office of the Chairman, 1996.

———. *National Military Strategy of the United States of America.* Washington, DC: Office of the Chairman, 2004.

———. *National Military Strategy of the United States of America: A Strategy of Flexible and Selective Engagement.* Washington, DC: Office of the Chairman, 1995.

———. *Publication 1,* as amended. Washington, DC: Office of the Joint Chiefs of Staff, 1984.

Joint Forces Command. *Irregular Warfare Special Study.* Norfolk, VA: JFCOM, 2006.

———. *Stability Operations Joint Operating Concept.* Norfolk, VA: JFCOM/J9, 2004.

Jurado, Carlos Caballero, and Nigel Thomas. *Central American Wars, 1959–1989.* Men-at-Arms Series. Oxford: Osprey Publishing, 1990.

Kagan, Frederick W. *Finding the Target: The Transformation of American Military Policy.* New York: Encounter Books, 2006.

Kagan, Kimberley. "ISW Interview with COL J.B. Burton, Commander of Dagger Brigade, Baghdad, Iraq." *Institute for the Study of War,* November 14, 2007.

Kaplan, Fred. "Challenging the Generals." *New York Magazine,* August 26, 2007.

———. "How Many Government Agencies Does It Take to Teach Soldiers Arabic? A Pathetic Case of Pentagon Incompetence." *Slate,* April 6, 2005. slate.msn.com/id/2116330.

———. "The Professional." *The New York Times,* February 10, 2008.

———. "Secretary Gates Declares War on the Army Brass." *Slate,* October 12, 2007.

———. "What's Really in the U.S. Military Budget? Much More than the Oft-Cited $515.4 Billion." *Slate,* February 4, 2008.

Kaplan, Robert D. "Imperial Grunts." *The Atlantic Monthly,* October 2005.

———. "Petraeus Wins." *The Atlantic.com,* April 24, 2008.

Karp, Jonathan. "Pentagon Redefines 'Emergency.'" *Wall Street Journal,* January 3, 2007.

Kelly, Lorelei. *Unbalanced Security: The Divide between State and Defense.* Silver City, NM, and Washington, DC: Foreign Policy in Focus, 2007.

Kennedy, President John F. Address before the American Newspaper Publishers Association, New York City. April 27, 1961. Transcript available at www.jfklibrary.org.

———. NSAM 2, February 3, 1961. The Papers of John F. Kennedy, Presidential Papers, National Security Files, Meetings, and Memoranda Series, National Security Action Memoranda. John F. Kennedy Presidential Library, and Museum, Boston, MA.

Kilcullen, David. "Anatomy of a Tribal Revolt." *Small Wars Journal,* August 29, 2007, www.smallwarsjournal.com.

———. "Counter-insurgency. *Redux.*" *Survival* 48, no. 4 (2006).

———. "Countering Global Insurgency." *Journal of Strategic Studies* 28, no. 4 (August 2005).

———. "Edward Luttwak's 'Counterinsurgency Malpractice.'" *Small Wars Journal,* April 15, 2007, www.smallwarsjournal.com.

Kipp, Jacob, Lester Grau, Karl Prinslow, and Capt. Don Smith. "The Human Terrain System: A CORDS for the 21st Century." *Military Review* 86, no. 5 (September-October 2006).

Kirkpatrick, Jeane. "The Role of the Soviet Union in Low-Intensity Warfare." In *Proceedings of the Low-Intensity Conference.* Ft. McNair. Washington, DC: Department of Defense, January 14–15, 1986.

Kiszely, John. *Post-Modern Challenges for the Modern Warrior,* The Shrivenham Papers, no. 5. Cranfield: Defence Academy, 2007.

Kitson, Frank. *Bunch of Five.* London: Faber and Faber, 1977

Klare, Michael T., and Peter Kornbluh, eds. *Low Intensity Warfare: Counterinsurgency, Proinsurgency, and Antiterrorism in the Eighties.* New York: Pantheon Books, 1988.

———. "The New Interventionism: Low-Intensity Warfare in the 1980s and Beyond." In Klare and Kornbluh, eds. *Low Intensity Warfare: Counterinsurgency,*

Proinsurgency, and Antiterrorism in the Eighties. New York: Pantheon Books, 1988.

Koch, Noel. "Objecting to Reality: The Struggle to Reform U.S. Special Operations Forces." In Thompson, ed. *Low Intensity Conflict: The Pattern of Warfare in the Modern World*. Lexington, MA: Lexington Books, 1989.

Kosiak, Steven M. *Analysis of the FY 2008 Defense Budget Request*. Washington, DC: CSBA, 2007.

———. *Analysis of the FY 2009 Defense Budget Request*. Washington, DC: CSBA, 2008.

———. "The Cost and Funding of the Global War on Terror (GWOT)." Testimony before the U.S. House of Representatives Committee on the Budget, January 18, 2007.

Krepinevich, Andrew F. Jr. *The Army and Vietnam*. Baltimore, MD: Johns Hopkins University Press, 1986.

———. "The Future of U.S. Ground Forces: Challenges and Requirements." Testimony before the Senate Armed Services Committee. Washington, DC: Center for Strategic, and Budgetary Assessments, April 17, 2007.

———. "How to Win in Iraq." *Foreign Affairs* 84, no. 5 (September/October 2005).

———. "The 'New' Counterinsurgency Doctrine and the Baghdad Surge: Formula for Success?" Presentation given on February 27, 2007. Available at www.csbaonline.org/4Publications/PubLibrary/S.20070228.New_Counterinsurge/S.20070228.New_Counterinsurge.pdf.

Krepinevich, Andrew F., and Dakota L. Wood. *Of IEDs and MRAPs: Force Protection in Complex Irregular Operations*. Washington, DC: CSBA, 2007.

Krulak, Gen. Charles C. "Operational Maneuver from the Sea." *Joint Force Quarterly* (Spring 1999).

———. "The Strategic Corporal: Leadership in the Three Block War." *Marines Magazines* (January 1999).

Krulak, Victor H. *First to Fight: An Inside View of the U.S. Marine Corps*. New ed. Annapolis, MD: Naval Institute Press, 1999.

Laird, Melvin. "Iraq: Learning the Lessons of Vietnam." *Foreign Affairs* 84, no. 6 (November/December 2005).

Landay, Jonathan. "Congress, Rumsfeld at Odds on Army; Increasing the Force's Size Is the Main Issue." *The Philadelphia Inquirer*, October 26, 2003.

Lawrence, T. E. *Seven Pillars of Wisdom: A Triumph*. London: Penguin Books, 1971.

Levite, Ariel E., and Elizabeth Sherwood-Randall. "The Case for Discriminate Force." *Survival* 44, no. 4 (2002).

Lind, William S. "Proposing Some New Models for Marine Mechanized Units." *Marine Corps Gazette* 62, no. 9 (March 1978).

Linn, Brian McAllister. "The Impact of the Imperial Wars (1898–1907) on the U.S. Army." *Heritage Lectures*. Washington, DC: Heritage Foundation, June 18, 2005.

Lischer, Sarah Kenyon. "Winning Hearts and Minds in the Horn of Africa: Humanitarian Aid in the War on Terror." *Harvard International Review* (2007).

Long, Austin. "The Anbar Awakening." *Survival* 50, no. 2 (2008).

Lovell, John P. "Vietnam and the U.S. Army: Learning to Cope with Failure." In George Osborn, Asa A. Clark IV, Daniel J. Kaufman, and Gouble E. Lute, eds. *Democracy, Strategy, and Vietnam: Implications for American Policymaking.* Lexington, MA: Lexington Books, 1987.

Luttwak, Edward N. "Dead End: Counterinsurgency Warfare as Military Malpractice." *Harpers* (February 2007).

———. "Give War a Chance." *Foreign Affairs* 78, no. 4 (July/August 1999).

MacFarlane, Neil. *Intervention in Contemporary World Politics,* Adelphi Papers, No. 350. Oxford: OUP for International Institute for Strategic Studies, 2002.

MacGregor, Douglas A. *Breaking the Phalanx: A New Design for Landpower in the 21st Century.* Westport, CT: Praeger, 1997.

———. "Reforming the Army and Marine Corps." Commentary for Straus Military Reform Project, Center for Defense Information, June 26, 2008.

———. *Transformation under Fire: Revolutionizing How America Fights.* Westport, CT: Praeger, 2003.

Mackey, Robert R. *The Uncivil War: Irregular Warfare in the Upper South, 1861–1865.* Norman: University of Oklahoma Press, 2004.

Maechling, Charles Jr. "Counterinsurgency: The First Ordeal by Fire." In Michael T. Klare and Peter Kornbluh, eds. *Low Intensity Warfare: Counterinsurgency, Proinsurgency, and Antiterrorism in the Eighties.* New York: Pantheon Books, 1988.

Mahon, John K. *History of the Second Seminole War.* Rev. ed. Gainsville: University of Florida Press, 1967.

Malenic, Marina. "Hard Skills Going Soft: Army Concerned That COIN Is Displacing Conventional Training." *Inside Defense,* July 2, 2007.

Malkasian, Carter. "Did the United States Need More Forces in Iraq? Evidence from Al Anbar." *Defence Studies* 8, no. 1 (March 2008).

Mancuso, Mario. "Irregular Warfare Roadmap." *Special Operations Technology* 4, no. 7 (October 2006).

Mandelbaum, Michael. "Foreign Policy as Social Work." *Foreign Affairs* 75, no. 1 (Jan./Feb. 1996).

Mannon Brig. Gen. Otis G. (USAF). Deputy Director, Special Operations, J-3 Joint Staff. Statement before the 109th Congress Committee on Armed Services Subcommittee on Terrorism, Unconventional Threats, and Capabilities. U.S. House of Representatives. September 27, 2006.

Manwaring, Max G., and Court Prisk. *A Strategic View of Insurgencies: Insights from El Salvador,* McNair Paper 8. Washington, DC: National Defense University Press, 1990.

Mazarr, Michael J. "The Folly of 'Asymmetric War.'" *The Washington Quarterly* 31, no. 3 (Summer 2008).

———. *Light Forces and the Future of U.S. Military Strategy.* McLean, VA: Brassey's 1990.

McCaffrey, Gen. Barry R. (ret.). "After Action Report—Visit Iraq and Kuwait, March 9–15, 2007." Memorandum to Col. Michael Meese, Professor and Head of the Department of Social Sciences, U.S. Military Academy, March 26, 2007.

McClintock, Michael. *Instruments of Statecraft: U.S. Guerrilla Warfare, Counterinsurgency, and Counterterrorism, 1940–1990.* New York: Pantheon Books, 1992.

McFate, Montgomery. "Anthropology and Counterinsurgency: The Strange Story of Their Curious Relationship." *Military Review* 85, no. 2 (March-April 2005).

———. "Iraq: The Social Context of IEDs." *Military Review* 85, no. 3 (May-June 2005).

McFate, Montgomery, and Andrea Jackson. "An Organizational Solution for DoD's Cultural Knowledge Needs." *Military Review* 85, no. 4 (July-August 2005).

McMaster, H. R. "On War: Lessons to Be Learned." *Survival* 50, no. 1 (February-March 2008).

Metz, Steven. *Learning from Iraq: Counterinsurgency in American Strategy.* Carlisle, PA: U.S. Army War College, Strategic Studies Institute, 2007.

———. *Rethinking Insurgency.* Carlisle, PA: Strategic Studies Institute, 2007.

Metz, Steven, and Raymond Millen. *Insurgency and Counterinsurgency in the 21st Century: Reconceptualizing the Threat and Response.* Carlisle, PA: U.S. Army War College, Strategic Studies Institute, 2004.

Miles, Donna. "Gates Asks Congress to Transfer More Funds to MRAP Program." *Armed Forces Press Service,* July 18, 2007.

———. "Petraeus-Odierno Team Nominated to Lead in CentCom, Iraq." *American Forces Press Service,* April 23, 2008.

Miller, Capt. Stephen W. "Winning through Maneuver: Part I—Countering the Offense." *Marine Corps Gazette* 63, no. 10 (October 1979).

———. "Winning through Maneuver: Conclusion—Countering the Defense." *Marine Corps Gazette* 63, no. 12 (December 1979).

Mueller, Chuck. "Counterinsurgency Training at Fort Irwin." *San Bernardino Sun,* April 10, 2006.

Mueller, John "The Iraq Syndrome." *Foreign Affairs* 84, no. 6 (2005).

Mulrine, Anna. "The Culture Warriors." *U.S. News and World Report,* November 30, 2007.

Multi-National Force–Iraq. "Charts to Accompany the Testimony of Gen. David H. Petraeus." April 8–9, 2008.

Munoz, Carlo. "JFCOM Chief Says Training Too Focused on Coin, Irregular Warfare." *Inside the Air Force,* October 19, 2007.

Nagl, John A. *Institutionalizing Adaptation: It's Time for a Permanent Army Advisory Corps.* Washington, DC: Center for a New American Security, 2007.

———. *Learning to Eat Soup with a Knife: Counterinsurgency Lessons from Malaya and Vietnam.* Chicago: University of Chicago Press, 2005.

Nash, William L., and Ciara Knudsen. "Reform and Innovation in Stabilization, Reconstruction, and Development." Princeton Project on National Security, unpublished paper, 2005.

National Priorities Project. *Military Recruitment 2006,* December 22, 2006.

Naylor, Sean. "More than Door-Kickers: Special Ops Forces Are Misused as Man-Hunters, Critics Say." *Armed Forces Journal* (March 2006).

Nelson, Lt. Col. John D. "Swiftly Defeat the Efforts, Then What? The 'New American Way of War' and the Transition from Decisive Combat Operations to Post-Conflict Security Operations." In Williamson Murray, ed. *A Nation at War in an Era of Strategic Change.* Carlisle, PA: U.S. Army War College, Strategic Studies Institute, 2004.

Nixon, Richard. "Address to the Nation on the War in Vietnam." November 3, 1969. Transcript obtained courtesy of John Woolley and Gerhard Peters at The American Presidency Project. University of California at Santa Barbara. Available at www.presidency.ucsb.edu.

Nordland, Rod. "A Radical Cleric Gets Religion." *Newsweek,* November 10, 2007.

Norman, Lloyd, and John B. Spore. "Big Push in Guerrilla Warfare: The Army Beefs Up Its Counter-Insurgency Doctrine." *Army* 12, no. 9 (March 1962).

O'Hanlon, Michael. "The Need to Increase the Size of the Deployable Army." *Parameters: U.S. Army War College Quarterly* 34, no. 3 (Autumn 2004).

O'Hanlon, Michael E., and Jason H. Campbell. *Iraq Index Tracking Variables of Reconstruction and Security in Post-Saddam Iraq.* Washington, DC: Brookings Institution, July 24, 2008.

Office of Force Transformation. *Elements of Defense Transformation.* Washington, DC: Department of Defense, 2004.

Office of Management and Budget, Executive Office of the President. *Fiscal Year 2008 Budget of the U.S. Government, Analytical Perspectives.* Washington, DC: U.S. Government Printing Office, 2007.

———. "Statement of Administration Policy, S.2766—National Defense Authorization Act for Fiscal Year 2007." Washington, DC, June 14, 2006.

Office of the Special Inspector General for Iraq Reconstruction (SIGUR). *Status of the Provincial Reconstruction Team Program in Iraq,* SIGIR-06-034. Arlington, VA: SIGIR, October 29, 2006.

Office of the Undersecretary of Defense (Comptroller). *National Defense Budget Estimates for FY 2006.* Washington, DC: Department of Defense, 2005.

———. *National Defense Budget Estimates for FY 2008.* Washington, DC: Department of Defense, 2007.

Oleszycki, Charles. "Update on Department of State and Department of Defense Coordination of Reconstruction and Stabilization Assistance." *Army Lawyer,* May 2006.

Olsen, Howard, and John Davis. *Training U.S. Army Officers for Peace Operations: Lessons from Bosnia.* Washington, DC: USIP Press, October 1999.

Olson, Vice Admiral Eric T. U.S. Navy, Deputy Commander, U.S. SOCOM. Statement before the Senate Armed Services Committee, Subcommittee on Emerging Threats, and Capabilities, April 5, 2006.

Osborn, Kris. "Gates Urges Ramping Up MRAP Acquisition." *Army Times,* May 10, 2007.

Owens, William A. *Lifting the Fog of War.* New York: Johns Hopkins University Press, 2000.

Packer, George. *The Assassin's Gate: America in Iraq.* New York: Farrar, Strauss, and Giroux, 2005.

———. "Knowing the Enemy: Can Social Scientists Redefine the 'War on Terror.'" *The New Yorker,* December 18, 2006.

———. "The Lessons of Tal Afar." *The New Yorker,* April 10, 2006.

Paley, Amit R. "U.S. Deploys a Purpose-Driven Distinction." *Washington Post,* May 21, 2008.

Peck, Maj. Gen. Allen G., USAF. "Airpower's Crucial Role in Irregular Warfare." *Air and Space Power Journal* 21, no. 2 (Summer 2007).

Perito, Robert M. *Where Is the Lone Ranger When We Need Him? America's Search for a Postconflict Stability Force.* Washington, DC: USIP Press, 2004.

Peters, Ralph. "Heavy Peace." *Parameters: U.S. Army War College Quarterly* 29, no. 1 (Spring 1999).

"Petraeus Cites Areas of Improvement in Baghdad." *The Online NewsHour,* April 4, 2007.

Petraeus, Gen. David. "Multi-National Force–Iraq Counterinsurgency Guidance." Released in June 2007 as unclassified guidance to be circulated to MNF-I for counterinsurgency operations in Iraq. Copy available at www.force aerienne.forces.gc.ca/cfawc/Contemporary_Studies/2007/2007-Jun/2007-06-06_MNFI_.

———. Opening Statement at "Hearing on Nomination to Be Commander of US Forces in Iraq." Senate Armed Services Committee. Washington, DC. January 23, 2007.

———. Commander, MNF-I. "Report to Congress on the Situation in Iraq." September 10–11. 2007. Available at www.defenselink.mil/pubs/pdfs/Petraeus-Testimony20070910.pdf.

———. "Transcript of *The Times* Interview with David Petraeus." *Times Online,* February 21, 2008.

Pleming, Sue, and Arshad Mohammed. "Bush Team Grilled by Hostile Democrats over Iraq Plan." *Washington Post,* January 11, 2007.

Posen, Barry R. *The Sources of Military Doctrine: France, Britain and Germany between the World Wars.* Ithaca, NY: Cornell University Press, 1984.

Powell, Colin. "U.S. Forces: Challenges Ahead." *Foreign Affairs* 71, no. 5 (Winter 1992).

"President Bush on Iraq, Elections, and Immigration." *Washington Post,* December 20, 2006.

Putrich, Gayle S. "U.S. House Panel Seeks FCS, JSF Cuts to '08 Authorization." *DefenseNews.com,* February 5, 2007.

Raghavan, Sudarsan, and Karin Brulliard. "April Toll Is Highest of '07 for U.S. Troops; Over 100 Killed in Month; Iraqi Deaths Far Higher." *Washington Post,* May 1, 2007.

Ramsey, Robert D. III. *Advising Indigenous Forces: American Advisors in Korea, Vietnam, and El Salvador.* Global War on Terrorism Occasional Paper 18. Ft. Leavenworth, KS: Combat Studies Institute Press, 2006.

Raz, Guy. "Army Focus on Counterinsurgency Debated Within." *NPR.com,* May 6, 2008.

Record, Jeffrey. "The American Way of War: Cultural Barriers to Successful Counterinsurgency." *Policy Analysis*, no. 577 (September 1, 2006).

———. *Revising U.S. Military Strategy: Tailoring Means to Ends*. McLean, VA: Pergamon-Brassey, 1984.

Reynolds, Col Kevin P. (ret.). "Insurgency/Counterinsurgency: Does the Army 'Get It?'" Paper for Presentation at the International Studies Association Annual Convention, February 28–March 3, 2007, Chicago, IL.

Rice, Condoleezza. "Campaign 2000: Promoting the National Interest." *Foreign Affairs* 79, no. 1 (January/February 2000).

———. "Iraq and U.S. Policy." Opening Remarks before the Senate Foreign Relations Committee. Washington, DC, October 19, 2005.

Ricks, Thomas E. *Fiasco: The American Military Adventure in Iraq*. London: Allen Lane, 2006.

———. "Officers with PhDs Advising War Effort." *Washington Post*, February 5, 2007.

———. "Situation Called Dire in West Iraq." *Washington Post*, September 11, 2006.

———. "U.S. Counterinsurgency Academy Giving Officers a New Mind-Set." *Washington Post*, February 21, 2006.

Ricks, Thomas E., and Michael Abramowitz. "A Meek Departure from the War Cabinet." *Washington Post*, November 9, 2006.

Robert H. Kupperman and Associates. *Low Intensity Conflict, Main Report*, vol. 1, ADA 137260. Washington, DC: Defense Technical Information Services, 1983.

Rohde, David. "Army Enlists Anthropology in War Zones." *New York Times*, October 5, 2007.

Romjue, John L. "The Evolution of the AirLand Battle Concept." *Air University Review* (May-June 1984).

Roosevelt, Ann. "FCS Would Bring Significant Advantages to Future Insurgency-Type Operations, Harvey Says." *Defense Daily*, January 23, 2007.

Rosen, Stephen P. *Winning the Next War: Innovation and the Modern Military*. Ithaca, NY: Cornell University Press, 1991.

Rothstein, Hy S. *Afghanistan and the Troubled Future of Unconventional Warfare*. Annapolis, MD: Naval Institute Press, 2006.

Roy, Olivier. "Development and Political Legitimacy: The Cases of Iraq and Afghanistan." *Conflict Security and Development* (Special Issue) 4, no. 2 (2004).

Rumsfeld, Donald. Secretary of Defense. "Beyond Nation Building." 11th Annual Salute to Freedom, New York, February 14, 2003.

———. "Special Briefing on the Unified Command Plan." Arlington, VA, April 17, 2002.

———. Official Welcoming Ceremony to Secretary of Defense Rumsfeld. Remarks as Delivered by Secretary of Defense Donald Rumsfeld. Washington, DC. January 26, 2001.

Salmoni, Barak A. "Advances in Pre-Deployment Culture Training: The U.S. Marine Corps Approach." *Military Review* 86, no. 6 (November-December 2006).

Sanger, David. "In White House, Debate Is Rising on Iraq Pullback." *New York Times*, July 9, 2007.

Sarkesian, Sam C. "Commentary on 'Low Intensity Warfare': Threat and Military Response." In *Proceedings of the Low-Intensity Conference.* Ft. McNair. Washington, DC: Department of Defense, January 14–15, 1986.

Scarborough, Rowan. *Rumsfeld's War.* Washington, DC: Regnery, 2004.

Schmidle, Brig. Gen. Robert E., USMC, and Lt. Col. Frank G. Hoffman (ret.), USMC. "Commanding the Contested Zones." *Proceedings*, September 2004.

Schmitt, Eric. "U.S. to Intensify Its Training in Iraq to Battle Insurgents." *New York Times*, November 2, 2005.

Schoomaker, Gen. Peter J. U.S. Army. "Foreword." In John A. Nagl, *Learning to Eat Soup with a Knife: Counterinsurgency Lessons from Malaya and Vietnam.* Chicago: University of Chicago Press, 2005.

———. Statement before the Commission on National Guard and Reserves. Washington, DC, December 14, 2006.

Scully, Megan. "Changes to Army's Modernization Program Come amid Congressional Concern." *Government Executive*, August 21, 2008.

———. "Conway Says Larger Marine Corps Will Be a 'Challenge.'" *Congress Daily*, March 13, 2007.

Senanayake, Sumedha. "Iraq: Al-Sadr Prepares for the Post-Coalition Era." *RFE/RL*, May 10, 2007.

"Senate Passes Iraq Withdrawal Bill; Veto Threat Looms." *CNN.com.* April 26, 2007.

Sepp, Kalev I. "Best Practices in Counterinsurgency." *Military Review* 85, no. 3 (May-June 2005).

Serafino, Nina M. *Peacekeeping: Issues of U.S. Military Involvement*, CRS Issues Brief for Congress, IB94040. Washington, DC: Congressional Research Service, August 6, 2003.

———. *Peacekeeping and Related Stability Operations: Issues of U.S. Military Involvement*, CRS Issues Brief for Congress, IB94040. Washington, DC: Congressional Research Service, June 25, 2005.

Sewall, Sarah. "A Radical Field Manual." Introductory note to *The U.S. Army/Marine Corps Counterinsurgency Field Manual.* Chicago: University of Chicago Press, 2007.

Shafer, Michael D. *Deadly Paradigms: The Failure of U.S. Counterinsurgency Policy.* Princeton, NJ: Princeton University Press, 1988.

Shanker, Thom. "Army Is Worried by Rising Stress of Return Tours to Iraq." *New York Times*, April 6, 2008.

———. "Mideast Commander Retires after Irking Bosses." *New York Times*, March 12, 2008.

Sherman, Jason. "New Blueprint for Irregular Warfare." *InsideDefense.com*, May 16, 2006.

Sherman, Maj. Gen. William T. Letter to the Mayor and City Council of Atlanta. September 12, 1864.

Shultz, Richard H. Jr. *In the Aftermath of War: U.S. Support for Reconstruction and Nation-Building in Panama following Just Cause.* Maxwell Air Force Base, AL: Air University Press, 1993.

———. "Low-Intensity Conflict: Future Challenges and the Lessons from the Reagan Years." *Survival* 31, no. 4 (1989).

Simon, Steven. "The Price of the Surge: How U.S. Strategy Is Hastening Iraq's Demise." *Foreign Affairs* 87, no. 3 (2008).

Smith, Maj. Neil, and Col. Sean MacFarland. "Anbar Awakens: The Tipping Point." *Military Review* 88, no. 2 (March-April 2008).

Spiegel, Peter. "Gates, White House Appear to Differ on Iraq Surge." *Los Angeles Times*, May 7, 2007.

Stanton, John. "US Army's Human Terrain System: From Super Concept to Absolute Farce." *Online Journal*, August 18, 2008.

———. "US Army Human Terrain System in Disarray." *Online Journal*, August 15, 2008.

Stewart, Richard W. "CORDS and the Vietnam Experience: An Interagency Organization for Counterinsurgency and Pacification." In Kendall D. Gott and Michael G. Brooks, eds. *Security Assistance: U.S. and International Historical Perspectives.* Proceedings of the Combat Studies Institute 2006 Military History Symposium. Ft. Leavenworth, KS, and Washington, DC: Combat Studies Institute Press, 2006.

Stringham, Col. Joseph S. III. "The Military Situation from the Fall of 1983 to the Turning Point." In Max G. Manwaring and Court Prisk, eds. *El Salvador at War: An Oral History of Conflict from the 1979 Insurrection to the Present.* Washington, DC: National Defense University Press, 1988.

Summers, Harry G. Jr. *On Strategy: The Vietnam War in Context.* Carlisle Barracks, PA: U.S. Army War College, 1981.

"Taking Shock Out of Culture." *Press Enterprise*, January 29, 2004.

Taw, Jennifer Morrison. *Operation Just Cause: Lessons for Operations Other than War.* Santa Monica, CA: RAND, 1995.

Terriff, Terry. "'Innovate or Die': Organizational Culture and the Origins of Maneuver Warfare in the United States Marine Corps." *Journal of Strategic Studies* 29, no. 3 (June 2006).

———. "Of Romans and Dragons: Preparing the U.S. Marine Corps for Future Warfare." *Contemporary Security Policy* 28, no. 1 (April 2007).

———. "Warriors and Innovators: Military Change and Organizational Culture in the U.S. Marine Corps." *Defence Studies* 6, no. 2 (June 2006).

"Terrorism: General Support for Military Action." *Americans and the World: Public Opinions on the World.* Available at www.americans-world.org/digest/global_issues/terrorism/terrorism_milAct.cfm.

Thompson, Loren B., ed. *Low Intensity Conflict: The Pattern of Warfare in the Modern World.* Lexington, MA: Lexington Books, 1989.

Thompson, Mark. "Why Our Army Is at the Breaking Point." *Time*, April 16, 2007.

Thompson, Robert. *Defeating Communist Insurgency: The Lessons of Malaya and Vietnam.* New York: Frederick A. Praeger Publishers, 1966.

Tilghman, Andrew. "The Army's Other Crisis: Why the Best and Brightest Young Officers Are Leaving." *Washington Monthly*, December 2007.

Tiron, Roxana. "Real-World Missions Shape Army Training." *National Defense,* March 2004.

Towell, Pat, and Stephen Daggett. *Defense: FY2009 Authorization and Appropriations,* CRS Report for Congress, RL34473. Washington, DC: Congressional Research Service, June 18, 2008.

Towell, Pat, Stephen Daggett, and Amy Belasco. *Defense: FY2008 Authorization and Appropriations, CRS Report for Congress,* RL33999. Washington, DC: Congressional Research Service. May 11, 2007.

Traub, James. "Making Sense of the Mission." *New York Times Magazine,* April 11, 2004.

Tyson, Ann Scott. "Pentagon Adds Initiatives, Retains Old Ones." *Washington Post,* February 7, 2006, p. A11.

———. "Petraeus Helping Pick New Generals: Army Says Innovation Will Be Rewarded."

———. "U.S. Tests New Tactics in Urban Warfare." *Christian Science Monitor,* November 9, 2004.

"USA TODAY/Gallup Poll on Iraq." *USA Today,* September 18, 2007.

U.S. Army-Air Force Center for Low-Intensity Conflict. *Joint Low-Intensity Conflict Final Report.* Langley AFB, VA: Center for Low-Intensity Conflict, 1986.

U.S. Department of the Air Force. Air Force Doctrine Document 2-3. *Irregular Warfare.* Washington, DC: Department of the Air Force, August 1, 2007.

U.S. Department of the Army. *2007 Army Posture Statement.* Washington, DC: U.S. Army, 2007.

———. *Army Action Plan for Stability Operations,* Army Campaign Plan Decision Point 105. Washington, DC: G-35 Strategy, Plans, and Policy, Department of the Army, August 2, 2007.

———. *Army Strategic Policy Guidance.* January 14, 2005. Available at www.army.mil/references/APSG14Jan05.doc.

———. FM 31-16. *Counterguerrilla Operations.* Washington, DC: Government Printing Office, 1967.

———. FMI 3-07-22. *Counterinsurgency Operations.* Washington, DC: U.S. Army, 2004.

———. FM 100-5. *Field Service Regulations: Operations.* Washington, DC: Government Printing Office, 1962.

———. FM 100-20. *Internal Defense and Development (IDAD).* Washington, DC: Government Printing Office, 1972.

———. FC 100-20. *Low-Intensity Conflict.* Ft. Leavenworth, KS, U.S. Army CGSC, 1986.

———. FM 100-23. *Peace Operations.* Washington, DC: U.S. Army, 1994.

———. FM 100-5. *Operations.* Washington, DC: Government Printing Office, 1986.

———. FM 100-5. *Operations.* Washington, DC: U.S. Army, 1993.

———. FM 3-0. *Operations.* Washington, DC: U.S. Army, 2001.

———. FM 3-0. *Operations.* Washington, DC: U.S. Army, 2008.

————. FM 3-07. *Stability Operations and Support Operations*. Washington, DC: U.S. Army, 2003.

U.S. Department of the Army. Army Training and Doctrine Command (TRADOC). *Army Comprehensive Guide to Modularity*. Ft. Monroe, VA: Department of the Army, 2004.

U.S. Department of the Army and United States Marine Corps. FM 3-24/MCWP 3-33.5. *Counterinsurgency*. Washington, DC: U.S. Army, 2006.

————. "Defense Department Operational Briefing: Secretary of Defense Donald H. Rumsfeld." Arlington, VA, January 13, 2004.

————. *Defense Language Transformation Roadmap*. Washington, DC: Department of Defense, 2005.

————. "Defense Secretary Gates Announces Recommendations to the President on Key Leadership Positions." Arlington, VA, January 5, 2007.

————. *Directive 3000.05: Military Support for Stability, Security, Transition, and Reconstruction (SSTR) Operations*. Washington, DC: Department of Defense, 2005.

————. *Directive 5100.1: Functions of the Department of Defense and Its Major Components*. Washington, DC: Department of Defense, 2002.

————. "DoD Media Roundtable with Secretary Gates and Gen. Pace in the Pentagon Briefing Room." Arlington, VA, June 21, 2007.

————. "DoD News Briefing—Secretary Rumsfeld and Gen. Myers." Arlington, VA, April 11, 2003.

————. "DoD News Briefing with Gen. Petraeus from the Pentagon." Arlington, VA, April 26, 2007.

————. "DoD News Briefing with Secretary Gates and Under Secretary Jonas from the Pentagon." Alexandria, VA, February 5, 2007.

————. "DoD News Briefing with Secretary of Defense Robert Gates and Adm. Mullen from the Pentagon, Arlington, Va." July 31, 2008.

————. "DoD News Briefing with Under Secretary of Defense David Chu, Lt. Gen. Stephen Speakes, and Lt. Gen. Emerson Gardner from the Pentagon." Arlington, VA, January 19, 2007.

————. *Fiscal Year 2009 Budget Request: Summary Justification*. Arlington, VA: Department of Defense, February 4, 2008.

————. *Irregular Warfare Joint Operations Concept*. Washington, DC: Department of Defense, 2007.

————. *National Defense Strategy of the United States of America*. Washington, DC: Department of Defense, 2005.

————. "President Bush Meets with Senior U.S. Defense Officials on Iraq." Arlington, VA, December 13, 2006.

————. *Quadrennial Defense Review Report*. Washington, DC: Department of Defense, 2001.

————. *Quadrennial Defense Review Report*. Washington, DC: Department of Defense, 2006.

————. *Report of the Quadrennial Defense Review*. Washington, DC: Department of Defense, 1997.

————. *Restricted Engagement Options.* Washington, DC: Government Printing Office, 1973.

————. "Rumsfeld and Myers Briefing on Enduring Freedom." Arlington, VA, October 7, 2001.

————. "Secretary Gates Addresses the Marine Corps Association." Arlington, VA, July 18, 2007.

————. "Secretary Rumsfeld Media Availability with Jay Garner." Arlington, VA, June 18, 2003.

————. *Transformation Planning Guidance.* Washington, DC: Department of Defense, 2003.

U.S. Department of Defense. Office of the Under Secretary of Defense for Policy. *Interim Progress Report on DoD Directive 3000.05: Military Support for Stability, Security, Transition, and Reconstruction (SSTR) Operations.* Washington, DC: Department of Defense, 2006.

U.S. Department of State. "About S/CRS." May 18, 2006. Available at www.state.gov/s/crs/c12936.htm.

————. "State Department Stands up Active Response Corps." Fact Sheet. August 23, 2006. Available at www.state.gov/s/crs/rls/71038.htm.

————. *U.S. Government Counterinsurgency Guide.* Washington, DC: Bureau of Political-Military Affairs, January 2009.

U.S. Government Accountability Office. *Peace Operations: Effect of Training, Equipment, and Other Factors on Unit Capability,* NSIAD-96-14, October 18, 1995.

————. *Peace Operations: Heavy Use of Key Capabilities May Affect Response to Regional Conflicts,* NSIAD-95-51, October 18, 1995.

————. *Stabilization and Reconstruction: Actions Needed to Improve Governmentwide Planning and Capabilities for Future Operations.* GAO-08-228T. Washington, DC: GAO, 2007.

U.S. House of Representatives. House Armed Services Committee. *Agency Stovepipes vs Strategic Agility: Lessons We Need to Learn from Provincial Reconstruction Teams in Iraq, and Afghanistan,* 41-409. Washington, DC: HASC Subcommittee on Oversight, and Investigations, April 2008.

U.S. Marine Corps. *Center of Excellence Charter.* January 14, 2006. Center for Advanced Operational Culture Learning. Available at www.tecom.usmc.mil/caocl/Includes/CAOCL%20COE.pdf.

————. "Joint Urban Warrior 05 Fact Sheet." Warfighting Laboratory. Available at www.mcwl.usmc.mil/factsheets/JUW05.pdf.

————. "Marine Corps Operating Concepts for a Changing Security Environment." 2006.

————. FMFM 8-2. *Operations against Guerrilla Forces.* Quantico, VA: USMC, 1962.

————. *Small-Unit Leaders' Guide to Counterinsurgency.* Quantico, VA: Marine Corps Combat Development Command (MCCDC), 2006.

————. *Small Wars Manual.* Washington, DC: Government Printing Office, 1940.

————. *Tentative Manual for Countering Irregular Threats: An Updated Approach to Counterinsurgency Operations.* Quantico, VA: Marine Corps Combat Development Command (MCCDC). 2006.

U.S. Senate. "Foreign Affairs Authorization Act, Fiscal Years 2006 and 2007." U.S. Senate Report 109-035, 109th Congress, 1st Session. March 10, 2005.

U.S. Senate Armed Services Committee. Hearing to consider nomination of Lt. Gen. David H. Petraeus to be General and Commander, Multi-National Forces-Iraq, January 23, 2007. Transcript available at www.armed-services.senate.gov /statemnt/2007/January/Petraeus%2001-23-07.pdf.

Ucko, David. "Countering Insurgents through Distributed Operations: Insights from Malaya." *Journal of Strategic Studies* 30, no. 1 (February 2007).

———. "Innovation or Inertia: The U.S. Military and the Learning of Counterinsurgency." *Orbis* 52, no. 2 (Spring 2008).

———. "Militias, Tribes and Insurgents: The Challenge of Political Reintegration in Iraq." *Conflict, Security and Development* 8, no. 3 (2008).

———. "Upcoming Iraqi Elections Must Consolidate Security Gains of 'Sons of Iraq,'" *World Politics Review*, May 20, 2008.

———. "U.S. Counterinsurgency in the Information Age." *Jane's Intelligence Review* 17, no. 10 (December 2005).

Ullman, Harlan, and James P. Wade. *Shock and Awe: Achieving Rapid Dominance.* Washington, DC: National Defense University Press, 1996.

United Nations. "Report of the Secretary General Pursuant to Paragraph 30 of Resolution 1546 (2004)." S/2007/330, June 5, 2007.

Vanden Brook, Tom. "Redeploy Troops in Iraq Soon, Brass Say." *USA Today*, December 14, 2006.

von Drehle, David. "Rumsfeld's Transformation: There's Been a Small Change in Plan." *Washington Post*, February 12, 2006.

Waghelstein, Col. John D. "What's Wrong in Iraq? Or Ruminations of a Pachyderm." *Military Review* 86, no. 1 (January-February 2006).

Wagner, Spc. Jim. "Gardez Office Opening Signals Shift in Afghanistan Mission." *DefendAmerica.com*, February 4, 2003.

Warner, Volney J., and James H. Willbanks. "Preparing Field Grade Leaders for Today and Tomorrow." *Military Review* 86, no. 1 (January-February 2006).

Watson, Brian G. *Reshaping the Expeditionary Army to Win Decisively: The Case for Greater Stabilization Capacity in the Modular Force.* Carlisle, PA: U.S. Army War College, Strategic Studies Institute, 2005.

Weigley, Russell F. "American Strategy from the Beginning through the First World War" In Peter Paret, ed., *The Makers of Modern Strategy.* Princeton, NJ: Princeton University Press.

———. *The American Way of War: A History of United States Military Strategy and Policy.* Bloomington, IN: Indiana University Press, 1973.

Weinberger, Caspar W. *Annual Report to Congress,* fiscal year 1988 (Washington, DC: Department of Defense), January 1987.

———. "The Uses of Military Power." Remarks to the National Press Club, November 28, 1984. News Release No. 609-84.

Westervelt, Eric. "Iraqi Tribal Leaders Work to Improve Security." *NPR.com*, November 12, 2007.

White House, "Management of Interagency Efforts Concerning Reconstruction and Stabilization." NSPD 44, December 7, 2005.

————. *The National Security Strategy of the United States of America.* Washington, DC: White House, 2006.

————. *The National Strategy for Combating Terrorism.* Washington, DC: White House, 2006.

————. "A Period of Consequences." Address given at the Citadel, South Carolina, September 23, 2003.

————. "President Bush Discusses Iraq." Washington, DC, April 10, 2008.

————. "President Discusses War on Terror and Operation Iraqi Freedom." Renaissance Cleveland Hotel, Cleveland, OH, March 20, 2006.

————. "President Speaks on War Effort to Citadel Cadets." South Carolina, December 11, 2001.

————. "President's Address to the Nation." Washington, DC, January 10, 2007.

————. "Press Conference by the President." Washington, DC, November 8, 2006.

————. "Remarks by the President at U.S. Naval Academy Commencement." Annapolis, MD, May 25, 2001.

White, John C. Jr. "American Military Strategy in the Second Seminole War." Research paper submitted to Marine Corps Command and Staff College, April 1995.

Wilson, James Q. *Bureaucracy.* New York: Basic Books, 1989.

Woodward, Bob. *Plan of Attack.* New York: Simon and Schuster, 2004.

————. *State of Denial.* New York: Simon and Schuster, 2006.

Wright, Robin, and Ann Scott Tyson. "Joint Chiefs Advise Change in War Strategy." *Washington Post,* December 14, 2006.

Yingling, Lt. Col. Paul. "A Failure in Generalship." *Armed Forces Journal* (May 2007).

ABOUT THE AUTHOR

David H. Ucko is a Transatlantic Fellow at the Stiftung Wissenschaft und Politik in Berlin, Germany. A former research fellow at the Department of War Studies, King's College London, Dr. Ucko has also enjoyed fellowships with the RAND Corporation, the Institute for National Strategic Studies of the National Defense University (NDU), and with the International Institute for Strategic Studies in Washington, D.C. He earned his PhD at the Department of War Studies with a thesis that examines the U.S. military's institutional learning of counterinsurgency and stability operations.

INDEX

Abizaid, John, 115, 120
Abrams, Creighton, 156
Abrams Doctrine, 156–57
"Absalon" training simulation, 32
Abu Sayyaf Group (ASG), 90–91
Active Corps (AC), rebalance of Reserve Corps and, 156–58, 173
Active Response Corps, 97
adaptation, 16–17, 28–29
advisory approach to counterinsurgency, 36–40
Afghanistan operations: best practices, 16; HTTs, 165; Operation Enduring Freedom, 56–57; postwar stabilization plans, 12–13; PRTs, 163, 164; security operations, 69; setbacks to U.S., 2–3; shift of military approach, 59; stability operations, 57–58
AFP, 90–91
Aideed, Mohamed Farrah, 48–49
Air Force Doctrine Center, 132
Air Force Doctrine Document 2-3, 132–33
Air Force Joint Tactical Air Control program, 86
Air University, 132
al-Askari Mosque (Samarra) bombing attack, 104, 112
Allison, Graham, 15
All Marine Messages (2003, 2005), 67
al-Maliki, Nouri, 122–23
al-Qaeda, 54–57, 104
al-Qaeda in Iraq (AQI), 126, 127

anticipation, in counterinsurgency syndrome, 27–28
AQI, 126, 127
Armed Forces of the Philippines (AFP), 90–91
Army Action Plan for Stability Operations, 132
Army Comprehensive Guide to Modularity (2004), 155
Army Focus Areas, 67
Army National Guard recruitment, 160, 215n107
Army of the Republic of Vietnam (ARVN), 38
Army Posture Statement (2007), 148
Army Strategic Policy Guidance (2005), 67
Army War College, 144
ARVN, 38
ASG, 90–91
Association of the United States Army, 134
asymmetric armed threats, 2. *See also* irregular warfare/operations
Atlacatl battalion, 38
Atonal battalion, 38
Aviation Captains Career Course (Army), 143–44
Aylwin-Foster, Nigel R. F., 78, 104

Bacevich, Andrew J., 39
Badr Organization, 129

Baghdad Security Plan, 171

balance of military priorities, 141–67; budget as indicator of, 145–51; and force structure, 151–66; institutional constraints in, 142–45

Balkans peace operations, 49–51, 57

Basic Officer Course (USMC), 144

BCTs. *See* brigade combat teams

Belloso battalion, 38

Berdal, Mats, 14

"Best Practices in Counterinsurgency" (Kalev I. Sepp), 76–77

Binnendijk, Hans, 152

Blaufarb, Douglas, 4, 32, 40, 41, 43, 44

Board for Low Intensity Conflict (National Security Council), 33

Boot, Max, 87, 93, 125, 150, 213n59

Bosnia peace operations, 49–51

bottom-up learning, 16, 17

Breaking the Phalanx (Douglas A. Mac-Gregor), 153

brigade combat teams (BCTs), 85–86, 152–56, 161, 162, 173

British Army, 11, 16, 76, 181

budget(s), 173; and 2006 QDR decisions, 84–85; 2007 defense budget requests, 87; and future successes, 181–82; as indicator of priorities, 145–51; for technologies, 19–20

Bush, George W., 4, 47; and ground forces increase, 120, 158, 159; Iraq situation blamed on, 179; on McMaster, 75; military priorities/strategies of, 51–54, 99; and new Iraq strategy, 112–15, 177; and Petraeus's promotion, 131; and positive effects of surge, 131; and Rumsfeld's resignation, 113, 177; transformation supported by, 193n32; veto of military funding bill by, 121

C4ISR, 55

CAOCL, 72, 73

capability for counterinsurgency, 18–21; during 1960s, 31–32; during 1980s, 32–33

CAP program, 28, 43

Capstone Concept for Joint Operations (CCJO), 71

Captains Career Course (Army), 143

Caraher, Leigh C., 21

Casey, George W., Jr., 76, 115, 120

Cassidy, Robert, 42

CCJO, 71

CENTCOM, 131, 177, 178

Center for Advanced Operational Culture Learning (CAOCL) (Quantico, Virginia), 72, 73

Center for Low-Intensity Conflict (CLIC), 32–33

Center for Strategic and Budgetary Assessments (CSBA), 145

"Changing the Army for Counterinsurgency Operations" (Nigel R. F. Aylwin-Foster), 78

Chapman, Leonard F., 30

Chiarelli, Peter W., 77, 106, 131–32, 134

civilian agencies: availability/capability of, 68, 94–100; counterinsurgency tasks conducted by, 12; division of labor with, 110, 169; FM 3-24/MCWP 3-33.5 input from, 105; military's criticism of, 180; Response Readiness Reserve, 97; *Stability Operations JOC* provisions for, 68–69

Civilian Reserve Corps, 97–98

Civil Operations and Revolutionary Development Support. *See* CORDS program

Civil War (U.S.), 28

CJTF-HOA, 90

clear, hold, and build strategy, 74–75, 84, 115

CLIC, 32–33

Clinton, Bill, 49, 50

Cody, Richard, 135

COIN. *See* counterinsurgency campaigns/operations

COIN Academy (Camp Taji, Iraq), 76

COIN community, 78, 103; and counterinsurgency conference, 108–9; and FM 3-24, 112, 114, 116, 119; and future events in Iraq War, 178;

Gates's association with, 134; learning by, 170; resistance to, 134, 137, 172–74; and success of the surge, 121

Cold War, 31, 173–74, 181

collective punishment, 28

Combined Action Platoon (CAP) program, 28, 43

Combined Arms Operations Research Activity, 32

Combined Joint Task Force Horn of Africa (CJTF-HOA), 90

Command, Control, Communications, Computers, Intelligence, Surveillance, and Reconnaissance (C4ISR), 55

Command and General Staff College (Fort Leavenworth), 75–76

Commandant's Planning Guidance (USMC), 136

communist subversion, threat of, 30–31

concept papers, as evidence of learning, 18, 20

conflation of irregular operations, 34–36, 51, 88–89

Conflict Response Fund, 98

conventional warfare, 1; budget requests supporting, 147–48; as core mission, 40–41; fear of losing capability for, 135–36; historical concentration on, 26; and military training courses, 143–44; in Vietnam, 43

Conway, James T., 136, 146–47

CORDS program, 28, 43, 163–64

Counterguerrilla Operations (FM 31-16), 35

counterguerrilla operations (in 1960s), 30–32, 40–41, 43–46; and advisory approach, 36–38; appearance of learning from, 33–34; and conflation of irregular operations, 34–35; as learning process, 25–26

"Countering Global Insurgency" (David Kilcullen), 78

Counterinsurgency Center (Fort Leavenworth), 108

counterinsurgency (COIN) campaigns/operations, 1–4, 10–13; complexity of, 110–12; counterterrorism vs., 88; JCS definition of, 183n2. *See also* learning of counterinsurgency

Counterinsurgency Era, The (Douglas Blaufarb), 4

Counterinsurgency (FM 3-24/MCWP 3-33.5), 103–5, 109–16, 170; assumption of troop deployment in, 109–10; and complexity of counterinsurgency, 110–12; conference on, 104–5; deviation of surge conditions from, 123–24; field implementation of, 112–16, 178; and need to take on nonmilitary tasks, 110

"Counterinsurgency in the 21st Century" conference, 108–9

Counterinsurgency Operations (FMI 3-07.22), 66–70

counterinsurgency syndrome, 25, 27–30, 186n10

counter network operations, 138

counterterrorism operations, 10, 88–90

Crocker, Ryan C., 131

Crowell, Lorenzo, 44

Cruz, Ginger, 164–65

CSBA, 145

cultural knowledge and awareness, 72, 87, 165

Culture Center (TRADOC), 108

Cuomo, Scott, 143, 144, 161

Dagger Brigade (1st Infantry Division), 127, 128

Defense Authorization Act (1987), 37

defense budget (FY07), 87

defense industry, in Iron Triangle, 20

Defense Language Office, 72

Defense Language Transformation Roadmap, 72, 73

Defense Science Board (DSB): 2004 Summer Study by, 44, 65, 154; 2005 report of, 73

Depuy, William, 43

direct action, 93–94, 138, 200n44

direct engagements, 11, 36, 137

Dobbins, James, 179

doctrine: of the 1960s, 34–35; bias against MOOTW in, 50; as

doctrine: of the 1960s *(cont'd.)*
  evidence of learning, 17–18, 20. *See
  also specific publications*
DoD. *See* U.S. Department of Defense
*DoD Directive 3000.05: Military Sup-
  port for Stability, Security, Transition,
  and Reconstruction (SSTR) Operations,* 73–74, 98, 139, 143–45,
  170–71
Doughty, Robert, 43
Downie, Richard, 4, 16, 44–45
DSB. *See* Defense Science Board

Edelman, Eric S., 17
education: as evidence of learning, 18,
  20–21; initiatives of the 1960s, 35
El Salvador, advisory approach in,
  38–39
El Salvador Armed Forces (ESAF), 38,
  39
England, Gordon, 137, 147, 211n112
ESAF, 38, 39
European Command Counterterrorism
  Initiative, 90
extrabudgetary funding, 145–47, 173

Fallon, William J., 131
Farabundo Marti National Liberation
  Front (FMLN), 38, 39
Fastabend, David, 152
FCS. *See* Future Combat System
FID, 89, 138
1st Infantry Division, 127, 128
1st Special Operations Command, 37
First Air Commando Group, 37
Fleet Marine Force Manual 8-2, 32, 35
Flournoy, Michèle, 84, 160–61
FM 3-0, 58, 69, 133–34
FM 3-07, 69
FM 3-24/MCWP 3-33.5, See *Coun-
  terinsurgency* (FM 3–24/MCWP
  3–33.5)
FM 31-16, 35
FM 100-5, 32, 36
FM 100-20, 32, 190n89
FM 100-23, 48
FMI 3-07.22, 66–70
FMLN, 38, 39

force structure, 151–66; ad hoc innovations in, 162–66; as evidence of prioritization, 18, 141, 173; increase in
  ground forces, 158–62; modularization, 152–56; rebalance of Active
  and Reserve Corps, 156–58
foreign ground troops: in advisory approach, 37; deployment of, 11
foreign internal defense (FID), 89, 138
Freedman, Lawrence, 23
full-spectrum operations concept, 106,
  133, 156
Future Combat System (FCS), 86, 149,
  150, 155, 200n34

Galula, David, 96
GAO brief, 142–43
Gates, Robert, viii, 113–14, 130–31; on
  asymmetric capabilities, 141; and
  funding of military programs,
  150–51; HTT funding by, 165;
  and increase in ground forces, 159;
  and MRAP production/fielding,
  146; and Next-War-itis, 136; as
  proponent for irregular operations,
  134
Gentile, Gian, 136
Giambastiani, Edmund, 98
Golden Battalion, 129
Goldwater-Nichols Reorganization Act
  (1986), 41
Gorman, Paul F., 42
governance, establishment of, 2
Government Accountability Office
  (GAO) brief, 142–43
Grissom, Adam, 16
ground forces, increase in, 158–62, 173
guerrilla tactics, 2; Army officers' perception of, 41; doctrine and training
  for, 32, 34–35; in Revolutionary
  War, 26; in U.S. Civil War, 28. *See
  also* counterguerrilla operations

Hagee, Michael, 67
Haiti peace operations, 49
Henry, Ryan, 81–82, 87, 97
Hoffman, Frank, 149, 150, 162
Howard, Michael, 14, 176

HTTs, 165–66
human terrain, 72, 142
Human Terrain Teams (HTTs), 165–66

IDA, 154
improvised explosive devices (IEDs), 146
Indian Wars, 28
indirect approach to irregular warfare, 89–92, 94, 137, 173–75
Infantry Officer Course (USMC), 144
Infantry Squad Leader Course (USMC), 144
innovation, 15–16, 21, 177
Institute for Defense Analyses (IDA), 154
institutional constraints on reorientation, 142–45
institutional learning: bottom-up and top-down, 16–17; broad framework for, 18; concept papers as evidence of, 20; culture, education, and training as evidence of, 20–21; doctrine as evidence of, 17–18, 20; drivers of, 15–16; integrative approach to, 16; organizational structures as evidence of, 21–22; perspectives on, 15; prerequisites for, 16; and success of surge, 132; technology as evidence of, 19–20. *See also* learning of counterinsurgency
insurgents, 2
integrative approach to military learning, 16
Interim Progress Report on DoD Directive 3000.05, Military Support for Stability, Security, Transition, and Reconstruction (SSTR) Operations, 142
Internal Defense and Development (FM 100-20), 190n89
International Crisis Group, 130
International Security Assistance Force, 57
"Iraq: The Social Context of Improvised Explosive Devices" (Montgomery McFate), 77
Iraq Counterinsurgency Guidance (2007), 163

Iraq Study Group (ISG), 113, 115
Iraq Syndrome, 23
Iraq War, 59–60; al-Askari Mosque attack, 104; best practices in, 16; blame for results of, 179–80; casualties in, 123, 125, 207n21; clear, hold, and build strategy for, 74–75, 84, 115; early assumptions about, 212n21; funding for, 145; and increase in ground forces, 158, 159; learning of counterinsurgency during, 66, 171–72, 176–78; ongoing adaptation in, 17; operationalization of FM 3-24 in, 112–16; Operation Together Forward II, 115–16; postwar stabilization plans for, 12–13; PRTs in, 163–65; as representative of future wars, 176–79; security operations in, 69; setbacks to U.S. in, 2–3; stabilization operations in, 3, 60–61
Iron Triangle, 20
Irregular Warfare (Air Force Doctrine Document 2-3), 132–33
Irregular Warfare Joint Operating Concept (IWJOC), 132
irregular warfare/operations: and 2001 QDR, 55–56; and 2006 QDR, 82–83; antipathy toward, vii; challenges of, 2; conflation of, 34–36, 51, 88–89; definitions of, 88, 133; frequency and duration of, 1, 27, 175–76; indirect approach to, 89–92, 94, 173–75; institutionalizing adaptations to, vii–viii; likelihood of facing, 13–14; military's avoidance of, 2; in policy statements/publications, 67; and transformation process, 53. *See also* counterinsurgency campaigns/operations; stability operations
Irregular Warfare Roadmap, 137–39
Isenberg, David, 86
ISG, 113, 115
IWJOC, 132

Jaffe, Greg, 148
JFCOM. *See* Joint Forces Command

Joint Chiefs of Staff (JCS): CCJO, 71; Joint Counter-Insurgency Concept and Doctrinal Guidance, 32; progress report of 1962, 33; on the surge, 119–20

Joint Counter-Insurgency Concept and Doctrinal Guidance (JCS), 32

Joint Doctrine for Military Operations Other than War (Joint Publication 3-07), 48

Joint Forces Command (JFCOM), 56, 66, 68–70, 73

Joint Low-Intensity Conflict Project Final Report, 32–33

Joint Publication 3-0, 107–8

Joint Publication 3-07, 48

Joint Readiness Training Center (Fort Polk, Louisiana), 66

Joint Strike Fighters (JSF), 147

Joint Urban Warrior 05, 73

Joint Urgent Operational Needs Statement (for HTTs), 165

Joint Vision 2010 (JV 2010), 82

JSF, 147

JV 2010, 82

Kagan, Frederick W., 82, 148–49

Kaplan, Fred, 134, 143, 148, 181

Kaplan, Robert, 91

Kennedy, John F., 30–31, 34

Khrushchev, Nikita, 31

Kilcullen, David, 77–78, 116

Kiszely, John, 176

Kosiak, Steven M., 145, 147, 181, 182

Kosovo peace operations, 49–51, 58

Krepinevich, Andrew, 10, 74–75, 160, 162

Krulak, Charles, 54, 73

Krulak, Victor H., 32

Kupperman, Robert, 41

language skills/training, 72, 87, 197n46

Learning from Conflict (Richard Downie), 4

learning (in general): appearance of learning vs., 30, 33–39; bottom-up, 16, 17; by COIN community, 170; concept of, 4; institutionalization of, 16–17; organizational, 3, 4; top-down, 16–17. *See also* institutional learning

learning of counterinsurgency, 104–9, 169–82; as applicable to modern wars, 4; bottom-up approach to, 16; in counterinsurgency syndrome, 29–30; within the DoD, 170–75; Downie's framework for, 17; in guerrilla warfare of 1960s, 25–26, 30–38, 40–41, 43–46; and indirect approach to irregular warfare, 174–75; institutional hindrance to, 3; and Iraq as representative of future wars, 176–79; knowledge and skills of, 4; in low-intensity threats of 1980s, 25–26, 30–33, 35–46; military's future pursuit of, 179–82; operationalization of, 171; previous studies of, 4; questionable assumptions in, 169; reasons for, 12–14; resistance to, 134–36, 172–73. *See also* reorientation of the military

Lebanon peacekeeping mission, 53

"lesser-included" cases, 50, 82

LIC. *See* low-intensity conflict

LID, 41–42

light infantry division (LID), 41–42

Low Intensity Conflict (FM 100-20), 32

low-intensity conflict (LIC) (in 1980s), 30–33, 40–46; and advisory approach to counterinsurgency, 36–39; appearance of learning from, 33; and conflation of irregular threats, 35–36; as learning process, 25–26

low-intensity conflict (LIC) (in general), 4, 35

MacFarland, Sean B., 127, 131

MacGregor, Douglas A., 135, 153

Maechling, Charles, Jr., 34

Mahdi Army, 128–30

Malaya, British campaign in, 11, 16, 76

"maneuver warfare" concept (USMC), 42

Mansoor, Peter, 116

Marine Corps Advisor Group, 162

Marine Corps Association, 134
Marine Corps Operating Concepts for a Changing Security Environment, 105–6
Marks, Thomas A., 94
Mattis, James N., 72, 104
McCaffrey, Barry, 125
McFate, Montgomery, 77
McMaster, H. R., 13, 17, 75, 116, 131, 184n10
McNamara, Robert S., 53
Michaelis, Patrick R., 77
military occupational specialties (MOS), 21, 156, 157
Military Operations Other Than War (MOOTW), 48–51, 107
Military Review, 76–78
Mine Resistant Ambush Vehicles (MRAPs), 146–47
mixed messages, 71–74
MNF-I. *See* Multinational Force Iraq
mock villages, for urban operations, 66
modern wars, learning process for, 4, 14
modularization of forces, 85–86, 152–56
MOOTW, 48–51, 107
MOS. *See* military occupational specialties
motivation for learning counterinsurgency, 30–31
MRAPs, 146–47
Multinational Force Iraq (MNF-I), 114, 115, 131, 177

Nagl, John, 76, 104–5, 162
National Defense Strategy (NDS) (2005), 70–71
National Front for the Liberation of South Vietnam (NLF), 33
National Guard, 161
National Military Strategy (NMS) (2004), 70
National Security Action Memorandum (NSAM) 2, 31
National Security Presidential Directive (NSPD) 44, 99
National Training Center (Fort Irwin, California), 66

nation-building, 12, 21, 52. *See also* state-building
NDS (2005), 70–71
Next-War-itis, 136
Nixon Doctrine (1969), 40
NLF, 33
NMS (2004), 70
nonpermissive operational environments, 9, 49, 54, 69, 169
Noriega, Manuel, regime, 43, 44
Norman, Lloyd, 41
NSAM 2, 31
NSPD 44, 99

Odierno, Raymond T., 131
Office of Force Transformation (OFT), 56
Office of Reconstruction and Humanitarian Assistance (ORHA), 60
Office of the Coordinator for Reconstruction and Stabilization (S/CRS), 96–98
Office of the Inspector General on Iraq Reconstruction, 164
Office of the Secretary of Defense (OSD): DSB study request by, 65; internal stability operations report, 99, 100; mismatch in rhetoric and provisions of, 70–71; Office of Force Transformation, 56; Office of Reconstruction and Humanitarian Assistance, 60; Stability Operations Office, 74
OFT, 56
"oil-spot" technique, 74
101st Airborne Division, 75
Operational Maneuver from the Sea, 150
Operation Blind Logic, 44
Operation Enduring Freedom, 56–57, 58
Operation Fardh al-Qanoon, 103–4, 119, 121–22, 128, 169, 171
Operation Just Cause, 44
Operation Restore Democracy, 49
Operations against Guerrilla Forces (Fleet Marine Force Manual 8-2), 32, 35

Operations (FM 3-0), 58, 69, 133–34
Operations (FM 100-5), 32, 36
Operations (JP 3-0), 107–8
Operation Together Forward II, 115–16
organizational decision making, 15
organizational learning, 3, 4
organizational structures, 21–22
ORHA, 60
OSD. *See* Office of the Secretary of
    Defense

Pace, Peter, 123
Panama invasion (1989), 43–44
paradoxes of counterinsurgencies, 111
Parameters, 77
PDD 25, 49
Peacekeeping Institute, 48
Peace Operations (FM 100-23), 48
peace (peacekeeping) operations, 10,
    48; in the Balkans, 49–50, 57, 58; in
    Haiti, 49; in Lebanon, 53; military
    distaste for, 51; PDD 25, 49; Rice's
    statement on, 21, 50, 52; in Soma-
    lia, 48–49
Pentagon. *See* U.S. Department of De-
    fense
pentathlete soldier concept, 159, 160
permissive peacekeeping environments,
    49–50
Peters, Ralph, 2, 25
Petraeus, David: and counterinsurgency
    manual conference, 104; at Fort
    Leavenworth, 75; limitations on,
    124; promotion of, 131; and PRTs,
    163; and Sadr's Mahdi Army,
    129–30; and strategy for Iraq, 112,
    114–16, 130–31, 171; and success
    of the surge, 120–23, 178
phased operational planning, 107
Philippines counterinsurgency, 27–29,
    90–91
PME programs, 18, 185n37
Powell, Colin, 53, 97
precision bombing, 51
Presidential Decision Directive (PDD)
    25, 49
priorities of the military: budget as in-
    dicator of, 87, 145–51; for coun-

terinsurgency, 18–19; mismatch of
    formal initiatives and, 67–71; mis-
    match of operations and, 26
professional military education (PME)
    programs, 18, 185n37
Project Metropolis, 54
Provincial Reconstruction Team (PRT),
    59, 163–65, 195n67

Quadrennial Defense Review (1997
    QDR), 82
Quadrennial Defense Review (2001
    QDR), 52, 55, 82
Quadrennial Defense Review (2006
    QDR), 81–202; anticipation of,
    81–82; assumption of non-DoD sta-
    bility initiatives in, 94–100; concept
    of irregular warfare in, 88–94; con-
    tradictions in, 83–88; irregular war-
    fare emphasis in, 82–83; major
    decisions in, 84; on modularization,
    153
Quadrennial Defense Review (QDR),
    81

Ramsey, Robert, 39
rational-actor perspective, 15
RC. *See* Reserve Corps
Ready First Combat Team (RFCT—1st
    Brigade, 1st Armored Division),
    126–28
Reagan, Ronald, 33, 37
rebels, 2
reconstruction activities, 2
recruitment of forces, 160, 215n107
reorientation of the military, 47–63,
    65–80; change in approach to,
    74–78; initiatives for, 65–67; institu-
    tional constraints on, 142–45; mis-
    match of priorities and initiatives
    for, 67–71; mixed messages in,
    71–74; MOOTW, 48–51; motiva-
    tion for, 3; and permissive peace-
    keeping environments, 49–50;
    RMA, 51–52; types of missions in-
    volved in, 9–10; for the War on Ter-
    ror, 54–61. *See also* learning of
    counterinsurgency

Reserve Corps (RC): borrowing of forces from, 152; rebalance of Active Corps and, 156–58, 173; recruitment shortage for, 160
Response Readiness Reserve, 97
Restricted Engagement Options study (1973), 41
Revolutionary War, 26
Revolution in Military Affairs (RMA), 51–52, 82
Reynolds, Kevin P., 144, 148
RFCT—1st Brigade, 1st Armored Division, 126–28
Rice, Condoleezza, 21, 50–52, 74, 97, 177
RMA, 51–52, 82
Root, Elihu, 26
Rothstein, Hy S., 92–94
Rumsfeld, Donald, 47, 52–59, 61, 113, 158–59, 177
Russo-Japanese War, 29

Sadr, Moqtada al-, 128–30
Samarra bombing attack, 104, 112
Schoomaker, Peter, 67, 76
Schultz, Tammy, 160–61
S/CRS, 96–98
SEALs, 37, 90
Second Seminole War, 27–29
Sepp, Kalev I. "Gunner," 76–77
September 11, 2001 terrorist attacks, 47–48, 54, 55
Shafer, Michael, 19
Sherman, William Tecumseh, 29
Shias, 128, 129
Shinseki, Eric, 153, 179, 217n11
Small Wars Center of Excellence, 72, 73
Small Wars Manual (USMC), 29, 187n23
Smith, Lance, 136
SOCOM. *See* Special Operations Command
SOF. *See* Special Operations Forces
Somalia intervention, 48
Sons of Iraq, 128
Soviet Union, 29–31. *See also* Cold War
Special Air Warfare Center (Fort Bragg), 37

Special Forces (SF), 36, 90
Special Group (Counter-Insurgency), 31
specialized units, for stability operations, 152
Special Operations Command (SOCOM), 37, 90, 93
Special Operations Forces (SOF), 14, 36–37, 58, 89–94, 138, 174–75
"special warfare," 35
Special Warfare units, 37
SPG 2006-11, 65–66
Spore, John B., 41
SSTR operations, 73–74, 95–100
Stability, Security, Transition, and Reconstruction Division (U.S. Army), 108
stability, security, transition, and reconstruction (SSTR) operations, 73–74, 95–100
stability operations, 1–2, 10–11; in Afghanistan, 12–13, 57–58; Army training for, 21–22; characteristics required for, 21; counterinsurgency campaigns vs., 10; DoD 2005 directive on, 96; in DSB report, 65; and experience with MOOTW, 48; as growth business, 12; as integral to national security, 19; in Iraq, 12–13, 60–61; JCS definition of, 183n2; joint conceptual understanding of, 66; in Panama, 44; as population-centered, 10–11; specialized units for, 151–52; in SPG 2006-11, 65–66; tasks involved in, 2; unanticipated engagements in, 13; as valuable to long-term success, 110
Stability Operations and Support Operations (FM 3-07), 69
Stability Operations Joint Operating Concept (Stability Operations JOC), 66, 68–70
Stability Operations Office, 74
state-building, 9–10, 68. *See also* nation-building
Stewart, Richard, 163–64
strategic corporal concept, 159–60
"strategic pause," 51, 52

Strategic Planning Guidance 2006-11 (SPG 2006-11), 65–66
Strategic Transformation Assessments, 56
Sullivan, Gordon, 48
Sunnis, 126–28
the surge, 114–15, 119–40; inauspicious circumstances for, 121–25; and learning of counterinsurgency, 130–39, 177–78; Pentagon opposition to, 119–20; public support for, 121; security gains made by, 125–30; troop shortfall for, 124
SWET operations, 77

Taliban, 56, 57
technology(-ies): associated with RMA, 51, 52; as evidence of learning, 19–20; in transformation process, 53
Tentative Manual for Countering Irregular Threats, 106–7
Terriff, Terry, 150
3rd Armored Cavalry Regiment, 75
third world, 30–31
three-block war, 54, 73
Thurman, Max, 44
Tighe, Dennis, 135–36
Tillson, John, 38
top-down learning, 16–17
Total Force Concept, 156
TRADOC. *See* Training and Doctrine Command
training: as evidence of learning, 18, 20–21; initiatives of the 1960s for, 35; for stability operations, 21–22
Training and Doctrine Command (TRADOC), 41–42, 67, 108
transformation, 52–56, 58, 59, 154
Transformation Planning Guidance (DoD), 59
Traub, James, 49

unconventional conflict, 58. *See also* irregular warfare/operations
understanding of counterinsurgency, 18
Unified Command Plan (2004), 90

United National Operation in Somalia (UNOSOM), 48–49
unmanned aerial vehicles, 90
UNOSOM, 48–49
urban operations, 14, 19, 66
Urban Warfare Training Center (UWTC), 143
"Urban Warrior" experiment, 54
U.S. Agency for International Development (USAID), 68, 94–95, 98
U.S. Air Force (USAF), 32; Air Force Joint Tactical Air Control program, 86; Doctrine Document 2-3, 132–33; funds allocated to, 148, 212n44; special forces of, 37
U.S. Army: 2005 Army Strategic Policy Guidance, 67; Active Component, 22; *Army Action Plan for Stability Operations*, 132; Aylwin-Foster's critique of, 78; budget issues for, 149, 150, 212n44; CLIC, 32–33; Command and General Staff College, 75–76; conventional warfare training focus of, 143–44; counterinsurgency campaigns of, 27–28; Counterinsurgency Center, 108; 1st Special Operations Command, 37; FM 3-0, 58, 69, 133–34; FM 3-07, 69; FM 3-24, 103–5, 109–16; FM 31-16, 35; FM 100-5, 32, 36; FM 100-20, 32; FM 100-23, 48; FMI 3-07.22, 66–70; full-spectrum operations concept, 106; in Haiti peace operations, 49; increase in forces, 120, 158–62; light infantry division, 41–42; mock villages for urban operations, 66; modularization of forces in, 85–86, 152–56, 173; 101st Airborne Division, 75; opposition to learning counterinsurgency in, 135–36; primary functions of, 1; promotion system of, 41; rebalancing of AC and RC, 156–58, 173; Reserve Component, 21–22; Special Forces school, 90; Stability, Security, Transition, and Reconstruction Division, 108; and strategy for Iraq War, 179–80; structure of, 21–22; 3rd Ar-

mored Cavalry Regiment, 75; underfunding of, 148–49; and Vietnam War, 30

U.S. Code of Federal Regulations, 1, 96

U.S. Department of Defense (DoD) (Pentagon): and 2006 QDR (*see* Quadrennial Defense Review [2006 QDR]); 2007 defense budget requests, 87; and counterinsurgency conference, 108–9; counterinsurgency initiatives of, 3, 34; Defense Language Transformation Roadmap, 72, 73; differences of opinion within, 14; *DoD Directive 3000.05*, 73–74, 98, 139; institutional culture of, 19; institutional learning at, 132; interpretation of counterinsurgency in, 71; Iraq war planning and doctrine of, 60, 61; in Iron Triangle, 20; learning of counterinsurgency in, 170–75, 181; low prioritization of irregular operations by, 67–68; marginalization of MOOTW by, 50; mismatch in rhetoric and provisions of, 70; Petraeus' influence within, 131; policy- and priority-setting sections of, 14; priorities of (*see* balance of military priorities); RMA-related investments by, 51; SPG 2006-11, 65–66; stability operations efforts of, 65; theories of future war in, 51; *Transformation Planning Guidance*, 59; transformation process in, 56

U.S. Department of State, 94–95; and counterinsurgency conference, 108–9; NSPD 44 stability operations mandate for, 99; S/CRS, 96–98

U.S. Marine Corps (USMC): All Marine Messages (2003, 2005), 67; budget issues for, 148–50, 217n3; CAOCL, 72, 73; collateral functions of, 1; *Commandant's Planning Guidance*, 136; conventional warfare training focus of, 143, 144; Counterinsurgency Center, 108; Fleet Marine Force Manual 8-2, 32, 35; in Haiti peace operations, 49; human terrain emphasis of, 72; improving counterinsurgency skills in, 66; increase in forces, 120, 158–62, 173; Joint Urban Warrior 05, 73; maneuver warfare concept of, 42; *Marine Corps Operating Concepts for a Changing Security Environment*, 105–6; MCWP 3-33.5, 103–5, 109–16; MRAPs for, 147; opposition to learning counterinsurgency in, 136; Project Metropolis, 54; Small Wars Center of Excellence, 72, 73; *Small Wars Manual*, 29; Special Operations Command, 90; and strategy for Iraq War, 179–80; structure of, 21; *Tentative Manual for Countering Irregular Threats*, 106–7; "Urban Warrior" experiment, 54; UWTC, 143; and Vietnam War, 30; Wargaming Division, 72

U.S. military: avoidance of irregular warfare by, 1–3; challenge of reorientation for, 3; composition of, 14; DoD allocation of funds among services, 148; drivers of learning in, 15–16; institutionalization of learning in, 17; interpretations of counterinsurgency within, 71; learning by (*see* institutional learning); as a learning organization, 14–17; three perspectives on, 15; War on Terror role of, 12. *See also* U.S. Department of Defense; *individual services*

U.S. Navy: collateral functions of, 1; funds allocated to, 148, 212n44; SEALs, 37, 90

U.S. Overseas Internal Defense Policy, 32

USAF. *See* U.S. Air Force

USAID. *See* U.S. Agency for International Development

USMC. *See* U.S. Marine Corps

UWTC, 143

V-22 Osprey, 150

Vietnam, advisory approach in, 38

Vietnam Syndrome, 23, 34

Vietnam War, 11; adaptation of methods in, 28; blame for results of, 179; conventional operations during, 191n113; CORDS program in, 163–64; counterinsurgency element in, 33; inability to shift gears in, 43; loss of learning from, 29–30

Waghelstein, John D., 27
Wall Street Journal, 148
Wargaming Division, USMC Warfighting Laboratory (Quantico, Virginia), 72
War on Terror: funding for, 145; inappropriate preparation/configuration for, 2–3; and increase in ground forces, 158, 159; military's role in, 12; new strategic environment of, 3; reorientation needed for, 54–61;

SOCOM as lead command for, 90. *See also* Afghanistan operations; Iraq War
Washington, George, 26
Washington Post, 123
Watson, Brian W., 155–56
Weigley, Russell F., 27–28
Weinberger, Caspar, 33, 42
Weinberger Doctrine, 42–43, 49, 52–53
Weyand, Fred C., 28–29
Williams, Robert, 135
Wilson, James Q., 15
"Winning the Peace" (Peter W. Chiarelli and Patrick R. Michaelis), 77
Wolfowitz, Paul, 77
Woodward, Bob, 87

Zelikow, Philip, 15